Fourth Edition

EDUCATIONAL ORGANIZATION *and* ADMINISTRATION

Concepts, Practices, and Issues

EDGAR L. MORPHET
University of California, Berkeley

ROE L. JOHNS
University of Florida

THEODORE L. RELLER
University of California, Berkeley

PRENTICE-HALL, INC., Englewood Cliffs, New Jersey 07632

Library of Congress Cataloging in Publication Data

Morphet, Edgar Leroy, (date)
  Educational organization and administration.

  First published in 1959 as: Educational
administration / Edgar L. Morphet, Roe L. Johns,
Theodore L. Reller.
  Bibliography: p.
  Includes index.
  1. School management and organization.
I. Johns, Roe Lyell, (date). II. Reller,
Theodore Lee. III. Title.
LB2805.M68 1982   371.2   81–10641
ISBN 0–13–236729–7   AACR2

Editorial production/supervision
  and interior design: *Edith Riker*
Cover design: *Miriam Recio*
Manufacturing buyer: *Edmund W. Leone*

To our wives
Camilla, Gladys, and Margery

Prentice-Hall International, Inc., *London*
Prentice-Hall of Australia Pty. Limited, *Sydney*
Prentice-Hall of Canada, Ltd., *Toronto*
Prentice-Hall of India Private Limited, *New Delhi*
Prentice-Hall of Japan, Inc., *Tokyo*
Prentice-Hall of Southeast Asia Pte. Ltd., *Singapore*
Whitehall Books Limited, *Wellington, New Zealand*

CONTENTS

PREFACE

In the third edition of this book (1974), the authors stated the following: "Although many of the developments and concepts discussed in the first two editions are still pertinent, it has become apparent to the authors that major revisions are again needed because during the past few years (1) on the basis of new information and insights, there have been many significant changes in the perspectives, value systems, attitudes, and expectations of most citizens in the nation and even further changes seem inevitable; (2) there has been a growing recognition of the fact that, even though improvements have been made in some aspects of education, these changes have been inadequate to meet the needs of a dynamic society; and (3) further systematically planned changes in education are essential to meet the emerging as well as presently recognized needs."

This statement is as appropriate today as it was in 1974. The public schools in 1980 received more unfavorable criticism than they had received during any of the past twenty years. Taxpayer resistance to financing the public schools is greater at this writing than at any time since the Great Depression in the 1930s. Inflation, unemployment, the energy crisis, and crises in international relations have created an uneasiness in public morale. A great increase in single-parent families, the use of drugs by school-aged students, the increase in sexual activity of teenaged students, racial conflict and an increase in teenaged crime have all created problems for the public schools. Although the public schools did not cause these problems, the schools are sometimes blamed for their existence. Technology offers a challenge and opportunity to both schooling and education. Furthermore, technology is causing rapid changes in business and industry, which in turn cause changes in the competencies needed by employees. One's education today is becoming obsolete at a more rapid rate than ever before. It is now increasingly apparent that learning and even formal schooling can no longer be confined to the young. Learning must continue throughout one's lifetime in the hope that it may be adequate for the times.

The development of educational leadership competent to deal with these problems is vital to the welfare of the nation. The modern educational administrator is a future-oriented leader. The administrator is knowledgeable about and sensitive to the changes in society that call for changes in the schools. He or she understands social systems, their norms, their values, and their goals. He or she understands the norms, values, and the goals of the individuals in the social system. He or she understands the resistance of social systems to change and what inputs are most promising in effecting needed changes. He or she provides the leadership that reconciles the goals of the society and the school social system with the needs of the individuals in that system. In a democracy, major policy decisions in the school social system are made by political processes. The educational leader, to be effective, must understand and participate in these processes. Furthermore, in the school social system, both the professional and support personnel are insisting that they be given the opportunity to participate in policy decisions that affect them.

The authors have made a comprehensive revision of *Educational Organization and Administration: Concepts, Practices, and Issues* for the fourth edition. Many new insights and new developments have been incorporated. Three new chapters have been added to the fourth edition as follows: Chapter 6, Decision Making and Communication; Chapter 8, The Politics of Education; and Chapter 18, Collective Bargaining and Administration. All other chapters have been revised, combined, or replaced by the new chapters.

This volume should be helpful to school administrators, school board members, and graduate students preparing to be school administrators and to teachers and other staff members concerned about educational policies.

Part 1 of this volume is concerned primarily with basic theories, concepts, and principles; Part 2, with the major provisions and implications for organization and administration; and Part 3, with the development and implementation of relevant provisions and programs.

Educational administration has not yet become a science, but progress is being made in developing some knowledge based on theory which has been tested by research. Knowledge of educational organization and administration perhaps can be divided into three categories: (1) things that we know; (2) things that we believe but can't quite prove; and (3) things that we have a hunch might be true. For that reason we have a section at the end of many chapters on pertinent problems and issues which are drawn largely from categories 2 and 3. The purpose of including this feature is to challenge the thinking of the reader, to stimulate research, and to reveal that no one knows the solution to many of the problems and issues of educational organization and administration. Educational administration is the interaction of the society (people) and its institutions (persons) in the search for usable knowledge and interactive knowledge with which to guide the school and education.

Edgar L. Morphet
Roe L. Johns
Theodore L. Reller

Part 1

BASIC PRINCIPLES, CONCEPTS, and ISSUSES

1

MASTERING *the* PROBABLE *and* MANAGING *the* UNPREDICTABLE [1]

The most certain thing about the situation that confronts the American educational system in the 1980s is, it seems, the lack of certainty. Everywhere the society faces what appear to be extremely difficult or insoluble problems such as the limitation of economic resources and our questionable ability to distribute them reasonably; the decline in the strength of the family and resultant questions regarding the education of children and youth; the decline of belief of the people in the responsibility and effectiveness of governmental agencies and other organizations and groups which have had authority roles; the growth of technology and its present and potential relationship to humanity; the lack of consensus regarding goals and policies that lead toward their attainment; the role of the state and of the individual; the knowledge explosion; a hostile world in which the people lack trust in each other; and the competency of people to meet the challenges and avoid self-destruction.

[1] From *Facing the Future: Mastering the Probable and Managing the Unpredictable*, (Paris: OECD 1979).

Having accepted considerable responsibility for their own destiny, humans are in a period of great uncertainty regarding their ability "to deliver." Belief in the idea of progress, once widely accepted in our society, has faded. The future is not faced with confidence but, rather, frequently with feelings of inability to cope or even of futility.

In this period even the remarkable achievements of persons and institutions tend to be passed over, greatly undervalued, or reinterpreted to support the view that the worst elements of human nature have always prevailed. Thus the revisionists may see the development of public education in our society as a planned effort to produce the needed "slaves" for industry.

This chapter is designed to provide a context in which the education service and educational administration will be operating. Brief attention will be given to selected factors in the society that help to establish the situation in which schooling will be carried forward, a few conditions within the education service itself that have significant impact on administration, and important facts and forces pertaining to administration itself. First, however, attention will be given to some background (historical) factors which provide a base or explanation for many current conditions.

SOME BACKGROUND CONSIDERATIONS

It has been said that, if one is to understand the present, one must know something of the past. Public education in our society developed over a long period of years and as a result of the interplay of many forces. It was long characterized by a wide range of provisions—from very poor to excellent. Whereas equality of educational opportunity was often spoken of as a central goal, provisions varied widely among states, within most states, and within many districts. The concept of equality of opportunity provided a lever against which practice could be evaluated and steps toward improvement could be planned.

The common school thus gradually grew, with better educated teachers and improved offerings and materials of instruction and with greater attention being given to the needs of the individual child. It was generally extended to include the high school and eventually the community college in some states.

Although common schools developed in accord with the provisions of state constitutions and statutes, many such provisions were permissive rather than mandatory. As a result developments were uneven and the developments in any community were substantially the product of the efforts of people in the community. This contributed to the belief that the schools were local agencies and that they were highly responsive to the people. This responsiveness to at least some segments of the population had important positive results as well as negative ones. The relative insecurity of the teacher was an important negative condition. However for many years the schools provided significant opportunity for upward mobility for substantial numbers of young people. This opportunity was related to the growth of the economy as the nation developed and as commerce, industry, and agriculture expanded. Provisions for immigrant children were generally limited, and yet in the course of a generation or two the public schools were an extremely important contributor to their advancement. Provisions for black children were far less adequate or successful in making it possible for them to enter the mainstream of society.

In the nineteenth century the activity of the states in education was rather limited. The states, however, did establish the bases for the local authorities or the local authorities themselves and took modest steps to finance schools, to provide teachers, and to ensure minimum curricular offerings. In the early decades of the twentieth century we witnessed a great growth of state activity in matters pertaining to schools. High schools developed widely, and compulsory school attendance laws with higher attendance ages were established. More attention was given to teacher education, especially through certification. State action regarding educational finance increased. The movement regarding preparation of professional personnel included administrators.

During this period local school districts were expanding and developing their programs to provide more adequately for elementary and secondary school-aged children, and significant beginnings occurred in vocational education. In the cities boards of education were reduced in size, and they directed their attention more largely to policy. Fiscal independence of school districts from city government was sought in an effort to remove schools from the impact of traditional party politics. School administration was substantially professionalized, and the administrative bureaucracy developed strength and respect—it was not viewed then as an aspect of a "cult of efficiency" or as a barrier to responsiveness.

The years following World War II until the early 1970s were characterized by large challenges, considerable achievement, and optimism. The *Brown* decision and various federal programs related to education such as efforts at national curricular reform and the poverty program spoke of the great belief in schooling. The number of local school units was reduced from over 100,000 to 15,000 in a few decades. Foundation grants centered attention upon improving programs for preparing educational administrators. Research, experimentation, and development were viewed more favorably than at any time in the past. It appeared to many that the golden age for schooling had arrived—the educative society was just ahead.

In recent years, the problems in the society, especially in the large cities but in no sense restricted to them, the malaise related to the war in Vietnam, and the "failure" of schooling and of hastily devised federal programs to meet expectations and to produce overt, significant, positive results had an enormous impact on public attitudes toward governmental efforts in the social program area including schools.

UNIQUE FEATURES OF EDUCATION IN THE UNITED STATES

The policies and plans that have been developed for the organization and administration of education in the United States have a number of unique features. These features grew out of the beliefs, attitudes, and experiences of the people who helped to develop the nation and its institutions.

Some of the unique features of education in the United States are discussed briefly in the paragraphs that follow.

The system of education has been relatively decentralized. The people in their respective states (not the federal government) have the basic responsibility for the organization and control of education (see Chapter 11). Each state, in fact, has developed a system of education which differs in some respects from that developed by other states. In most states, much of the responsibility for the organization and administration of public schools has been delegated to local school districts. However, the increasing concern of the federal government about education has been indicated by provisions for financial assistance and regulation of categorical programs, by U.S. Supreme Court decisions concerning the implications of constitutional provisions, and in many other ways. The extent of decentralization (the important role of local districts) in the United States contrasts sharply to the marked centralization of control found in many other nations. However, it has declined significantly in recent decades—and the decline threatens to continue or even to accelerate.

The people, not the educators or government officials, are ultimately responsible for all basic policies relating to education. Although in practice many policies are developed cooperatively, the decisions as to what policies are to be adopted and followed are usually delegated to the legislature and the state board of education (for state policies) and to local lay boards of education selected by the people (for local policies); in some cases, the decisions are made by the people themselves. The recommendations of educators are usually considered and often followed. In many countries, most operating policies are determined nationally. An increasing number of policies are now established in the United States by the federal government through legislation, administrative regulation, and court action. Many of these policies are general rather than specific regarding schools, for example, the basic rights of minorities, women, and the handicapped. However they impact heavily on schools.

A system of education open freely to all has been established. This system, contrasting sharply to the dual systems formerly found in many countries, is one logical outgrowth of the concept of equal opportunity in and through education for all citizens. Thus every person, regardless of his or her social, economic, political, religious, or racial background or mental or physical handicaps, has a constitutional right (not yet fully recognized in practice) to an equal opportunity to develop his or her talents fully so as to become a socially and economically productive citizen and a self-renewing person. These opportunities are provided primarily through a system of public education extending in many states from early childhood or kindergarten education through comprehensive secondary schools and higher education.

Although primary emphasis is placed on public schools, provision is also made for private and parochial schools. Most people believe that public schools have a special and necessary contribution to make to the development and unity of the nation. Schools are supported by public tax funds to be available to all, and special efforts are being made to ensure that they are organized and operated in the interest and for the benefit of all people. Parents may, however, send their children to public or nonpublic schools. Private and religious agencies have been given considerable freedom to establish, control, operate, and support schools and other educational institutions in accordance with their own beliefs and concepts.

The public schools and educational institutions are safeguarded insofar as possible from partisan political control. Control of the schools or other public educational institutions by any partisan political group is considered not only undesirable but potentially dangerous. Therefore, provision has generally been made for the schools to have a comparatively independent status, so there is an opportunity to resolve educational issues separately from other issues, thus freeing school boards and educators from domination or control by partisan political agencies or groups and even by other governmental agencies.

Education in the public schools and educational institutions is nonsectarian. No religious creed or doctrine may be taught in the public schools. Special provisions are made to ensure that these schools on all levels are safeguarded against domination or control by any religious organization. Such provisions make it possible for the public schools to "teach" about religions and to instruct in moral and ethical values, but not to present these matters from the point of view of any sect or religious organization.

Most citizens believe that those who are responsible for the administration of their schools, as well as those who teach in the schools, should be especially prepared to meet their responsibilities. The idea that educational administrators should have special preparation developed slowly but is now accepted in practically all states. The significance attached to public schools, which has provided a unique valuing of and commitment to them, has resulted in high expectations regarding administrators.

SELECTED SOCIETAL FACTORS

Developments regarding population and the family. One of the most significant of the changes in our society in recent years relates to demographics. Ours has become an aging society, with relatively few children, many young adults, and growing numbers of elderly. A couple of decades of high fertility, followed by years of very low birthrates and increased longevity, have produced a changing and distorted age composition. In nearly 40 percent of our homes, there are no children. The trend is toward later marriage and less childbearing in the long run.

Among other forces, changes in the economic realm have large impact on population. This has been a major cause of the increased participation of women in the labor force. Two-worker families with children have become common. This can have important benefits in addition to economic-broadening horizons of women and increasing their self-confidence and providing children with new perceptions of roles. It can also add greatly to physical and emotional strain and without adequate child care can lead to neglect of children.

The society has also seen a sharp increase in single-parent families—now more than one in five. Generally such families are headed by a woman, often of minority background, and in many instances poor.

The in-migration of peoples and fertility rates indicate that a larger percentage of the child population will be minority.

Further, there has been a change in social values and attitudes toward children. These changes relate in one way or another to the tendency to live for the present rather than to defer gratification in the interest of children, the struggle between or among age groups as the elderly, for example, seek an increased share of public spending, the disillusionment with the great social programs many of which relate to children. Thus a more negative or indifferent climate of opinion exists toward children—especially children from disadvantaged backgrounds.

Certainly birth rates and attitudes can change. However, major challenges from developments in this area appear certain to those who are interested in children and youth—both because of the dignity and worth of the individual and the future renaissance of the society.

A more pluralistic society. A major change in thinking about our society in recent years is suggested by the wide usage of the term "pluralism." It is used with a wide variety of meanings and frequently without essential definition if understanding or communication is to be facilitated. It has highly significant implications regarding the purposes of education as well as its organization and functioning. It has been used especially with reference to ethnic and language groups, although religious commitment or orientation may also be an important factor involved in it.

Pluralism is also seen as the opposite of the expressed view (myth) of our society as a melting pot. Clearly there are many arrangements in between a highly segmented society (on the basis of ethnicity, language, or religion) and the uncritical acceptance of the melting pot theory. Regrettably there has been too little attempt at defining pluralism and at exploring its implications. Proponents and opponents of it may give too little thought to the essential common commitments of the people of a society—common commitments without which all decline.

Probably the most basic reason for being very skeptical of proposed voucher plans is that they would encourage each group (economic, social, religious, or other) to be primarily concerned with its own group at a time in our history when there is great need for being concerned about all children and when there is great need for building a society in which each group may, if it wishes, be relatively autonomous but in which there is a system of authority and a unity of values. We have had a substantial measure of success in building a nation with an adult or mature system of values out of many peoples. This would not appear to be the appropriate time in which to give up the quest.

Declining belief in the idea of progress and governmental action. During most of the current century there has been a strong belief in our society in the idea of progress. Through hard work, innovation, schooling, science, and commercial and industrial enterprise, and in recent decades through governmental programs, it has been widely believed that the quality of life would be continuously improving. Our society has been an optimistic one. In recent years this idea of inevitable progress has been seriously challenged. Doubts have risen as the result of many factors such as continued world population expansion, recognition of limited natural resources, serious environmental forces impinging on health, possible inability to utilize the results of science in the interest of the people, the questioning of authority in all organizations and concurrently the quest for certainty, and decline in belief in nearly all governmental forms and social-economic institutions.

While this decline in belief in the idea of inevitable progress may be seen as a sign of maturity, it also must be recognized as a possible barrier to the development of essential common goals and mobilization of the resources of a society to facilitate movement toward their realization. Although there may be dangers in institutions which have a sense of mission and identity, it is also true that schools and school systems without strong identity feelings and commitment may be severely handicapped.

An increasingly litigious society. The last decade has been marked by an increasing tendency to find "solutions" to problems through the courts. This is probably the result of such factors as the difficulty that individuals and groups may experience in getting legislative action, the perceived success of litigation in matters such as desegregation, the distance between the governmental bureaucracies and the people, the growing kinds of issues accepted by the courts, the establishment of public agencies to assist individuals and groups in securing their legal rights, and the lack of trust between and among various individuals and groups involved with public services.

The development of the more litigious society has and may contribute significantly to the improvement of justice in our society. However, it may also have substantial costs in terms of increasing the effort to control or live by overregulation or of avoiding innovative approaches to avoid challenge. Further, expectations regarding the value of litigation may be too high. The problem of integration is basically an educational one. While the courts have assisted in a highly significant manner in desegregation, they find it difficult to prescribe or to provide the attitudes, understandings, resources, and actions which will result in integration. The long-run implications of a highly litigious society upon a person-to-person, caring, interactive service such as schooling are difficult to assess, but not particularly promising.

A burgeoning (educational) technology. The development of technology in our society as it relates to education and schooling may in the long run be the most important of the major forces impinging upon the development of schools. Even today the impact of television on student learning is difficult to assess—although it has been having a major impact on attitudes toward learning as well as on the learning processes. Indeed there are those who believe that the techniques and strategies used in the instructional program in most schools do not compare favorably with those used in television. But technology is expanding extremely rapidly in areas such as microprocessing, which may permit people to learn many things at home more effectively than in the school. Are we on the threshold of an "information society" made possible by a merger of computer technology, low-cost electronic products, and communication systems and devices? Do these developments portend a new sort of partnership between the home and the school in the educational process? Who will make the decisions regarding the utilization of these new technological developments—regarding the goals toward which they will be committed? Highly significant issues of governance and process emerge in this field.

SELECTED EDUCATIONAL ISSUES

A Local System or a Federal-State-Local System

In the United States education (schools) has been generally regarded as a state responsibility—administered locally. During recent decades there has been a marked shift toward a federal-state-local system. The local district has lost much of its traditional freedom to develop programs and spend funds as it has wished with little or no outside monitoring. This has resulted from the attempt (legislative, judicial, administrative) to improve equality or adequacy of educational opportunity, to promote accountability, and to provide for the needs of various individuals or groups whose needs were not being met adequately. This highly significant trend has far-reaching implications for many aspects of educational administration.

Interestingly this movement has not done a great deal to strengthen the local partner. For more than a decade there has been too little concern on the part of the states regarding local districts, although strengthening them by ensuring adequacy in size, organization, and resources might well have been a viable avenue by which to achieve the goals sought. There have been very important gains through these trends toward a federal–state–local system but also probably some significant losses. Can or should any of these trends be simply maintained or reversed? Have they or will they produce unacceptable unanticipated consequences? Can federal and state programs be developed and administered in such a manner that the local partner (district) becomes more competent and innovative and more likely to take the initiative in the development of an outstanding educational program? How can the local system operate to challenge (and facilitate) the individual school (principal, staff, students, public) to become an outstanding, inspired learning center?

For a quarter of a century discretion in educational policy making by professionals and politicians has been constrained by law—court decisions, state and federal statutes, regulatory apparatuses such as rule-making and hearing requirements, and tighter standard setting. What has been the impact of these actions on the "system"?

The Growth of Teacher Power

Traditionally the teacher has had less power in our society than in many others. In recent years this power has grown significantly. It is exhibited in the collective negotiations movement in many states. Through it the organized teachers have won a recognized right to participate in the decision-making process regarding many aspects of the educational service. This power has tended to grow in such manner that many administrators and boards of education have become concerned about management rights.

Teacher power may be exercised at the site level, the system level, the state level, and the federal level. It was exercised at the federal level in the case of the establishment of the Department of Education. At the site level it can change the role of the principal and contribute to reducing the principal to a manager or even a contract manager.

The question of how teacher power will be used is of great significance to the school system. In some societies it has been a highly conservative force, holding to traditional practice rather than to the development of excellence. There is the genuine possibility that through their organizations teachers may indeed contribute importantly to the development of much more highly regulated and routinized schools rather than to that professional discretion which they have professed to be seeking.

An Increasingly Bureaucratic School System

Bureaucracy is not new to our school system. It has been developed rather extensively in some large city systems—exhibiting important positive and negative results. With the rapid growth of state and federal intervention in schools, its significance for education has increased dramatically. Wise states that bureaucratic

> rationalization occurs when the relationship between means and ends is known, when the ends are attainable given the means, or when the means are reasonable given the ends. When the relationship between means and ends is not known and bureaucratic rationalization persists, we shall say that we are witnessing the phenomenon of hyperrationalization—that is, an effort to rationalize beyond the bounds of knowledge. This involves imposing means which do not result in the attainment of ends, or the setting of ends which cannot be attained, given the available means—imposing unproven techniques on the one hand, and setting unrealistic expectations on the other.
>
> Ensuring that a practice conforms to norms requires replacing the exercise of administrative discretion either with procedures or rules. Rationalization occurs when procedure and regulations ensure conformity to norms and have the intended effects of fairness and equality. Hyperrationalization occurs, when conformity to norms is not achieved by the procedures and rules imposed—when procedures are followed but the norm of fairness is not necessarily attained, when rules are obeyed but the norm of equality is not necessarily attained.[2]

While the continued growth of incremental bureaucratic centralization appears probable, it should be noted that a mix of central and local control is theoretically possible. Past performance suggests that equity cannot be expected with local control—and that to date the science and technology of education does not provide an adequate basis for excessive policy intervention by the state and federal governments—that indeed legislating learning may be highly counterproductive.

General Education or Categorical Programs

The educational service in the United States has traditionally been administered locally. Thus the organization of the schools, the methods employed and even the subjects taught, and the teachers employed have been determined by the local authorities in accordance with rather broad state laws or guidelines and with little or no supervision or monitoring. Generally the states have not followed the administration of state funds in the districts to determine how they were expended. Most state funds were provided for general elementary and/or secondary education. Educators and boards of education have favored this practice of general state aid, believing that it made it possible for them better to meet educational needs. In recent decades, however, it has been increasingly recognized that many local districts have not provided equitably for all children. One result has been a great growth in categorical programs. These have been federal and state programs sponsored by special interest groups. Those who have sought these programs have been far more successful than have those who unsuccessfully sought general federal aid for education for several decades.

The growth of the categorical programs has indeed been most notable and has

---

[2] Arthur E. Wise, *Legislated Learning: The Bureaucratization of the American Classroom* (Berkeley: University of California Press, 1979), pp. 65–66.

resulted in highly significant contributions to large numbers of children. During the last decade or two these programs have been in the forefront of public school developments. Even as their success is noted, however, important unanticipated consequences should be recognized. What is or will be the impact of the detailed regulations and attempts at monitoring which accompany many of these programs? What is the effect of these programs on general education? Are the needs of all children being met more effectively as a result of these programs? Have boards of education and local school systems lost substantially regarding their feeling of responsibility and actual responsibility for the education of all children? Do they see themselves primarily as following mandates and regulations rather than as setting policy for educational advancement? In fact one may wonder whether the strong commitment to special interests, which has resulted in this legislation, may have been accompanied by a significant decline of public interest in and support for general education. Have the categorical programs increased the tendency for the principal and the superintendent to be administrators of regulations rather than educational leaders?

The integration of general education and categorical programs remains a major challenge. How it is done has major implications for educational governance, finance, boards of education and administrators, teachers, and especially the education of children and youth. If categorical programs become essentially separate systems within the system, the education of children suffers.

The Reconstruction of Education and Schooling

The 1980s promises to be a period in which highly significant decisions regarding schooling will be made. To what extent are the trends of the previous decade or two going to be reversed, modified, or institutionalized? Do regulations inevitably expand? Is direct or indirect action on curriculum and programs by the federal and state governments the answer?

The question, *What are schools for?*, is a most fundamental one. In a comprehensive treatment of this issue Goodlad states

> Unfortunately, much of what we have done and continue to do has resulted in trivialization of the ends and means of schooling. Recent research suggests that schools spend an inordinate amount of time on noninstructional activities. Regrettably, much of the time spent on instruction is devoted to training. As a consequence, today's schools are only marginally educational institutions.[3]
>
> Not surprisingly, the improvement of learning figures more prominently in the rhetoric than in the time allocation of school administrators, including principals.[4]

He makes a plea that those in administrative positions put curricular and instructional matters at the center of their leadership role, noting that there are no cur-

---

[3] John I. Goodlad, *What Schools Are For* (Bloomington, Ind.: Phi Delta Kappan Educational Foundation, 1979), Preface, p. vi.
[4] *Ibid.*, p. 12.

ricular and instructional panaceas and that good instruction involves "the orchestration of a dozen or more factors."

Further, the problem of balance between meeting the needs of individuals and society remains a difficult and crucial one. What kind of society do we seek to provide for that individualism which is fundamental? How can the development of individuals contribute most effectively to the society desired—and to be desired?

A growing number of people have been seeking a role in curriculum and program matters. Various organized special interest groups have sought more power as have teachers. The respective levels of government—from the school site to the federal government—have been engaged in a struggle. Direct and indirect federal action has demonstrated that changes can be initiated rather easily. To sustain the desired change and realize the intended aims, however, is extremely difficult. Given the facts that even the experts have limitations, that the precise relationship between curriculum and instruction and educational results remains unclear, and that the interventions do not assure excellence in teaching or learning, there are many who are not unhappy about the difficulty. Possibly enough may be learned through the analysis of past experience to provide a more defensible basis for action now.

Minimum Competency Testing

While the debate continues regarding the reconstruction of schools and their goals and programs, the understandable demand for accountability has grown. This demand expressed itself in recent decades through programs such as PPBS, performance-based teacher education, competency-based education, and state teacher evaluation systems. For each of these, much was claimed by proponents, and although each made some contribution it was much less than anticipated. More recently minimum competency testing has grown rapidly and by too many has been regarded as a panacea.

The impact of minimum competency testing is not established. It must be seen as another of the many efforts to improve schooling through regulatory practices. Questions which are raised about it include: Would the funds involved be better invested in improved services to children? Will it further disenfranchise teachers and administrators in instructional matters? Will basic skills and minimum competency become synonymous and with what impact? Will it exacerbate social and economic class differences through causing the parents of children economically able and deeply interested in the education of their children to turn to private schools? Will tests dictate the curriculum and centralize control of curriculum? Are the programs being pursued based upon adequate study of their probable effect? These are among the social and political questions; there are also many technical ones related to the design and operation of the programs.

Decision Making or Social Problem Solving

The complexity, spread, and variation of involvement in decision making regarding schooling—if consideration is given both to influence and power—is almost overwhelming. All levels of government—federal, state, intermediate, local, and site—are involved. Legislatures, administrators, and courts act. Boards, committees, and bureaucracies concerned primarily with education are involved, but increasingly other general or special governmental bodies are also powerful participants. The idea of being fiscally independent or nonpolitical appears remote. While new or additional agencies become involved, the authority of all is questioned.

In the earlier period, schooling appeared to develop through one community's trying out a program which upon being found helpful or valuable spread to other communities and eventually became mandated by the state. Then lighthouse schools and school systems were regarded favorably. The effort during the last couple of decades at finding direction through research and development was built upon exaggerated expectations and resulted in "failure" in relation to expectations. This "failure" was accepted by many even though there had indeed been substantial achievements.[5]

In an important treatise related to the problem of social problem solving, Lindblom and Cohen note the gap between those engaged in professional social inquiry and the practitioners. They state that society must continue to rely heavily upon *ordinary knowledge,* "knowledge that does not owe its origin, testing, degree of verification, truth status or currency to distinctive PSI (professional social inquiry) professional techniques but rather to common sense, casual empiricism, or thoughtful speculation and analysis."[6] This is not to deny that PSI may be an important supplement to ordinary knowledge.

They further draw a distinction between analytical and interactive problem solving. "Since people never stop thinking, the alternatives are a frontal analytical attack on some identified problem, or interaction in which thought and analysis is adapted to the interaction and is therefore on some issues displaced by interaction."[7]

The issues confronting society and educational practitioners regarding instruction, curriculum, organization of classroom and schools, outcomes, and relation of schooling to education are extremely difficult. How can they be met more adequately? How can administrators be better prepared to engage in interactive problem solving?

A Steady State or Contracting Service

Few societies have enjoyed the opportunities of an educational service connected with economic growth or expansion to a greater degree than ours. Over a long period of time there have been increasing numbers of children and youth, extension of service to younger children and to a larger percentage of youth and adults, and relatively ample opportunities for young people to enter the world of employment. Although there were problems involved in securing an adequate supply of competent teachers, providing facilities, and in financing the service, they were of a different and less difficult order than the problems of contraction. In

---

[5] See, for example, Patrick Suppes, ed., *Impact of Research in Education* (Washington, D.C.: National Academy of Education, 1978).

[6] Charles E. Lindblom and David K. Cohen, *Usable Knowledge* (New Haven, Conn.: Yale University Press, 1979), p. 12.

[7] *Ibid.,* p. 20.

part this difficulty may be the result of inexperience in dealing with the issue; in fact, previous experience with expansion may conceivably be a barrier to success in meeting contraction.

It can be argued that contraction may provide positive benefits resulting from smaller numbers and lowered expectations. However, it also involves important conceptual and political issues. "Success in tackling the task of revising the scale on which an activity is carried out, in establishing some kind of new (and possibly short-run) equilibrium at a new level, will come only if the potentially disruptive forces that are generated by contraction can be controlled, if individual expectations can be substantially revised, and if structures and procedures geared to growth can be adapted for other purposes.[8]

Contraction may in some instances provide an opportunity for innovation—it may in fact demand it. However, anyone familiar with the problems of effecting innovation will recognize that contraction provides many conditions and forces which militate against promising development. Central to this question is the teaching staff—more experienced, more mature, and with the advantage of continuity; but what about the problems of an aging profession? Further, it must be recognized that the limiting of opportunity through contraction produces sharp conflicts with the efforts of society to open the doors to individuals and/or groups which have known too little opportunity even in the growth period.

Contraction demands planning even though it is even more difficult than planning in periods of growth. It requires that alternatives be developed. Decisions must be made—decisions cannot be delayed as readily as in growth periods—and they may be less modifiable or reversible. Confidence in the acceptability of the future must be maintained while there is recognition of the limits of our ability for social control. New or more appropriate styles of administration need to be developed to avoid what otherwise could be debilitating conflict or even loss of commitment to central values of a democratic society.

The Role of School Administrators

The consideration of issues in educational administration involves not only the changing society with its diffuse values, its shifts in the exercise of power, and the problems of schools; it also involves administrators. Struggles regarding structure and policy are not new. Perhaps because of a change in attitudes toward authority and because of the incredible complexity of decision-making processes in the educational service, administration has grown more difficult even as excellence in it has grown more imperative. In any case the principal, at the site, and the superintendent, at the district level, have been and are in extremely crucial positions.

The question of whether those in these positions should be *educators,* that is, persons with such understanding and knowledge of educational processes that they can effectively participate (or even lead) in shaping them, is not new. Even as the superintendency was developing in the nineteenth century, some chose to be

---

[8] William Taylor, "Managing Contraction," in Robin Farquhar and Ian Housego, eds., *Canadian and Comparative Educational Administration* (Vancouver, B.C.: The University of British Columbia, 1980), p. 160.

managers (primarily of finance and facilities), some sought only to be involved with matters directly pertaining to curriculum and instruction, and others, with strong interest in and competence in matters of educational process, led and administered all aspects of the service in terms of educational needs. Today many forces are pushing the administrator to become a manager, with little or no competence or energy to devote to learning or the impact of varied forces upon learning and child development. If the administrator is not highly sensitive to and most fundamentally concerned with learning (educational processes), who will offer leadership in this area? The proverbial bureaucrat in the highly centralized organization is not an adequate answer.

In recent decades we have witnessed a remarkable development of concern for and action in the area of preparing administrators—pre- and in-service. Universities became more involved as did the profession. New knowledge developed, aided by a search for defensible theoretical constructs in and from related disciplines. Much remains to be achieved in this field in terms of theory, of usable knowledge, and of effective cooperative relationships between state and local school systems, universities, and the profession. One of the most important keys to the future may indeed be very substantial advancement in the processes of selecting and continuously preparing administrators.

CONCLUSION

While we are aware of the enormous issues which confront us—the social–economic issues of our society, the diversity of peoples and values, the problems of our schools, the lack of a clear course ahead, inadequate theory of administration, too limited usable knowledge, professional preparation programs in need of much further development—we need also to see the positive side. We can take pride in our heritage as a "free" people with strong commitment to common basic values gradually expanding opportunities to those once denied, a common school system with remarkable public involvement which has grown enormously in its goals and services over more than a century and has contributed in a highly significant manner to the individual attainments and the development of our society. A lack of certainty (fixedness) regarding who makes decisions and controls—parents, the state, local authorities, teachers' organizations, the federal government, courts, students, administrators—is a lack which hopefully keeps the door open for fresh initiatives and recognizes that no one can or should plan (determine) the future in irreversible terms. While immeasurably difficult, it is an unrivaled, endless opportunity providing (in view of inevitable changes socially, technologically, environmentally) for renewal with a drive toward discovery and "truth approximation" which recognizes that humanization requires that perfection be sought even though it is not to be found. It is in this context that educational organization and administration is examined in this volume.

2

THE LEGAL BASIS
for EDUCATION*

In this chapter, major attention is devoted to the origin, evolution, and implications of constitutional provisions, laws, board policies, administrative regulations, and court decisions relating to education. There must be a rational authority—that is, a legal basis—for all decisions in or relating to formal education. In this country the legal basis for education, as well as for other aspects of government, is the Constitution, other legal provisions adopted to implement the Constitution, and interpretations of those bases by court decisions. These determine the kinds of educational programs that must or can be provided and the provisions that can be made for organizing, administering, financing, and operating these programs. Of course the perceptions and attitudes of state and local school board members and the competencies and points of view of the educational personnel they employ also have an important and often a significant influence on the effectiveness and quality of the programs provided. An understanding of the major legal provisions is important for

*Prepared with the collaboration of Thomas M. Griffin, chief counsel, State Department of Education, California.

all who are concerned with education and is essential for those who have administrative responsibilities.

BASES FOR LEGAL PROVISIONS

In all nations the legal provisions (ranging from those incorporated in the constitution—if there is one—through enactments of a legislative body, decrees, or other official policy statements, administrative regulations, and court decisions) grow out of the values, beliefs, and concerns of the people or their rulers. The legal system may be designed primarily to protect the privileges of the governing group and its supporters, to ensure the perpetuation of certain customs or practices, or to provide the basis for orderly progress.

In the United States, the federal and state provisions that relate to education are a direct outgrowth of the value systems and beliefs of the citizens of the nation and of the various states. These value systems and beliefs relate to the place and role of education in the lives of people and in the governmental structure and also to the process of how educational decisions are made. These provisions are an integral part of a comprehensive legal system that constitutes a body of guides and rules for many aspects of human conduct and relations that are prescribed and enforced by legally authorized representatives of the organized society.

The Conceptual Design

In general, the legal provisions for education are based on what Hamilton and Mort have termed the "conceptual design" for education, which is an outgrowth of the beliefs, values, and aspirations of the people.[1] This conceptual design is based on the stated or implied purposes to be achieved through education and includes, by implication, the generally accepted perspectives and concepts concerning the place and role of education in society and government, the scope and major goals, and the basic guidelines or policies considered necessary to ensure adequate and effective provisions and programs. These legal provisions are organized into a more or less consistent and rational system that provides for policies and practices considered "good" or desirable and a basis for rejecting those that are considered "bad" or undesirable. Although the conceptual design for education is not static, many of the basic elements are relatively constant.

The evolving design is influenced by changes in society that have implications for education and by new information, ideas, and concepts relating to education. Basically, the design is affected by such factors as the following, which are often interrelated: (1) a new or revised theory concerning education and its organization and administration, (2) findings and conclusions based on important research studies in areas ranging from learning through finance, (3) the evaluation of experiences resulting in conclusions as to what works well and what does not, (4) new and challenging ideas and concepts which seem to hold promise, and (5) the changing beliefs and aspirations of the people. The design is also modified and given greater

[1] Robert R. Hamilton and Paul R. Mort, *The Law and Public Education,* 2nd ed. (New York: Foundation Press, Inc., 1959), Chap. 2.

specificity by court decisions which apply constitutional concepts (such as equality) to education.

Neither the people of the nation nor those in the areas that later became states began with laws relating to education. They started with beliefs, attitudes, and ideas—with the elements of a conceptual design—that constituted the basis for legal provisions. Some of their aspirations for education became statutorily sanctioned; others resulted in, or were the result of, decisions by courts of law, a process still in use today. This conceptual design which is still evolving with some differences noted from state to state, continues to be inconsistent and irrational in some respects, moves at inconstant rates within the nation as a whole, and in some aspects continues to be controversial. To the extent that standards are set by the courts—and especially by the U.S. Supreme Court—the process tends to be relatively uncontrolled by state interests except in those areas not subject to constitutional strictures.

As a result of having to design education without a fully developed model to guide them, early citizens and educators tended to grope idealistically toward a future system of education that no one really envisioned but that began to be expressed in purposes and goals to be attained and ends to be achieved. For example, Horace Mann wrote in the 1840s

> I believe in the existence of a great, immortal immutable principle of natural law, or natural ethics—a principle antecedent to all human institutions, and incapable of being abrogated by any ordinance of man—which proves the *absolute right* to an education of every human being that comes into the world, and which, of course, proves the correlative duty of every government to see that the means of that education are provided for all.[2]

This aspiration of Mann's (universal education at public expense) has become the cornerstone for most of the state systems of education since the 1840s and continues to challenge citizens and state planning agencies or commissions in the 1980s.

The Sources of Law

It is precisely because of the deep and abiding faith of the people in universal education at public expense that the states were able to obtain the cooperation of parents and students in attempting to implement Mann's concept. Through compulsory attendance, compulsory taxation, and related statutes, the legislative bodies preempted some aspects of the personal preferences of individuals on the grounds that the American way of life depended on an enlightened citizenry and that such measures were necessary to achieve the "great American dream." The states controlled these aspects of public education until 1954, when the "Warren court" was requested, and attempted, to bring about a better balance *between the responsibility assumed by the states and individual freedoms* under the Constitution.

Prior to the Warren court decisions, the courts had exercised "judicial restraint";

[2]Horace Mann, *Tenth Annual Report to the Massachusetts State Board of Education,* 1846, pp. 177–180.

that is, they had hesitated to act in support of an individual's rights in or for education, doing so only when a board of education clearly acted outside its legal powers or in an arbitrary or capricious manner in denying individual rights. But the U.S. Supreme Court, beginning in 1954, instituted a line of decisions which protected and expanded individual liberties. The court developed the rule that, to limit individual rights in schools, school officials must show "an overriding public purpose to be served" which made such limitation necessary. As a result of its decisions relating to educational policy, the Warren court wielded considerable power in shaping some important aspects of current policy.

The fact that some important educational policies have been determined by the courts, however, does not minimize or eliminate the need for better educational planning. On the contrary, the need for such planning is heightened by the court's willingness to balance the interests of the state against those of each individual teacher, student, and lay citizen, for two reasons. First, there are inherent weaknesses in the judicial determination of educational policy. It can determine only one issue at a time between one plaintiff (or class of plaintiffs) and one defendant; it never is presented with the entire school policy in one case. Second, in the adversarial forum, each side either wins or loses. A court is not in a position to formulate a "middle ground" policy which strikes a balance between competing interests. School authorities are likely to lose in court when they cannot show that they gave careful consideration to the rights of the children, parents, teachers, and taxpayers that the plaintiffs seek to have enforced by the courts. In short, when educators and others fail to plan carefully programs which balance the rights of all parties, including society, they create a vacuum which courts are now willing to fill.

Continuing or periodic study and review of the basic purposes and goals of education should be considered essential in every state and community. To the extent that agreement can be reached, there is an acceptable basis for developing legislation and for planning educational programs. New purposes and goals or new emphases will emerge from time to time, and these, of course, will have implications for developments throughout the state.

The Structural Pattern

Public education is "one instrumentality of society for the carrying out of a function which society has decreed to be a desirable one."[3] It is not surprising, therefore, that the basic provisions for the organization and operation of education are determined by the society in which it operates. Thus, the society determines not only the conceptual design for education but also the structure for implementing that design. Educators, through their concepts, ideas, and studies, undoubtedly influence both the design and the structure in many ways, but they do not necessarily determine what either is to be. Educators are trained specifically to develop and implement educational programs. For example, if a strong program in mathematics is desired, the educator is trained in administration and pedagogy to develop and implement an effective and efficient mathematics curriculum. But the basic concept—whether mathematics is more or less desirable as an educational objective

---

[3] Hamilton and Mort, *Law and Public Education*, p. 3.

than is reading or music—is generally seen as a public policy decision which, although influenced by the educator, is a prerogative of lay representatives of society, either the legislature or the local board of education.

Ideally, the structural pattern for education should emerge from the conceptual design and be consistent with it. Actually, the structural pattern often is determined basically by the legal and political systems that establish the plan for organization and operation by creating the agencies to be utilized in attaining the desired goals and allocating functions among them within prescribed limits.

The structural pattern tends, in certain respects, to lag behind the evolving conceptual design for education. In other words, constitutional provisions, laws, and even court decisions are based on elements of the conceptual design *at a particular time*. As the design changes, the legal system usually retains some practices and concepts that are outmoded. Moreover, the structural pattern, for one reason or another, often omits important elements of the conceptual design and often includes nonrational or inconsistent aspects that prevent the development of an effective program of education, at least in certain parts of the state.

Such inconsistencies and limitations should not be surprising. Often, the conceptual design is not articulated clearly, particularly in the balance of conflicting principles such as state monitoring versus local control. Constitutional conventions and legislatures often include some people who do not subscribe to the generally accepted conceptual design for public education or do not understand the implications of some of the provisions they advocate. The problem is likely to be particularly acute when people in the states have sharp differences of opinion concerning elements of the conceptual design, when the design itself is vague or poorly formulated in certain respects, or when the people are relatively uninformed or indifferent about changing needs and the characteristics of an effective program of education.

Some steps that might well be taken in any state to ensure that the structural pattern is as consistent as possible with the evolving conceptual design include the following:

1. Educational and lay leaders should review systematically, and if necessary revise, the conceptual design for education periodically to ensure that it will facilitate the attainment of the desired purposes of education, that it is consistent internally, and that it is stated clearly.

2. Legislators and other citizens should be encouraged to discuss this tentative statement and to propose revisions or clarification. This procedure should result not only in improving the statement and in making it more meaningful but also in facilitating understanding, agreement, and support.

3. All major legal provisions should then be reviewed as a means of identifying any handicapping constraints, lags, or inconsistent aspects and as a means of proposing revisions.

4. The legislature should be encouraged to incorporate into the legal structure all basic elements that seem to be substantiated by evidence and experience, so as to make the structure as consistent as possible with the design.

5. The legislature should be expected to refrain from mandating any aspect of structure that is inconsistent with the design or is based on an emerging concept that has not yet been adequately tried out or tested.

6. As a basis for ensuring greater flexibility in introducing locally promising

innovations, the legislature should provide for considerable local discretion and should refrain from restricting local boards to those educational policies and practices that are authorized specifically by statute.

CONSTITUTIONAL PROVISIONS

The basic legal provisions relating to or having implications for education are found in the federal and state constitutions. Those in the federal Constitution are of significance for education throughout the nation, whereas provisions found in each state constitution are applicable only to the educational program within the state.

The Federal Constitution

As far as education is concerned, the most significant provisions of the federal Constitution are found in the Tenth Amendment, which—like other sections of the Constitution—does not even mention education. This amendment reserves to the states or to the people all powers not delegated to the federal government by the Constitution.

In the case of *San Antonio Independent School District* v. *Rodriguez*[4] the U.S. Supreme Court concluded that education, although important, is not a right that is protected by the federal Constitution in the sense that freedom of speech, religion, press, and so on are rights that are so protected. Therefore, as far as the federal Constitution is concerned, states are free to provide an educational system to their citizens or not, as they see fit.

However, four other provisions in the federal Constitution and its amendments noted in the paragraphs that follow are commonly recognized as having considerable significance for education. Most of them are concerned with the protection of what is often referred to as the inherent rights of individuals. Sections 8 and 10 of Article I prescribe, respectively, that Congress shall have power to provide, among other things, for the general welfare and that no state shall pass any law impairing the obligation of contracts. The First Amendment prohibits Congress from making any law "respecting an establishment of religion, or prohibiting the free exercise thereof." (Later, the Bill of Rights, including the First Amendment, was held to apply to the states as well as to the Congress.) One clause of the Fifth Amendment, which is concerned with the protection of individuals against self-incrimination in criminal cases, has been invoked in cases in which investigation committees have sought to inquire into connections that teachers and others may have had with what some people may consider to be "subversive organizations." Of particular importance is the Fourteenth Amendment, which prohibits any state from making or enforcing any law abridging "the privileges or immunities of citizens of the United States," or from depriving any person of "life, liberty, or property, without due process of law," or from denying "to any person within its jurisdiction the equal protection of the laws." Each of these provisions has been the basis for a number of controversies and challenges involving education.

[4] *San Antonio Independent School District* v. *Rodriguez*, 411 U.S. 1 (1973).

The "equal protection" clause of the Fourteenth Amendment has been inter-preted by the courts as prohibiting a state from denying to a child a state right to an equal education merely because he or she was handicapped[5] or emotionally disturbed.[6] The "due process" clause has been invoked by the U.S. Supreme Court to prohibit a state from removing from a student his or her state right to an educa-tion through suspension for misconduct without affording him or her a funda-mentally fair hearing.[7] The general rule of federal constitutional law derived from this amendment is that, whereas a state need not make education a legal right, if it does so it must make it available to all citizens equally and may not deprive a citizen of this state right without "due process of law."

Although each state has the responsibility for developing its own public school program, it cannot through its constitutional provisions or laws violate (without the probability of challenge in the courts) any of the provisions of the federal Consti-tution including its amendments. There are thus important controls on what states may do in certain respects, but as long as these limitations are observed, the people of each state are free to develop their own education program as they see fit.

State Constitutional Provisions

The people of each state have incorporated in their constitution some of their basic beliefs about, and policies for, education as well as other aspects of govern-ment for which they are responsible. However, as new information has become available, insights and points of view have gradually changed. Some of these chang-ing concepts have tended to be reflected in most states either in new constitutions adopted by the people or in amendments to the original constitution.

Ideally, the constitution should include only the fundamental policies and basic provisions concerning education and other aspects of government. The more spe-cific and detailed provisions are usually included in the statutes, policy statements, and regulations. All of these, as supplemented or modified by court decisions, con-stitute the presumably rational—and legal—authority for organizing and operating school systems and schools. Constitutional provisions are usually more difficult to revise or repeal than are statutes.

One policy that has found expression in some form in every state constitution is that the state legislature must provide for a uniform and effective system of pub-lic schools. Thus the people generally have not left the legislature any discretion as to whether public schools shall be established. Usually, however, it has had con-siderable discretion as to steps and procedures that may be used in establishing such schools. Other policies relating to education that have been expressed in the consti-tution of nearly every state include the following: the permanent school fund is to be kept sacred and inviolate and only the income from the fund may be used for public school purposes; public schools are to be provided at public expense; and

---

[5] *Pennsylvania Assoc. for Retarded Children* v. *Commonwealth of Pennsylvania,* U.S. Dist. Ct., E. Dist. Pa., 334 F. Supp. 1257 (1971).

[6] *Mills* v. *Board of Education of the District of Columbia,* U.S. Dist. Ct., Dist. Col., 348 F. Supp. 866 (1972).

[7] *Goss* v. *Lopez,* 419 U.S. 564 (1975).

public tax funds made available for educational purposes are to be used only for the support of public education.

Although one objective of the people in each state seems to have been to incorporate in their constitution those provisions that require and facilitate the development of an adequate program of public education, experience has shown that restrictive or handicapping provisions have from time to time been included. For example, constitutional provisions in some states prescribe such rigid limits on taxes or bond issues for school purposes that the people in many communities have not been permitted to make the effort they would be willing to make to support schools. Thus the provisions relating to education that are incorporated in a state constitution have vital significance. They may either stimulate and facilitate the development of an adequate program of public education or make such a program difficult, if not impossible, to attain until they are repealed.

The legislature of a state has full power, commonly referred to as *plenary* power, to enact laws regarding the schools as well as other aspects of government. However, such legislation should not conflict with provisions of the state or federal Constitution. If any such conflict exists and the matter is taken to the courts, the statute will be declared unconstitutional. The following statement in a New York court decision is significant:

> The people, in framing the constitution, committed to the legislature the whole law making power of the state which they did not expressly or impliedly withhold. Plenary power in the legislature for all purposes of civil government is the rule.[8]

LAWS AND ADMINISTRATIVE POLICIES
RELATING TO EDUCATION

Laws as well as constitutional provisions relating to education vitally affect provisions for education and should be of concern to everyone interested in education or government. Statutes (commonly referred to as "laws") enacted by the legislatures of the respective states are enforced as long as they are not in conflict with the state's constitution or the federal Constitution and its amendments. Such statutes presumably express the majority beliefs and intent of the people of the state and, in certain respects, may be as significant as constitutional provisions in determining the scope and adequacy of the educational program that can be provided. Narrowly restrictive or unwise statutes may be as serious as limiting constitutional provisions.

Majority rule must give way, however, where the courts indicate that the state has overstepped its authority and infringed upon the individual rights of any citizen. The philosophical question as to whether "majority rule should predominate in all things" is too involved to be treated here. Suffice it to say that our "law" comes from two sources, neither of which is exclusive: (1) enactments of public policy by majority legislative decision and (2) decisions by the courts and ad-

---

[8] *The People* v. *Draper*, 15 N.Y. 532 (1857).

ministrative bodies upholding the rights of individuals or minorities as contrasted to those of the state. The model, an apothecary's scale, sees justice in this framework as balancing the interests of the individual in relationship to those of the state (all the other individuals).

Federal Laws

Since education has been established as a function of the respective states, the basic laws relating to the organization, administration, and operation of schools are state rather than federal laws. However, the people of the entire nation have always been interested in education and, as a consequence, from the time of the early land grants there have been federal laws relating to one aspect or another of education (see Chapter 10). Although some of these laws are concerned with direct responsibilities of the federal government (for education of the military forces or wards of the federal government and education in certain federal areas and territories), others are designed to aid or stimulate education in and through the states. These laws have provided for grants and services to the states for various educational purposes. These laws are passed under the general "police" power of Congress to provide for the general welfare.[9]

The chief problems from the point of view of many people have arisen over the narrow categorical financial provisions and the requirements or controls that have been incorporated in some laws relating to financial assistance. Congress undoubtedly has a right to establish requirements that are not inconsistent with provisions of the federal Constitution. The issue is basically one as to the kind of policies and the extent of controls that seem to be needed and are prudent. Usually, states have been given the right (theoretically, at least) to decide whether they will accept the funds authorized. However, if a state is willing to accept the funds authorized by any law, it must observe the conditions attached to the acceptance.

Congress has seen fit to impose two different types of conditions. The first type are the specific conditions relating to the specific program. For example, a recipient of funds under Title I of the Elementary and Secondary Education Act of 1965 must meet the specific program requirements of that program, including pupil and school eligibility, maintenance of effort, accounting of funds, and so on. The second type of condition is that under the civil rights statutes and applies to recipients of federal funds regardless of the program. Thus, a recipient, as a condition of receiving any federal assistance at all, may not discriminate on the basis of race, color, religion, national origin,[10] sex,[11] or physical or mental handicap.[12] The U.S. Supreme Court has held it to be a violation of this nondiscrimination provision for a school district to fail to take steps to remedy the language barrier of national origin minority children.[13]

[9] U.S. Constitution, Article I, Section 8.
[10] 42 U.S.C. § 2000d (Title VI of the Civil Rights Act of 1964).
[11] Title IX (Section 901–907 of P. L. 92–318).
[12] 29 U.S.C. § 794 *et seq.* (P. L. 93–112, Title V, § 504).
[13] *Lau* v. *Nichols,* 414 U.S. 563 (1974).

State Statutes

Three major questions underlying educational legislation in each state are: What kinds of statutes are desirable to provide for the development of an adequate and effective program of public education? What procedures can be utilized to help to ensure that changes in statutes or new legislation are planned as carefully as most legislators would expect changes in educational programs or procedures to be? How much detail should be delegated to state or local school boards rather than specified in the law? Appropriate statutes are those that facilitate the attainment of these goals; those that do not should be challenged. Undoubtedly, every state has some statutes that, properly assessed, would be found indefensible.

The process of evaluating statutes is taking place constantly in every state. Sooner or later, unwise or hastily enacted statutes are likely to be found unsatisfactory on the basis of studies and experiences in various parts of the state and may be repealed or modified materially. Unfortunately, however, once statutes are enacted, the process of evaluation often tends to be slow or ineffective. Many inappropriate or restrictive laws tend to be continued indefinitely.

Some state legislatures have accepted quite literally the concept that education is a function of the state and tend to assume that local school systems should have no responsibility or authority unless it is specifically granted by the state. Such states have developed very detailed statutes because such detail has been considered necessary to enable school systems to operate satisfactorily. A system of statutes prepared on the basis of this premise is referred to as a "mandatory" system or code. California is a good example of a state that has had (but has recently abandoned) a mandatory system of school legislation, as school districts have been prohibited from doing anything that is not authorized or clearly implied by legislation. Some years ago, the state attorney general advised that

> The question is not whether the payment of expense (as proposed by a school board) would contribute to the education of pupils, but whether the authority is vested in the board to make such an expenditure. . . . School districts are *quasi* municipal corporations of the most limited power known to law.[14]

Such a system results in a vast volume of detailed legislation that places a burden not only on the legislature but also on school officials who are attempting to observe the provisions of statutory law. Perhaps even more significant, it tends to stifle initiative and may prevent local school systems from experimenting or instituting some promising innovations until the legislature has authorized the action. Especially during this period of rapid change and search for helpful innovations, such a policy can be defended only on the basis of tradition.

Several states have attempted to observe the principle that, while basic policies and responsibilities must be prescribed, some discretion should also be granted to local school systems to assume responsibilities not inconsistent with law that are found necessary for an effective program of education. Provisions of this type, sometimes called a "mandatory-discretionary" system of laws, seem to be favored by an increasing number of states. In a study of the powers and duties of local

[14] California Attorney General Opinion 47-38, 1947.

26

school boards in selected states with "mandatory" and others with "mandatory-discretionary" types of school codes, Hall found the difference in wording to be small but significant.[15] In the latter group of states, a clause, worded somewhat as follows, was added to the section listing the powers and duties allocated to local school boards: "and in addition thereto, those which it may find to be necessary for the improvement of the school system in carrying out the purposes and objectives of the school code." After analyzing court decisions in these states, Hall concluded that, in the absence of abuse of discretion, the courts generally ruled in favor of the board in its use of the discretionary authority granted.

In delegating authority to local boards to make specific decisions, the legislature may dictate a process which brings others—teachers, parents, members of the community, and sometimes students—into the decision-making process. Two recent trends point to decision making in educational policy matters by a broader base of participants. First is collective bargaining for teachers and noncredentialed staff which gives them a voice in matters within the scope of bargaining that once was the sole prerogative of the local board. Second is the use of parent and community advisory councils at both the school and district levels. Originating with district committees under Title I of the Elementary and Secondary Education Act of 1965, they can now be found at school sites under Title I and in the state aid programs in some states such as California.

Statutes pertaining to schools, unlike those on many other subjects, have to be used for guidance by both professional educators and laypersons serving on boards of education. Few of them have had much legal training. Even well-drafted statutes may have relatively little meaning for laypersons or even lawyers unless they are well organized, written so they can be readily understood, presented so they can be easily located, and properly indexed.

For this reason, all states have found it necessary to organize their statutes relating to education into a code. Several plans have been proposed for organizing and codifying the statutes relating to education. One of the simplest of these provides for a code comprising two or three major parts. The first part would include statutes that have implications for all aspects of education, with appropriate divisions, chapters, and sections; the second part would include the more specific provisions with divisions, chapters, and sections incorporating statutes dealing with personnel, students, program, plant, finance, and so on; a third part, or a separate code, would include statutes relating to institutions of higher learning and other aspects of education.

Board Policies, Standards, and Regulations

Some legislation has included details that have resulted in needless handicaps to the educational program. An extreme illustration is afforded by a statute enacted some years ago in one of the states providing that a course on safety education be "taught by lectures." A more common illustration is found in statutes providing

---

[15] Donald Ellis Hall, "Discretionary and Mandatory Provisions of State Education Law," (unpublished doctoral dissertation, University of California, Berkeley, 1959).

that a designated number of minutes each day be devoted to a certain subject in every school.

Experience has shown that it is not practicable and usually not desirable to include minor policies or details in legislation. The general practice of the U.S. Congress is to enact rather general policy statements into law, with an authorization to the federal administration to enact implementing regulations. To have the force and effect of law, these regulations must be adopted in a prescribed way which assures notice to the public and an opportunity for interested persons to comment on the proposal and offer suggestions for amendment. Once adopted, the regulations are published in the *Code of Federal Regulations.*

Similarly, in every state provision is made for the development and adoption by some state agency (usually the state board of education) of policies, standards, and regulations that have the effect of law. The state board also has the authority to adopt guidelines which are suggested but not binding on local education agencies. The process for adopting a regulation which is binding, as compared with a policy or guideline which is not, is dictated by the legislature in state law. In addition, local boards are authorized to adopt policies and regulations that are not inconsistent with state laws or regulations and which, if properly developed and adopted, have the effect of law in the local school system.

If the legislature were to attempt to grant unlimited powers to a state board of education or to a chief state school officer, the courts could be expected to hold that that legislature cannot delegate its responsibilities and that the powers granted are too broad and, therefore, are null and void. When the legislature prescribes the general policies and establishes definite limits within which administrative policies or regulations must come, difficulties should be avoided. But the policies and regulations adopted as authorized by law must be consistent with the provisions of law and must be reasonable.[16]

A good example of legislation that requires the adoption of administrative policies and regulations can be found in the field of teacher certification. In many states the statutes set forth the purposes of certification, the general procedures to be used, and, perhaps, the major kinds or classes of certificates authorized. The responsibility for prescribing detailed policies, standards, and regulations is usually delegated to the state board of education. The state board should establish application procedures and prescribe requirements to be met before a certificate can be issued. These regulations, however, would have to be reasonable and consistent with the purpose of the statutes to assure fair treatment for all applicants.

All major policies and directives should, therefore, be incorporated in legislation, but details that might retard improvements in education or may need to be changed from time to time should be avoided. The statutes should clearly delegate responsibility, when appropriate, for administrative policies and regulations but should carefully define the limits. Boards or agencies to which such responsibilities are delegated should take steps to ensure that their actions are authorized by and are consistent with provisions of law, are reasonable, and do not constitute an impulsive or arbitrary exercise of delegated power.

The process of developing policies in a local school system often involves some

[16] Newton Edwards, *The Courts and the Public Schools,* rev. ed. (Chicago: University of Chicago Press, 1955), p. 31.

difficulties. Each proposed policy must be considered in relation to other policies; otherwise, there may be conflicts and crosscurrents with resultant confusion, dissention, or inefficiency. Studies by a competent and representative committee in advance of board consideration should mean that, if the board adopts the recommended policy, it is not only likely to be sound and defensible but also to have a reasonably good prospect of being accepted by the staff and by the community. Adoption of the policy by the board means that the board then has a guide for action in that field, subject to possible revision on the basis of further studies. Once a policy has been adopted, a board should not need to spend time in considering individual problems that arise in that area. Nor should it have to risk the possibility of inconsistent action while attempting to work out a solution for each problem without reference to previous decisions.

The board of education of the district should not enact, nor should the administrator prescribe, restrictive or detailed rules and regulations governing the implementation of board policies. Unless reasonable flexibility is provided for management, there will be little innovation in a school system. It is not good policy for the legislature, the state board of education, the local board of education, or the administrator to prescribe in detail the activities of principals and teachers. Better educational programs tend to be found in those systems which provide for a considerable amount of decision making at the operating level.

COURT DECISIONS

Any statute or any board regulation may be constitutional or unconstitutional. Any board regulation may be consistent or inconsistent with the underlying statute. When a question arises, either the statute or the board regulation bears the presumption of constitutionality unless or until a court of competent jurisdiction has declared otherwise. This means that any untested statute or regulation must be presumed to be valid until such time as it has been declared unconstitutional and all appeals to higher courts, including those to the U.S. Supreme Court, have been exhausted or abandoned.

Ordinarily, courts will not of their own volition test the constitutionality of a statute or public law; they interpret only *concrete* examples of the applicability, or misapplicability, of the statute or public law in question. Inasmuch as each case differs in some or perhaps many respects from other cases, a school administrator needs to be familiar with related adjudicated cases of recent vintage to develop a reasonably defensible position for dealing with legal problems that arise in his or her work and should seek to work closely with the board's legal counsel on all major legal problems with which the school system is or may be concerned.

The Role of the Courts

Because education affects practically all people in one way or another at some time during their lives, there are many differences of opinion regarding the rights, privileges, and obligations of people relating to schools. As society becomes more complex, as attempts are made to adapt education to the rapidly changing needs, and as laws relating to education increase in number and scope, more and more questions regarding the purposes and intent of those laws are likely to arise. Thus, the courts in every state and, in some cases, federal courts, are called upon from time to time to interpret one aspect or another of the laws relating to schools.

The courts have been established to attempt to resolve the many controversies that are certain to arise in a pluralistic society. They function in accordance with established rules or criteria in an effort to assure equity and justice for all in every aspect of life, including education. Fortunately, courts do not always decide issues merely by precedent or weight of evidence. As the U.S. Supreme Court stated in a landmark decision holding that the Social Security Act was not in conflict with the Tenth Amendment, "Nor is the concept of general welfare static. Needs that were narrow or parochial a century ago may be interwoven in our day with the well being of the Nation. What is critical or urgent changes with the times."[17]

In this way, controversies are rationalized in the legal and judicial frame of reference. The result has been a slowly changing conceptual pattern to which the courts have made significant contributions. At times, they have helped to free education from some outmoded legislative constraints and, in a way, have served as an adapting agency between legislation and educational administration.[18]

In addition to the federal system of courts (to which recourse may usually be had only when a constitutional issue or a federal policy or statute is involved), each state has its own judicial system.

Because the Constitution of the United States is the supreme law of the land, no law can be contrary to its provisions. The statement concerning the supremacy of the Constitution (Article VI) presupposes the power of some agency or body to declare acts of the president and the Congress unconstitutional. Such power is vested in the U.S. Supreme Court. The Supreme Court, which is the court of final appeal in the system, is given final jurisdiction over all constitutional cases that arise. When the U.S. Supreme Court exercises its granted jurisdiction by accepting a case (often from a lower federal or a state court) involving an interpretation of the Constitution, and this court finds that a law—federal or state—is contrary to the court's interpretation, this law is declared void for that reason. This is what is meant by declaring an act "unconstitutional."

There is a common misapprehension that the Supreme Court frequently declares acts of the Congress unconstitutional. However, throughout its history, the Supreme Court has held only eighty-two[19] acts of the Congress unconstitutional in whole or in part through 1975. Considering the immense volume of congressional legislation enacted during this long period in the nation's history and the limited number of restraints imposed on congressional power, it seems evident that the highest court in the nation has exercised considerable "judicial restraint" and self-control.

The controversy over whether a court is "legislating" when it is deciding legal controversies undoubtedly will continue for some time to come. An important issue, however, is whether or not this way of regulating the power of the other two

---

[17] *Helvering* v. *Davis,* 301 U.S. 619, (1937).

[18] Hamilton and Mort, *Law and Public Education,* pp. 1, 11.

[19] Paul C. Bartholomew, *Summaries of Leading Cases on the Constitution* (Totowa, N.J.: Littlefield, Adams & Co., 1977), p. 13.

branches of government is likely to remain. There is no doubt that basic public policy, including that pertaining to the public schools, will continue to be determined to a large extent by the courts of law. This fact in no way minimizes the necessity for adequate planning by the states and the federal government in matters relating to public education. In fact, if there were more state-level planning and leadership, the role of the courts in educational decision making probably would be somewhat more limited than it is at present.

During recent years, the chief concern of the courts has been with those problem areas related to the rights of individuals—teachers, students, administrators, and others—vis-à-vis the schools as an agency of government. As our society becomes more pluralistic, the need for judicial interpretation and review tends to become more evident. Through a system of *stare decisis* (let the decision stand), landmark cases are accepted as precedents to be followed in future cases of the same kind. The courts, however, can and often do overrule prior decisions, so the doctrine of *stare decisis* is by no means ironclad.

State courts are also charged with judicial review responsibility, especially with respect to the state constitutionality of statutory enactments by legislatures, and often act as screening devices in the early stages of litigation. For example, the *Serrano*[20] case in California in 1971 contributed significantly to the development of cases and court decisions relating to provisions for financing schools in a number of other states. The issue was whether the state's plan for funding public education denied "to the child in a poor district equal protection of the laws because it makes the quality of that child's education a function of the wealth of his parents and neighbors." The California Supreme Court held that the provisions being challenged did deny equal protection.

In the light of a 1972 New Jersey Supreme Court decision (*Robinson* v. *Cahill*), which is similar to the California decision, and of recent developments in several other states, it seems apparent that most progress for improving provisions for financing schools is likely to be made in those states in which the constitution and laws clearly require reasonable equity for taxpayers and equality of educational opportunities for students.

U.S. Supreme Court Decisions

Because education is not mentioned in the federal Constitution, it is never involved directly in questions that come before the U.S. Supreme Court. The involvement is always incidental, coming through other questions, but often is quite significant.

According to Spurlock, forty-five cases involving education to a rather significant extent came before the Supreme Court between the time the Constitution was adopted and 1954.[21] Most of these cases were concerned with questions relating to (1) state or federal power and functions, (2) civil rights under the First and Fifth Amendments, and (3) due process of law and equal protection of law under

---

[20] *Serrano* v. *Priest*, 5 C. 3d 584; 96 Cal. Repr. 601; Cool, 487 P.2d 1241 (Calif. 1971).

[21] The authors are indebted to Clark Spurlock, *Education and the Supreme Court* (Urbana: University of Illinois Press, 1955), for much of the basic information presented in this section.

the Fourteenth Amendment. The cases were classified under the following headings: (1) contests involving rights of parents and students, (2) contests involving rights of teachers and touching on property rights and personal freedoms, (3) contests involving rights of races in schools in states maintaining segregated schools, (4) contests involving powers of school authorities in fiscal matters or in matters involving powers of school authorities in fiscal matters or in matters involving rights of citizens, and (5) contests involving rights of nonpublic schools.

It is interesting to note that most of these cases occurred after 1925. Before that time, only eighteen cases had important implications for education. Of these, only nine occurred before the beginning of the present century. Between 1925 and 1954, however, there were twenty-seven cases. Many of these touched on conflicts between individual rights and state requirements and conflicts relating to separation of church and state.

During the period 1953 to 1969, the "Warren court" decided thirty-three cases involving education (eight relating to religion in the public schools, thirteen relating to segregation of the races, and twelve relating to academic freedom).[22] Of the eight cases dealing with separation of church and state, five concerned the practice of Bible reading and/or prayers in the schools' opening exercises. The remaining three cases dealt with lending textbooks to children in parochial schools, teaching Darwin's theory of evolution, and allowing individuals to contest the expenditure of federal funds for related purposes.

The thirteen decisions concerning segregation and integration included the landmark case of *Brown* v. *Board of Education,*[23] which established the controlling legal principle that *racial discrimination in the public schools is in violation of provisions of the Constitution.* Significantly in this decision the court also emphasized the *importance of education:*

> Today, education is perhaps the most important function of state and local government . . . in these days it is doubtful that any child may reasonably be expected to succeed in life if he is denied the opportunity of an education. Such an opportunity, when the state has undertaken to provide it, is a right which must be made available to all on equal terms.

Between 1953 and 1969, the Supreme Court dealt with freedom of speech and association (seven cases) and loyalty oaths for teachers and other state employees (five cases). The five loyalty oath laws were declared to be unconstitutional, teacher affiliation with certain organizations was decided on the narrow issues in each case, and free speech protection was upheld for both teachers and students in two separate cases. Later statutes reinstating a loyalty oath were subsequently upheld, and the scope of teachers' freedom of speech widened by the Burger court. Because many of the decisions of the Warren court were the result of a divided court, later courts might reverse any of them. The school administrator should keep abreast of the latest decisions involving education handled by the Supreme Court as the scene changes.

[22] H. C. Hudgins, Jr., *The Warren Court and the Public Schools* (Danville, Ill.: Interstate Publishers, 1970), p. 155.

[23] *Brown* v. *Board of Education of Topeka,* 347 U.S. 483 (Kans. 1954).

Three landmark cases involving students' rights are noteworthy. In 1967[24] the Supreme Court held that the state may not maintain two legal standards, one for adults and another for children. In declaring that "due process [of law] is not for adults alone," the court established the principle that children are entitled to the constitutional guarantee of due process despite juvenile codes to the contrary in many states. In 1969 the court widened and clarified its window on student rights[25] by declaring that

> In our system, state-operated schools may not be enclaves of totalitarianism. School officials do not possess absolute authority over their students. Students in school as well as out of school are "persons" under our Constitution. They are possessed of fundamental rights which the State must respect, just as they themselves must respect their obligations to the State. . . . In the absence of a specific showing of constitutionally valid reasons for regulating their speech, students are entitled to freedom of expression of their views.

Thus the Supreme Court has set a new standard by which the courts will judge the propriety of a local board's rules and regulations. In the future, if a local board attempts to restrict personal freedoms of its students in any way, *it must show that there is an overriding public purpose to be served thereby.* In the absence of such a showing, the courts will intervene to uphold individual rights where denial of a guaranteed constitutional freedom is involved.

In 1975 the court expanded the right of students to procedural due process of law. In *Goss* v. *Lopez*,[26] the court held that the right of students to an education was a property right under the Fourteenth Amendment. Thus, a student is entitled to minimum procedural safeguards before that interest is taken away through suspension for misconduct.

In some cases the Supreme Court has indicated that it is reluctant to consider matters that might pertain to state educational policies, in view of the fact that education is clearly recognized as a function of the respective states. Nevertheless, it is apparent that the court has exercised significant influence in a number of respects on the design and pattern for American education. Without such decisions, the American system of education would undoubtedly have been different in many respects than it is today. Thus the federal government, through Supreme Court decisions, has controlled more aspects of the development of education in the various states than many people realize. This control has been in the direction of stabilization and of unification in certain aspects of the conceptual design for education.[27]

In a case some years ago, one of the justices expressed concern that the Supreme Court might be tending to become a national board of education. However, it seems apparent that the Supreme Court, in its expressed philosophy underlying decisions, has uniformly tended to avoid questions involving state policy except where provisions of the federal Constitution are at issue.

[24] In the matter of *Gault*, 387 U.S. 1, 87 S. Ct. 1428 (Ariz. 1967).
[25] *Tinker* v. *Des Moines School Board*, 393 U.S. 503 (Iowa 1969).
[26] 419 U.S. 565 (1975).
[27] Spurlock, *Education and the Supreme Court*, p. 238.

The complex body of law on the subject of integration remains almost exclusively a product of court decisions. The way in which the courts fashioned remedies to the Southern dual school systems and the ways in which these principles of constitutional duty and remedies were applied to Northern school districts is a story too long to be detailed here. It is sufficient to point out that this story is still being written as new cases are brought to the U.S. Supreme Court. At the present time, districts have an obligation to alleviate whatever segregation has been caused by intentional government action—a form of segregation called *de jure*—but do not have an obligation under the Fourteenth Amendment to alleviate segregation caused by housing patterns or other nongovernmental factors—called *de facto* segregation. Whether or not this distinction will remain will depend upon the way in which the "conceptual design" of the Fourteenth Amendment is articulated by the courts. Similarly, other issues in this area such as the need for metropolitan desegregation plans, the responsibility of the state administration for enforcing and financing compliance, and the development of educational components to desegregation plans such as multicultural education can be expected to be addressed by the courts in the years ahead.

State Supreme Court Decisions

U.S. Supreme Court decisions, by implication at least, affect education throughout the United States. On the other hand, a decision by a state supreme court is of direct significance for education only in that state, although it may have indirect significance in other states if it is used or cited by courts in those states. Courts do not legislate, but their decisions have the effect of law. Consequently, reference is frequently made to *statute law*, or law enacted by legislature, and to *case law*, or law interpreted in specific instances through court cases.

Ordinarily, the role of the state courts is to interpret state statutes in the light of the state's constitution. A state court, however, is not responsible for determining the *wisdom* of the particular law but is concerned, instead, with whether it is consistent with the constitution. In deciding the legality of a local board policy or action, a court will not intervene unless the board has acted outside its legal powers or in an arbitrary and capricious manner.

Almost every aspect of the educational program has at some time been involved in court decisions in each of the states. The laws among the states differ so widely and there are so many different types of court decisions that generalization would seem to be difficult if not impossible. Yet there are many basic similarities in state laws and, likewise, many basic similarities in court decisions relating to fundamental issues. Although it is necessary to consult the laws and court decisions of a particular state before authoritative statements can be made regarding many aspects of the educational program, certain legal principles have become sufficiently well established to permit generalization. Among the most important are the following:

- The courts are generally agreed that education is a function of the state and that the control and management of the public schools is an essential aspect of state sovereignty.
- The legislature has full and complete power to legislate concerning the control and management of the public schools of the state, except in respects in which that power is restricted by the state constitution or by the federal Constitution.

- The legislature may delegate certain powers and responsibilities for education to designated state and local agencies, but it may not delegate all its powers. It must give reasonable direction to the administrators and establish reasonable limits that are required to be observed by state or local agencies as they exercise their delegated responsibilities.
- Public schools are state, not local, institutions. In reality the public school program is a partnership program between the state and local unit created by the state. The state may create and reorganize local school districts and delegate to them definite powers for the organization, administration, and operation of schools. These districts may be created especially for school purposes or may be municipal or county districts. However, the municipality or county has no authority or power over the schools within its boundaries except as such authority or power is definitely granted by the state.

SOME IMPORTANT PROBLEMS AND ISSUES

A few of the many important issues relating to the legal aspects of education are discussed briefly in this section.

How Much Educational Policy Should Be Incorporated into Law?

Although it may not be possible in any state to get complete agreement on educational policies, majority concurrence on all or most aspects of the conceptual design for education is both feasible and desirable. Without such concurrence, some policies and laws would probably be likely to deviate sharply from a rational pattern, and the educational program could be handicapped seriously.

One of the first concerns of many who want to change educational policies or practices seems to be to incorporate their "idea" into law. Some apparently believe that, when a "law" has been enacted, the problem has been solved. However, those who understand the situation recognize that laws do not necessarily solve problems. A statute requiring counseling in all schools, providing for environmental education or even for accountability, does not necessarily mean that all local school boards, administrators, or teachers are in a position to implement rationally the intent of the law or will do so.

Laws, of course, are necessary if local school systems are to operate, because their basic authority and responsibilities must be established by the state. For example, because of differences in wealth among school districts, legal provision must be made for equitable financial support. Beyond such basic provisions, what other laws are necessary? How can the number of laws be kept to a reasonable minimum when there are so many demands by different groups for laws designed to protect or promote their interests?

What Criteria Should Be Utilized in Evaluating Proposals for Legislation?

Laws originate in many different ways. Sometimes they grow out of careful studies by some appropriate group concerned with the conceptual design and with needs and ways of meeting those needs. In other cases, some individual or group may become concerned because school expenditures have increased rapidly or because some board has inaugurated a controversial type of program, or for some other reason, and may seek legislation designed to prevent the schools from doing those things the person or group considers undesirable. In other instances, a local board may decline to adopt a desired program or course of action so the proponent may seek legislation requiring the board to do so. Ignorance, selfishness, and provincialism are likely to lead to bad legislation in any state. While there is probably no way to prevent some unwise or handicapping laws, there are some important safeguards. The most fundamental safeguard is widespread understanding of the role and significance of high-quality education. However, even this understanding needs to be supplemented by effective political activity by those who believe in and support public education and by vigorous leadership by competent leaders who understand the conceptual design and appropriate means of achieving it. This kind of climate should contribute to the development of a "conscience" by the people and in the legislature that will be favorable to sound legislation for education. What criteria should be used in determining whether proposed legislation is needed?

When educators fail to agree, the legislature finds itself in the position of having to decide what it believes to be the best educational policy. In several states, reasonably effective plans have been developed for coordinating the interests and efforts of major lay and educational groups. What steps should be taken to avoid serious conflicts concerning legislation among lay and educational groups?

The point of view and attitude of the public and of the legislators they select is usually a decisive factor in determining the kind of legislation relating to education that is enacted in each state. Hamilton and Mort suggested the need for a legislative "code of ethics" with reference to education.[28] Would such a code be feasible and helpful? If so, how should it be developed and what should be included?

How Can the Responsibilities of School Boards and the Rights of Individuals Involved in Educational Programs Be Reconciled?

The Supreme Court's mandate that "state-operated schools may not be enclaves of totalitarianism" suggests that individual students and teachers of the future will be protected in their right to speak and write freely, to associate with groups of their choice, and otherwise to conduct themselves as first-class citizens while in attendance or teaching in the public schools. Nevertheless, these rights, as with all other constitutional freedoms, are relative and not without limits: There must be a proper balance between the right of a state or local school system to operate "orderly" schools and the right of an individual student or teacher to be himself or herself, to dress and conduct himself or herself in an individualized manner, and otherwise to enjoy his or her constitutional rights while in school.

A clue to possible future court rulings may be gleaned from these statements by the Supreme Court in the *Tinker* case[29] in 1969:

Under our Constitution, free speech is not a right that is given only to be so circumscribed that it exists in principle but not in fact. . . . It can hardly be

[28] Hamilton and Mort, *Law and Public Education*, pp. 619–620.
[29] *Tinker* v. *Des Moines School Board*, 393 U.S. 503 (Iowa 1969).

argued that either students or teachers shed their constitutional rights to freedom of speech or expression at the schoolhouse gate.

Undifferentiated fear or apprehension of disturbance is not enough to overcome the right to freedom of expression. Any departure from absolute regimentation may cause trouble. Any variation from the majority's opinion may inspire fear. Any word spoken, in class, in the lunchroom or on the campus, that deviates from the views of another person, may start an argument or cause a disturbance. But our Constitution says we must take this risk. Our history says that it is this sort of hazardous freedom—this kind of openness—that is the basis of our national strength and of the independence and vigor of Americans who grow up and live in this relatively permissive, often disputatious society.

What guidelines should be used in attempting to resolve these issues? What, if any, steps should be taken by student organizations, parents, the school board and staff, the legislature, or the courts? An individual not only has rights; an individual also has obligations. What are some of them?

To What Extent Should the Judiciary Be Involved in Making Educational Decisions?

Some people have expressed considerable alarm about the propensity of the judiciary to hand down educational decisions affecting the public school systems of the nation. Yet it seems fair to say that many of the changes the courts have made in school interrelationships would not have occurred without the intervention of the courts. Improving education is everybody's business, so everyone has a right to "get into the act." "Everybody" includes, but is not limited to, the legislatures in the various states, other lay citizens including taxpayers, educators, *and* the courts (who have a stake in balancing the interests when controversies arise). This is not to say that "judge-made" law is best—it only occurs when any failure or cessation of the leadership by the governor, the legislature, or others in a state raises the need for judicial intervention.

Judges are no more interested in solving education's problems than they are in resolving other social issues—welfare, abortion, and similar problems. Generally, the courts hesitate to hand the states any set program to follow, preferring instead to put their stamp of approval on those proposals which the states themselves originated and the courts thought fell within the constitutionally permissible area. This policy has been observed by the courts in the *Brown* progeny cases. Where the local districts have made good faith attempts to resolve integration problems, the courts have been cooperative. On the other hand, the courts will not approve a plan which clearly violates the constitutional protection of individual rights. Moreover, the court must draw a plan to guarantee the rights of plaintiffs where school authorities fail to do so.

The issue of judicial involvement in educational decision making will continue to prove challenging to educators in the future, even though they may take a more active part in educational planning in their respective states. The reason for this is that the judiciary is a viable and much needed member of the team without which orderly development of the school system would be impossible.

Should the courts ever attempt to give the "answers" to educational problems (such as finance and student rights)? Have they attempted to do so? What are the best safeguards against such a possibility?

At What Level Should Decisions Relating to Education Be Made?

As was noted earlier in this chapter, some states have highly prescriptive education codes (mandatory codes), whereas others give a good deal of flexibility to local education agencies (permissive codes). Most legislatures strike a balance between these extremes by regulating some areas with statewide uniformity (e.g., school finance) while delegating other matters to local school boards (e.g., pupil disciplinary rules). With respect to each program or activity, how much detail should be prescribed centrally by the legislature? How much should be prescribed on a statewide basis by the state boards of education? How much should be delegated to the local boards of education? What is the proper balance between state control and local control? To what extent should groups other than local boards be involved in the decision-making process, as, for example, is done by employee groups through collective bargaining or community advisory councils?

Is the Concept of "Equal Educational Opportunity" for All America's Children Practically or Legally Attainable?

Horace Mann's dream—his belief in the *absolute right* of every human being to an education and in the duty of every government to see that the means of that education are provided for all—has been only partly realized. Although his belief that education is a "fundamental interest of every citizen" has been declared valid by many courts, the duty of the government to see that the means of that education are provided for all remains largely unfulfilled. Should the government seriously attempt to equalize educational opportunity, or are the states only obligated to live up to their own constitutions, which in the main guarantee only "a uniform system" of public education at taxpayer expense? Although education is considered a responsibility of the states, what does "equal protection of the laws" mean for those students who happen to live in the poorer districts? What are the implications for state policies and provisions for school support? For other kinds of provisions for education?

Perhaps no more pressing issue has presented itself in this century than the question, "How can the state system for school district organization, for funding schools, or other provisions for education be designed to ensure every child equal protection of the laws?" What steps should be taken in a serious effort to attain this goal?

SELECTED REFERENCES

Alexander, Kern, and K. Forbis Jordan, "Constitutional Alternatives for School Finance," in *Financing Education: Fiscal and Legal Alternatives,* eds., Roe L. Johns, Kern Alexander, and K. Forbis Jordan, Chap. 13. Columbus, Ohio: Charles E. Merrill Publishing Company, 1972.

Bolmier, Edward C., *Teachers' Legal Rights, Restraints and Liabilities,* Chaps. 4, 9. Cincinnati: W. H. Anderson Co., 1971.

Drury, Robert L., and Kenneth C. Ray, *Principles of School Law with Cases.* Englewood Cliffs, N.J.: Prentice-Hall, Inc., 1965.

Edwards, Newton, *The Courts and the Public Schools* (rev. ed.), Chaps. 1, 7, 21. Chicago: University of Chicago Press, 1971.

Gauerke, Warren E., *School Law.* New York: Center for Applied Research in Education, 1965.

Hamilton, Robert R., and Paul R. Mort, *The Law and Public Education* (2nd ed.), Chaps. 1, 2, 4, 17. New York: The Foundation Press, 1959.

Hooker, Clifford P., ed. *The Courts and Education.* The National Society for the Study of Education, 77th Yearbook, Part I, 1978. Chicago: University of Chicago Press.

Nolte, M. Chester, *School Law in Action: 101 Key Decisions with Guidelines for School Administrators.* Part One. *Landmark Cases.* West Nyack, N.Y.: Parker Publishing Co., 1971.

Reutter, E. Edmund, Jr., and Robert R. Hamilton, *The Law of Public Education,* Chap. 1. Mineola, N.Y.: The Foundation Press, 1970.

Wise, Arthur E., *Legislated Learning: The Bureaucratization of the American Classroom,* Chaps. 1, 4, 5. Berkeley: University of California Press, 1979.

3

THEORY *and* RESEARCH RELATING *to* EDUCATIONAL ADMINISTRATION

Some executives have been inclined to scoff at the use of theory in educational administration. The expression "That is all right in theory but it won't work in practice" has been used frequently by self-styled "practical" school administrators. The myth that theory and practice are incompatible has been attacked by Coladarci and Getzels. "Theorizing is not the exclusive property of the laboratory or the ivory tower. Everyone who makes choices and judgments implies a theory in the sense that there are reasons for his action. When an administrator's experiences have led him to believe that a certain kind of act will result in certain other events or acts, he is using theory."[1] The authors also state that when an administrator learns from experience, he is theorizing," it may be poor theorizing, but it is theorizing nevertheless."[2]

[1] Arthur P. Coladarci and Jacob W. Getzels, *The Use of Theory in Educational Administration* (Stanford, Calif.: Stanford University Press, 1955), p. 5.
[2] *Ibid.*

40

Getzels has presented some convincing evidence concerning the usefulness of basic or theory-oriented research. After reviewing most of the basic research related to education that had been produced during the last fifty years, he concluded in brief as follows: (1) Basic or theory-oriented research can have a powerful effect on the operation of schools; (2) it contributes to broad conceptions of human behavior; (3) it alters preparation programs for teachers and administrators conceptions; and (4) it helps to define accurately educational problems.[3]

Much progress has been made in recent years in laying the foundations for a science of educational administration. No systematic science in any discipline has ever been developed by the trial-and-error process; however, until comparatively recently that was the principal method used to develop our knowledge of educational administration. Progress in the physical sciences was very slow as long as knowledge was derived primarily from trial-and-error methods, folklore, and superstition. When the scientific method was applied, our knowledge of the physical sciences developed at an astounding rate.

In recent years, we have begun to apply the scientific method to develop knowledge in the social and behavioral sciences. The scientific method involves the conceptualization of theories from which hypotheses may be formulated and tested. The development of theory and research in the disciplines of psychology, sociology, social psychology, anthropology, political science, and economics has provided a number of useful theoretical bases for developing a science of educational administration. Some of these theories will be presented and discussed briefly in this chapter. These theories and some other concepts will be applied to organizations in Chapter 4 and to leadership in Chapter 5.

GENERAL SYSTEMS THEORY

One of the most significant innovations in the study of the social and behavioral sciences during the last half of the twentieth century is the application of general systems theory to those sciences. Ludwig von Bertalanffy, an Austrian biologist, is generally considered the original proponent of the application of general systems theory to all the sciences. He noted that the sciences were being split up into narrower and narrower specialized fields with little intercommunication. He also observed that the same general formulas were being derived to explain phenomena in many diverse fields by experimenters who were usually unaware that they had been stated previously in another field. He then set about to formulate general systems theory to describe systems in general to provide a framework for unifying the sciences. Bertalanffy stated

> . . . the aims of general systems theory can be indicated as follows: (1) There is a general tendency towards integration in the various sciences, natural and social; (2) Such integration seems to be centered in a general theory of systems; (3) Such theory may be an important means for aiming at exact

---

[3] Adapted from Jacob W. Getzels, "Paradigm and Practice," Chap. 7 in *Impact of Research on Education—Some Case Studies,* ed. Patrick Suppes (Washington, D.C.: National Academy on Education, 1978).

theory in the non-physical fields of science; (4) Developing unifying principles running vertically through the universe of the individual sciences, this goal brings us nearer to the goal of the unity of science and (5) This goal can lead to a much needed integration in scientific education.[4]

It is now generally recognized that there is a discernible linkage among all the sciences and that systems theory provides an important part of that linkage. According to Hearn,

> General systems theorists believe that it is possible to represent all forms of animate and inanimate matter as systems; that is all forms from atomic particles through atoms, molecules, crystals, viruses, cells, organs, individuals, groups, societies, planets, solar systems, even the galaxies, may be regarded as systems. They are impressed by the number of times the same principles have been independently discovered by scientists working in different fields.[5]

The journal *Behavioral Science* is devoted to general systems theory. The following statement was made in an editorial appearing in the first issue published in January 1956.

> Our present thinking—which may alter with time—is that a general theory will deal with structural and behavioral properties of systems. The diversity of systems is great. The molecule, the cell, the organ, the individual, the group, the society are all examples of systems. Besides differing in the level of organization, systems differ in many other crucial respects. They may be living, nonliving, or mixed; material or conceptual and so forth.[6]

Griffiths defines a system as follows:

> A system is simply defined as a complex of elements in interaction. Systems may be open or closed. An open system is related to and exchanges matter with its environment, while a closed system is not related to nor does it exchange matter with its environment. Further, a closed system is characterized by an increase in entropy, while open systems tend toward the steady state. (Given a continuous input, a constant ratio among the components is maintained.) All systems except the smallest have subsystems and all but the largest have suprasystems, which are their environment.[7]

Each system and subsystem is conceptualized as having a *boundary*. There is more interaction among the units included within the boundary of a system than between units within the boundary and units outside it. It also requires more energy to transmit energy across the boundary from within to without or from

[4] Ludwig von Bertalanffy in *General Systems: Yearbook for the Society for the Advancement of General Systems Theory,* Vol. 1 (Ann Arbor, Mich.: Braun-Brunfield, Inc., 1956).

[5] Gordon Hearn, *Theory Building in Social Work* (Toronto: University of Toronto Press, 1958), p. 38.

[6] Editorial, *Behavioral Science,* 1, no. 1 (1956).

[7] Daniel E. Griffiths, ed., *Behavioral Science and Educational Administration,* Sixty-third Yearbook of the National Society for the Study of Education (Chicago: University of Chicago Press, 1964), p. 116.

without to within than to exchange matter or information among the units in-cluded within the boundary of a system.[8]

The environment of a system, subsystem, or suprasystem is everything external to its boundary. There are numerous factors both within a system and its environment that affect the behavior, structure, and function of both the system and its environment.[9]

In Chapters 1 and 2, considerable attention was given to the value structure of our society. There has been much controversy concerning whether scientific research should be "value free." Because values are factors both in a social system and in its environment, the social scientist cannot ignore values. But the social scientist will treat a value in the same manner as any other factor affecting a system or its environment.

Some Characteristics of Social Systems

The school system is a social system. Following are some characteristics of social systems.

Organizational equilibrium. Any system has a tendency to achieve a balance among the many forces or factors operating upon the system and within it.[10] Chin distinguishes between different types of equilibriums as follows: "A *Stationary equilibrium* exists when there is a fixed point or level of balance to which the system returns after a disturbance. . . . A *dynamic* equilibrium exists when the equilibrium shifts to a new position of balance after disturbance."[11] Current literature on systems theory usually refers to stationary equilibrium as "equilibrium" and to dynamic equilibrium as "steady state." In this chapter, steady state and dynamic equilibrium will be used as synonymous terms. Chin theorized that a system in equilibrium reacts to outside impingements "(1) By resisting the influence of the disturbance, by refusing to acknowledge its existence, or by building a protective wall against the intrusion, and by other defensive maneuvers. . . .; (2) By resisting the disturbance through bringing into operation the homeostatic forces that restore or re-create a balance. . . .; (3) By accommodating the disturbance through achieving a new equilibrium."[12] Strategies 1 and 2 are designed to attain a stationary equilibrium without making changes; strategy 3 is designed to attain a dynamic equilibrium or steady state by making changes.

The concepts of stationary equilibrium and dynamic equilibrium or steady state are of great significance to educational administrators because of the consequences of alternate strategies to the social system called the school system, which is at the present time receiving more signals from its environment than ever before.

---

[8] James G. Miller, "Toward a General Theory for the Behavioral Sciences," *American Psychologist,* 10 (1955), pp. 516–517.

[9] Hearn, *Theory Building,* p. 42.

[10] Robert Chin, "The Utility of Systems Models and Developmental Models for Practitioners," in *Planning of Change,* eds. Warren G. Bennis, Kenneth D. Benne, and Robert Chin (New York: Holt, Rinehart and Winston, Inc., 1969), pp. 297–312.

[11] *Ibid.,* p. 205.

[12] *Ibid.*

The concept of "feedback" is closely related to the concept of equilibrium. "Cybernetics" is the study of feedback control. Lonsdale defines feedback as follows: "As applied to organization, feedback is the process through which the organization learns: it is the input from the environment to the system telling it how it is doing as a result of its output to the environment."[13] It is hypothesized that, if any social system (including the school system) fails to learn from its environment, it will eventually fail to survive in that environment or the environment will force changes in the system. If research sustains this hypothesis, what will be the eventual fate of a school system that makes continuous use of strategies 1 and 2?

There are other concepts of equilibrium which are of great importance to administrators. As has been pointed out already, every living system strives to maintain a steady state. It will resist a disturbance if it can and adjust to it if it must. Every system produces entropy, but at a minimal rate when the system is in a steady state. *Entropy in a social system is a tendency toward disorganization or chaos.* When a system is under such stress or strain that its components cannot bring it back into a steady state, the system may collapse. Systems under threat will usually use first the most available and least costly processes to relieve the strain on the system by removing the variable disturbing a steady state. Later, the less quickly available and more costly processes will be utilized if necessary to restore the equilibrium of the system.[14] Thus, any living system, including such social systems as the school system, has a precarious existence. It needs feedback to receive the information necessary for the system to serve the environment and to adjust to it, if the system is to survive. But the feedback disturbs the equilibrium, and, if the steady state cannot be restored, the system will break down. Change is necessary for the survival of the system, but it usually causes stress and strain. These times, which require a rate of change greater than ever before, present an unparalleled challenge to the educational administrator to provide leadership for making desirable innovations and at the same time maintain a dynamic equilibrium in the school system.

Entropy. One of the limitations of general systems theory is that the concept of entropy varies for different types of systems. Systems can be classified in many ways, such as open and closed, living and nonliving, social and nonsocial, mechanical and nonmechanical, material and conceptual, and so forth. The impact of entropy differs for open and closed systems. Immegart has pointed out that open systems can combat entropy and remain in a dynamic life state by exchanging matter and energy with their environment. Closed systems are isolated from their environment and inevitably move toward entropy, a death state.[15]

The tendency of an open living system to combat death or disorganization (entropy) is called *negentropy*. Thus, the living animal maintains a steady state (dy-

---

[13] Richard C. Lonsdale, "Maintaining the Organization in Dynamic Equilibrium," Chap. 7 in *Behavioral Science in Educational Administration*, Part II, p. 173.

[14] See James G. Miller, "Living Systems: Cross-Level Hypotheses," *Behavioral Science*, 10, no. 4 (1965), pp. 394–397.

[15] G. L. Immegart, "Systems Theory and Taxonomic Inquiry into Organizational Behavior in Education," in *Developing Taxonomies of Organizational Behavior in Education Administration*, ed. D. E. Griffiths (Chicago: Rand McNally & Company, 1969).

namic equilibrium) by receiving energy inputs in the form of food and air. The social system (including a school system) maintains a dynamic equilibrium by negentropy inputs from its environment in the form of feedback needed for survival. Furthermore, the social system usually includes actors who move the system toward entropy and also negentropy actors who move the system toward the steady state.

As was pointed out, entropy in a social system such as a school system can be defined as the tendency toward disorganization or chaos. The engineer considers entropy as the amount of energy generated in a system which is not available for producing useful work and is lost to the system or dissipated by some means, such as heat loss or friction.[16] In communications theory, noise is considered as entropy. In thermodynamics, entropy may be considered as the tendency toward homogeneity or static equilibrium. Although the concepts of entropy vary for different types of systems, there is a general thread of similarity running through all these concepts.

Equifinality. Open, self-regulatory systems have the property of equifinality. According to Granger, "in such systems identical output conditions appear to be derived from different initial inputs, and identical inputs appear to achieve different results."[17] This condition is common in complex social systems such as school systems which have many variables both within the social system and within the environment. Those developing management information systems for school administrators should study the concept of equifinality. Frequently, the school system may obtain substantially equal outputs in the form of measurable learning objectives from different inputs of money, teaching methods, and instructional delivery systems. Futhermore, widely different outputs may be obtained in different schools from substantially the same inputs of money, teaching methods, and instructional delivery systems. Therefore, useful management information systems should include information on all factors both within the school system and in its environment that affect output.

The School as a Social System

The systems theory discussed in this book deals only with open living systems. A school system is an open, living social system which can be conceptualized in a number of ways in terms of systems theory. For example, an individual school might be conceptualized as a system; its departments, sections, and divisions as subsystems; and the central staff, the board of education, the state education agencies, and, if present trends continue, even federal education agencies may all in the order listed be conceptualized as suprasystems. The environment of any given system consists not only of its subsystems and suprasystems but also of all the other systems in the society with their attendant beliefs, values, and purposes.

[16] Some of the concepts of this section were adapted from an unpublished paper entitled, "General Systems Theory: The Implications for Educational Administration" presented by John M. Turner at a seminar at the University of Florida, March 1972.

[17] Robert L. Granger, *Educational Leadership: An Interdisciplinary Perspective* (Scranton, Pa.: Intext Educational Publishers, 1971), p. 12.

Parsons has suggested a useful conceptualization of the formal school organization.[18] He proposed that the hierarchical aspect of school organization be broken down according to function or responsibility. Using this concept, Parsons classified the hierarchical levels of authority in school systems as the "technical" system, the "managerial" system, and the "community" or "institutional" system. The teaching function is in the technical system, the management system controls the technical system, and the community legitimizes the management system through creating agencies for the control of schools or by direct vote.

Systems theory can also be used to conceptualize informal organizations in social systems. This topic will be treated more completely in Chapter 4.

Research and Systems Theory

Systems theory has proven to be extremely useful for conceptualizing and organizing research dealing with organization and administration. It provides a systematic method for utilizing research from the social and behavioral sciences to understand and control organizational and administrative phenomena. Research on administration and organization conceptualized on meaningful theoretical bases will bring that research into the mainstream of valid research in the social and behavioral sciences and should eventually produce a science of administration.

Miller, after making an exhaustive study of research based on systems theory, listed 165 hypotheses which had been proposed by various researchers including himself.[19] He noted that some of these hypotheses had been confirmed by research but that some were probably entirely wrong or partially wrong and needed to be modified. Miller also observed that, undoubtedly, many other hypotheses relating to living systems could be formulated. His work is highly significant for practicing educational administrators and for researchers in educational organization and administration. Because of their significance, a few of the 165 hypotheses listed by Miller are quoted in the following paragraphs and their significance for educational systems is indicated.

1. "In general, the more numbers or components a system has, the more echelons it has."[20] The larger the school system, the more pupils and teachers and the longer the chain of command. As we lengthen the chain of command, it can be hypothesized that we retard communication and increase the internal friction of the system. There are many economies of scale that can be obtained by making school systems larger. If, however, as we make school systems larger, we must increase the echelons of control, how large can we make school systems until the disadvantages of internal friction and difficulty of communication arising from increasing the echelons of control outweigh the advantages of economy of scale gained by increasing the size of school systems? Available research on educational administration has not yet provided the answer to that question.

2. "System components incapable of associating, or lacking experience which

[18] Talcott Parsons, "Some Ingredients of a General Theory of Formal Organization," Chap. 3 in *Administrative Theory in Education,* ed. Andrew W. Halpin (Chicago: Midwest Administration Center, University of Chicago, 1958), p. 41.

[19] Miller, "Living Systems: Cross-Level Hypotheses," pp. 380–411.

[20] *Ibid.,* p. 383.

has formed such association, must function according to strict programming or highly standardized operating rules."[21] The armed services are sometimes criticized for the regimentation inevitably arising from "highly standardized operating rules." However, when consideration is given to the situation facing officers dealing with recruits and constantly changing personnel, it is probable that the armed services could not function efficiently by any other plan. Is the school system similar to or different from the army? Does the fact that the school system and the army have different purposes affect the validity of the processes of control of each? Those who believe that the purposes of a school system can best be achieved by strict programming and highly standardized rules probably assume a set of purposes for the schools different from those who disagree with them. If research sustains the hypothesis, then the educational administrator who wishes to avoid strict programming or highly standardized operating rules in any system or subsystem he or she is administering should select as components of that system or subsystem persons who are capable of working with each other and provide them with opportunities to do so in group situations.

3. "The larger a system is and the more components it has, the larger is the ratio of the amount of information transmitted between points within the system to the amount of information transmitted across its boundary."[22] A number of the largest city school systems in the United States have experienced serious crises in recent years. Is it possible that these large school systems have lost some public support because of failure to transmit sufficient information across their boundaries? It might also be hypothesized that the larger the school system, the greater the difficulty in getting information from the environment across the boundary into the school system.

4. Miller presented several hypotheses, supported by some research, concerning communication channels. Following are two examples: "The further away along channels a subsystem is from a process, the more error there is in its information about that process."[23] "The probability of error in or breakdown of an information channel is a direct function of the number of components in it."[24] The implications of these hypotheses to educational organization and administration are obvious. The farther the teachers are removed from contact with the central administration and the greater the number of echelons placed between the teacher and the central administration, the greater the chance of error in the teachers' perceptions of the actions of the central administration and the greater the number of errors in the factual information reaching the teachers. The same is true for the central administration.

SOME THEORETICAL MODELS

In the remainder of this chapter, some theoretical models will be presented and applied to problems of organization and administration.

---

[21] *Ibid.*, p. 384.
[22] *Ibid.*, p. 385.
[23] *Ibid.*, p. 388.
[24] *Ibid.*, p. 389.

A bold attempt was made in 1951 by a group of psychologists, sociologists, and anthropologists to develop a general theory of the social sciences.[25] Their frame of reference for a theory of action was based on personality, social system, and culture. Personality was defined "as the organized system of the orientation and motivation of action of one individual actor."[26] A social system was defined as "Any system of interactive relationships of a plurality of individual actors."[27] Although culture can be conceptualized as a body of artifacts and systems of symbols, it is not organized as a system of action and, therefore, is on a different plane from the personality and social systems. However, cultural patterns tend to become organized into systems.

The personality is viewed as a relatively consistent system of need dispositions which produce role expectations in social systems. Roles rather than personalities are conceptualized as the units of social structure.

Cultural patterns may be internalized both by the individual personality system and by the social system. These patterns are not always congruent, and the integration of personalities in social systems with different cultural patterns frequently presents serious difficulties.

Rewards, roles, and facilities in a social system are scarce and must be allocated. Therefore, the social system, or organization, must deal with the problems of allocation and integration. Furthermore, "The regulation of all of these allocative processes and the performance of the functions which keep the system or the subsystem going in a sufficiently integrated manner is impossible without a system of definitions of roles and sanctions for conformity or deviation."[28]

The formulation presented by Parsons and his associates seems highly general and abstract. But the conceptualization of the reciprocal integration of the personality, the social system, and the culture through interaction processes stimulated much creative thinking by other social scientists.

Can the theories of Parsons and his associates be applied to the development of solutions of educational problems? From what theoretical bases will we develop solutions to the problems of integration of the races in the schools? From what theoretical bases will we develop educational programs to accomplish the purposes of the Economic Opportunity Act of 1964 and Titles I and III of the Elementary and Secondary Education Act of 1965? The educational provisions of these acts both deal with the educationally and culturally disadvantaged. It may be inappropriate to refer to pupils as "culturally disadvantaged." It may be more appropriate to use the term "culturally different." For example, a child reared in a slum develops a culture which enables that child to cope with the environment in a slum. A child from the middle class has acquired a culture that ill equips that child to survive in a slum environment but serves well in his or her own environment. The problem of developing educational programs for culturally different children

---

[25] Talcott Parsons and Edward S. Shils, eds., *Toward a General Theory of Action* (Cambridge, Mass.: Harvard University Press, 1951).
[26] *Ibid.*, p. 7.
[27] *Ibid.*
[28] *Ibid.*, p. 25.

and adults and educationally disadvantaged children and adults is one of the greatest challenges to the educational leadership of the nation. Solutions to this problem by trial-and-error methods will be very slow. The intelligent application of appropriate theory should greatly speed up the development of education programs to alleviate this problem.

The Organization and the Individual

Perceptive administrators have long recognized that every administrator must deal with the organization, the individual, and the environment. The organization and the environment must come to terms with each other—the organization's establishing and attaining purposes wanted by the environment and the environment's supporting the organization that satisfies its wants. Similarly, the individual and the organization must come to terms with each other by the individual's accepting and facilitating the attainment of the purposes of the organization and the organization's satisfying the wants of the individual.

One of the earliest writers placing these propositions in theoretical form was a business executive, Chester Barnard.[29] He conceived of an organization as a system which embraced the activities of two or more persons coordinating their activities to attain a common goal. He considered organization as the binding element common to all cooperative systems. According to Barnard's theoretical formulation, the continuance of a successful organization depends upon two conditions: (1) the accomplishment of the purposes of the organization, which he termed "effectiveness," and (2) the satisfaction of individual motives, which he termed "efficiency." Two types of processes were required for meeting these conditions: (1) those relating to the cooperative system itself and its relationship to its environment and (2) those relating to the creation and allocation of satisfaction among individuals.[30]

Getzels has developed a model for explaining social behavior which has been extremely fertile in producing hypotheses and stimulating research.[31] He started with the assumption that the process of administration deals essentially with social behavior in a hierarchical setting: "we may conceive of administration *structurally* as the hierarchy of subordinate–superordinate relationships within a social system. *Functionally,* this hierarchy of relationships is the locus for allocating and integrating roles and facilities in order to achieve the goals of the social system."[32]

He conceived "the social system as involving two classes of phenomena which are at once conceptually independent and phenomenally interactive."[33] Those two

---

[29] Chester I. Barnard, *The Functions of the Executive* (Cambridge, Mass.: Harvard University Press, 1938).

[30] *Ibid.*, Chap. 1.

[31] Jacob W. Getzels, "Administration as a Social Process," Chap. 7 in *Administrative Theory in Education.* NOTE: Getzels credits Egon Guba with assisting him in developing his theoretical formulations.

[32] *Ibid.*, p. 151.

[33] *Ibid.*

phenomena are the institution with roles and expectations fulfilling the goals of the system, and the individuals with personalities and need dispositions who inhabit the system. The observed interaction he termed social behavior. He asserted that "social behavior may be understood as a function of these major elements: institution, role, and expectation, which together constitute what we shall call the *nomothetic* or normative dimension of activity in a social system, and individual, personality, and need-disposition, which together constitute the *idiographic* or personal dimension of activity in a social system."[34]

Getzels summarized this theoretical formulation in a simple model, which he presented pictorially as follows:[35]

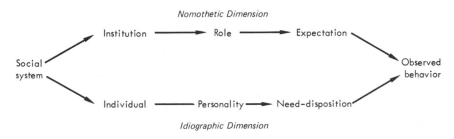

This model has already become a classic because of its simplicity and seminal properties. It demonstrates clearly the utility of models in presenting abstract theoretical concepts. A number of empirical research studies have been based on hypotheses originating in Getzels's formulation.[36]

Compliance Relationship

It is assumed that any formal organization must fulfill its purposes at least to the extent required by its environment or it will cease to exist or be substantially restructured. It is also assumed that the actors in an organization must accept the organizational roles assigned to them and comply with the directives of superordinates, if the organization is to accomplish its purposes. Etzioni has formulated a middle-range theory of organization, utilizing compliance as the primary variable for the classifications in his typology. He defines compliance as "a relation in which an actor behaves in accordance with a directive supported by another actor's power, and the orientation of the subordinated actor to the power applied."[37] Etzioni assumed that the exercise of power involved the manipulation of physical, material, and symbolic means to secure rewards and deprivations, depending upon a person's perception of the legitimacy of the exercise of power by his superordinate and the need disposition of his subordinate. These factors determine the involvement of the individual in the organization, ranging on a continuum from

---

[34] *Ibid.*, p. 152.

[35] *Ibid.*, p. 156.

[36] *Ibid.*, pp. 159–165.

[37] Amitai Etzioni, *A Comparative Analysis of Complex Organizations* (New York: Free Press of Glencoe, Inc., 1961), p. 3.

TABLE 3.1   A Typology of Compliance Relations

Kinds of Power	Kinds of Involvement		
	ALIENATIVE	*CALCULATIVE*	*MORAL*
Coercive	1	2	3
Remunerative	4	5	6
Normative	7	8	9

positive to negative. The term "alienative" was used to refer to an intensely negative orientation; "calculative" to a low-intensity involvement, either positive or negative; and "moral" to a high-intensity commitment.[38]

Another basic assumption of Etzioni's theory was that social order in an organization was accounted for by three sources of control: coercion, economic assets, and normative values. He constructed the typology of compliance relations based on these assumptions (see Table 3.1).[39]

The terms coercive and remunerative in his typology are self-explanatory. Normative power depends upon the regulation of symbolic rewards and deprivations involving esteem, prestige, social acceptance, ritualistic symbols, and other factors associated with values.

The numbers in Etzioni's typology model are used to identify the types of possible involvement resulting from the use of a kind of power. That is, type 1 is alienative involvement from the use of coercive power, type 2, calculative, and type 3, moral. Each number identifies a different type of power-involvement response.

Etzioni further theorized that organizations exhibiting similar compliance structures exhibit similar goals. Goals were classified as follows: (1) order goals to control actors considered deviant, (2) economic goals to provide production and services to outsiders, and (3) culture goals to institutionalize attempts to preserve and create culture and to create or reinforce commitments to these ends. A prison would be an example of an organization with an order goal, a factory, an organization with an economic goal, and a school system, an organization with a culture goal.

Following are some other hypotheses Etzioni derived from his formulation: (1) organizations tend to emphasize only one means of power, and, when two means of power are used on the same actors in an organization simultaneously, they tend to neutralize each other; (2) organizations exhibit all three kinds of power but emphasize only one kind or segregate the application of different kinds of power; (3) types 1, 5, and 9 from the preceding model represent the responses most likely to be received from the application of the different means of power.

Etzioni's theories have many applications to educational administration. Should the same means of power be used on all classes of personnel in an educational organization to obtain compliance? For example, should there be any differences in the types of power used with teachers, custodians, secretaries, and students?

[38] See Douglas Richard Pierce, "An Analysis of Contemporary Theories of Organization and Administration" (unpublished doctoral dissertation, University of Florida, 1963), for an interesting analysis of Etzioni's theories as well as a number of other contemporary theories.
[39] Etzioni, *Complex Organizations,* p. 12.

Assuming that the goal of the total school system is cultural, can it be assumed that the goal of each subsystem is cultural? If a new principal uses normative power at the first meeting of his faculty, coercive power at the second meeting, and normative power again at the third meeting, what kind of involvement on the part of the faculty can he anticipate at the third faculty meeting?

Innovation and Change

Numerous theoretical formulations have been developed to account for innovation and change. Only a few examples are discussed here.

Presthus has developed an interesting theory relating to the individual's reaction to the organization in which he or she is involved.[40] He assumes that organizations have manifest as well as latent goals. The manifest goals are in terms of the organizational purposes, particularly productivity. The latent goals are in terms of the need dispositions of members for security, recognition, and self-realization. He hypothesized that the attainment of the manifest goals would be promoted by recognition of the legitimacy of the latent goals of the actors in the organization. It is noteworthy that Presthus's formulation bears a close resemblance to the assumption on which Getzels's model was based.

Presthus developed a comprehensive analysis of complex hierarchical organizations and hypothesized that there are three types of personal accommodations of actors who remain with the organization: (1) upward-mobiles, (2) indifferents, and (3) ambivalents.

According to this hypothesis, the upward-mobiles become "organization men" and internalize organizational values that become the premises for action. Personal goals are synthesized with organizational goals. The upward-mobiles recognize authority as the most functional value and are sensitive to authority and status differences. They tend to perceive their superiors as nonthreatening models and their subordinates with organizational detachment.

Indifferents adapt to big organizations by withdrawal and redirecting their interest to nonorganizational activities. Because they lack identification with organizational values, they withdraw from organizational activities and decisions.

Ambivalents exhibit dysfunctional behavior in relation to both personal and organizational goals. They depend upon rational values that might be in conflict with the values of the hierarchical organization. The ambivalents are a source of conflict, but they provide the insight, motivation, and the dialectic that inspire change. Therefore, the conflict created by ambivalents is considered as a creative catalyst. Should school administrators deliberately include on a school faculty some ambivalent persons who disturb the "equilibrium" from time to time?

The concepts "local" and "cosmopolitan"[41] have some relationship to the formulations of Etzioni and Presthus. Local actors tend to identify closely with their organization and to have a stronger allegiance to the vertical institutional subcul-

---

[40] Robert Presthus, *The Organizational Society* (New York: Alfred A. Knopf, Inc., 1962).

[41] See Alvin W. Gouldner, "Cosmopolitans and Locals: Toward an Analysis of Latent Social Roles," *Administrative Science Quarterly,* 2, (December 1957), pp. 281–306; 2 (March 1958) pp. 444–480.

TABLE 3.2 Selectivity in Client–Organization Relationship
in Service Organizations

| | | Client Control over Own Participation in Organization | |
		YES	NO
Organizational control over admission	Yes	Type I	Type III
	No	Type II	Type IV

ture than do cosmopolitan actors. The latter tend to have a stronger allegiance to the horizontal subculture of the profession to which they belong than to the subculture of the particular organization in which they are actors. It can be hypothesized that the cosmopolitan actor is more likely to initiate change in an organization than is a local one. The former is also more likely to be ambivalent than either indifferent or upwardly mobile. It can also be hypothesized that normative power would be more effective than any other means of power in dealing with a cosmopolitan actor.

Thompson has theorized that the bureaucratic, hierarchical type of organization advocated by Max Weber retards innovation.[42] He hypothesized that "other things being equal, the less bureaucratized (monocratic) the organization, the more conflict and uncertainty and the more innovation.[43] Based on this hypothesis, Thompson proposed that the hierarchical organization be "loosened up" and made less tidy, if innovation and change are desired:

> In the innovative organization, departmentalization must be arranged so as to keep parochialism to a minimum. Some overlapping and duplication, some vagueness about jurisdictions, make a good deal of communication necessary. People have to define and redefine their responsibilities continually, case after case. They have to probe and seek for help. New problems cannot with certainty be rejected as *ultra vires*.[44]

Thompson assumed in his organizational model that some immediate production must be sacrificed to assure innovation within the organization.

Carlson has developed a typology of client–organization relationships in service organizations, as opposed to production organizations, from which he has formulated a number of useful hypotheses.[45] Table 3.2 outlines Carlson's typology.[46]

According to this classification, type I organizations select their clients and the clients select the organization. Type IV represents the opposite set of conditions under which the organization does not select its clients nor the clients the organiza-

---

[42] Victor A. Thompson, "Bureaucracy and Innovation," *Administrative Science Quarterly,* 10, no. 1 (1965).

[43] *Ibid.,* p. 4.

[44] *Ibid.,* p. 15.

[45] Richard O. Carlson, "Environmental Constraints and Organizational Consequences: The Public School and Its Clients," Chap. 12 in *Behavioral Science and Educational Administration.*

[46] *Ibid.,* p. 265.

tion. Private universities, hospitals, and legal firms are examples of type I; public schools, state mental hospitals, and reform schools are examples of type IV.

Carlson designated type IV organizations as "domesticated" for the following reasons: "By definition, for example, they do not compete with other organizations for clients; in fact, a steady flow of clients is assured. There is no struggle for survival for this type of organization. Like the domesticated animal, these organizations are fed and cared for. Existence is guaranteed."[47] (See discussion in Chapter 1.)

He classified type I organizations as "wild" because "they do struggle for survival. Their existence is not guaranteed, and they do cease to exist. Support for them is closely tied to quality of performance, and a steady flow of clients is not assured. Wild organizations are not protected at vulnerable points as are domesticated organizations."[48]

It was hypothesized "that domesticated organizations because of their protected state, are slower to change and adapt than are wild organizations."[49] Following are some of the hypotheses that Carlson formulated from his model concerning how an organization adapts itself to unselected clients: (1) An adaptive response of domesticated organizations to not being able to select its clients is segregation, for example, "dumping" students unsuited to academic programs into vocational areas, special sections, or even special schools. (2) Segregation may lead to goal displacement, which is the replacement of the original goal by some other goal, for example, discipline may be substituted for learning. (3) Preferential treatment may be given the clients that accommodate themselves to the purposes of the organization, for example, research has shown that preferential treatment is frequently given in the public schools to middle- and upper-class children in such matters as discipline, punishment, and curriculums.[50]

It was also hypothesized that the inability of the student client to select his or her organization resulted in the following adaptations: (1) receptive adaptation, (2) dropout adaptation, (3) situational retirement, (4) rebellious adjustment, and (5) side-payment adaptation.

There is much interest at the present time in innovation and change in education. Griffiths has identified some propositions aiding or inhibiting change which have been derived from the system theory model. They are as follows:

> The major impetus for change in organizations is from the outside.
>
> The degree and duration of change is directly proportional to the intensity of the stimulus from the suprasystem.
>
> Change in organization is more probable if the successor to the chief administrator is from outside the organization than if he is from inside the organization.
>
> When change in an organization does occur, it will tend to occur from the top down, not from the bottom up.
>
> Living systems respond to continuously increasing stress first by a lag in

[47] *Ibid.*, p. 266.
[48] *Ibid.*, p. 267.
[49] *Ibid.*
[50] *Ibid.*, pp. 269–273.

response, then by an over-compensatory response, and finally by catastrophic collapse of the system.[51]

The number of innovations expected is inversely proportional to the tenure of the chief administrator.

The more hierarchical the structure of an organization, the less the possibility of change.

The more functional the dynamic interplay of subsystems, the less the change in an organization.[52]

In this chapter, we have presented only an introduction to some of the theoretical formulations which are useful in studying the phenomena of change. Some additional concepts relating to innovation and change are applied to organizational and leadership problems in the chapters immediately following.

Theories from Economics

There are many theoretical formulations from economics that have significance for educational organization and administration. Theories of investment, input–output, division of labor, economic growth, the allocation of resources, marginal utility, taxation, and credit are only a few examples. Fortunately, in recent years a number of economists have directed their research toward a study of the economics of education. For example, Fabricant in 1959 presented estimates showing that a large portion of the economic growth of the nation between 1889 and 1957 could not be explained by increased inputs of land, labor, and capital.[53] The classical economists had long used an economic model that included land, labor, and capital as the only factors for explaining production. Fabricant hypothesized that investments in education, research, and development and other intangible capital might account for the unexplained difference in economic growth. In 1961, Schultz tested this hypothesis and found that approximately one half of the unexplained increase in national income could be attributed to investment in education.[54] He concluded that a large part of the resources allocated to education could be classified as an investment, because it resulted in the formation of human capital.

The educational literature on school finance is beginning to include numerous concepts based on theories from economics.[55] Space does not permit discussion of these concepts.

[51] Miller, "Toward a General Theory for the Behavioral Sciences," p. 525.

[52] Griffiths, "The Nature and Meaning of Theory," Chap. 5 in *Behavioral Science and Educational Administration,* pp. 117–118.

[53] Solomon Fabricant, *Basic Facts on Productivity Change,* Occasional Paper No. 63 (New York: National Bureau of Economic Research, 1959).

[54] Theodore W. Schultz, "Education and Economic Growth," Chap. 3 in *Social Forces Influencing American Education,* Sixtieth Yearbook, National Society for the Study of Education (Chicago: University of Chicago Press, 1961).

[55] See Charles S. Benson, *The Economics of Public Education* (Boston: Houghton Mifflin Company, 1961), Chaps. 1, 2, 3, 11, and Roe L. Johns and Edgar L. Morphet, *The Economics and Financing of Education,* 2nd ed. (Englewood Cliffs, N.J.: Prentice-Hall, Inc., 1969), Chaps. 3, 4.

Economics is the first of the social and behavioral sciences in which theoretical models were developed and utilized for formulating hypotheses to be tested by scientifically acceptable methods of research. Economists discovered that many concepts in economics could be expressed in mathematical form. This was a great advantage. The preciseness of the language of mathematics made it possible for researchers to express hypotheses exactly in mathematical equations and to test these hypotheses by valid methods. The extensive use of this approach to the study of economics gave rise to a new specialty in economics called econometrics.

Recently, there has been a trend toward the use of mathematical models in research on organization and administration. Simon was one of the first social scientists to make extensive use of mathematical formulations for expressing theoretical concepts in administration and organization. For example, Simon expressed in mathematical form Homans's theoretical system of group relationships.[56] Subsequently, March and Simon made extensive use of mathematics in presenting a comprehensive theoretical approach to organization.[57] Miller used a considerable number of mathematical formulas in presenting 165 cross-level hypotheses on living systems.[58] Griffiths has been the pioneer among professors of educational administration in using mathematical formulations of organizational theory.[59] It is probable that mathematical formulations for research in educational organization and administration will be used even more extensively in the future. Furthermore, mathematical formulations adapted to computers are already used widely in decision making by the armed services and some types of business and industry. It is anticipated that a considerable amount of middle-management decision making may be done by computers in the near future. Thus, as so often happens, theoretical mathematical formulations, which were originally applied primarily to pure research problems, are now being applied to day-to-day operations.

However, there are certain dangers in using computer simulation models for evaluation of educational outputs and the determination of accountability.

SOME IMPORTANT PROBLEMS AND ISSUES

In this chapter we have presented only a sampling of the rich body of significant theory already available. No general field theory of educational organization and administration has yet been formulated. Nor is this likely to occur soon. However, systems theory does provide an extremely useful means by which it is possible to tie together much significant research in educational organization and administration. In the following paragraphs, some further applications of theoretical formulations to educational problems and issues are presented.

[56] Herbert A. Simon, "Some Strategic Considerations in the Construction of Social Science Models," in *Mathematical Thinking in the Social Sciences,* ed. Paul F. Lazarsfeld (New York: Free Press of Glencoe, Inc., 1954).

[57] James C. March and Herbert A. Simon, *Organizations* (New York: John Wiley & Sons, Inc., 1958).

[58] Miller, "Living Systems: Cross-Level Hypotheses," No. 4.

[59] Daniel E. Griffiths, *Administrative Theory* (New York: Appleton-Century-Crofts, 1959).

How Can Change Be Initiated in a Junior College Faculty?

The public junior college in a thriving, growing city of 100,000 has been in existence for seven years, but it was started by taking over the facilities and staff of a private junior college. That college had been in existence for thirty-seven years when it was changed to a tax-supported institution. The private junior college had selective admissions and a good academic reputation, but it was designed to provide only a two-year program equivalent to the first two years of a four-year college. The board of trustees of the private junior college was willing to turn the institution over to a new, publicly elected board of trustees for operation as a public institution because of financial difficulties.

When the institution became a public junior college, the new board continued the president, his administrative assistants, the deans, and the faculty in their positions. However, additional faculty members were provided because of a large increase in enrollment.

When the publicly elected board of trustees assumed responsibility for the junior college, it inaugurated nonselective admissions and defined the purposes of the junior college as including vocational, technical, and general adult education as well as the two-year college parallel program. It requested the president of the junior college to change the curriculum of the institution to include these purposes, and it provided the necessary funds for staff and facilities.

The broad-purpose program and the open-door policy were privately opposed by the president of the junior college and most of his staff. The new facilities were constructed and some staff members provided for implementing the additions to the program. But the new programs in vocational, technical, and general education for adults did not flourish. The new faculty members added for these new purposes were not accepted by the other faculty members as peers. The president, instead of promoting the new programs, seemed to apologize for their existence. No effort was expended to inform the pupils and to recruit students for these new programs.

A new situation developed when the president of the junior college resigned and accepted the presidency of a senior college. He took two of his deans with him. When the president resigned, he recommended one person on his staff to succeed him and two other persons on his staff to succeed to the vacant deanships. His recommendation, submitted to the board, was accompanied by a petition signed by 85 percent of the faculty.

The board desired some substantial changes in the program and in the general climate of the junior college. What theoretical concepts would help the board to bring about change in this junior college? What are some strategies that would be consistent with these formulations?

How Can the Recent Increase in Teacher Unrest Be Explained?

During recent years, classroom teachers in the public schools have become increasingly vocal, active, and aggressive. The membership of teachers in labor unions has increased, and many local education associations have adopted some of the tactics of labor unions, such as collective bargaining and withholding of services for certain functions. Sanctions have been imposed on entire states as well as on a number of local school systems. Teachers have been demanding a more aggressive professional leadership at local, state, and national levels. In one school system of 400,000, the classroom teachers by a majority of 90 percent voted to censure their superintendent, their board of education, their legislative delegation, the state superintendent of schools, the state legislature, and the governor and then voted to impose sanctions on their local school system.

What theories can be used to conceptualize this problem? What hypotheses can be derived from these theories to explain this phenomenon?

What Is the Present Role of Theory in Research on Administrative Problems?

Griffiths, one of the principal leaders in building abstract theories of educational administration, has concluded that there is little theory building at present in educational administration but considerable useful theorizing.[60] Following are his insightful conclusions concerning the use of administrative theory in education.

1. The emphasis now is on theorizing, not on theory building. Studies are being done in which concepts are developed, related to each other, and tested against empirical data.

2. Theorizing is proceeding in a variety of ways—a highly desirable development. The study of administration should proceed through as many methodological approaches as possible.

3. There appears to be little theorizing concerning some of the major problems of educational administration: collective negotiation, integration, and more effective ways of organizing to provide education. The realm of public policy making has received little attention.

4. Significant bits of research, theory, and theorizing are not being "followed-up." Much research which opens an area gets no further because no one picks it up.

5. The search for one encompassing theory (if anyone is searching) should be abandoned. There is need for a number of theories concerning the various aspects of administration. Just as there is no one theory of anatomy, but theories of circulation, the nervous system, etc., similarly there should be theories of decision-making, personal relations, structure, etc., etc. Each theory may help in the understanding of the totality.

6. We have learned that a modest approach to theory pays off. Theorizing in terms of basic understanding of administration is proving more fruitful than did the highly abstract and formal theories of a decade ago.[61]

It has been alleged that educational administration as taught in many universities is not very relevant to the solution of problems of practicing school administra-

[60] Daniel E. Griffiths, "Theory in Educational Administration: 1966," in *Educational Administration: Internal Perspectives,* eds. George Bacon, Dan H. Cooper, and William G. Walker (Chicago: Rand McNally & Company, 1969), p. 154.

[61] *Ibid.,* pp. 166–167.

tors. Will the use of theory in the solution of administration problems make the science of educational administration more relevant or less relevant to the solution of problems in the field?

SELECTED REFERENCES

Barnard, Chester I., *The Functions of the Executive.* Cambridge, Mass.: Harvard University Press, 1938.

Bennis, Warren G., Kenneth D. Benne, and Robert Chin, *The Planning of Change.* New York: Holt, Rinehart and Winston, Inc., 1961.

Berelson, Bernard, and Gary A. Steiner, *Human Behavior: An Inventory of Scientific Findings.* New York: Harcourt, Brace Jovanovich, 1964.

Bertalanffy, Ludwig von, "General System Theory—A Critical Review," in *Modern Systems Research for the Behavioral Scientist,* ed. M. W. Buckley. Chicago: Aldine Publishing Co., 1968.

Buckley, Walter, *Sociology and Modern Systems Theory.* Englewood Cliffs, N.J.: Prentice-Hall, Inc., 1967.

——, *Modern Systems Research for the Behavioral Scientist.* Chicago: Aldine Publishing Co., 1968.

Culbertson, Jack A., and Stephen P. Hencley, *Educational Research: New Perspectives.* Danville, Ill.: Interstate Printers and Publishers, Inc., 1963.

Etzioni, Amitai, *A Comparative Analysis of Complex Organizations.* New York: Free Press of Glencoe, Inc., 1961.

Griffiths, Daniel E., ed., *Behavioral Science and Educational Administration.* Sixty-third Yearbook of the National Society for the Study of Education. Chicago: University of Chicago Press, 1964.

——, *Taxonomies of Organizational Behavior.* Chicago: Rand McNally & Company, 1967.

Likert, Rensis and Jane B. Likert, *New Ways of Managing Conflict.* New York: McGraw-Hill, 1976.

Miller, James G., "Living Systems: Basic Concepts," *Behavioral Science,* 10, no. 3 (July 1965).

——, "Living Systems: Structure and Process," *Behavioral Science,* 10, no. 4 (October 1965).

——, "Living Systems: Cross-Level Hypotheses," *Behavioral Science,* 10, no. 4 (October 1965).

Parsons, Talcott, and Edward A. Shils, eds., *Toward a General Theory of Action.* New York: Harper & Row, Publishers, Inc., 1962.

Presthus, Robert, *The Organizational Society.* New York: Alfred A. Knopf, Inc., 1962.

Suppes, Patrick, ed., *Impact of Research on Education—Some Case Studies.* Washington, D.C.: National Academy of Education, 1978.

Tope, Donald E., et al., *The Social Sciences View School Administration.* Englewood Cliffs, N.J.: Prentice-Hall, Inc., 1965.

4

CONCEPTS *and* PRINCIPLES *of* ORGANIZATION *and* ADMINISTRATION

A number of authorities on organization and administration have insisted that most, if not all, of the currently accepted principles of administration are unscientific. For example, Simon wrote in 1950 that the currently accepted principles of administration are "little more than ambiguous and mutually contradictory proverbs."[1] He found many so-called principles of administration to be mutually incompatible when applied to the same situation. For example, it had been stated as a principle that administrative efficiency is improved by keeping the number of persons supervised (span of control) at any given level to a small number. It had also been stated as a principle that administrative efficiency is improved by keeping to a minimum the number of levels through which a matter must pass before it is acted upon. Simon considered these two principles contradictory. He asked, how is it possible to keep the span of control at any given hierarchical level to a small number and at the same time hold the number of hierarchical levels to

[1] Herbert A. Simon, *Administrative Behavior* (New York: Macmillan Publishing Co., Inc., 1950), p. 240.

a minimum? One can agree with Simon that current statements of principles of span of control and number of hierarchical levels leave much to be desired. Nevertheless, every administrator of an organization, especially a large complex organization, must make decisions on how many persons to place under the control of one administrator at each level in the organization, how many persons for each type of task to place under the control of one administrator, and how many hierarchical levels to establish in the organization. Perhaps research based on systems theory discussed in Chapter 3 might develop a principle (or perhaps valid criteria) incorporating both the concept of span of control and number of hierarchical levels, which would be useful in making decisions on these matters.

Another example of contradiction is the statement of principles presented by a number of writers relating to "flexibility" and "stability." These two concepts seem to be contradictory. Actually, many concepts of administration and organization are like some mathematical functions that are valid only within certain limits. Unfortunately, the limits of the applicability of many concepts of administration and organization have not yet been determined. When these limits are defined, it should be possible to state more generalizations in the form of principles that can be used as reliable guides for decision making.

Griffiths wrote in 1957, "At the present time, there appear to be no established principles of administration."[2] He generally agreed with the point of view expressed by Simon.

Blau and Scott commented as follows concerning the development of principles:

> The object of all science is to explain things. What do we mean by a scientific explanation? An observed fact is explained by reference to a general principle, that is, by showing that the occurrence of this fact under the given circumstances can be predicted from the principle. To first establish such an explanatory principle as theoretical generalization, many particular events must be observed and classified into general categories that make them comparable. To explain a principle requires a more general proposition from which this and other specific principles can be inferred.[3]

Very few (if any) principles of administration have been developed in strict compliance with the standards proposed by Blau and Scott. Nevertheless, the literature on administration contains many statements of principles of administration.[4] In this chapter, some of the most commonly accepted "principles" will be presented and discussed. These cannot be considered as scientifically determined; rather, they should be viewed as operating rules of thumb which have been developed largely from experience. They constitute a part of the "folklore" of administration and should be studied because they point to the areas in which principles of administration are needed.

[2] Daniel E. Griffiths, "Toward a Theory of Administrative Behavior," Chap. 10 in *Administrative Behavior in Education,* ed. Roald F. Campbell and Russell T. Gregg (New York: Harper & Row, Publishers, Inc., 1957), p. 368.

[3] Peter M. Blau and W. Richard Scott, *Formal Organizations: A Comparative Approach* (San Francisco: Chandler Publishing Co., 1962), p. 10.

[4] One of the earliest of these statements of principles was made by Frederick Taylor in *The Principles of Scientific Management* (New York: Harper, 1911).

Principles of administration developed in accord with the standards proposed by Blau and Scott are value free. That is, such principles should be equally applicable in authoritarian and democratic societies. However, values are variables and, because democratic administrators and authoritarian administrators have different value structures, administrative processes and organizational structures will vary even though the same principles are applied. The implementation of principles of organization will vary widely in different countries and different communities, depending largely upon the philosophical assumptions and values of those in a position to make decisions. The administrator holding an authoritarian philosophy will make many assumptions concerning the implications of theories of administration and organization that differ from those made by the person holding a democratic philosophy. Therefore, some of the assumptions underlying contrasting philosophies of administration will be presented.[5]

No attempt is made in this chapter to distinguish between the principles of organization and the principles of administration. In accord with systems theory, the school administrator is conceptualized as an actor in a social system interacting with the environment. Because the administrator is always an actor in an organization, it is extremely difficult to distinguish between principles of organization and principles of administration.

SOME CHARACTERISTICS OF ORGANIZATIONS

In this chapter, we are concerned primarily with the administration of certain types of formal organizations, although certain propositions and theories are probably applicable to all types of organizations. It is difficult to define a formal organization in precise terms. March and Simon observed that "It is easier, and probably more useful to give examples of formal organizations than to define them."[6] Thus, a business firm and a public school system are examples of formal organizations, as contrasted to such face-to-face groups as work groups in a factory or office and groups of interacting influential persons in the community power structure, which are examples of informal organizations.

Classification of Organizations

With reference to formal organizations, Blau and Scott stated, "Since the distinctive characteristics of these organizations is that they have been formally established for the explicit purpose of achieving certain goals, the term 'formal organization' has been used to designate them."[7] These authors have developed a useful typology for classifying organizations. They started with the assumption that the following four basic categories could be distinguished in relation to any formal organization: the members or rank-and-file participants, the owners or

---

[5] Some of the concepts presented in the following pages were adapted from Chap. 9 of *Better Teaching in School Administration* (Nashville, Tenn.: Southern States Cooperative Project in Educational Administration, George Peabody College for Teachers, 1955).

[6] James C. March and Herbert A. Simon, *Organizations* (New York: John Wiley & Sons, Inc., 1958).

[7] Blau and Scott, *Formal Organizations*.

managers, the clients, and the public at large.[8] The following typology was then developed in terms of who benefits from the organization: "(1) 'mutual benefit associations' where the prime beneficiary is the membership; (2) 'business concerns' where the owners are the prime beneficiary; (3) 'service organizations' where the client group is the prime beneficiary; and (4) 'commonweal organizations' where the prime beneficiary is the public at large."[9] Examples of mutual benefit associations are unions, teachers associations, and clubs; examples of business concerns are factories, stores, and private utilities; examples of service organizations are public schools, hospitals, and social work agencies; and examples of commonweal organizations are the armed services, police forces, and fire departments.

Crucial Problems of Different Types of Organizations

Blau and Scott made the following observations concerning the crucial problems of these different types of organizations:

> Thus the crucial problem in mutual benefit associations is that of maintaining internal democratic processes—providing for participation and control by the membership; the central problem for business concerns is that of maximizing operating efficiency in a competitive situation; the problems associated with the conflict between professional service to clients and administrative procedures are characteristic of service organizations; and the crucial problem posed by commonweal organizations is the development of democratic mechanisms whereby they can be externally controlled by the public.[10]

Attention is directed to the fact that these observations concerning the crucial problems of the different types of organizations are applicable only to organizations located in countries with a capitalistic economy and a democratic value system, such as the United States. These are not the crucial problems of the same types of organizations in a country with a socialist economy and an authoritarian value system.

It seems that all these problems for different types of organizations are crucial in a public school organization, with the possible exception of "maximizing operating efficiency in a competitive situation." However, a crucial problem of public school administration is competition with other governmental services and also with the private sector of the economy for allocation of the national product. Furthermore, public school administrators are under pressures quite as severe as administrators of private firms to make efficient use of resources.

Relationship of Information Organizations to Formal Organizations

Attention has already been directed in Chapter 3 to a number of other typologies by which organizations may be studied. It is obvious that the study of organiza-

[8]*Ibid.*, p. 42.
[9]*Ibid.*, p. 43.
[10]*Ibid.*, p. 43.

tion is a very complex matter. Because we are concerned primarily in this chapter with the phenomena of formal organizations, it would seem that our problem should be simplified. However, numerous authorities have pointed out that it is impossible to ignore informal organizations in the study of formal organizations, because informal organizations of actors are factors in the functioning of formal organizations. Therefore, considerable attention will be given to informal groups in Chapter 5.

One of the important distinctions between formal and informal organizations is that formal organizations usually have a longer life than the actors in the organization, while the informal organization usually has a shorter life than the actors in it. In a formal organization such as a school system, the organization will continue after the services of a particular group of teachers are terminated, but the informal organization of a particular group of teachers ceases to exist when that group of teachers severs its connection with the school system. The formal organization has long-term purposes which must be continuously met, and the personnel of the organization must be replenished to do this. The informal group usually has a short-term purpose directed toward satisfying the personal needs of the actors in the informal organization. When those needs are met, the group may disappear. Differences between formal and informal organizations that affect organizational structure are discussed in the sections that follow.

Need for Organizations

The purpose of an organization is to provide the means by which the actors in the organization may cooperate. An organizational structure is necessary when any group has a common task.[11] This is true for gregarious animals as well as for human groups.[12] An unorganized group is only a mass of people. It can neither determine its purposes nor accomplish its ultimate objectives. Therefore, to survive, the group must organize. The organization, no matter how simple, must provide for at least the following procedures for making decisions and taking action:

1. A procedure for selecting a leader or leaders.
2. A procedure for determining the roles to be played by each member of the group.
3. A procedure for determining the goals of the group.
4. A procedure for achieving the goals of the group.

Advocates of democratic procedures sometimes infer that organization and administration are less necessary in a democracy than in an authoritarian government. Thomas Jefferson's statement, "The least governed is the best governed," is sometimes quoted as authority for that belief. Even Plato, who was not an advocate of democracy, contemplated in *The Republic* the idea of a simple com-

---

[11] George C. Homans, *The Human Group* (New York: Harcourt, Brace Jovanovich, 1950), Chaps. 4, 5.

[12] W. C. Allee, "Conflict and Cooperation: Biological Background," in *Approaches to National Unity, Fifth Symposium,* ed. Lyman Bronson, Louis Finkelstein, and Robert MacIver (New York: Harper & Row, Publishers, Inc., 1945).

munistic society without government. He rejected the idea, because he believed that human beings were naturally ambitious, acquisitive, competitive, and jealous. The researches of social psychologists, anthropologists, political scientists, and authorities in business and educational administration do not reveal less necessity for organization and administration in democratic than in authoritarian government. Patterns and procedures of organization and administration will differ, of course, but organization and administration are equally necessary in all forms of human society.

Decision Making

Every organization must make provisions for decision making. Decisions must be made concerning what goals, purposes, objectives, policies, and programs will be accepted by the organization as legitimate. Decisions need to be rendered continuously with respect to the implementation of policies and programs. Therefore, every organization, to be effective, must have the ability to make decisions. These decisions may be made by the leader, by the group, by authorities external to the group, or by a combination of methods. Regardless of how decisions are made or who makes them, an organization cannot operate unless decisions are rendered.

The processes of decision making are so vital to the understanding of administration and organization that significant progress has been made in their theoretical analysis. Simon has suggested that the understanding of the application of administrative principles is to be obtained by analyzing the administrative process in terms of decisions.[13] He theorized that the effectiveness of organizational decisions could be maximized by increasing the rationality of organizational decisions. He assumed that there are limits to human rationality and that this creates a need for administrative theory. According to Simon,

> Two persons, given the same possible alternatives, the same values, the same knowledge, can rationally reach only the same decision. Hence administrative theory must be concerned with the limits of rationality, and the manner in which organization effects these limits for the person making the decision.[14]

Griffiths has formulated a theory of administration as decision making based on the following assumptions:

1. Administration is a generalized type of behavior to be found in all human organization.
2. Administration is the process of directing and controlling life in a social organization.
3. The specific function of administration is to develop and regulate the decision-making process in the most effective manner possible.
4. The administrator works with groups or with individiuals with a group referrent, not with individuals as such.[15]

[13] Simon, *Administrative Behavior*, p. 240.
[14] *Ibid.*, p. 241. Also see Daniel E. Griffiths, *Administrative Theory* (New York: Appleton-Century & Appleton-Century-Crofts, 1959), pp. 57–60, for a discussion of Simon's theories.
[15] Griffiths, *Administrative Theory*, p. 91.

He presented a set of concepts on decision making, perception, communication, power, and authority, and formulated the following major propositions:

1. The structure of an organization is determined by the nature of its decision-making process.
2. If the formal and informal organization approach congruency, then the total organization will approach maximum achievement.
3. If the total organization is not approaching maximum achievement, then, in all probability, the formal and informal organization are divergent.
4. If the administrator confines his behavior to making decisions on the decision-making process rather than making terminal decisions for the organization, his behavior will be more acceptable to his subordinates.
5. If the administrator perceives himself as the controller of the decision-making process, rather than the maker of the organization's decisions, the decision will be more effective.[16]

Miller has proposed a number of significant hypotheses of decision making in social systems.[17] Further research on these and other hypotheses related to the processes of decision making will undoubtedly produce significant advances in understanding principles of administration and organization.

A more extensive analysis of decision making is presented in Chapter 6.

Selecting a Leader

There are many methods by which a group may be provided with leadership. The leader (here not distinguished from the administrator) may be selected by instinct, as in the case of bees, or by a test of physical strength, as in the case of the wolf pack. The leader may be selected by force or by chicanery, in accordance with the patterns usually followed in dictatorships. The leader may be selected by the group itself or by representatives of the group, as in a democracy or a republic. Regardless of the method of selection, an effective group will always have leadership. The role of the leader will vary widely in different types of groups, depending upon the goals and values of the group, the leader's perception of his or her role, the group's perception of the leader's role, and other factors.

The group cannot attain its maximum productivity and the maximum satisfaction of individual members unless functions, activities, interests, and assignments are coordinated. That is one of the principal functions of executive leadership. The executive head of an organization, to be of maximum usefulness to the organization, must also be a leader. The functions of leadership are many and varied. The definition of the term "leadership" itself is an involved undertaking. This subject is discussed in detail in the following chapter.

---

[16]*Ibid.,* pp. 89–91.

[17]James G. Miller, "Living Systems: Cross-Level Hypotheses," *Behavioral Science,* 10, no. 4 (October 1965), 394–397, 406.

Determination of Roles

The organization must also provide for the determination of the roles of each member of the group. Again, the method of determining these roles will vary widely among different groups, depending upon the nature of the group. In the lowest order of animals, the individual role of a group member may be assigned largely by instinct. In a higher order of animals, such as human beings, the roles of individual members may be determined arbitrarily by the leader, or largely by the choice of individual members of the group, or by various combinations of these methods. Regardless of how roles are determined, each member of the group or organization must have an appropriate role for the social system to function with maximum efficiency.

Determination of Goals and Purposes

An organization such as a school system must provide some method by which a group may determine its common goals. This is very easy in the case of some groups, such as the wolf pack. The common goal of obtaining food was the reason the group was formed. Even in animals of a higher order, such as human beings, common goals are usually the basis of group formation. When human beings are arbitrarily forced together, they cannot become an effective group until common goals have been determined. This phenomenon is sometimes observed in faculties of schools which do not have common purposes. Conflicts sometimes develop within a group over the determination of purposes. If these conflicts are not resolved, the group will either disintegrate or break into two or more factions.

Miller has stated the following two hypotheses concerning the determination of goals and purposes which have been supported by some research:

1. Lack of clarity of purpose or goals in a system's decisions will produce conflict between it and other components of the suprasystem.
2. If a system has multiple purposes and goals, and they are not placed in clear priority and commonly known by all components and subsystems, conflict among them will ensue.[18]

Attainment of Goals

All groups must develop procedures for taking action to attain goals. If these goals are not attained, the group will either disintegrate or be reorganized. The goals must include the goals of individual members as well as those of the organization if it is to maximize its production possibilities (see Getzels's model presented in Chapter 3). It is impossible to attain organizational goals with efficiency if there is a crucial conflict between organizational goals and the goals of the actors in the organization.

[18] *Ibid.*, pp. 404–405.

A distinction should be made at this point between goal attainment of formal organizations and of informal organizations. An effective organization must be an active one. In fact, activity is essential for organizational survival. Because formal organizations usually have long-range goals which must be continuously met, the need for activity is continuous. But informal organizations usually have short-range goals arising from the needs of the actors in the informal organization. If the goal is attained and no other goal is substituted for it, activity ceases and the organization disappears. The same thing is true even of some types of formal organizations, such as a political organization formed to elect a particular candidate at a given election. After the election, the goal is either attained or abandoned, activity ceases, and the organization dissolves. Thus, we have the paradox of the necessity for the organization to attain its goals to succeed but the probability of nonsurvival once it attains its goals.

Fortunately, the school organization does not face this kind of dilemma because, each year, each class or grade has new inputs of students with fresh goals to be attained for those students. A school organization is a dynamic system continuously seeking to attain its goals and at the same time continuously assuming responsibility for assisting maturing students and new entrants to attain their goals. Therefore, no school system has failed to survive because it attained all its goals. The critical problem with school organizations is failure to adopt goals relevant to the needs of students and the community or inadequate attainment of relevant goals.

Nature of Organizational Structures

The tendency in formal organizations is to develop pyramidal, hierarchical structures with superordinate–subordinate relationships among the actors in the organization. This phenomenon has been observed in all societies, regardless of stage of civilization, economic system, or political philosophy. The larger and more complex the organization, the more bureaucratic and hierarchical the structure of the organization tends to become. For example, the organizational structure for a rural elementary school district that provides educational services for only 150 pupils in a six-teacher school is far less hierarchical and bureaucratic than the organizational structure for a municipal district with a population of 500,000 providing numerous elementary and high schools, a junior college, and many special educational services. Further attention will be given to the structure of formal organizations later in this chapter.

Informal organizations are usually small in size and have a very simple structure with few organizational hierarchies. Berelson and Steiner have reported that most informal groups have an upper limit of fifteen to twenty persons.[19] Informal organizations usually have face-to-face relations in small groups.

CONCEPTS OF ORGANIZATION AND ADMINISTRATION

In the following sections of this chapter, a number of concepts of organization and administration are presented, Although each of these "principles" is stated

[19] Bernard Berelson and Gary A. Steiner, *Human Behavior: An Inventory of Scientific Findings* (New York: Harcourt, Brace Jovanovich, 1964), p. 325.

in terms of its relationship to the effectiveness of the organization in surviving in its environment and attaining its goals, it could just as readily be stated in terms of "administrative efficiency." For example, the proposition concerning the single executive could be stated as follows: (1) administrative efficiency is increased by having a single executive head of an organization, or (2) the effectiveness of an organization is enhanced by having a single executive head. These two statements illustrate the relationship of principles of administration to principles of organization. However, the ultimate purpose of an organization is not to establish conditions that increase administrative efficiency but to establish conditions that will enhance the effectiveness of the organization in attaining its goals. Sometimes this important point has been forgotten by an administrative hierarchy snarled in red tape. *Administrative efficiency is valid only to the extent that it contributes to the attainment of the goals of the organization, the goals of the actors in the organization, and the extent that it meets the requirements of the environment for the survival of the organization.* In the future, more meaningful and useful principles of administration and organization than those presented here will no doubt be developed from current and future research, much of it based on systems theory. Educational administrators administer social systems usually comprising a complex of suprasystems and subsystems. Therefore, useful principles must deal with cross-level factors as well as factors at one system level.[20]

The generally recognized "principles" of organization are presented in the following paragraphs. As was pointed out, some theorists insist that there are no principles in the scientific sense. That may be true. Perhaps they should be called criteria or guides. Regardless of what they are called, they are concepts useful for the study of organization and administration.

Single Executive

The effectiveness of an organization is enhanced by having a single executive head. The executive must provide central coordination for the activities of an organization. Although an organization may have a number of leaders, one of these leaders must serve as the coordinating head of the group. Unless this is done, no organization can achieve its purposes, because division of central leadership will prevent the coordination of its activities. The necessity for the recognition of this principle becomes more imperative as the size of the organization's membership increases. This principle of administration was among the earliest generally recognized. Despite the fact that numerous experiments in divided central executive leadership have failed, proposals are still being advanced to provide an organization with two executive heads. In educational administration numerous attempts have been made to divide the executive functions for education into educational and business administration. Boards of education have sometimes employed two superintendents, one for educational and one for business administration, each directly responsible to the board and neither responsible to the other. These experiments have almost invariably resulted in friction and in the failure of the organization to attain its goals effectively. The activities of any effective organization must be coordinated, and this can best be achieved through a single executive head.

[20] See Miller, "Living Systems."

Unity of Purpose

The effectiveness of an organization is enhanced by clear definition of goals and purposes. The processes of determining goals and purposes may be formal or informal. The members of a simple organization may have tacitly agreed upon its purposes before the organization was formed. However, a complex organization such as an educational structure has many purposes and goals. In such an organization these must be carefully determined. Unless that is done, the organization is likely to operate with conflicting purposes. Such an organization will almost inevitably end in conflict among members of the group or between the group and the official leadership. Unresolved conflicts will eventually destroy informal organizations and "wild" formal organizations (defined in Chapter 3). The members of a public school organization are members of a "domestic" organization. Such a group, with undetermined or conflicting purposes, may legally continue in existence past its period of usefulness. The turnover in such a group is high and the group is ineffective. Therefore, it is vital that any organization determine its purposes and goals if it wishes to continue serving a useful function.

Unity of Command

The effectiveness of an organization is enhanced when every person in the organization knows to whom and for what he is responsible. This principle, as its name implies, was first recognized by the armed services. As pointed out later in this chapter, there is much disagreement concerning the validity of this proposition. Following are some of the assumptions underlying it.

The organization should provide for the definition of the role of each individual. It is demoralizing to the individual and destructive to the productivity of the organization to have individuals uncertain of their duties. Whether the individual is assigned duties by the status leader or participates personally in their selection, the individual will not be an effective member of the organization unless that individual knows what his or her obligations are. Unless the lines of responsibility and authority are defined clearly, chaos is inevitable. It follows that no individual in the organization should be compelled to take direct orders from more than one person, because conflicts will inevitably arise.

Delegation of Authority and Responsibility

The effectiveness of an organization is enhanced when superordinates delegate authority to subordinates. It would seem that this is a self-evident fact rather than a principle. However, the problem of delegation of authority and responsibility has plagued humankind since the development of organizations. One of the assumptions back of this principle is that, when an administrator delegates responsibility for a task to a subordinate, the administrator should at the same time delegate to the subordinate the necessary authority to accomplish the task.

As is true with many principles of organization and administration, there are limits to the operation of this principle. Miller has hypothesized that segregation (compartmentalization) increases conflict among subsystems.[21] He cited in support of that hypothesis the observation of March and Simon that the delegation of authority to departments in firms increased the disparity of interests and created conflict among them.[22]

Division of Labor

The effectiveness of an organization is enhanced by the division of labor and task specialization. Provision for an appropriate division of labor to increase productivity was the basic reason private firms were established. Adam Smith presented an excellent illustration of this principle in his famous book, *The Wealth of Nations,* published in 1776. In his illustration, he demonstrated that, if a group of people making pins divided the labor and each specialized on a task, the same number of people could greatly increase their production of pins in a given length of time.

Much of the increase in the productivity of the economy of Western civilization during the past two centuries has been due to the formation of large numbers of complex organizations which have applied the division-of-labor principle. The growth in technology and the industrialization of society have greatly increased the emphasis on division of labor and specialization during the past twenty-five years. This trend has created some critical problems, which will be treated later in this chapter.

Miller has hypothesized that the segregation of functions in a system is increased by structurally increasing the types of its members or components.[23]

Standardization

The effectiveness of an organization is enhanced by the development of standardized procedures for routine administrative operation. Standardized procedures are applicable to such operations as accounting, data gathering, statistical reporting, and record keeping. Standardization of routine operations saves labor on the part of all members of the organization. Such procedures are also essential to collecting much of the data necessary for establishing management information systems.

Span of Control

The effectiveness of an organization is enhanced by assigning to each administrator no greater a number of persons than the administrator can supervise directly. This is an extremely controversial principle, as will be shown later. However it is a time-honored principle, generally accepted by military and business organizations. Perhaps this principle is applicable to some types of organizations and not applica-

---

[21]*Ibid.,* p. 403.
[22]March and Simon, *Organizations,* pp. 41–42.
[23]Miller, "Living Systems," p. 384.

ble to others. Or perhaps the most efficient span of control differs for different types of organizations and for different types of tasks within an organization.

Stability

The effectiveness of an organization is enhanced by continuing policies and programs until results can be evaluated. An organization that changes its policies or programs capriciously is almost certain to be an ineffective organization. If policies and programs are defined carefully and are given a thorough trial before being abandoned or changed, "sunken costs" are minimized and the probability of establishing a favorable ratio between input and output is increased.

Flexibility

The effectiveness of an organization is enhanced when it makes provision for innovation and change. Innovation and change are facilitated when policies are stated in broad enough terms to permit reasonable flexibility in management. The principle of flexibility also implies that, once a program or policy has been continued long enough for evaluation, provision should be made for needed changes. Therefore, the principle of flexibility might be interpreted as a contradiction of the principle of stability. However, these two principles do not contradict each other as much as they tend to balance one another. What is sought in effective administration is an appropriate balance between stability and flexibility. The need for flexibility of administration and organization increases in these times of rapid change.

Security

The effectiveness of an organization is enhanced when the organization provides security for its members. Different members of the group have many different individual needs, but the need for security is universal. This universal craving for security makes it essential that this need be met in any group, regardless of its political philosophy. As a matter of fact, security itself is frequently the goal or purpose for which informal groups are formed. The need for security is no less present in formal groups, such as educational organizations, than in informal groups.

Personnel Policies

The effectiveness of an organization is enhanced by personnel policies, which include selecting the competent, training the inexperienced, eliminating the incompetent, and providing incentives for all members of the organization. Even informal organizations such as street gangs follow these procedures. Personnel policies in formal groups, such as school faculties, must be defined carefully. Selecting the competent is essential to recruiting potentially effective group members. Training the inexperienced is essential to obtaining maximum productivity from individual members of the group. Eliminating the incompetent is essential to maintaining the integrity, cohesiveness, and effectiveness of the group. Providing incentives by meeting the individual needs of group members is essential to maintaining group morale and assuring maximum productivity.

Evaluation

The effectiveness of an organization is enhanced when provision is made for evaluating not only the products of the organization but also the organization itself. Activity without evaluation may be fruitless. The ability to evaluate is one of the characteristics which distinguishes the human species from lower orders of animals. Evaluation is provided not only by actors within the organization, but also by the environment of the organization if evaluation is effective. Evaluation by the environment is obtained by making provision for the organization to receive feedback, as was pointed out in Chapter 3.

Leavitt has presented evidence indicating that two-way communication in an organization providing feedback reduces error.[24] Feedback provides one means of continuous evaluation.

There are numerous technical and scientific methods available for evaluation of the material products of an organization. The instruments available for the evaluation of the nonmaterial products of the educational system are far less precise. This does not relieve the educational system of the necessity for evaluation. It only makes the problem more difficult.

TRADITIONAL AND EMERGING CONCEPTS
OF ORGANIZATION AND ADMINISTRATION

There are two principal competing concepts of organization and administration, which we will call the traditional monocratic, bureaucratic concept and the emerging pluralistic, collegial concept. The use of the terms "traditional monocratic, bureaucratic concept" and "emerging pluralistic, collegial concept" should not be interpreted as suggesting that we have a clear dualism in types of administration and organization. As Bennis has said, "So we hear of 'Theory X vs. Theory Y,' personality vs. organization, democratic vs. autocratic, task vs. maintenance, human relations vs. scientific management, and on and on. Surely life is more complicated than these dualities suggest, and surely they must imply a continuum—not simply extremes."[25]

Therefore, in this section we will describe not dual concepts of administration and organization but the extreme ends of a continuum. The principles of adminis-

[24] Harold K. Leavitt, *Managerial Psychology* (Chicago: University of Chicago Press, 1958), p. 123.
[25] Warren G. Bennis, "Theory and Method in Applying Behavioral Science to Planned Organizational Change," *Journal of Applied Science,* 1, no. 4 (1965), 356.

tration discussed in the previous section are equally applicable throughout this continuum. However, as will be shown in this chapter, the structure of the organization and administrative procedures will vary greatly, depending upon the assumptions made and the value systems of those applying these principles.

The Traditional Monocratic, Bureaucratic Concept

The traditional monocratic, bureaucratic concept of organization and administration is defined as a pyramidal, hierarchical organizational structure, in which all power for making decisions flows from superordinates to subordinates. This concept has been described by Weber.[26]

We are indebted to Abbott for the following succinct description of Weber's monocratic, bureaucratic model:

> For Weber, the essential and distinctive characteristics of a bureaucracy were somewhat as follows:
>
> 1. The regular activities required for the purposes of the organization are distributed in fixed ways as official duties. Since the tasks of an organization are too complex to be performed by a single individual, or by a group of individuals possessing a single set of skills, efficiency will be promoted by dividing those tasks into activities which can be assigned to specific offices or positions. This division of labor makes posssible a high degree of specialization which, in turn, promotes improved performance in two ways. First it enables the organization to employ personnel on the basis of technical qualifications; second, it enables employees to improve their skills by limiting their attention to a relatively narrow range of activities.
> 2. The positions in an organization are arranged on the principle of office hierarchy and of levels of graded authority. This means that there is a firmly ordered system of superordination and subordination in which the lower offices are supervised by the higher ones. Although specialization makes possible the efficient performance of specific tasks, specialization also creates problems of coordination. To achieve the required coordination, it is necessary to grant to each official the requisite authority to control the activities of his subordinates.
> 3. The management of activities is controlled by general rules which are more or less stable, more or less exhaustive, and which can be learned. These rules are general and abstract, and they constitute standards which assure reasonable uniformity in the performance of tasks. They preclude the issuance of directives based on whim or caprice, but require the application of general principles to particular cases. Together with the hierarchical authority structure, rules provide for the coordination of organizational activities and for continuity of operations, regardless of changes in personnel.

[26] Max Weber, *The Theory of Social and Economic Organization,* trans. A. M. Henderson and Talcott Parsons, ed. Talcott Parsons (New York: Free Press of Glencoe, Inc., 1947). NOTE: Max Weber (1864–1920) was a remarkably productive German scholar. He began with the study of law but soon went on to study economics. After writing a number of outstanding works on economics, he turned to the development of a science of sociology. Every serious student of administration should read *The Theory of Social and Economic Organization.*

4. Bureaucracy develops the more perfectly the more completely it succeeds in eliminating from official business love, hatred, and all purely personal, irrational, and emotional elements which escape calculation. The essence of bureaucratic arrangements is rationality. A spirit of formalistic impersonality is necessary to separate organizational rights and duties from the private lives of employees. Only by performing impersonally can officials assure rationality in decision making, and only thus can they assure equitable treatment for all subordinates.

5. Employment in a bureaucracy is based upon technical competence and constitutes a career. Promotions are to be determined by seniority, or achievement, or both; tenure is to be assured; and fixed compensation and retirement provisions are to be made. Since individuals with specialized skills are employed to perform specialized activities, they must be protected from arbitrary dismissal or denial of promotion on purely personal ground.[27]

Weber wrote as follows concerning the superiority of his model for human organization:

> Experience tends universally to show that the purely bureaucratic type of administrative organization—that is, the monocratic variety of bureaucracy— is, from a purely technical point of view, capable of attaining the highest degree of efficiency and is in this sense formally the most rational known means of carrying out imperative control over human beings. It is superior to any other form in precision, in stability, in the stringency of its discipline, and in its reliability. It thus makes possible a particularly high degree of calculability of results for the heads of the organization and for those acting in relation to it. It is finally superior both in intensive efficiency and in the scope of its operation, and is formally capable of application to all kinds of administrative tasks.[28]

Weber was definitely at one end of the continuum. He insisted that, considering the needs of mass administration, the only choice was between bureaucracy and dilettantism in the field of administration. His opinion of "collegiality"— the formal requirement that legitimate acts of a body require the participation of all its members in decision making—was expressed as follows:

> Furthermore, it divides personal responsibility, indeed in the larger bodies this disappears almost entirely, whereas in monocratic organizations it is perfectly clear without question where responsibility lies. Large-scale tasks which require quick and consistent solutions tend in general, for good technical reasons, to fall into the hands of monocratic "dictators" in whom all responsibility is concentrated.[29]

Strangely enough, Weber did not consider his idealized bureaucracy as authoritarian. On the contrary, he thought that it foreshadowed mass democracy, be-

[27] Max G. Abbott and John T. Lovell, eds., *Change Perspectives in Educational Administration* (Auburn, Ala.: School of Education, Auburn University, 1965), pp. 42–43.
[28] Weber, *Social and Economic Organization,* p. 337.
[29] *Ibid.,* p. 399.

cause, according to his model, technical experts would be placed in the executive, decision-making positions in the hierarchy, instead of staffing these positions through the traditional methods of patriarchalism, patrimonialism, and charisma. Viewed from this standpoint, the development of the modern bureaucracy was considered a step toward democracy because, theoretically, positions of power in the hierarchy would be opened to experts who could come from the masses.

Thompson has pointed out, however, that at the present time one of the crucial problems in modern organizations is the reconciliation of conflicts between specialists on the staff of an organization who know and executives in the power structure of the line organization who do not know.[30]

Weber's monocratic, bureaucratic model has been severely criticized in ways discussed later in this chapter. Despite such criticism, the monocratic, bureaucratic concept of administrative organization is the prevailing model of organization found in every advanced country of the world, regardless of its political philosophy or economic organization. It has been the basic model for organizing the public school systems of the United States, especially the larger systems.

In the following section, some of the assumptions underlying the monocratic, bureaucratic concept are presented. It will be noted that a number of these assumptions are not value free.

✱ Some Assumptions Underlying the Traditional Monocratic, Bureaucratic Concept

Administrators differ widely in theory concerning the application of the principles of organization and administration to, first, those activities relating to the formulation of goals, programs, and policies; second, those activities relating to goal attainment through the implementation of programs and policies; and third, those activities relating to maintaining the group. There is no recognized field theory of administration. Furthermore, it is difficult for the student to find anywhere in the literature of educational administration a coherent statement of theory on how the principles of organization and administration should be implemented.

Critics of administrators, sometimes administrators themselves, have tended to categorize administration as good or bad, efficient or inefficient, without attempting to differentiate carefully between different concepts of administrative theory. In this chapter, an attempt is made to distinguish between the traditional monocratic, bureaucratic and the emerging pluralistic, collegial concepts of administration and organization, but for many people even these words, unfortunately, have good and bad connotations.

Sometimes the arbitrary classification of administrative theory by labels that have value connotations retards a scholarly analysis. It is better to assume that administrators are neither good nor bad but that they differ in their assumptions concerning these concepts. In the following paragraphs, an analysis is made of some of the important assumptions underlying the monocratic, bureaucratic concept.

[30] Victor A. Thompson, *Modern Organization* (New York: Alfred A. Knopf, Inc., 1961), pp. 81–113.

(1) **Leadership is confined to those holding positions in the power echelon.** Those accepting such a premise generally assume that the population is divided into two groups, the leaders and the followers. The leaders should be assigned to power positions in the hierarchy, where it is their responsibility to exercise leadership. If persons other than power holders exercise leadership, conflicts are bound to arise. A capable person should obtain a power position if he or she wants to be a leader. If such a person attempts to exercise leadership when not holding a power position, that person will become a troublemaker and will interfere with the administrative leadership of the person holding the superordinate position. If the superordinate permits leadership outside of the power structure to develop, his or her own position is threatened. If a person does not exercise his or her authority, that person will lose it. The superordinate must carefully protect his or her prerogatives, or he or she is likely to lose the leadership position.

(2) **Good human relations are necessary in order that followers accept decisions of superordinates.** The decisions of the officials in the power hierarchy must be accepted and implemented, or the enterprise fails. The power holder can use force on the followers and require them to accept decisions, but force requires rigorous inspection and supervision, which is expensive in time and energy. Therefore, the power holder should establish good relations between followers and himself or herself so that they will voluntarily follow without question.

(3) **Authority and power can be delegated, but responsibility cannot be shared.** The top executive may delegate power and authority to subexecutives, and he or she may hold them responsible for the proper exercise of the power and authority delegated to them. Nevertheless, all responsibility is ultimately the top executive's if things go wrong.

(4) **Final responsibility for all matters is placed in the administrator at the top of the power echelon.** The top executive in the organization is ultimately responsible for everything that happens. That person should receive the credit and also receive the blame. This assumption logically follows the assumption with respect to responsibility. Certainly, if the executive is ultimately responsible for everything, he or she should have the authority to veto any decision of subordinates.

(5) **The individual finds security in a climate in which the superordinates protect the interests of subordinates in the organization.** The person holding the top position in the power echelon should defend subordinates, right or wrong, so long as they take orders and are loyal. This assumption is similar to the assumptions of feudalism, whereby a person became a vassal of a feudal lord for protection. The success of the feudal system was based upon the loyalty of vassals and on the effectiveness with which the feudal lord protected those vassals.

Thompson made the following comment concerning this point:

> Bureaucratic hierarchy has inherited the rights and privileges of the early charismatic leader and his retainers, the traditionalistic king and his nobility, and the entrepreneurial owner-manager and his family protégés. Conse-

quently, to be socially defined as "successful" in our culture, one must proceed up some hierarchy.[31]

⑥ **Unity of purpose is obtained through loyalty to the administrator.** Because the administrator will protect subordinates, right or wrong, those subordinates owe the administrator their undivided loyalty. This loyalty requires that subordinates defend the administrator and also accept decisions without question. This, too, is an essential assumption of the feudal system.

⑦ **The image of the executive is that of a superman.** According to Thompson, "The impression is fostered that occupants of hierarchical positions are, of all people in the organization, the ablest, the most industrious, the most indispensable, the most loyal, the most reliable, the most self-controlled, the most ethical, which is to say the most honest, fair, and impartial."[32]

Because money is one of the most important factors in determining prestige and status, the person occupying the top position in the heirarchy should be paid the highest salary.

⑧ **Maximum production is attained in a climate of competition and pressure.** People excel in their efforts when they compete with each other. Life is a competitive struggle for survival, and greater rewards should be given to the persons who are successful. This competition should be supplemented by pressure, taking the form of either rewards or punishment. Competition and pressure are good for production.

⑨ **The line-and-staff plan of organization should be utilized to formulate goals, policies, and programs as well as to execute policies and programs.** Because the best leadership is placed in the line-and-staff structure, this leadership is most competent to formulate goals, policies, and programs. That structure has the responsibility for implementing the goals, policies, and programs and therefore should have the responsibility for formulating them.

⑩ **Authority is the right and privilege of a person holding a hierarchical position.** Authority is inherent in the position itself. The authority should be given to the person who has the greatest ability. Administrators have the greatest ability, or they would not be in positions of power in the hierarchy. This assumption can be traced back to the divine right of kings theory.

⑪ **The individual in the organization is expendable.** The purpose or goal of the organization is more important than the individual. For that reason, the individual should be sacrificed if necessary to accomplish the goals of the organization. The individual exists to serve the organization rather than the organization to serve the individual.

⑫ **Evaluation is the prerogative of superordinates.** Because the superordinate is finally responsible for everything, logically he or she should have the exclusive

---

[31] *Ibid.*, p. 96.
[32] *Ibid.*, p. 143.

authority to evaluate persons and production. Evaluation is one of the means by which the superordinate enforces discipline in the organization.

THE EMERGING PLURALISTIC, COLLEGIAL CONCEPT

Unfortunately, no scholar with the brilliance of a Weber has attempted to describe the model for the pluralistic, collegial concept of administration and organization. Many writers have described in detail the defects of the bureaucratic model, but none has suggested its complete abandonment.[33] The emerging pluralistic, collegial concept of organization can perhaps best be described as a modification of the monocratic, bureaucratic concept, providing for a pluralistic sharing of power to make policy and program decisions on a collegial basis. Under this concept, the organization is structured hierarchically, as in Weber's bureaucracy, to implement programs and policies, and is structured collegially on an egalitarian basis for making policy and program decisions. Perhaps the best example of this model is a college that (1) emphasizes academic freedom, scholarship, and the dignity of the individual, (2) provides that the faculty, and not the administrative hierarchy, shall make major policy and program decisions, and (3) pays distinguished professors salaries as high as or higher than those of persons holding positions in the administrative hierarchy. This is not a hypothetical case. This concept of organization and administration is actually found in many of the leading colleges and universities of the nation.

Thompson noted that the monocratic, bureaucratic organization is not innovative.[34] Following is a summary of his proposals for making a bureaucratic organization more innovative: (1) the organization will be more loosely structured, with less emphasis on a precise definition of duties and responsibilities; (2) jobs will be described in terms of professional responsibilities, as contrasted with duties; (3) communications will be freer; (4) appropriate types of decisions will be decentralized; (5) there will be less stratification in the organization, and salary scales will no longer reflect chiefly "awesome status differences"; (6) greater use will be made of group processes and less emphasis made of authority; (7) work assignments will be made broader; (8) more opportunities will be provided for multiple group membership and interpersonal communication; (9) departmentalization will be so arranged as to keep parochialism to a minimum; (10) the organization will not be as tidy as the monocratic bureaucracy, because some overlapping of functions and vagueness concerning jurisdictions promote interdepartmental communication.[35] While Thompson did not attempt to conceptualize the pluralistic, collegial organizational model, he made the following proposals, which take us a considerable distance on the continuum toward this model.

> If formal structures could be sufficiently loosened, it might be possible for organizations and units to restructure themselves continually in the light of

[33] For example, see Thompson, *Modern Organization;* Chris Argyris, "The Individual and Organization: Some Problems of Mutual Adjustment," and Wallazz B. Eaton, "Democratic Organization: Myth or Reality" in *Educational Administration: Selected Readings,* ed. Walter G. Hack et al. (Boston: Allyn & Bacon, Inc., 1965).

[34] Victor A. Thompson, "Bureaucracy and Innovation," *Administrative Science Quarterly,* 10, no. 1 (June 1965).

[35] Adapted from Thompson, "Bureaucracy and Innovation."

the problem at hand. Thus, for generating ideas, for planning and problem solving, the organization or unit would "unstructure" itself into a freely communicating body of equals. When it came time (as opposed to stimulation of novel or correct ideas), the organization would then restructure itself into the more usual hierarchical form, tightening up its lines somewhat.[36]

Some Assumptions Underlying the Emerging Pluralistic, Collegial Concept

Some of the assumptions underlying the pluralistic, collegial concept of administration differ sharply from those underlying the traditional monocratic, bureaucratic concept. Under the headings that follow an analysis is made of some of these assumptions.

① **Leadership is not confined to those holding status positions in the power echelon.** Any person who helps a group to formulate goals, programs, and policies, any person who assists a group to attain its goals, or any person who helps maintain the group, is providing leadership. Therefore, leadership is not a narrow or restricted function, reserved exclusively to superordinates, but leadership potential is widely dispersed throughout the organization. The person holding authority will be more effective if he or she develops, rather than restricts, this leadership potential throughout the group. Instead of losing leadership by sharing it, that person will increase his or her own potential. The individual can prevent conflicts from multiple leadership by the appropriate use of the coordination function of executive leadership.

② **Good human relations are essential to group production and to meeting the needs of individual members of the group.** Good human relations improve group morale, and high group morale generally facilitates production. Individual members of the group feel the need for acceptance by other members. When individual needs as well as group needs are met, the organization is more productive.

③ **Responsibility, as well as power and authority, can be shared.** If leadership can be shared, responsibility can be shared. If potential leaders in the organization are permitted to exercise their leadership potential, they will voluntarily accept responsibility as well as authority and power. Because all responsibility is not placed in the executive at the top of the power echelon, the executive should not receive all the credit or all the blame.

④ **Those affected by a program or policy should share in decision making with respect to that program or policy.** This assumption is stated as follows in the Declaration of Independence: "Governments are instituted among men, deriving their just powers from the consent of the governed." Lincoln stated basically this same assumption in the following words: "Government of the people, by the people, for the people." Perhaps traditional and emerging administration theo-

[36] *Ibid.*, p. 16.

ries differ more on this assumption than any other. Due to the development of large, complex educational organizations, not all members can participate directly in all types of policy decisions. But all members can participate through their representatives.

(5) **The individual finds security in a dynamic climate in which responsibility for decision making is shared.** A person is more secure in implementing goals, policies, and programs if the person understands them. The person will understand them better if he or she helps to formulate them. A person is more secure if he or she helps to determine his or her own fate. A free person is more secure than a vassal.

(6) **Unity of purpose is secured through consensus and group loyalty.** When members of a group participate in the formulation of goals, policies, and programs, the group is more likely to accept them than if they are handed down through the hierarchy. As the group works together, interactions occur which make the group more cohesive. If the leader works effectively with the group, he will be accepted by the group as a member. When the group develops goals, policies, and programs, they tend to be the property of the group, and the group will be loyal to what it has developed and to the members who have shared in that process. Unity of purpose is secured through these interactional processes.

(7) **Maximum production is attained in a threat-free climate.** The by-products of competition and pressure may ultimately reduce, rather than increase, production. A threat-free climate does not mean a problem-free situation.

> The solution of problems promotes the growth of the individual and also gives him a feeling of satisfaction. External pressures are sometimes exerted on an individual in order to force him to accept a value or achieve a goal. A pressure is a threat if it is resented by the individual concerned and is destructive of his personality. A threat is particularly destructive to the individual if the pressure is exerted to force him to accept a value or attain a goal which he does not believe is valid. If the individual participates in the determination of acceptable values and goals and they become his own values and goals, he will be under pressure to attain goals that are consistent with his values, but the pressure will be internal rather than external. This internal pressure will then become a felt need of the individual. As he meets his needs, he will solve problems which promote his growth and give him satisfaction.
>
> The emerging theory of administration provides a climate which avoids the use of external pressures that are destructive of human personality. The traditional theory of administration does not hesitate to use external pressures in order to attain production.[37]

(8) **The line-and-staff organizations should be used exclusively for the purpose of dividing labor and implementing policies and programs developed by the total group affected.** It will be noted that the emerging collegial concept, as well as the traditional monocratic concept of administration, accepts the necessity of a line-and-staff organization. However, these two concepts differ in the way the line-

[37]*Better Teaching in School Administration,* pp. 92–93.

and-staff organization is used. Under the monocratic concept, it is assumed that the line-and-staff organization determines and also executes policies and programs. The emerging collegial concept of administration calls for group participation in decision making. Therefore, the line-and-staff organization alone will not meet the requirements of emerging theory. Two structures are needed under the emerging theory of administration: one for determining goals, policies, and programs and another for executing policies and programs. Under the emerging theory of administration, the structure for implementing policies and programs is usually a line-and-staff organization. The structure for developing policies and programs is usually some type of a committee organization in which all members of the organization have a peer status, regardless of position in the power echelon.

Law and regulations legitimizing authority recognize that the need for authority arises from the situation. Authority arises out of the situation rather than out of the position. For example, routine operating decisions are made as near the scene of action as possible. The situation itself frequently demands that authority be exercised by someone. The administrator finds himself or herself in a situation in which he or she must exercise authority to attain the goals of the organization or to meet the needs of its members. Therefore, the administrator exercises that authority because of the necessities of the situation, not because of the prerogatives of the position. The teacher is also in a situation that requires that authority over certain matters be exercised. That authority is exercised not because of prerogatives held by reason of being a teacher, but because the situation requires that the teacher exercise authority if the organization is to function properly.

The individual in the organization is not expendable. The ultimate purpose of an organization is to meet the needs of individuals in human society. The individuals in the organization are a part of that society. Government was created to serve people, and not people to serve government. Therefore, the worth of the individual should not be ignored by the organization. Furthermore, the organization can better achieve its own purpose by conserving and improving the members of the organization.

Evaluation is a group responsibility. If there is broad participation in the formation of goals, policies, and programs, then there must be broad participation in evaluation. Participation in evaluation by the group is necessary to develop the competencies of the group. Collegial group evaluation is more valid and reliable than evaluation by one individual. Furthermore, broad participation in evaluation provides valuable feedback.

SOME CONTRASTS BETWEEN THE MONOCRATIC, BUREAUCRATIC AND THE PLURALISTIC, COLLEGIAL CONCEPTS

As has already been pointed out, the assumptions made and the values held by those in a position to formulate the structure of an organization and to administer it determine largely the point on the monocratic, bureaucratic–pluralistic, collegial continuum (hereafter shortened to monocratic–pluralistic continuum) on which an organization can be located. Although the principles of formal organization are generally applicable to all types of formal organization, there are vital differences between school systems on one end of the monocratic–pluralistic continuum and those on the other end. Some of those differences are discussed under the headings that follow.

Climate

The climate of human relations is different in school systems operating under the monocratic and pluralistic concepts of administration. The absence of fear of the hierarchy, the feeling of equality, and the knowledge that one is master of one's own fate beget different personalities in systems at the opposite ends of the monocratic-pluralistic continuum. The monocratic school system tends toward a *closed climate*, as contrasted to the tendency toward an *open climate* in a pluralistic system.[38]

Structure

It has already been pointed out that there are wide differences in organizational structures developed in accordance with the assumptions underlying the monocratic concept and with the pluralistic concept. Structures based on the monocratic concept of administration emphasize centralized authority for planning, controlling, and decision making. Such structures also usually exercise a close inspectional type of supervision. Because the executives in such organizations are responsible for all decision making and planning and, at the same time, for exercising highly centralized control over all operations, the span of control or the number of persons supervised by the executive in the monocratic organization is usually less than the executive span of control in the pluralistic organization. Therefore, the monocratic organization requires more echelons of authority and tends to have longer chains of command supervised by each executive.

There has been some misunderstanding concerning the line-and-staff structure. Some writers have even inferred that the line-and-staff structure is outmoded and should be abandoned. This reasoning seems to be based on the assumption that structure is inherently undemocratic. Actually, the line-and-staff structure is not at fault; the fault lies with the way in which it is used. For instance, in one organization the line-and-staff structure may be so used as to require that all decisions, even routine ones, be cleared with the executive head of the organization before action is taken. This method of operating ignores the possibility of increasing the efficiency of the organization by a judicious delegation of authority. Furthermore, it violates the principle that *operating decisions should be made as near the point of action as practicable.* In another organization, line-and-staff structure

---

[38] See Andrew W. Halpin and Don B. Croft, "The Organizational Climate of Schools," *Administrators Note Book,* 2, no. 7 (March 1963). These researchers did not specifically study the variations in climate of school systems at opposite ends of the monocratic–pluralistic continuum; they did define carefully the characteristics of schools with open and closed climates. Although not intended to do so, those descriptions rather accurately distinguish between the climates of school systems at opposite ends of the continuum.

for the implementation of programs and policies is accompanied by proper delegation of authority and supplemented by machinery for broad participation in decision making with respect to policy and program. Both organizations use a line-and-staff structure, one inappropriately and the other appropriately.

Structures for pluralistic, collegial administration emphasize wide sharing of authority for planning, controlling, and decision making and such centralized authority as is necessary for coordinating the total organization. The organizational structure may actually be more complex than that for the monocratic, bureaucratic organization. However, this additional complexity is introduced for the purpose of making the arrangements necessary for broad participation in decision making.

It is sometimes said that there is less emphasis on structure in pluralistic than in monocratic organizations. It is probably true that the skeleton of the monocratic structure is more stark, because of its constraints, than is the skeleton of the pluralistic structure. On the other hand, the structure for the pluralistic organization is designed to give maximum freedom to the individual; therefore, the individual is less conscious of the structure itself.

Communication

The communication patterns differ widely in monocratic and pluralistic organization. The communication pattern for monocratic organization is quite simple. It goes up and down a vertical line organization. A communication from the top must pass through all *intermediate echelons* of authority before it reaches the bottom, but no *intermediate echelon* can stop the communication from the top down. A communication from the bottom to the top must also pass through each *intermediate echelon,* but any *intermediate echelon* can stop the communication from a lower level from reaching the top. Therefore, the channel of communication is not strictly a two-way channel. Furthermore, great emphasis is given to "going through channels," and any communication from the bottom to the top which does not go through channels is frowned upon. The administrator in the monocratic hierarchy uses control over communications to increase his or her status, power, and prestige.

There are many channels of communication in pluralistic organizations. Such organizations have provisions for communicating through a vertical channel, but it is a two-way channel. Communication is also circular and horizontal in pluralistic organization. The organization provides for a committee structure or some other arrangement whereby members at the bottom of the line structure may communicate in a face-to-face relationship with the top executives. Because communication is much freer among all members of the organization in a pluralistic structure, the opportunity for beneficial interactions is much greater.

Administrative Behavior

For want of better terminology, we have already referred to democratic and authoritarian administration. The assumptions underlying traditional monocratic, bureaucratic concepts of administration are largely authoritarian, and the assumptions underlying emerging pluralistic, collegial concepts of administration are largely democratic by popular definition. It should not be inferred, however, that democratic administration is *ipso facto* good and that authoritarian administration is *ipso facto* bad. History provides numerous examples of successful and unsuccessful democratic administration and successful and unsuccessful authoritarian administration. Furthermore, it is not strictly accurate to classify administration as democratic and authoritarian. It would be difficult, if not impossible, to find an administration which is completely authoritarian or completely democratic. It is more accurate to think of democracy and authoritarianism as part of the same continuum. Democratic and undemocratic behavior of school principals were defined in a series of studies at the University of Florida. The definitions are as follows:

Democratic behavior:
a. Action involving the group in decision making with respect to policy and program.
b. Implementation in line with democratically determined policy.
c. Action promoting the group or individual creativity, productivity, and satisfaction without harm to other groups or individuals.
d. Behavior or attitude respecting the dignity of individuals or groups.
e. Action that indicates that the principal seeks to become an accepted member of the group.
f. Action that indicates that the principal seeks to keep channels of communication open.

Undemocratic behavior:
a. Action that indicates that decision making is centered in the status leader or his inner circle.
b. Implementation that ignores democratically determined policy.
c. Action that frustrates group or individual creativity, productivity, and satisfaction.
d. Action that indicates that the principal attains objectives by pressures that jeopardize a person's security.
e. Action that indicates that the principal considers himself above or apart from the group.
f. Action that indicates that the principal discourages or blocks free communication.[39]

These definitions were developed to describe the behavior of school principals, but they are equally applicable to other types of administrators. According to these definitions, the words "undemocratic" and "authoritarian" are synonymous terms.

Innovation and Change

Attention has already been directed to the fact that a number of investigators have found that monocratic, bureaucratic organizations are not as innovative as

[39] Carroll D. Farrar, "Refinement of an Instrument to Determine Certain Characteristics of the Working Patterns of School Principals" (unpublished doctoral dissertation, University of Florida, 1956), pp. 14–15.

pluralistic, collegial organizations. This is not surprising, because monocratic control limits feedback both from the environment and from the subsystems of an organization. Furthermore, in monocratic organization the upwardly mobile person must become an organization "man"; follow the chain of command, observing closely all rules, regulations, and norms of the organization; and above all things avoid becoming a threat to superordinates by being an innovator. Consequently, innovation and change, when it does come, usually comes from the top of the hierarchy downward.

In pluralistic, collegial organization, there is more feedback from the environment and from subsystems in the organization. Leadership which promotes change is encouraged at all hierarchical levels. Therefore, in the pluralistic organization, there tends to be more change and innovation, and it may come from the bottom of the hierarchy as well as the top.

Assumption Concerning People

McGregor,[40] one of the leaders of the human relations movement, developed an interesting theory of management which he called Theory X and Theory Y. He distinguished these two theories by analyzing the assumptions behind each theory. According to McGregor, Theory X is based on the following assumptions:

1. The average human being has an inherent dislike of work and will avoid it if he can.
2. Because of this human characteristic of dislike of work, most people must be coerced, controlled, directed, threatened with punishment to get them to put forth adequate effort toward the achievement of organizational objectives.
3. The average human being prefers to be directed, wishes to avoid responsibility, has relatively little ambition, wants security above all.[41]

Following are the assumptions upon which Theory Y is based:

1. The expenditure of physical and mental effort in work is as natural as play or rest.
2. External control and the threat of punishment are not the only means of bringing about effort toward organizational objectives. Man will exercise self-direction and self-control in the service of objectives to which he is committed.
3. Commitment to objectives is a function of the rewards associated with their achievement.
4. The average human being learns, under proper conditions, not only to accept but to seek responsibility.
5. The capacity to exercise a relatively high degree of imagination, ingenuity, and creativity in the solution of organized problems is widely, not narrowly, distributed in the population.

[40] Douglas McGregor, *The Human Side of Enterprise* (New York: McGraw-Hill Book Company, 1960).
[41] *Ibid.*, pp. 33–34.

6. Under conditions of modern industrial life, the intellectual potentialities of the average human being are only partially utilized.[42]

It is noted that there is a marked similarity between the assumptions upon which Theory X is based and the assumptions upon which the monocratic, bureaucratic concept of organization and administration is based. The assumption behind Theory Y and the assumptions behind the pluralistic, collegial concept are also very similar in nature.

EVALUATION OF ALTERNATIVE ORGANIZATION MODELS

In Chapter 3, it was pointed out that the successful social system had to attain its goals and also meet the personal needs of the members of the social system (organization). Which type of organization model best meets the needs of the members of the educational organization—the monocratic, bureaucratic model or the pluralistic, collegial model?

Maslow's Model

Maslow developed a hierarchy of needs model which is useful for determining which organization model is more useful for educational organizations.[43] His hierarchy of needs is (1) self-actualization, (2) esteem, (3) belongingness and love, (4) safety and security, and (5) physiology. Porter later modified Maslow's model by inserting "autonomy needs" between self-actualization and esteem.[44] It is impossible to make an exhaustive list of the examples of needs under each hierarchical level. However, a few examples of needs are listed under each level of Maslow's model as modified by Porter.

- *Level 6—Self-actualization:* Development of maximum potential, creativity, self-expression.
- *Level 5—Autonomy:* Independence, find solutions to own problems, self-determination of the way things are done.
- *Level 4—Esteem:* Self-respect and respect of others, achievement, recognition, status, appreciation.
- *Level 3—Belongingness and love:* Accepted group membership, have friends with whom love and friendship are reciprocated.
- *Level 2—Safety and security:* Protection against danger and threat; security from chaos, fear and anxiety.
- *Level 1—Physiological needs:* Satisfaction of need for food, drink, sleep, and the like.

[42] *Ibid.,* pp. 47–48.

[43] A. H. Maslow, *Motivation and Personality* (New York: Harper & Row, Publishers, Inc., 1954), Chap. 80 of first edition. Also see second edition published in 1970.

[44] Lyman W. Porter, "A Study of Perceived Need Satisfactions in Bottom and Middle Management Jobs," *Journal of Applied Psychology,* 45 (1961), 1–10.

Maslow theorized that higher-level needs emerge as the lower-level needs are satisfied. That is, if lower-level needs are satisfied, the individual is motivated to seek the gratification of higher-level needs. However, if lower-level needs reemerge after having been satisfied, then lower-level needs will again dominate behavior. Maslow admits that some individuals have motivating needs in different order from the hierarchies listed but that the motivation needs of most people are in the order listed.

It is interesting to note that economists have observed that, in a primitive civilization, practically all human effort is allocated to the production of goods that satisfy primary wants such as food and shelter.[45] But, when the civilization has advanced to the point at which its economy has some productive capacity remaining after satisfying primary wants, it begins to produce goods that satisfy cultural or secondary wants.

Organizations differ in the orientation of their members. Numerous authorities have pointed out that some organizations have a bureaucratic orientation and that others have a professional orientation.[46] For example, most individuals in a mass-production industry tend to have a bureaucratic orientation, and most individuals in the public schools and the institutions of higher learning have a professional or semiprofessional orientation. Most professionals have an extremely high motivational need for self-actualization, autonomy, and esteem. The pluralistic, collegial model of organization meets those needs much better than the monocratic, bureaucratic model does. The monocratic, bureaucratic model probably meets the lower-order motivational needs as well as the pluralistic, collegial model.

Schneider and Alderfer defined Maslow's and Porter's concepts in operational terms.[47] They developed a measure of those concepts based on the same hierarchical levels listed with the exception of "physiological needs" because those needs are not provided for operationally in the organization.

Herzberg's Two-Factor Theory

Herzberg developed a two-factor theory of job satisfaction called the motivator-hygiene theory.[48] Following are the items listed under each classification.

- *Motivators.* Achievement, recognition, work itself, responsibility, advancement.
- *Hygienes.* Salary, possibility of growth, interpersonal relations—subordinates, interpersonal relations—superiors, interpersonal relations—peers, company

---

[45] See Roe L. Johns and Edgar L. Morphet, *The Economics and Financing of Education* (Englewood Cliffs, N.J.: Prentice-Hall, Inc., 1975), p. 91.

[46] See, for example, Blau and Scott, *Formal Organizations,* pp. 206–214; Arthur L. Stinchombe, "Bureaucratic and Craft Administration of Production," *American Science Quarterly,* 4 (1959), 168–187; and Stanley H. Udy, "Bureaucracy and Rationality in Weber's Organization Theory," *American Sociological Review,* 24 (1959), 791–795.

[47] Benjamin Schneider and Clayton P. Alderfer, "Three Studies of Need Satisfaction in Organizations," *Administration Science Quarterly,* 18 (1973), 489–505.

[48] Frederick Herzberg, Bernard Mausner, and Barbara Snyderman, *The Motivation to Work* (New York: John Wiley & Sons, Inc., 1959).

policy (school policy) and administration, working conditions, personal life, and job security.

The research of Herzberg and others has shown that the gratification of the motivators increased job satisfaction beyond a neutral feeling. It was also found that, when hygiene factors were not gratified, negative attitudes were created which caused job dissatisfaction. It was assumed by Herzberg that job satisfaction promoted the motive to work and therefore increased production.

There is some similarity between Maslow's need hierarchy model and Herzberg's two-factor model. The motivators in the two-factor model are similar to some extent to the higher-level need motivators of Maslow's model and the hygienes are associated to some extent with the lower-level need motivators of Maslow's model. Therefore, the motivators in the two-factor theory are more likely to be gratified in educational organizations by the pluralistic, collegial organization than by the monocratic, bureaucratic organization.

Monocratic Bureaucracy and Human Personality

Argyris has presented an extremely interesting analysis of the conflict between the healthy human personality and a monocratic bureaucracy established in accord with the principles of formal organization already discussed in this chapter.[49] He did not accept the arguments of some advocates of formal organization that the choice is between the monocratic, bureaucratic organization or no organization at all. Nor did he accept the arguments of some human relations researchers that formal structures are "bad" and that the needs of the individual actors in the organization should be given priority over organizational goals. He assumed that, to date, no one has defined a more useful set of formal organizational principles than those discussed in this chapter. He then proceeded to demonstrate how each of the formal principles of organization, such as division of labor, unity of chain of command, unity of purpose, and span of control, is in conflict with the psychological needs of a mature, healthy human personality. He cited research showing that the self-actualizing personality through the process of growth passes from a state of being passive as an infant to a state of increasing activity as an adult, tends to develop from a state of dependency upon others as a child to relative independence as an adult, tends to develop from being able to use only a few of his or her capacities as an infant to the ability to use many capacities as an adult, tends to grow from a subordinate position as an infant toward an equal position as an adult, and tends to grow and mature in many other ways.[50] After comparing the needs of the human personality with the requirements for strict application of the principles of formal organization, Argyris observed

If the principles of formal organization are used as ideally defined, then the employees will tend to work in an environment where (1) they are

[49] Chris Argyris, "The Individual and Organization: Some Problems of Mutual Adjustment," Chap. 14 in *Educational Administration: Selected Readings,* ed. Walter G. Hack et al. (Boston: Allyn & Bacon, Inc., 1965).
[50] *Ibid.,* pp. 161–162.

provided minimal control over their work-a-day world, (2) they are expected to be passive, dependent, subordinate, (3) they are expected to have a short-time perspective, (4) they are induced to perfect and value the frequent use of a few superficial abilities, and (5) they are expected to produce under conditions leading to psychological failure.[51]

Argyris concluded that these conditions lead to conflict. He made no proposals for major changes in the bureaucratic organization. But he stated that the basic problem is the reduction in the degree of dependency, subordination, and submission required of the employee and suggested that "job enlargement and employee centered (or democratic or participative) leadership are elements which, if used correctly, can go a long way toward ameliorating the situation."[52]

SOME IMPORTANT PROBLEMS AND ISSUES

A summary of some of the most commonly accepted concepts and principles of organization and administration was presented in the first part of this chapter. It is apparent that many of these concepts and principles are not sure guides to administrative action because of possible wide differences in interpretation and application. Additional problems associated with the interpretation of these concepts and principles are presented in the following paragraphs.

How Can Assumptions Be Tested?

It has already been pointed out that traditional monocratic concepts are based on somewhat different assumptions than are emerging pluralistic concepts of administration. How can these assumptions be tested? Some are philosophical and cannot be tested by objective research. Philosophical assumptions must be tested against the value system of the society in which the organization finds itself. This test of philosophical assumptions would yield somewhat different results in the United States than in the Soviet Union. For instance, the assumptions underlying traditional monocratic administration are fairly consistent with the assumptions of Plato and Nietzsche. Emerging concepts of administration, however, are fairly consistent with the philosophy of John Dewey and the philosophy expressed in the great political documents of this country, such as the Declaration of Independence and the Constitution with its amendments.

Assumptions dealing with such factors as production, group morale, and human relations can be tested by objective research. As a matter of fact, a considerable body of research dealing with these assumptions is already available.[53] The weight of available evidence indicates that the assumptions underlying pluralistic, collegial

---

[51] *Ibid.,* pp. 176.

[52] *Ibid.,* p. 182.

[53] See, for example, Berelson and Steiner, *Human Behavior,* and Darwin Cartwright and Alvin Zander, *Group Dynamics: Research and Theory* (New York: Harper & Row, Publishers, Inc., 1960).

concepts of administration relating to production, group morale, and human relations are more valid than are the assumptions of monocratic concepts. Some of that research is reviewed in the following chapter. However, this research has been done largely in the United States, a country with a democratic orientation. Whether the same research would yield the same results in a country such as Russia with an authoritarian orientation is unknown. Much additional research needs to be done on identifying the assumptions underlying different concepts and theories of administration. Furthermore, those assumptions should be subjected to much more rigorous testing and examination than has been the case up to the present time. This will involve the development of more precise theoretical models than have yet been developed, from which appropriate hypotheses may be formulated and tested.

The testing of assumptions is not as simple a matter as it might seem. For instance, before assumptions with respect to production can be tested, production itself must be defined. Production may be defined solely as the output of the organization, or the definition may include what happens to members of the organization along with the output. If one accepts the first definition, process and product are separable, because members of the organization are expendable. If one accepts the second definition, process and product are inseparable, because members of the organization are not expendable. To state the problem in another way, if one accepts the second definition, production will be measured not only in terms of the quantity and quality of production over a definite period of time, but it will also include the future production potential of the organization. Similar difficulties will no doubt be encountered as other assumptions are tested. Can values be ignored when testing assumptions?

How Can Individuals and Minorities Be Protected from Group Domination?

The group can be quite as authoritarian as the executive in suppressing individuals and minorities. The group itself, if it so chooses, can exercise powerful sanctions against its members to force compliance with group norms, values, and goals. The rights of individuals and minorities are likely to be jeopardized if the administrative group shifts suddenly from the benevolent, paternalistic, directive authoritarian style to a permissive, democratic style. A sudden change from monocratic decision making to pluralistic decision making is likely to create a power vacuum. Group members with authoritarian tendencies are likely to rush into this power vacuum and take over. Thus, a group inexperienced in democratic group operation will hardly become democratic overnight, simply because the administration is changed. There is no assurance that the group will act democratically, unless group members are dedicated to democratic values. Even such dedication does not always protect individuals and minorities from capricious group action. The government of the United States is based on a constitution with amendments that incorporate a bill of rights protecting individuals and minorities from capricious group action. Should educational organizations also develop constitutions incorporating a bill of rights and an internal judicial system for protecting the rights of individuals and minorities?

How Much Collegiality in Decision Making Is Practicable?

When large numbers of people are involved, it is impracticable to submit all matters to the total group for decision. The government of the United States is a republic rather than a pure democracy. Nevertheless, certain matters are submitted to a vote of the total electorate.

In large school systems and even in large schools, it is impractical to submit all matters to the total faculty. The problem that arises as to what matters should be decided by the total faculty, what matters should be decided by committees representing the faculty, and what matters should be decided by the executive head.

There are also problems relating to lay participation in decision making. Boards of education are selected to represent the people. But the existence of thousands of citizens committees and parent-teacher associations throughout the nation is evidence that present legal means of lay participation in decision making with respect to the schools do not meet the demand for wider participation. This problem is so important that it is treated more extensively in other chapters of this book.

What criteria could be used to determine the matters that should be decided by the faculty or its representatives and the matters that should be decided by the hierarchy?

Are the Monocratic, Bureaucratic and Pluralistic, Collegial Concepts of Administration Equally Suitable for All Types of Organizations?

Earlier in this chapter, reference was made to Blau and Scott's typology of organization based upon who benefits.[54] These authors classified organizations as mutual benefit, business concerns, service organizations, and commonweal organizations.

A public school system is a service organization operated for the benefit of its clients, as contrasted to a business concern operated for the benefit of its owners and a commonweal organization operated for the benefit of the general public. Will organizations with such widely different functions as a labor union serving its members, a factory making automobiles to provide profits for the stockholders, a school system serving children, or an army protecting the general public be equally effective in utilizing either the monocratic, bureaucratic concept of organization or the pluralistic, collegial concept?

Teachers are becoming "cosmopolitans" rather than "locals" in their orientation.[55] Therefore, teachers may be oriented to the goals of the profession quite as much as to the goals of an organization. Most college professors are also cosmopolitans. There is considerable evidence that teachers and professors are more productive in pluralistic, collegial organizations than in monocratic organizations. Would the same thing be true of army personnel? Would the type of organization

---

[54] Blau and Scott, *Formal Organizations,* p. 43.

[55] Alvin W. Gouldner, "Cosmopolitans and Locals: Toward an Analysis of Latent Social Roles," *Administrative Science Quarterly,* 11 (December 1957), 281–306; 11 (March 1958), 444–480.

that is most effective for producing automobiles be equally effective for educating students?

SELECTED REFERENCES

Anderson, James G., *Bureaucracy in Education.* Baltimore: The Johns Hopkins University Press, 1968.

Argyris, Chris, *Interpersonal Competence and Organizational Effectiveness.* Homewood, Ill.: Richard D. Irwin, Inc., 1962.

Berelson, Bernard, and Gary A. Steiner, *Human Behavior: An Inventory of Scientific Findings.* New York: Harcourt, Brace Jovanovich, 1964.

Blau, Peter M., and W. Richard Scott, *Formal Organizations: A Comparative Approach.* San Francisco: Chandler Publishing Company, 1962.

Blau, Peter M., and Richard A. Schoenberr, *The Structure of Organization.* New York: Basic Books, Inc., Publishers, 1971.

Carzo, Rocco, and John W. Yanouzas, *Formal Organization, A Systems Approach.* Homewood, Ill.: Richard D. Irwin, Inc., 1967.

Etzioni, Amitai, *A Comparative Analysis of Complex Organizations.* New York: Free Press of Glencoe, Inc., 1961.

——, *Modern Organizations.* Englewood Cliffs, N.J.: Prentice-Hall, Inc., 1964.

Levinson, Harry, Janice Molinari, and Andrew G. Spohn, *Organizational Diagnosis.* Cambridge, Mass.: Harvard University Press, 1972.

Lippitt, Gordon L., *Organizational Renewal.* New York: Appleton-Century-Crofts, 1969.

March, James G., *Handbook of Organization.* Chicago: Rand McNally & Company, 1966.

——, and Herbert A. Simon, *Organizations.* New York: John Wiley & Sons, Inc., 1958.

Maslow, Abraham H., *Motivation and Personality,* 2nd ed. New York: Harper & Row, Publishers, Inc., 1970.

Mouzelis, Nicos P., *Organization and Bureaucracy: An Analysis of Modern Theory.* Chicago: Aldine Publishing Co., 1968.

Presthus, Robert, *The Organizational Society.* New York: Alfred A. Knopf, Inc., 1962.

Thompson, Victor A., *Modern Organization.* New York: Alfred A. Knopf, Inc., 1961.

Townsend, Robert, *Up the Organization.* New York: Alfred A. Knopf, Inc., 1970.

5

ROLE of EDUCATIONAL LEADERSHIP

Concepts of leadership and administration are changing rapidly. Since 1925, hundreds of research studies on group characteristics, leader behavior, human relations, and formal and informal organization have been creating a new and exciting body of knowledge. The implications of these studies are so significant that the demand for new theoretical concepts of administration and organization is widespread. Such interest is not limited to educational administrators. In fact, much of the significant research in these areas has been conducted by business and industry, the armed services, the National Training Laboratories, and university research centers such as the Personnel Research Board at Ohio State University, the Research Center for Group Dynamics at the University of Michigan, the Laboratory of Social Relations at Harvard University, and the Yale Labor and Management Center.

This movement has had a significant impact on educational administration. An organization called the National Conference of Professors of Educational Administration was formed in 1947 primarily to improve preparation programs for school administrators. This organization meets annually and serves as a vehicle for disseminating research findings and innovative practices which have significance not only for those engaged in training school administrators but also for practicing administrators.

An organization called the University Council for Educational Administration was formed in 1956. The council encourages basic research and the dissemination of important research findings through seminars and publications including the *Educational Administration Quarterly*. It has also fostered the use in educational administration of theoretical concepts developed in the social and behavioral sciences. This policy has contributed significantly to the beginnings of a science of educational administration, because most of the significant research on leadership, organizations, and social systems has been done by social and behavioral scientists.

The American Association of School Administrators, the National Association of Secondary Principals, and the National Association of Elementary Principals have been active in promoting improved practices in educational administration and organization and the educational program generally since early in this century. These organizations have not produced much significant research, but they have functioned to disseminate research findings and innovative practices.

SOME CONCEPTS OF LEADERSHIP

In Chapter 3, major attention was given to systems theory and the value of theory and research in dealing with problems of organization and administration. In Chapter 4, systems theory was applied to the examination of concepts and principles of organization. In this chapter, attention will be given to the leader's role in the social system. This is not a simple task for a number of reasons. In the first place, there is no general agreement among researchers and writers on the meaning of the word "leader." For example, some writers, especially historians, do not distinguish clearly between a leader and the holder of a position with status in the organizational hierarchy. These persons, as well as laypersons generally, assume that the holder of an important position in the heirarchy is, by virtue of position, a leader. Most behavioral scientists do not hold that view.[1] Lipham has attempted to solve this problem by suggesting in effect that the term *leader* be restricted to the role of change agent and that the term *administrator* be used to denote the role of maintaining the organization. Some valid reasons exist for accepting this definition, but it is not the concept of leadership utilized in the research designs of most behavioral scientists. It is the position of the authors of this book that leadership can be provided by an administrator in acts of maintaining an organization as well as in acts as a change agent. Furthermore, leadership can operate to prevent change as well as to facilitate it. Therefore, Lipham's typology is not used in this book.

Cartwright and Zander in 1953 wrote

> It is not possible at the present stage of research on groups to develop a fully satisfactory designation of those group functions which are peculiarly functions of leadership. A more promising endeavor, at least for the present,

[1] James M. Lipham, "Leadership and Administration," Chap. 6 in *Behavioral Science and Educational Administration*, ed. Daniel E. Griffiths, The Sixty-third Yearbook of the National Society for the Study of Education, Part II (Chicago: University of Chicago Press, 1964).

is to identify the various group functions, without deciding finally whether or not to label each specifically as a function of leadership, and then to discover by empirical investigation such things as what determines this distribution within the group and what consequences stem from various distributions among members.[2]

In 1971 Phi Delta Kappa conducted a national symposium on leadership which was attended by many of the scholars engaged in leadership research. These scholars differed somewhat in their definition of leadership. For example, Lipham defined leadership "as that behavior of an individual which initiates a new structure in interaction within a social system."[3] Getzels criticized this definition as follows: "The missing ingredient is recognition that leadership depends on *followership,* and that the followership determining the leadership is a function of cooperation or mutuality *with* the leader rather than forcible domination and coercion by the leader."[4] He pointed out that the wardens of a prison initiated new structures to which prisoners must comply and that would be considered leadership under Lipham's definition.

Immegart also objected to Lipham's definition of leadership because it

misses the kind of leadership which often exists to maintain the status quo structure in the face of an external or internal force to change. With a definition that demands that we find change in order to assert that leadership has taken place, we have in fact missed a great deal of leadership behavior that goes on in the organization of the social system.[5]

The scholars at the symposium did not develop a definition of leadership agreed to by all participants, but there seemed to be general agreement on the following characteristics of leadership:

1. Leadership is not domination or coercion but the promotion of followership.
2. Leadership promotes change but it may also resist change to maintain the school social system from forces both within and external to the system which are pressing for undesirable change.

Burns, in commenting on different definitions of leadership, stated the following:

Some define leadership as leaders making followers do what *followers* would not otherwise do, or as leaders making followers do what the *leaders* want them to do. I define leadership as leaders inducing followers to act for certain goals that represent the values and the motivation—the wants and needs, the

[2] Darwin Cartwright and Alvin Zander, eds., *Group Dynamics—Research and Theory* (New York: Harper & Row, Publishers, Inc., 1960), p. 494.

[3] Luvern L. Cunningham and William G. Gephart, eds., *Leadership, The Science and Art Today* (Itasca, Ill.: F. E. Peacock Publishers, Inc., 1973), p. 6.

[4] *Ibid.,* p. 16.

[5] *Ibid.,* pp. 28–29.

aspirations and expectations *of both leaders and followers.* . . . Leadership, unlike naked power-wielding, is thus inseparable from followers needs and goals.[6]

Burns's definition of leadership meets most of the objections raised to Lipham's definition in the symposium.

Since 1953, considerable research has been based on role differentiation in a social system. Many behavioral scientists now conceptualize leadership in that context.[7] In this chapter *we conceptualize leadership as the influencing of the actions, behaviors, beliefs, and goals of one actor in a social system by another actor with the willing cooperation of the actor being influenced.* The willing co-operation of the other actors in the social system with the leader cannot be at-tained, as Burns has pointed out, unless the goals represent the values, motivations, wants, needs, aspirations, and expectations of both leaders and followers.

The top leader in any system, subsystem, or suprasystem is the actor who most often influences in critical matters the actions, behaviors, beliefs, and goals of the greatest number of other actors in that system with the willing cooperation of the actors being influenced. Under this concept, there are many leaders with different degrees and kinds of influence in a social system, and a leader may or may not hold a position in the hierarchy of the formal organization.

We are confining ourselves in this chapter to leadership in formal organizations and in informal groups. There are other types of leaders which are worthy of study, but they are beyond the scope of this book. Some examples are (1) opinion leaders such as interpreters of news events, (2) intellectual leaders such as Albert Einstein, and (3) societal leaders such as Marx and Engels.

In examining the leadership phenomena of educational organization and ad-ministration, we are concerned primarily with concepts and theories of leadership that are applicable to those who hold decision-making positions in the various hierarchies of educational organizations and in informal organizations that interact with formal educational organizations. These persons include state and local super-intendents of schools, school principals, college and university presidents, leaders in teacher organizations and federations, leaders in parent–teacher organizations, and leaders of informal organizations. Educational organizations commonly include suprasystems, subsystems, and numerous informal organizations or groups. Edu-cational administrators deal not only with a complex of systems within the educa-tional organization but also with a complex of social systems in the environment of the school system, all of which are exchanging inputs and outputs of informa-tion, energy, and matter with each other. Unfortunately, most research on leader-ship has been confined to leadership in small face-to-face groups. Most of the literature on group dynamics is based on research with small groups. Lipham com-mented on this situation: "Leadership roles in structure organizations are, indeed, complex. Thus, the methodology and findings of leadership studies concerned with small, unstructured, randomly selected groups are likely to be of only lim-

---

[6] James MacGregor Burns, *Leadership* (New York: Harper & Row, Publishers, Inc., 1978), p. 19.
[7] See Paul F. Secord and Carl W. Backman, *Social Psychology* (New York: McGraw-Hill Book Company, 1964).

ited value when transplanted indiscriminately to large, complex, hierarchical organizations."[8]

Berelson and Steiner published a comprehensive review of the research relating to human behavior in 1964.[9] They compiled from the research available in the behavioral and social sciences 1,045 propositions or hypotheses of moderate generality dealing with groups, organizations, social processes, and other phenomena of human behavior. Most of the propositions they advanced concerning leadership are based on research in small face-to-face groups.[10] Their propositions relating to leadership in organizations did not seem to be based on much research.[11]

Miller has pointed out that a hypothesis or proposition which does not apply to two or more levels of systems does not have much generality.[12] He listed 165 cross-level hypotheses (applicable across different levels of suprasystems and subsystems within a social system) which could reasonably be supported by available research. He did not list a single cross-level hypothesis on leadership.

Hoy and Miskel, after making an extensive survey of leadership research, concluded in 1977 that, although there is considerable concern about leadership among scholars and practitioners in diverse fields, comprehensive, empirically tested theories are still to be developed.[13]

How many of the conclusions concerning leadership that have been reached from research in small face-to-face groups are applicable to administrators of complex, bureaucratic, hierarchical organizations such as medium and large school systems, colleges, and universities? We will not know until more cross-level research is carried out, and this will require sophisticated designs conforming to rigorous standards.[14] With these limitations in mind, we present certain generalizations and phenomena relating to leadership in the remainder of this chapter.

TRENDS IN STUDIES OF LEADERSHIP

Leadership is very highly valued in human society, so it is not surprising that many books have been written and many studies conducted concerning leaders and leadership. Classical literature is filled with references to leaders and leadership. The need to lead and the need to be led is a pervasive characteristic of the human animal. Some approaches to the study of leadership are presented next.

The Great Man Approach

Historians and biographers have been largely responsible for this theory. Burlingame has stated that the "great man" theory rests on two foundations:

[8] Lipham, "Leadership and Administration," p. 125.

[9] Bernard Berelson and Gary A. Steiner, *Human Behavior: An Inventory of Scientific Findings* (New York: Harcourt, Brace Jovanovich, 1964).

[10] *Ibid.*, pp. 341–346.

[11] *Ibid.*, pp. 372–377.

[12] James G. Miller, "Living Systems: Cross-Level Hypotheses," *Behavioral Science,* 10, no. 4 (1965).

[13] Adapted from Wayne K. Hoy and Cecil G. Miskel, *Educational Administration, Theory, Research, and Practice* (New York: Random House, Inc., 1978), p. 208.

[14] *Ibid.*, pp. 382–384.

First that men have free will, hence history is a struggle to decide the course of the future. Second, that men may learn from the examples of the great men. . . . The explicit morality of the great man theory has suggested that *if* mankind could learn how they ought, or ought not, to act from great men, then mankind would act accordingly.[15]

The great man approach to the study of leadership is similar in some respects to "the times make the man approach." Washington, Napoleon, and Hitler all changed the course of history. Did they become great because of their individual characteristics or because they happened to live at certain times in history? There has been much speculation but little research on this question.

Burlingame, after making an exhaustive study of the relevance of the great man theory to the study of leadership, concluded that

the proponents of the great man theory present neither explanation nor accurate descriptions of what constitutes a great man. They present no rigorous criteria for the selection of greatness. . . . If theory must seek both prediction and explanation, then there appears to be no great man theory.[16]

② Studies of Traits

Prior to 1945, most of the studies of leadership were devoted primarily to the identification of the traits or qualities of leaders. These studies were based in part on the assumption that human beings could be divided into two groups— the leaders and the followers. Therefore, leaders must possess certain traits or qualities not possessed by followers. Some persons in each generation since the dawn of recorded history have believed that "leaders are born, not made."

In 1948, Stogdill examined 124 studies on the relationship of personality factors to leadership. A summary of his findings follows:

1. The following conclusions are supported by uniformly positive evidence from fifteen or more of the studies surveyed:
   A. The average person who occupies a position of leadership exceeds the average members of his group in the following respects: (1) intelligence, (2) scholarship, (3) dependability in exercising responsibilities, (4) activity and social participation, and (5) socioeconomic status.
   B. The qualities, characteristics, and skills required in a leader are determined to a large extent by the demands of the situation in which he is to function as a leader.
2. The following conclusions are supported by uniformly positive evidence from ten or more of the studies surveyed:
   A. The average person who occupies a position of leadership exceeds the average member of his group to some degree in the following respects: (1) sociability, (2) initiative, (3) persistence, (4) knowing how to get things done, (5) self-confidence, (6) alertness to and insight into situations, (7) cooperativeness, (8) popularity, (9) adaptability, and (10) verbal facility.[17]

[15] Cunningham and Gephart, eds., *Leadership,* pp. 46–47.

[16] *Ibid.,* pp. 48–49.

[17] Ralph M. Stogdill, "Personal Factors Associated with Leadership, A Survey of the Literature," *Journal of Psychology,* 25 (1948), 63.

Stogdill, however, after further study of the evidence, concluded that

> A person does not become a leader by virtue of the possession of some combination of traits, but the pattern of personal characteristics of the leader must bear some relevant relationship to the characteristics, activities, and goals of the followers. Thus, leadership must be conceived in terms of the interactions of variables which are in constant flux and change.[18]

Therefore, leadership is not a matter of passive status, nor does it devolve upon a person simply because he or she is the possessor of some combination of traits. Rather, the leader acquires leader status through the interactions of the group in which he or she participates and demonstrates capacity for assisting the group to complete its tasks.[19]

In 1971, Stogdill, Nickels, and Zimmer reviewed the findings of 136 trait studies conducted between 1948 and 1969.[20] In this survey they made three classifications of traits as follows: (1) self-oriented—physical characteristics, intellectual characteristics, personality; (2) task oriented—achievement drive, initiative, persistence, and the like; (3) socially oriented—cooperativeness, tact, and sociability. Stogdill, in summarizing the findings from the 1948 and 1969 surveys of trait studies, concluded the following:

> The self oriented traits yield a picture of the leader as self assured and somewhat more intelligent than the average member of his group. He is physically active, fluent of speech, independent, original, adaptable, tolerant of stress, uses good judgment, and in the case of outstanding leaders, exhibits firm personal integrity. He may or may not differ from his followers in age, physique, extroversion and emotional stability.
>
> The findings of the task oriented traits are uniformly positive. These items provide a picture of the leader as an individual who is responsible in the pursuit of goals, exhibits a strong drive for responsibility and achievement, and is persistent in the face of obstacles.
>
> Results from task oriented traits are also positive without exception. They picture the leader as participative, popular, sociable, tactful, cooperative and able to enlist cooperation.[21]

Stogdill has objected to conclusions drawn by his studies and the studies of others that (1) the traits of leaders are irrelevant to leadership and (2) leadership is determined entirely by the situation. He stated that the following conclusions are supported by the surveys that have been made of trait studies:

1. Several clusters of traits have been identified that clearly differentiate leaders from followers, and
2. A pattern of traits that is acceptable in one situation will not necessarily be acceptable in another situation.[22]

[18] *Ibid.*, p. 64.

[19] *Ibid.*, p. 66.

[20] Cunningham and Gephart, eds., *Leadership,* pp. 88–90.

[21] *Ibid.*, pp. 89–90.

[22] *Ibid.*, p. 91.

The study of personality traits alone will not explain leadership. These studies have shown clearly that the assumption, "leaders are born, not made," is largely false. The only inherited trait that has been identified as having some relationship to leadership is intelligence. Even this relationship is frequently quite low.

Stogdill investigated thirty-three separate research studies on the relationship of intelligence to leadership.[23] He found that the average of the coefficients of correlation between intelligence and leadership was only 0.28. A coefficient of correlation this low is only slightly better than a chance guess.

All the other personality traits identified as being related to leadership are acquired traits and, as such, are subject to modification by training and experience. Actually, most of the personality traits or characteristics that have been found to be associated with leadership should be classified as skills or competencies rather than as personality traits. Therefore, it should be possible within limits to attain these skills and competencies through an appropriate program of learning experiences. This emphasizes the importance of preparation programs for school administrators.

It must not be assumed that the many studies of personality traits in relation to leadership have been totally unproductive. Although the traits approach has not provided a comprehensive description of leadership, it has opened the way for further research that gives promise of great significance. Researchers in this area have had great difficulty in defining and measuring leadership and the traits being studied. Different researchers have used different definitions and different instruments. Situational factors have been ignored in most studies. It is not surprising that the conclusions of a number of studies have been contradictory. With sharper definitions, improved instruments, and better control of conditions, researchers in the future will undoubtedly contribute additional knowledge needed in this area.

③ *The Interactional or Group Approach*

Another approach is known as the interactional or group approach to the study of leadership. It is generally accepted as being the most productive to the understanding of leadership. Although the individual leader is still an important object of study, it is now generally recognized that he or she cannot be studied in isolation. The focus of most research on leadership is now on "leader behavior" in a social system rather than on "leader traits."

Attention in Chapter 3 was directed to Getzels's nomothetic-idiographic model for explaining social behavior in a social system. Applying this model to the behavior of the leader in interaction with the group (or organization) which he or she is leading, the leader must deal with two dimensions—achievement of organization or group goals and meeting the needs of the members of the organization or group. Numerous studies have been made of the dimensions of leadership, and most of those studies classify the dimensions of leadership in two categories.[24] Different terms are used for these two categories, but they are synonymous in meaning. For

[23] Stogdill, "Leadership Literature," p. 44.
[24] See Hoy and Miskel, *Educational Administration,* p. 180.

example, Cartwright and Zander use the terms goal achievement and group maintenance; Halpin, initiating structure and consideration; Kahor, production orientation and employee orientation; Brown, system orientation and person orientation.

As has been pointed out, a leader with certain traits and leadership style may be a successful leader in one situation and unsuccessful in another situation. The situation has the same two dimensions as the dimensions of leadership. These are the goals of the organization and the needs, beliefs, and aspirations of the members of the organization. If the leader has goals that are different from the accepted goals of the organization or if the leader's values and beliefs differ widely from the group's norms, the leader will not likely succeed in that situation. Therefore, the interaction of the leader with the other actors in the social system (group or organization) largely determines the effectiveness of leadership.

Fiedler postulates that leadership effectiveness depends upon the appropriate matching of the individual's leadership style of interacting and the influence which the group situation provides. Fiedler concludes

> that leadership effectiveness—that is, effective group performance—depends just as much on the group situation as it does on the leader. If the theory is right this means that a personnel program that deals only with the personality aspects of the leader or only with the situational aspects of the organization is bound to fail. One style of leadership is not in itself better than the other, nor is one type of leadership behavior appropriate for all conditions.[25]

The remainder of this chapter presents some generalizations concerning leadership that have been derived principally from studies of leadership in relation to a social system.

THE LEADER AND THE SOCIAL SYSTEM

School administrators spend much of their time working with groups. These groups may be informal groups or formal organizations. The informal group sometimes called an informal organization, has the following characteristics:

1. Each member of the group is able to interact with every other member of the group.
2. The group develops its own structure and organization.
3. The group selects its own leader or leaders.
4. The group has been voluntarily formed to achieve certain common tasks, goals, and purposes.
5. It does not have an officially prescribed hierarchical structure.

The formal organization, sometimes called the formal group, has the following characteristics as contrasted to the informal group:

[25] Fred E. Fiedler, *A Theory of Leadership Effectiveness* (New York: McGraw-Hill Book Company, 1967), p. 247.

1. Each member of the organization usually is not able to interact with every other member.
2. The formal organization is usually structured by external authority or by a suprasystem.
3. The holders of positions of status in the organization are usually determined by external authority or by the suprasystem.
4. The tasks, goals, and purposes of the group may be determined in part by authority external to the group.
5. It usually has an officially hierarchical structure.

There are many variations in types of human groups other than those identified. For example, a state education association is a voluntary group with some of the characteristics of an informal group and some of a formal organization. Attention was directed in Chapter 4 to four types of formal organizations based on who benefits. It would require an extensive treatment to present a comprehensive analysis of all types of human groups. Much of the research on leadership has been done in small informal groups and only a limited amount in large formal organizations. However, all educational administrators deal with informal groups as well as with a formal organization. Furthermore, if the assumptions back of general systems theory are valid, it is possible that more of the findings concerning leadership in small groups are applicable to leadership in formal organizations than has been assumed by some behavioral scientists. Therefore, in the next section we will examine some group phenomena that are important to an understanding of leadership.

THE GROUP

School administrators spend much of their time working with groups. The most effective administrators are leaders as well as holders of "headships." Effective administrative leadership involves an understanding of the behavior of people in groups. Many studies of group behavior and structure have been made. Some principal findings of one of the most significant of these studies, that of Homans, are presented in the following paragraphs.[26]

Homans, after studying numerous small groups sometimes called "face-to-face groups," concluded that the underlying human relationships differ from group to group in degree rather than in kind. This concept is of great significance because, if it is valid, it is possible to make a systematic analysis of group behavior.

Each group is conceived of as having a boundary, outside of which lies the group environment. Each person may belong to many different groups, and large groups may be subdivided into smaller groups and cliques. Each group has an external environment that differs for every group, and the behavior of each group must be such that it can survive in its environment. Each group interacts with its environment. The group changes the environment at times and at other times the environment changes the group.

[26] George C. Homans, *The Human Group* (New York: Harcourt, Brace Jovanovich, 1950).

The members of the group as they work together develop norms which, if violated by a leader, will likely cause his or her rejection. A norm is an idea in the minds of the members of a group, an idea that can be put in the form of a statement specifying what the members or other participants should do, ought to do, or are expected to do under given circumstances.

Homans presented some hypotheses concerning these interactions that are of great significance to the understanding of leadership. Some of these hypotheses are as follows:

1. If the frequency of interaction between two or more persons increases, the degree of their liking for one another will increase, and vice versa.
2. If the interactions between the members of the group are frequent in the external system, sentiments of liking will grow up between them, and these sentiments will lead in turn to further interactions over and above the interactions of the external system.
3. A decrease in the frequency of interaction between the members of a group and outsiders, accompanied by an increase in the strength of their negative sentiments toward outsiders, will increase the frequency of interaction and the strength of positive sentiments among the members of a group, and vice versa.[27]

Let us apply these hypotheses to a school. We might generalize as follows:

1. The more all people—faculty, students, and parents—interact with each other, the more opportunity they have to like each other.
2. Sentiments of liking grow up between teachers and administrators who work on the job together, and these sentiments will lead to other activity beyond the requirements of the job.
3. If the communications between a faculty group and a community group are reduced and this lessening of communications is accompanied by an increase in the negative sentiments of each group toward the other, then the members of each group are drawn closer together, but intergroup hostility is increased.

Let us apply this same reasoning to the relationships between the superintendent or principal and the teacher group. If the administrator is not accepted by the teachers as a member of the teacher group, then he or she is an outsider and a part of the external environment of the group. As already pointed out, a group has sentiments and norms in its internal system. A group endeavors to survive in its environment. To do so, it protects its norms and sentiments. Any attack on these norms and sentiments, especially from an outsider, solidifies the group and develops negative group sentiments toward the source of the attack. If a member of a group violates or offends the norms and sentiments of the group, the group itself disciplines the group member. The group may discipline the administrator by making him or her an "outsider."

But group norms and sentiments are not likely to be positively changed by interaction unless the sentiment climate is positive. This seems to be a defect in Homans's hypotheses. He assumes that the liking of group members for each other

---

[27]*Ibid.*, p. 112–113.

will always increase as interactions increase. It is conceivable that the negative sentiments of group members for each other might increase with an increase in interactions if the climate of the group is such as to stimulate negative sentiments.

Within a formal organization such as a large school system, groups tend to increase in number. For instance, the board, the superintendent and his or her central staff, the principals, and the teachers might each be a tight, separate group. This is especially true if interactions between these groups are minimized. In addition, there will be innumerable informal groups. Intergroup hostility is not constructive conflict. It inhibits cooperation and collegial cooperation facilitates both the attainment of organizational goals and the meeting of the needs and aspirations of the members of the organization.

Behavioral scientists have formulated a number of hypotheses based on evidence produced by research on group behavior. Following are some hypotheses proposed by Berelson and Steiner, which they derived from their inventory of scientific findings in the behavioral sciences:

1. A small group after discussion finds a more satisfactory solution to a problem than individuals working alone when the problem is technical rather than attitudinal, when a range of possible solutions is available, when the task requires each member to make a judgment, when rewards and punishments are given to the group as a whole, when the information and skills needed are additive, when the task can be subdivided, and when the task includes "traps" that might be missed by individuals.[28]
2. Active participation in the communicating itself is more effective for persuasion and retaining information than is the passive reception of information.[29]
3. The more people associate with one another under conditions of equality, the more they come to share values and norms and the more they come to like one another.[30]
4. The more interaction or overlap there is between related groups, the more similar they become in their norms and values; the less communication or interaction between them, the more tendency there is for conflict to arise between them. And vice versa; the more conflict, the less interaction.[31]

Hemphill has studied attempted leadership. He defined these terms as follows:

1. Attempted leadership acts are acts accompanied by an intention of initiating structure-in-interaction for solving a mutual problem.
2. Successful leadership acts are acts that have initiated structure-in-interaction during the process of mutual problem solution. An attempted leadership act may or may not become a successful leadership act depending upon subsequent observation of its effect upon the structure of interaction.
3. Effective leadership acts are acts that have initiated structure-in-interaction and that have contributed to the solution of a mutual problem. An effec-

[28] Adapted from Berelson and Steiner, *Human Behavior,* p. 355.
[29] *Ibid.,* p. 548, adapted.
[30] *Ibid.,* p. 327.
[31] *Ibid.,* p. 331.

tive leadership act is always also a successful leadership act, but a leadership act may be successful without being effective for solving mutual problems.[32]

SOME GENERALIZATIONS ON LEADERSHIP

A number of generalizations and hypotheses concerning leadership have developed from studies in this area. Although these propositions have not all been confirmed fully by research, they are worthy of study.

Motives and Behavior

McClelland divided people into three main classes—those who were achievement motivated, those who sought power, and those who had a need to be liked.[33] He concluded that different patterns of behavior result from different motivations.

McClelland and Burnham found that better managers had a higher need for power than for affiliation (the need to be liked) coupled with a moderate need for achievement.[34] They concluded that power is not inherently bad. If the desire for power on the part of the leader (or the manager) was for the good of the organization, it had a positive effect on the organization. However, if the desire for power was for personal reasons, it might have a negative effect on the organization. They also found that a person who had a high need for power was more effective with a democratic leadership style.

Fiedler concluded from his studies that a person's leadership style reflects the individual's basic and motivational need structure and that it is very difficult to change a person's leadership style.[35]

Generalizations Proposed by Myers

As has already been pointed out, a great number of studies have been made of leadership and the relationship of leadership to the group. Myers, after making an extensive analysis of these studies, proposed the following generalizations which are supported by two or more studies:

1. Leadership is the product of interaction, not status or position.
2. Leadership cannot be structured in advance. The uniqueness of each combination of persons, of varying interactional patterns and of vary-

---

[32] John K. Hemphill, "Administration as Problem Solving," Chap. 5 in *Administrative Theory in Education,* ed. Andrew W. Halpin (Chicago: Midwest Administration Center, University of Chicago, 1958).

[33] D. C. McClelland, *Power, The Inner Experience* (New York: Irvington Publishers, 1975).

[34] D. C. McClelland and D. H. Burnham, "Good Guys Make Bum Bosses," *Psychology Today* (December 1975), and "Power Is the Great Motivator," *Harvard Business Review* (March 1976).

[35] Fiedler, *A Theory of Leadership Effectiveness,* p. 248.

ing goals and means, and of varying forces within and without impinging upon the group will bring forth different leaders.

3. A leader in one situation will not automatically be a leader in another situation.
4. Leadership does not result from a status position, but rather [from] how a person behaves in the organization.
5. Whether a person is a leader in a group depends upon the group's perception of him.
6. The way a leader perceives his role determines his actions.
7. Most groups have more than one person occupying the leadership role.
8. Leadership fosters positive sentiments toward the group activity and persons in the group.
9. Leadership may be democratic or autocratic but never laissez-faire.
10. Leadership protects the critical group norms.
11. Leadership is authority rendered to some who are perceived by others as the proper persons to carry out the particular leadership role of the group.
12. Program development that involves only persons of a single position (such as principals, or supervisors, or teachers) is not as comprehensive or lasting as that which involves people of various positions in the organization.[36]

Although each of these generalizations is supported by some research, it must not be assumed that each generalization is completely valid. Much additional research needs to be done for the further validation of these and other generalizations.

Some Hypotheses Formulated by Berelson and Steiner

Berelson and Steiner made an extensive survey of the scientific findings in the behavioral sciences and formulated a number of propositions and hypotheses. Following are a few of their most important formulations related to leadership in small groups:

1. The closer an individual conforms to the accepted norms of the group, the better liked he will be; the better liked he is, the closer he conforms; the less he conforms, the more disliked he will be.
2. The higher the rank of the member within the group, the more central he will be in the group's interaction and the more influential he will be.
3. In general, the "style" of the leader is determined more by the expectations of the membership and the requirements of the situation than by the personal traits of the leader himself.
4. The leadership of the group tends to be vested in the member who most closely conforms to the standards of the group on the matter in question, or who has the most information and skill related to the activities of the group.
5. When groups have established norms, it is extremely difficult for a new leader, however capable, to shift the group's activities.

[36] Robert B. Myers, "A Synthesis of Research in Leadership" (unpublished paper presented to A.S.C.D., March 1957), pp. 4-9.

6. The longer the life of the leadership, the less open and free the communication within the group and probably the less efficient the group in the solution of new problems.
7. The leader will be followed more faithfully the more he makes it possible for the members to achieve their private goals, along with the group's goals.
8. Active leadership is characteristic of groups that determine their own activities, passive leadership of groups whose activities are externally imposed.
9. In a small group, authoritarian leadership is less effective than democratic leadership in holding the group together and getting its work done.[37]

Berelson and Steiner also formulated some hypotheses concerning leadership in organizations. However, these authors did not distinguish between leaders as defined early in this chapter and holders of power positions in the hierarchy of an organization. But their formulations do point up some of the difficulties of an executive in the hierarchy when attempting to provide leadership. They point out that holders of intermediate positions in the hierarchy are under pressure from their superiors for productivity and under pressure from their subordinates for human consideration and that this cross-pressure is the source of actual or potential conflict in their behavior.[38] Following are a few of the hypotheses proposed by Berelson and Steiner relating to leadership (more properly, headship) in formal organizations:

1. The leader's style of leadership tends to be influenced by the style in which he is led.
2. The more the member holds to the organization's professed values, the more likely he is to be promoted within the organization.
3. The requirements for organizational leadership change with the life of the organization: at the start the leader is characterized more by doctrinal loyalty, aggressiveness, and personal quality ("the charismatic leader"); later, when the organization is well established, by administrative skills ("the bureaucratic leader").
4. Within an organization, conflict between leader and subordinates tends to increase the number and the concreteness of the organization's regulations, and vice versa—i.e., regulations go along with conflict.[39]

Although these hypotheses relate to management rather than to leadership, they are quite provocative.

Homans's Exchange Theory of Leadership Determination

Homans has developed an interesting theory of exchange for explaining social behavior.[40] It can be used to explain when a person decides to lead and when he or

---

[37] Berelson and Steiner, *Human Behavior,* pp. 341-344. NOTE: This important work should be read by every serious student of administration.

[38] *Ibid.,* p. 372.

[39] *Ibid.,* pp. 376-377.

[40] George C. Homans, *Social Behavior: Its Elementary Forms* (New York: Harcourt, Brace Jovanovich, 1961).

she decides to follow. The exchange theory is a complex formulation. Homans attempts to explain behavior in terms of costs incurred and rewards exchanged by actors interacting in a social system. He incorporates some of the market exchange concepts from economics and reinforcement concepts from psychology. Exchange theory incorporates four basic concepts: reward, cost, outcome, and comparison level.

Let us apply these concepts to a leadership situation. Let us assume that an actor in a group is contemplating initiating a leadership act in a problem situation. The actor considers what rewards may be received if he or she provides leadership in terms of increased status, need for dominance, desire to see the problem solved, and so on. The actor then considers the cost in terms of loss of status if the group rejects him or her or his or her solution fails, increased effort and responsibility on his or her part, and so on. The actor then attempts to determine the outcome by subtracting the costs from the rewards. If the outcome is positive, it is a profit, and if negative, a loss. The actor's decision to act will also depend on the comparison level. The profit must be sufficiently above a "break-even" point and past experiences in comparable situations must have been successful often enough to take the chance of leadership. The more frequently the actor has succeeded in leadership attempts in the past, the more likely is the actor to attempt another leadership act (reinforcement).

In a similar manner, the actor in a social system who decides to follow also seeks a fair exchange. The actor weighs the costs against the rewards, considers the qualifications of the person offering to lead, and how successfully he or she has led in similar situations in the past. The actor then decides whether there is a fair profit for following rather than leading.

Conflict in Perceptions

Campbell has described the conflicting expectations faced by administrators.[41] Different groups within the community and within the school system have different perceptions of the role that should be played by the administrator. The board of education also has its perception of the administrator's role. Individuals even within the same group have different perceptions of the role of the administrator. The administrator has a perception of the role, and somehow the administrator must reconcile all these differences in role perceptions. Therefore, many situational factors condition the behavior of the educational administrator.

The job of educational administration is complicated further by the following factors.

1. The school system's task may be defined largely by authorities external to the group by means of laws and regulations.
2. The administration's perception of the school system's task may be different from the perceptions of other members of the organization. This is a potential source of conflict.
3. Different groups within the system may have goals that are in conflict with the task of the organization. This is a potential source of difficulty.

[41] Roald F. Campbell and Russell T. Gregg, eds., *Administrative Behavior in Education* (New York: Harper & Row, Publishers, Inc., 1957), Chap. 7.

4. The administrator, to be effective, must be a group leader, and this may be difficult if the goals of primary groups are in conflict with the goals of the formal organization. When such a situation occurs, informal organizations develop to achieve the goals of primary groups. The task of the administrator-leader is then to bring the formal and informal groups into congruence with respect to goals, in order to be an effective leader.

Coffey and Golden have made the following observations concerning the formal and informal structures:

Along with the formal structure are the informal functions which have much less structure, are characterized by more spontaneous flow of interpersonal relationships, and are often effective in either aiding the formal structure in reaching goals or working as a very antagonistic core and in a private way against the public goals of the institution. An institution is likely to function more effectively and with greater satisfaction to its employees if the needs which are expressed in the informal social relationships are dealt with in the formal structure.[42]

Power and Authority

There has been a tendency on the part of some to reject the terms "power" and "authority" as being inconsistent with democracy. Those who hold that belief seem to assume that, if proper leadership is provided, power and authority are not essential to the social system. Let us take a look at power and authority.

For the purposes of this chapter, it is best to conceive of power in terms of behavior. Hunter has presented such a definition. Power, according to Hunter, is "the acts of men going about the business of moving other men to act in relation to themselves or in relation to organic or inorganic things."[43]

Dubin defines authority as "institutionalized power."[44] Simon defined authority in behavioral terms. According to him, "a subordinate may be said to accept authority whenever he permits his behavior to be guided by a decision reached by another, irrespective of his own judgment as to the merits of that decision."[45] Authority is always backed by power. Therefore, it might be said that a person has authority when he is perceived by the group to have the institutionalized right to "move other men to act in relation to themselves or in relation to organic or inorganic things."[46]

Griffiths has presented a thoughtful analysis of power and authority as affecting

[42] Hubert S. Coffey and William P. Golden, Jr., *In-Service Education for Teachers, Supervisors, and Administrators,* Fifty-sixth Yearbook of the National Society for the Study of Education, Part I (Chicago: University of Chicago Press, 1957), pp. 101–102.

[43] Floyd Hunter, *Community Power Structure* (Chapel Hill: University of North Carolina Press, 1953).

[44] Robert Dubin et al. *Human Relations in Administration* (Englewood Cliffs, N.J.: Prentice-Hall, Inc., 1951), p. 188.

[45] Herbert A. Simon, *Administrative Behavior* (New York: Macmillan Publishing Co., Inc., 1951), p. 22.

[46] Hunter, *Community Power Structure.*

human relations.[47] Following are two of his conclusions concerning power which are of particular significance to the study of leadership:

1. Power is the cement which holds our society together as well as the societies of totalitarian states such as Soviet Russia and Nazi Germany.
2. A democratic society is one in which the power command is held by a large number of people and is subject to the will of all of the people.[48]

We see that power cannot be ignored in a democracy any more than in an authoritarian state. School administrators certainly are not the only wielders of power in the school systems of the United States. In back of the superintendent is the board, and in back of the board are the people. Teachers and pupils also have power in certain situations.

Wiles has pointed out that power is used differently by persons with different concepts of leadership.[49] He distinguishes between "power over" and "power with" the group. "A "power over" approach decreases the possibilities of releasing the full power of the group. It limits the potential accomplishment of the group."[50] Wiles states his concept of "power with" the group as follows:

Under the group approach to leadership, a leader is not concerned with getting and maintaining personal authority. His chief purpose is to develop group power that will enable the group to accomplish its goal. He does not conceive of his power as something apart from the power of the group. He is concerned with developing the type of relationships that will give him "power with" the group.[51]

Because authority in an organization is backed by institutionalized power, it cannot be exercised effectively unless the person exercising the authority is perceived by the members of the organization as having the right to do so. There are further limitations on authority. Griffiths makes this point:

Although there is a line of authority in each organization, there are also modifying conditions which change the effectiveness of the power being exerted. We note that the authority of an administrator is affected and modified by the board of education, the teachers, non-teaching staff, parents, students, patrons, the state school law, the customs and traditions of the community, and the authority of the profession.[52]

This concept is also extremely important to each group within the school faculty. No school group is completely autonomous in authority. All school groups,

---

[47] Daniel E. Griffiths, *Human Relations in School Administration* (New York: Appleton-Century & Appleton-Century-Crofts, 1956), Chaps. 5, 6.
[48] *Ibid.*, p. 105.
[49] Kimball Wiles, *Supervision for Better Schools,* 2nd ed. (Englewood Cliffs, N.J.: Prentice-Hall, Inc., 1955), pp. 161–167.
[50] *Ibid.*, p. 163.
[51] *Ibid.*, p. 164.
[52] Griffiths, *Human Relations,* p. 142.

both formal and informal, are subgroups of the total organization. The ultimate "group" that has the final authority to determine school goals is the people. Therefore, no group within a school system has the legal or moral right to consider itself a completely autonomous primary group. Participation in decision making by all groups and individuals concerned is now being widely advocated. As groups participate in decision making, it is vital that the limits of authority of each group be clearly defined. The administrator-leader must also make clear to groups and individuals participating in decision making the decisions reserved for executive decision making and the decisions in which they can share. To do otherwise would result in chaos. These implications are important for state school administration as well as for local school administration.

EXECUTIVE BEHAVIOR

The behavior of the executive (who may or may not be a leader) in the hierarchy is influenced by personal values or beliefs and by the values and beliefs of superordinates. The executive's behavior is also influenced by environment and interaction with other actors in the organization and perhaps other factors. We are interested here, however, primarily in the values and beliefs of the executive and the superordinates and subordinates in the hierarchy. If the executive's values and beliefs are in conflict with the values and beliefs of the mass of actors in the social system which he or she administers, conflict in the system is inevitable and the executive no longer is a leader in the social system. The executive may continue to hold a command position because of institutionalized power but the executive is not a leader as defined in this chapter. At the present time many school superintendents and boards of education are in conflict with the classroom teachers in their systems. A number of college presidents are also in conflict with either their faculties or their students or both. In Chapter 4 we discussed McGregor's[53] Theory X and Theory Y relating to differing assumptions with respect to the nature of workers in the organization. If the executive of an organization assumes that Theory X describes the nature of most of the workers in his or her organization and if the majority of these workers are more like Theory Y, destructive conflict will surely arise and the executive cannot be a leader in that organization. In the following paragraphs, a number of concepts and beliefs are presented which may affect favorably or unfavorably the leadership potential of the executive.

Scientific Management Theory

The public school system made great strides between 1900 and 1925. Public elementary and secondary education was well on its way to becoming available everywhere in the United States. Professional school administrators were employed to serve most of the larger school districts. A literature on school administration was being written. The words "efficient" and "businesslike" appeared

---

[53] Douglas McGregor, *The Human Side of Enterprise* (New York: McGraw-Hill Book Company, 1960).

frequently in that literature. The dynamic, bustling, aggressive administrator was confident that he or she could use the proven methods of business and industry to solve all the important problems of educational administration.

The "gospel of efficiency" dominated the thinking in the first third of the twentieth century.[54] Frederick Taylor, Henri Fayol, Luther Gulick, and Lyndall Urwick were all influential promoters of administrative and organizational efficiency. All these men, with the exception of Gulick, were identified primarily with engineering. The efficiency formulations developed by these men did not conceptualize human beings as living systems but rather as inanimate parts of an organization. Consequently, these men gave little emphasis to human relations and the interactions of social systems. They were concerned primarily with getting more from the workers, the managers, and the organizational structures, without giving much consideration to what happened to the human components of organizations.

Callahan[55] made a brilliant analysis of this movement in his study of the social forces that have shaped the administration of the public schools. He was particularly intrigued with the concepts of Taylor.[56] He described Taylor's system as follows:

> When Taylor introduced his system into any shop, his first step was to make a careful, detailed, and exhaustive study of the various aspects of the jobs being done. For example, in a machine shop Taylor would observe, time with a stop watch, and record the times of various motions of a group of the most skillful men in the shop. After studying his data, he would then select a worker he regarded as being potentially a first-class man, offer him a bonus for working faster, and experiment. He would combine what he regarded as the best and fastest movements for each phase of the work that he had observed, and eliminate all useless motion. The experimental first-class man would then be taught all the proper motions and Taylor would have him repeat the process until he had satisfied himself that the job was being done in the best and fastest manner. This procedure would then be standardized and one by one the other workers would be taught and required to use this system. His belief was that there was one best way of doing any job and this method could be determined only through the scientific study of that job by experts with proper implements, i.e., a stop watch and recording card.[57]

There was much resentment among factory workers both here and abroad to "Taylorism." These workers were relatively uneducated. Nevertheless, there have been attempts in school systems to establish teacher rating and merit pay for persons who were relatively well educated. Teachers generally have associated this practice with "Taylorism" and deeply resented it. This resentment has usually bred unproductive conflict and impaired or destroyed the leadership potential of the school executives responsible for inaugurating that policy.

[54] See Bertram M. Gross, "The Scientific Approach to Administration," Chap. 3 in *Behavioral Science and Educational Administration.*

[55] Raymond E. Callahan, *Education and the Cult of Efficiency* (Chicago: The University of Chicago Press, 1962).

[56] Frederick Taylor, *Scientific Management* (New York: Harper, 1912).

[57] Callahan, *Education*, pp. 28–29.

Today there is a widespread demand for "accountability" and management by objective. Is this a revival of Taylorism?

The "Survival of the Fittest" Theories

The "survival of the fittest" theory of life reached a high point of acceptance during the latter part of the nineteenth century. It was even held by many to be the law of life. In fact, this theory has a powerful influence on the social thinking and actions of many people on the contemporary scene.

Malthus laid the foundation for the "survival of the fittest" theory in his famous *Essay on Population,* written in 1798. In that essay he stated the theory that poverty and distress were unavoidable, since population increases in geometric ratio whereas the food supply increases in arithmetic ratio. He accepted war, famine, and disease as necessary to human survival because the population must be kept in balance with the food supply.

Darwin, stimulated by the work of Malthus, wrote his *Origin of the Species* in 1859. He started with the assumption that more of each species are born than can possibly survive. The surplus starts a struggle for existence, and, if any individual in the species varies in any way profitable to itself, it has a better chance of survival. Thus, the surviving individual has been "naturally selected."

The scientist Huxley supported and advanced still further the theories of Darwin in his *Struggle for Existence,* written in 1888. But the theories of Darwin and Huxley needed philosophical justification. This was done in masterly fashion by Nietzsche in *The Will to Power,* written in 1889. He looked upon life as a battle in which strength rather than goodness, pride rather than humility, unyielding intelligence rather than altruism, and power rather than justice are needed. He concluded that theories of equality and democracy had been disproven by the laws of selection and survival; therefore, democratic procedures were decadent.

The "survival of the fittest" theories gave rise in the latter part of the nineteenth century to a school of thought known as Social Darwinism.[58] Herbert Spencer, a brilliant English thinker, was the intellectual leader of this movement. His *First Principles,* published in 1864, *The Study of Sociology,* published in 1872-1873, as well as his other publications, were widely read in the United States.

The Social Darwinists applied Darwin's theories of biological evolution directly to social institutions and the life of man in society. The "struggle for existence" and "survival of the fittest" concepts suggested that natural law demanded that these factors be permitted to operate in human society or that society would degenerate. Competition would eliminate the unfit, and this would assure continuing improvement.

Is the school executive of a large, urban school system, with a concentration of disadvantaged minority groups, likely to provide the leadership needed to raise the educational level of these disadvantaged groups if the executive and board hold a Social Darwinist point of view?

Ricardo, a close friend of Malthus, accepted Malthus's population theory

---

[58] Richard Hofstadter, *Social Darwinism in American Thought* (New York: George Brazeller, Inc., 1959).

(though not most of his economic theories) and published in 1817 a brilliant exposition of economic theory in *Principles of Political Economy.* Of interest here is Ricardo's "iron law" of wages. According to Ricardo, a worker should be paid only a subsistence wage, defined as a wage sufficient for the worker to survive and reproduce a sufficient number of workers to meet the needs of the economy. If a worker were paid wages above the subsistence level, the reproduction rate would increase to the point where a surplus of workers would be produced, which would drive wages back down to the subsistence level. At that level, poverty, misery, disease, and reduced reproductive activity would hold the number of workers down to the number needed. Ricardo saw little need for cooperation of workers with the managers and owners because, in his view, their interests were conflicting.

Is an executive holding Ricardo's views likely to be perceived as a leader by the teacher and other employees of the school system?

Nicolo Machiavelli

Nicolo Machiavelli presented some interesting theories of executive behavior in the fifteenth century.[59] Following are some quotations taken from *The Prince.*

1. The prince should choose the fox and the lion to emulate. . . . It is necessary to be a fox to discover the snakes and a lion to terrify the wolves.[60]
2. It is much better to be feared than loved. . . . This is to be assumed in general of men, that they are ungrateful, fickle, false, cowards, covetous, and as long as you succeed they are yours entirely but when need approaches they turn against you.[61]
3. Men have less scruples in offending one who is beloved than one who is feared for love is preserved by the link of obligation which owing to the baseness of men is broken at every opportunity for their advantage; but fear preserves you by a dread of punishment which never fails.[62]

Is a teacher or an administrator who holds that concept of people likely to provide leadership as defined by the authors of this book?

Mutual Aid Theories

It should not be thought that the "survival of the fittest" theory went completely unchallenged. Many voices were raised against the sweeping conclusions being drawn from this theory. Many religious leaders opposed the doctrine because of its association with the theory of evolution, which they considered atheistic.

[59] Nicolo Machiavelli, *The Prince,* trans. W. K. Merriott, 1st ed. (New York: E. P. Dutton and Company, 1908).

[60] *Ibid.,* p. 142.

[61] *Ibid.,* p. 134.

[62] *Ibid.,* p. 135.

The fact of evolution could not be refuted, so the opposition of the ministry was not very effective.

Some intellectuals soon began to reveal the fallacies of Social Darwinism. The early pragmatists were among this group. In 1867, William T. Harris started the *Journal of Speculative Philosophy,* in which he and others attacked many of Spencer's propositions. The pragmatists accepted evolution but rejected Social Darwinism. William James, the famous philosopher and psychologist of Harvard University, first accepted Spencer, but by the middle 1870s he was exposing the fallacies of Spencer's theories.[63] The influence of John Dewey and his *Democracy in Education,* published in 1916, has already been mentioned. Dewey was greatly influenced by Harris and James.

Kropotkin, an anthropologist, wrote a series of essays between 1890 and 1896 in which he attacked some of the theories of Darwin and Huxley.[64] He rejected the Darwinian concept that the struggle for existence pitted every animal against every other animal of the same species. He contended that competition within the same species was of only limited value and that mutual aid was the best guarantee for existence and evolution. Kropotkin's conclusions were based on studies of conditions for survival of animals, savages, barbarians, a medieval city, and of the times in which he lived. He found that the unsociable species were doomed to decay. But the species that reduced to its lowest limits the individual struggle for existence and developed mutual aid to the greatest extent were the most numerous, the most prosperous, and the most likely to develop further. His studies of human beings, regardless of the stage of civilization, led to the same conclusions.

Montagu, another anthropologist, has also boldly challenged the Darwin-Huxley thesis that the nature of man's life is a conflict for the survival of the fittest. He assembled an array of evidence from the investigations of many scientists and concluded that the true nature of man's life is cooperation. He stated his position as follows:

> Evolution itself is a process which favors cooperating groups rather than dis-operating groups and "fitness" is a function of the group as a whole rather than of separate individuals. The fitness of the individual is largely derived from his membership in a group. The more cooperative the group, the greater is the fitness for survival which extends to all its members.[65]

He studied the researches of Allee on lower-order animals[66] and concluded that animals confer distinct survival values on each other. For Montagu, the dominant principle of social life is cooperation, not the struggle for existence. The findings of Montagu are particularly significant because they are based on the researches of biologists, anthropologists, physiologists, psychologists, and many other scientists. He accepts the theory of evolution but insists that, for the human animal, the fitness to survive is based more on the ability to cooperate than on "tooth and claw." It is interesting to note that both Darwin and Huxley recognized in

[63] Hofstadter, *Social Darwinism.*
[64] Peter Kropotkin, *Mutual Aid, A Factor of Evolution* (London: William Heinemann, Limited, 1902).
[65] Ashley Montagu, *On Being Human,* 2nd ed. (New York: Hawthorn Books, 1966), p. 45.
[66] Ward C. Allee, *Animal Aggregations* (Chicago: University of Chicago Press, 1931).

their later years the importance of cooperation in the evolutionary process, but many of their followers would have none of it. Nietszche died holding firmly to his thesis.

LaBarre, an anthropologist, has presented a synthesis of the sciences of humans, an integration of human biology, cultural anthropology, psychiatry, and their related fields.[67] According to LaBarre, humans are polytypical anthropoids, not polymorphous anthropods. The polytypical anthropoid is a species in which all individuals have essentially the same characteristics. A polymorphous anthropod is an insect species that has been structured into many physical castes by evolution. Each of these castes is a proper slave to the codified instincts of the hive. Because humans are polytypical anthropoids, they cannot grow maximally under a rigid caste or class system. Biologically, "all men are brothers"; therefore, humans can grow best in a society of peers or equals.

He also concluded that racial traits have nothing to do with the survival of the individual or the races. Therefore, the ultimate survival of societies depends primarily on "what the people in them believe" and not on physical differences. Social organisms are the means of survival of humankind. The findings of LaBarre support the thesis that the evolution and growth of humankind depends primarily on cooperative procedures which assume that all members of human society are essentially equal.

The executive who believes in the essential equality of all people and their potentiality for growth will tend to develop a cooperative organization in which he or she is a leader as well as an executive.

SOME IMPORTANT PROBLEMS AND ISSUES

The emerging concepts of leadership described in this chapter have great significance for administrative action. Some of the problems and issues associated with the application of these concepts are discussed in the following paragraphs.

Can a Person Be a Leader and at the Same Time Hold an Executive Position in an Organization?

Attention has already been directed to the fact that the executive holding a position in the hierarchy of an organization is under pressure from superordinates to attain the goals of the organization and under pressure from subordinates to meet their personal needs (the nomothetic versus idiographic dimensions of the social system). Thompson commented as follows concerning this dilemma:

> Modern social scientists are coming to the conclusion that headship and leadership are incompatible or that their consolidation in the same hands is very unlikely. Leadership is a quality conferred upon a person by those who are led, and in this sense the leader is always elected. An appointed person on the other hand, must work to advance the interests of his sponsors.

[67]Weston LaBarre, *The Human Animal* (Chicago: University of Chicago Press, 1954), p. 225.

He cannot be a leader for his subordinates and still serve his sponsors, unless there is complete harmony between the two, an unlikely event.[68]

Is the situation as hopeless as Thompson implies? Would the application of the emerging pluralistic, collegial concepts of organization and administration help to resolve this dilemma? How does the exclusion of administrators from the AFT and NEA relate to this issue?

Is There a Need for Role Differentiation Among Leaders?

Leadership acts include those acts intended to help meet group goals and also acts intended to maintain the group by meeting group and individual needs. Berelson and Steiner have pointed out that even in small face-to-face informal groups the "intellectual leader" who structures the group and initiates action to attain group goals is usually not the same person as the "social leader" who meets group and individual needs by promoting mutual acceptance, harmony, liking, and so on.[69] That is, the top position in an informal group on both "liking" and "ideas" is not frequently held by the same person. If this hypothesis is sustained by research on informal face-to-face groups, can it be assumed that the same findings would be applicable to different leadership roles in formal organizations? Some organizations have placed a "tough" person to say no as second in command to the top executive. Is the purpose of this arrangement to give a better image to the top executive, so that it will be possible to play a leadership role when the situation seems to require it? Despite the myth that the top executive in an organization must assume final responsibility, sometimes a subordinate in the executive hierarchy is sacrificed when a serious mistake has been made, to preserve the favorable image of the top executive. This policy has been justified because "it was for the good of the organization." What would be the long-term effect of this policy on the leadership potential of the top executive?

What Officials Should Be Elected by the Group?

Research indicates that, if a group elects its head, the person elected is perceived by the group as being its leader. That person is accepted by the group as a group member, and is in a strategic position to provide leadership for the group. But research has also shown that the person chosen by a group to be its leader is likely to be the person who most nearly is representative of the norms of the group. Rate of production is one of the norms in a factory group. The production norm is the average rate of production that the group believes ought to be maintained. If a group member produces considerably more or considerably less than the group norm, that member is not likely to be accepted by the group as its leader.

A school faculty is a formal school group, but the elements of behavior of a face-to-face formal group are similar in some respects to the elements of behavior

[68] Victor A. Thompson, *Modern Organization* (New York: Alfred A. Knopf, Inc., 1961), p. 120.
[69] Berelson and Steiner, *Human Behavior,* pp. 244–245.

of a primary or informal group. The executive officer of the faculty is the school principal. The almost universal practice in the United States is for the principal to be appointed by the board of education upon the nomination of the superintendent. Considering the concepts of leadership presented in this chapter, should the present practice be continued, or would it be better for the principal to be elected by the faculty?

In some large high schools and in some institutions of higher learning, department heads are elected by the members of the department concerned. Is this good practice?

In some states the county superintendent of education, who is the executive officer of the board, is elected by the people. What are the advantages and disadvantages of this procedure?

The prevailing practice in the United States for the selection of board members is election by the vote of the people. The board of education is a legislative and policy-forming group. Do the concepts of leadership and group dynamics presented in this chapter justify that practice?

Committee members in school faculties are sometimes appointed by the principal and sometimes elected by the faculty. What criteria should be used to determine whether members of a committee should be elected or appointed?

When the Goals of Two Groups Are in Conflict, How Can They Be Harmonized?

Cooperative procedures involving group operation will very frequently result in conflict both within a group and among different groups. This is especially true if the membership of a group was deliberately selected to represent different points of view. However, conflict itself, if properly understood and dealt with, may present an opportunity for growth. Therefore, conflict can be either constructive or destructive. This point of view was orginally presented by Mary Parker Follett in 1925.[70] Miss Follett was one of the pioneer thinkers in the field of human relations. In her great paper on constructive conflict, she advanced the point of view that the three main ways of dealing with conflict are domination, compromise, and integration.[71] Domination, the victory of one side over the other, is the easiest and quickest but the least successful method for dealing with conflict. Compromise, the most commonly used method, involves each side moderating its demands to have peace, neither side obtaining all its objectives. If the ideas of both sides are integrated into a solution that encompasses the desires of both sides, the highest level of dealing with conflict is reached. Miss Follett's illustration of her point is worthy of repetition here.

It seems that a dairymen's cooperative league was on the point of breaking up over the question of precedence of unloading. The creamery was located on the side of a hill. The men who came uphill thought that they should have precedence, but the men who came downhill thought their claims to precedence were stronger.

[70] Henry C. Metcalf and L. Urwick, eds., *Dynamic Administration, The Collected Papers of Mary Parker Follett* (New York: Harper & Row, Publishers, Inc., 1940).
[71] *Ibid.*, pp. 30–49.

If the method of domination had been followed, one side or the other would have been given precedence. If the matter had been compromised, the uphillers and downhillers would each have been given precedence on alternate days. But a consultant suggested that the platform be so arranged that unloading could be done on both sides, in order that the uphillers could unload on one side and the downhillers on the other. This solution was adopted. Each side got what it wanted, and the conflict was resolved. She pointed out that thinking is too often confined between the walls of two possibilities. The integrator is inventive and examines all possible alternatives, not just the ones being advocated by the parties in conflict.

Unfortunately, more differences are settled by compromise than by integration. Undoubtedly, conflicts have been resolved many times by compromise when the possibilities of developing integrated solutions had not been fully explored. Incidentally, Nehru once suggested that compromise that represents a step toward attaining a desirable objective may be good; compromise that results in abandoning an objective or substituting an inferior principle may be bad. The most effective groups, however, will not resort to compromise to resolve conflicts without first attempting to find an integrated solution.

Conflict is destructive when it continues or increases social disorganization or is damaging to individual personalities. Conflict is constructive when it can serve as the impetus for growth in human relations and for bringing about desirable change.

What should be the role of the administrator in resolving conflicts? What procedures can be used to help groups grow in their ability to resolve conflicts constructively? Under what conditions are destructive conflicts likely to be encountered in educational organizations?

What Is the Relation Between Group Morale and Task Achievement in the Formal Organization?

Let us first consider informal groups that are subgroups of the formal organization. Each informal group, as has been pointed out, has two principal goals: group achievement and group maintenance. Each group defines its own achievement goals. The group maintenance goal is attained when both group and individual needs are substantially met and members get satisfaction from group membership. When a group continues to attain its two primary goals, the morale is high; but if it fails, the morale is low. An informal group with high morale is more productive in terms of its own standards of measuring production than a low-morale group. However, a high-morale group may not be productive as measured by the achievement of the tasks of the organization.

Let us now consider the formal organization of which the informal groups are subparts. The formal organization also has two principal functions: achievement of its goals and organizational maintenance. Let us assume, for example, that we have a formal organization such as a school faculty that has no real achievement goals accepted by its members. Let us assume further that the formal organization has been ineffective in meeting group and individual needs. In fact, the formal organization is not an entity, but rather a collection of individuals subdivided into primary groups and cliques. The informal organization, rather than the formal organization, holds the real power and authority. The morale of the actors in this organization is low.

What can the administrator-leader do to make the formal organization a real group?

How Can the Administrator-Leader
Bring About Change and Innovations?

The public school system must constantly change its tasks, goals, and purposes if it is to meet the changing needs of society. This involves changes in the curriculum, the organizational structure, and the services provided. But the administrator always encounters some resistance to change. This is especially true if the changes conflict with critical group norms or threaten the status roles of individuals in the organization. But the administrator, if he is to be a leader, cannot assume a laissez-faire role and avoid change, because change is inevitable. On the other hand, if the administrator in bringing about change ignores certain vital factors of human relations, he will lose the leadership of his group. Under what conditions can institutional changes be made? Coffey and Golden, after an extensive review of applicable research, suggested the following conditions for facilitating organizational change:

(a) When the leadership is democratic and the group members have freedom to participate in the decision-making process; (b) when there have been norms established which make social change an expected aspect of institutional growth; (c) when change can be brought about without jeopardizing the individual's membership in the group; (d) when the group concerned has a strong sense of belongingness, when it is attractive to its members, and when it is concerned with satisfying member needs; (e) when the group members actually participate in the leadership function, help formulate the goals, plan the steps toward goal realization, and participate in the evaluation of these aspects of leadership; (f) when the level of cohesion permits members of the group to express themselves freely and to test new roles by trying out new behaviors and attitudes without being threatened by real consequence.[72]

Recently, there has been much interest in planned change. Bennis, Benne, and Chin and their associates have presented a design for planned change.[73] Under this concept there is "the application of systematic and appropriate knowledge to human affairs for the purpose of creating intelligent action and change."[74] The process involves the deliberate collaboration of the change agent and the client system. These authors objected to the conceptualization of a change agent exclusively as a "free" agent brought in as a consultant from outside the client system. They comment on this issue as follows:

For one thing, client systems contain the potential resources for creating their own planned change programs under certain conditions; they have in-

---

[72] National Society for the Study of Education, pp. 101–102.

[73] Warren G. Bennis, Kenneth D. Benne, and Robert Chin, eds., *The Planning of Change* (New York: Holt, Rinehart and Winston, Inc., 1961).

[74] *Ibid.*, p. 3.

side resources, staff persons, applied researchers, and administrators who can and do act as successful change agents. For another thing, we contend that a client system must build into its own structures a vigorous change-agent function, in order for it to adapt to a continually changing environment.[75]

Is the change-agent role a leadership role when the change is made with the "willing cooperation" of the members of the client system? What theoretical concepts discussed in this chapter can be used to predict the by-products of imposing change on a group against its will? Should outside consultants be used as change agents as well as personnel within an organization?

SELECTED REFERENCES

Bennis, Warren G., Kenneth D. Benne, and Robert Chin, *The Planning of Change.* New York: Holt, Rinehart and Winston, Inc., 1961.

Berelson, Bernard, and Gary A. Steiner, *Human Behavior: An Inventory of Scientific Findings.* New York: Harcourt, Brace Jovanovich, 1964.

Burns, James MacGregor, *Leadership.* New York: Harper & Row, Publishers, Inc., 1978.

Carlson, Richard O., Art Gallaher, Jr., Mathew B. Miles, Roland J. Pellegrin, and Everett M. Rogers, *Change Processes in the Public Schools.* Eugene, Ore.: Center for the Advanced Study of Educational Administration, University of Oregon, 1965.

Cartwright, Darwin, and Alvin Zander, *Group Dynamics: Research and Theory.* New York: Harper & Row, Publishers, Inc., 1960.

Cunningham, Luvern, L., and William G. Gephart, eds., *Leadership, The Science and Art Today.* Itasca, Ill.: F. E. Peacock Publishers, 1973.

Fiedler, Fred E., *A Theory of Leadership Effectiveness.* New York: McGraw-Hill Book Company, 1967.

Griffiths, Daniel E., ed., *Behavioral Science and Educational Administration.* Sixty-third Yearbook of the National Society for the Study of Education. Chicago: University of Chicago Press, 1964.

Hare, A. Paul, Edgar F. Borgatta, and Robert F. Bales, *Small Groups: Studies in Social Interaction.* New York: Alfred A. Knopf, Inc., 1965.

Homans, George C., *The Human Group.* New York: Harcourt, Brace Jovanovich, 1950.

Hoy, Wayne K., and Cecil G. Miskel, *Educational Administration, Theory, Research and Practice,* Chap. 8. New York: Random House, Inc., 1978.

McClelland, D. C., *Power, the Inner Experience.* New York: Irvington Publishers, 1975.

---

[75] *Ibid.*

6

DECISION MAKING
and COMMUNICATION

Some of the basic theories and concepts of educational organization and administration have been presented in Chapters 3, 4, and 5. In this chapter some of those theories and concepts are applied to the day-to-day problems that administrators face as they make decisions and communicate with members of the school social system and members of the community.

Every successful organization must be capable of and must make decisions which enable the organization to achieve its goals and which meet the critical needs of the members of the organization. The administrative leader of the organization facilitates the processes of decision making and also facilitates the communication of those decisions to members of the organization and to the community.

DECISION MAKING

The type of decision being made affects the organizational level making the decision, the processes of making the decision, and the implementation of the decision after it is made.

123

Gore classified decisions by type as follows: (1) routinely occurring decisions, (2) adaptive decisions involving adjustments of existing policies, and (3) innovative decisions involving the establishment of new policies and goals.[1] This classification is convenient for the purpose of discussion.

Routine Decisions

It might be assumed that routine, recurring decisions are not an important phase of educational administration. However, the appropriate assignment of the authority to make routine decisions, the processes followed in making those decisions, and the evaluation of the decisions made may make the difference between an efficient, functioning organization and an organization characterized by strife and chaos.

Authority to make routine decisions governed by general policies. These decisions are made at all levels of the organization depending upon the type of routine decision being made. Some types of routine decisions start with policies made at a high level. Let us take as an example the operation of a school bus. State legislatures may enact laws regulating the speed at which school buses operate, laws prohibiting the passing of school buses while loading and unloading pupils, laws regulating the color of school buses, and laws authorizing the state board of education to make additional regulations concerning the safety and adequacy of school transportation. The local board of education has the authority to establish additional policies and rules regulating the operation of school buses. It is desirable for the state legislature to set certain policies regulating school bus operation so that citizens throughout the state as they travel from district to district may operate their private automobiles according to uniform policies which maximize the safety of school children. As a matter of fact, certain policies such as color of school bus and minimum specifications for school bus bodies and chassis by common consent are becoming nationwide.

The school bus driver makes routine decisions daily on the speed at which to operate the bus, the route to take, the stops to make, and similar matters, but all decisions of this type are made in accordance with policies established by higher levels of authority.

All persons in an organization have the authority to make some decisions. For example, the bus driver has the responsibility to check the bus daily and determine if it is operating properly and if the bus should be taken to the shop for repairs. The driver also must make many decisions regulating the behavior of pupils on the bus.

When policy decisions are made by higher levels of authority which govern the routine decisions made by persons in lower levels, the persons in the lower levels of authority should be consulted before the policy decision is made. When such policy decisions are made without consulting with persons in the lower echelons, the employees at the lower rungs of the ladder are likely to complain "They don't know what's really going on down here." The example of the bus driver is used for the

---

[1] William Gore, "Decision-Making Research: Some Prospects and Limitations" in *Concepts and Issues in Administrative Behavior* eds. Sidney Mailick and Edward Van Ness (Englewood Cliffs, N.J.: Prentice-Hall, Inc., 1962), pp. 55–57.

purpose of pointing out the desirability of employees in the lowest levels of authority to have the opportunity to make inputs into the decision-making process. All employees at all levels of authority should be given the authority to participate in the decision-making process in matters with which they are concerned.

Authority to make routine decisions not governed by general policies. In general, these decisions should be made by persons near the scene of action as possible. Let us consider classroom teachers. They perceive themselves as professionals with professional qualifications equal to and in some cases superior to the professional qualifications of their administrative superiors. Teachers are the administrators in their classrooms with legitimate authority to make many important recurring, routine decisions not governed by general policy. Examples of such decisions are what routine tests to give and when to give them, what audiovisual aids to use and when to use them, what marks to give pupils, what homework to assign pupils, what methods of teaching to use in presenting different types of materials and many similar matters. If the school principal or an administrator or supervisor from the central office attempts to make decisions of this type for the teachers, they will view this an invasion of their authority and conflict results. This conflict will increase the difficulty of the organization in attaining its goals and it lowers the morale of the teachers. This is an example of the application of the Getzels model discussed in Chapter 3.

The making of routine decisions. It is highly important that the person responsible for making a decision make that decision at the time at which it should be made, especially if it affects the persons lower in the echelons of authority. Procrastination in making routine decisions retards the attainment of organizational goals and is very frustrating to persons in the organization who cannot function until those decisions are made. The leadership quality of an administrator may become suspect if he or she procrastinates in making routine decisions which must be made if the organization is to function efficiently. Let us take the case of a disruptive pupil in the tenth grade who has caused trouble in a number of classes. Several teachers and the school counselor have requested the principal to take action. The principal and the counselor have conferred with the pupil and the pupil's parents but the parents have not been cooperative. The principal has the authority to suspend the pupil for ten days, the principal can recommend to the superintendent that the pupil be transferred to an alternative school, or the principal can recommend to the board that the pupil be expelled from school. If the principal delays making a decision on this matter, the situation may get worse and the members of the staff may lose confidence in his or her capacity for leadership.

Adaptive Decisions

Situations occasionally arise in the operation of a school system in which a decision needs to be made but no established policy fits the situation exactly. The administrator has the option of either making no decision or seeking an adaptation in the policy so that it will fit the situation. If the administrator fails to make the decision because the existing policy does not fit the situation, the administrator encounters the same difficulties experienced by the administrator who procrastinates making routine decisions.

If the situation is critical, the administrator should make the decision at once but he or she should promptly seek an adjustment in the existing policy. If the situation is not critical, the administrator should seek an adjustment of the existing policy before taking action.

Bureaucratic delays are extremely frustrating. The greater the number of echelons of authority in the chain of command, the greater the chance of bureaucratic delays. Each echelon has the opportunity to raise technical objections concerning whether or not approval is in accordance with existing policy. This "nit-picking" causes friction in the organization, which in general systems theory is called *entropy* as was pointed out in Chapter 3. Entropy hinders the organization from attaining its goals, and it is frustrating to the members of the school social system. If a decision needs to be made and action taken, the administrators at each level of the organizational hierarchy should seek ways to make a decision rather than to seek ways to thwart decision making. Much of the public opposition to government in general is due to unnecessary bureaucratic friction. Bureaucratic delays most frequently occur when adaptive decisions must be made.

Innovative Decisions

Innovative decisions involve the development of new policies, goals, and programs or the making of major changes in existing policies, goals, and programs. Such decisions cannot be wisely made speedily or intuitively. The movie version of the corporation president sitting behind a bank of telephones making profound decisions on policy by telephone after telephone without consulting anyone is not the way in which policy decisions are made in educational administration. It is no doubt a wrong image of the way decisions are made in business world.

The decision-making process. Hoy and Miskel have presented an analysis of the steps in the decision-making process. It is summarized briefly as follows:

1. Recognize and define the problem or issue.
2. Analyze the difficulties in the existing situation.
3. Establish criteria for problem resolution.
4. Develop a plan or strategy for action. This involves specifying alternatives, predicting consequences and deliberating and selecting the alternatives for action.
5. Initiate the plan for action which involves programming, communicating, monitoring and appraising.[2]

Griffiths presented the view that the central process of administration is decision making which is composed of the following aspects:

1. Recognize, define and limit the problem.
2. Analyze and evaluate the problem.

[2] Adapted from Wayne K. Hoy and Cecil G. Miskell, *Educational Administration, Theory, Practice, and Research* (New York: Random House, Inc., 1978), pp. 217–226.

3. Establish criteria or standards by which solutions will be evaluated or judged as acceptable and adequate to the need.
4. Collect data.
5. Formulate and select the preferred solution or solutions. Test them in advance.
6. Put into effect the preferred solution.
   a. Program the solution.
   b. Control the activities in the program.
   c. Evaluate the results and the process.[3]

Dill from the field of business administration has proposed the following phases of decision-making activity:

1. Agenda building—defining goals and tasks for the organization and assigning priorities for their completion.
2. Search—looking for alternative courses of action and for information that can be used to evaluate them.
3. Commitment—testing proposed "solutions" to choose one for adoption by the organization.
4. Implementation—elaborating and clarifying decisions so that they can be put into effect; motivating members of the organization to help translate decisions into action.
5. Evaluation—testing the results of previous choices and actions to suggest new tasks for the organizational agenda or to facilitate organizational learning.[4]

The similarity of the descriptions of the decision-making process by these different writers is obvious. If innovative decisions are made efficiently, the processes are probably very similar in all types of formal organizations. Hasty decisions on education made by the state legislatures sometimes injure the educational program. Such decisions are usually made when legislatures do not follow sound decision-making processes before enacting a law. The decision-making processes of state legislatures will be discussed more fully in Chapter 8 devoted to the politics of education.

The value framework of decision making. When decisions are being made among alternatives, values enter into the process, either consciously or unconsciously. The study of philosophy should be included in the program for training school administrators. However, the busy school administrator working with a group engaged in developing an important policy or program will not likely find much help by weighing the philosophical contributions of moral universalism, logical positivism, experimentation, pragmatism, existentialism, realism, and idealism to the solutions of the problem.

There is no universally acceptable set of values. Different acceptable values are frequently in conflict. That is, if the administrator makes a decision in accordance

---

[3] Daniel E. Griffiths, *Administrative Theory* (New York: Appleton-Century & Crofts, 1959), p. 113.
[4] William R. Dill, "Administrative Decision-Making" in *Concepts and Issues in Administrative Behavior*, p. 34.

with one value, the administrator may violate another important value. Leys has suggested that the administrator may resolve this dilemma in part by becoming aware of the different moral values that he or she should consider. He presented the six following moral values which have all been advocated by one or more of the classical philosophers:

1. Happiness—desirable results, maximized satisfactions, efficiency.
2. Lawfulness—precedents, customs, and contracts authorizations.
3. Harmony—logical consistency, platonic justice, order, plan, common good.
4. Survival—political power, effect on friend-foe relations.
5. Integrity—self-respect, the rationality of the individual, peace-of-mind.
6. Loyalty—institutional trends, social causes.[5]

When alternatives are being considered, the administrator might well consider the impact of each alternative on each value. In making many decisions, there is no perfect solution because the best that can be done is to "satisfice" rather than "satisfy." That is particularly true when the board is dealing with teachers in collective negotiations. This subject is treated more fully in Chapter 18.

Sometimes the board's values come into conflict with the community's values. Consider the case of a board of education that is contemplating the closing of an elementary school in a declining population area. In this urban community, the board's policy is to maintain a minimum enrollment of 600 in each elementary school to maintain financial efficiency in school operations. But the people served by that school are loyal to it and fight the closing of the school bitterly. The board next considers the alternative of transporting the pupils from some other schools to that school. But the people from the other schools object because they are loyal to their communities. The board has a conflict between the value of efficiency and the value of loyalty. There is no perfect solution. The board has the unpleasant task of giving one value a priority over the other value.

Boards of education and school administrators do not have unlimited power to make value choices. The federal constitution, state constitutions, federal and state statutes, and federal and state courts all place constrictions on the value choices of local authorities. For example, the Fourteenth Amendment, the *Brown* v. *Board of Education of Topeka* decision in 1954, the Civil Rights Act of 1964, Title I of the Elementary and Secondary Education Act of 1965, and the Education for the Handicapped Act of 1976 all place federal restrictions on the value choices of state and local governments. State governments and state courts also limit the value choices of boards of education. We place a high value on local self-government, but we place a higher value on the rights of the individual and, if the lower level of government violates those rights, the values of the higher levels of government prevail.

COMMUNICATION

When a decision is made, it must be communicated to all the subsystems of the school social system affected by the decision. Furthermore, the people of the com-

[5] Adapted from William A. R. Leys, "The Value Framework of Decision-Making" in *Concepts and Issues in Administrative Behavior*, pp. 87–88.

munity must be informed concerning the programs and policies with which they are concerned. On the other hand, before a decision is made or evaluated, information from the community should be communicated to the decision-making authority. Of great importance also are the day-to-day communications on routine decisions necessary for school operations. For an organization to function efficiently, communication channels should be available up and down the organizational hierarchy and also laterally at each organizational level. Informal organizations also provide important communications functions. Some policies with respect to communication will be discussed in the remainder of this chapter.

Participation in decision making and communication. School administrators or boards of education who make decisions on important policies and programs without adequate information do not facilitate the attainment of organizational goals and frequently lower the morale of members of the organization. Of course much information can be provided through a "management information system," but often this type of information does not communicate very much. This is particularly true of innovative policies and programs under consideration.

One of the most useful methods of communicating information is to provide opportunities for those vitally affected by programs to participate in the decision-making process. This does not mean that the board should delegate its legal decision-making authority to its employees or the general public, but it should provide the opportunity for those interested in a decision to provide information needed in making that decision.

Korda has stated that "information always comes from below, and the more important it is, the farther down one has to go to collect it."[6] The administrator can communicate from his or her level in the hierarchy downward to subordinates information on decisions that have been made, instructions on operating procedures, announcements, interpretation of events, approval or disapproval of requests, and similar matters. However, no real information relating to the evaluation of an existing policy or program or the institution of new policies originates in the superintendent's office or the principal's office. That information originates at the operating level, and the most important operating level is the classroom. If a superintendent or principal does not provide opportunities for teachers to participate in decision making on policies and programs that concern them, they are likely to feel "He doesn't know what's really going on down here." The failure of many boards of education to provide opportunities for teachers to participate in decision making has no doubt stimulated the formulation of teachers' unions for collective negotiations with an adversary relationship with the board of education. This is in contrast to the processes of cooperative procedures advocated in Chapter 4. The subject of collective negotiations is treated extensively in Chapter 18.

Participation in the decision-making process is a highly effective method of communication. If a person participates in the formulation of a program on policy, that person will understand it better and also is in a better position to implement it. Group participation is necessary for efficient decision making, but the formal organization is necessary for implementing the programs and policies developed.

Citizens' advisory committees at the systems level and at the local school level

[6]Michael Korda, *Power, How to Get It, How to Use It* (New York: Ballantine Books, Inc., 1975), p. 147.

have frequently been found very useful in decision making and also in transmitting information up and down communication channels. Various types of parent–teacher organizations have also facilitated decision making and communication.

It should not be assumed, however, that teachers should be invited or be requested to participate in making all decisions. This is especially true of routine decisions. If the teachers are not interested in the decision to be made, they should not be requested to participate in making it. They may consider it an imposition on them and a waste of time. On the other hand, if the decision to be made is controversial, the teachers may perceive the administrator as "passing the buck."

Organizational communication. Hoy and Miskel have made an insightful analysis of communication in organizations and have presented the following generalizations on communication theory:

1. Communication is purposive . . .
2. Meanings of messages are in people and not necessarily in the intended content . . .
3. Feedback is essential for high levels of understanding . . .
4. Formal and informal communication channels exist in all organizations . . .
5. The formal and informal communication channels are potentially complementary . . .
6. The messages carried by verbal and nonverbal media must be congruent for effective understanding . . .[7]

Organizational communication involves explaining, instructing, approving or disapproving, ordering, influencing, announcing, and so on. There is a sender and a receiver. The receiver may not receive the message intended by the sender because the sender and the receiver may interpret the meaning of the same words differently. If opportunity is provided for interaction or instant feedback, the message sent by the sender is more likely to be interpreted accurately by the receiver. For example, if a new form for reporting pupil attendance and membership by class or grade level, by transported and nontransported pupils, and by other classifications is being initiated, it is better for the principal to explain the new form in a faculty meeting and to receive immediate feedback from teachers than to try to explain it exclusively by a set of written instructions.

The principal is in the middle of the channel of communication from the central office to the staff and from the staff to the central office. Written or oral instruction sent by the superintendent to be transmitted to teachers may be interpreted differently by different principals. If these instructions or other types of communications are important, the principals should have the opportunity to interact directly with the central office. Social interaction in a group provides an error-correcting mechanism.[8]

On certain matters, the teachers should feel free to communicate with the central office without clearing with the principal. If the principal insists that all com-

[7] Adapted from Hoy and Miskel, *Educational Administration, Theory, Practice and Research* (New York: Random House, 1978) pp. 240–248.

[8] See Peter M. Blau and W. Richard Scott, *Formal Organizations—A Comparative Approach* (San Francisco: Chandler Publishing Company, 1962), pp. 118–119.

munications with the central office be cleared through him or her, the teachers are likely to perceive the administrator as a censor. In most school systems today of middle size and above, the teachers are so well organized that they will communicate with the central office and the general public through their unions if they are denied communicating with the central office by any means other than the "chain of command." The longer the chain of command, the greater the distortion in the information transmitted through it. This is particularly true of oral communication.

Administrators attempting to communicate through the media experience many communication difficulties. If the administrator talks to a reporter, sometimes the reporter places unintended inferences on what the administrator said. If the administrator writes an article or speaks on the radio or television, members of the public frequently "hear" or "infer" things that the administrator did not say or write. Therefore, the administrator should prepare press releases and speeches very carefully or communications will not have the intended effect.

Formal and informal channels of communication exist in all organizations and in a well-administered organization may be mutually helpful. Social groups of school employees discuss school matters on an informal basis. If the school system has established good channels of communication up and down hierarchical levels and also outside the hierarchy, informal groups tend to refine the development and the implementation of programs and policies. Teachers serving on committees that participate effectively in decision making at the system level need to confer with their peers informally to represent them adequately.

Groups of parents meeting socially frequently discuss school affairs. Uninformed parents frequently misinterpret school policies and programs and create undesirable conflict. School administrators who keep the public well informed through such methods as encouraging the establishment of community schools, by providing opportunities for school patrons to participate in decision making, and by providing a good system of public information find that informal groups of parents provide a channel of communication that assists the school organization to attain its goals and that provides a good community climate for the pupils and the teachers.

School administrators communicate much by their methods of operation and by their manner. The administrator may want to create an image of being democratic and understanding. The principal or superintendent may invite people to come to his or her office and proclaim, "my door is always open." But, when a teacher comes to see that administrator, the secretary may be instructed to say that the administrator is busy or that the administrator can be seen for only a few minutes. When the teacher does enter, there is the administrator sitting behind a huge desk with a chair for the teacher placed several feet in front of the desk as though the teacher were the culprit and the administrator was the judge. That is not the image that the administrator wishes to communicate but that is what the teacher feels. If the administrator puts the teacher on the defensive and does not listen respectfully and give adequate time to discuss the matter that the teacher wants to present, the administrator is communicating that "the door is not always open" despite the stated policy.

The administrator's contacts with the lay public are extremely important. If the administrator has a cold manner and resents parents asking questions about the school, parents get the impression that the administrator is operating a closed social system, that it is "his (or her)" school and not "their" school. Some administrators spend too much time talking about their own achievements and goals and neglect to give credit to others in the system who are making vital contributions to the achievement of organizational goals. Giving credit where credit is due promotes the achievement of organizational goals and also improves staff morale. An administrator who talks too much about himself or herself is reminiscent of the story told of the movie actor on a talk show who said to the host, "We have talked enough about me, let's talk about you. What do you think of my acting in my last play?"

SOME PROBLEMS AND ISSUES

Decision making may be the heart of administration, but it may also involve the administrator in some critical problems and issues. A few illustrations are presented in the following paragraphs.

What Alternatives Are Available to the Administrator if Community Values Conflict with His or Her Values and the Board's Values?

This is not an unusual situation. For example, the problem of racial integration involving court-ordered busing in some cases has faced many boards of education in recent years. The majority of the white community is bitterly opposing racial integration and forced busing. The black community supports racial integration but its members are in the minority. The community power structure is dominated by whites. The superintendent and the board both believe in the justice of integration. It is true that the federal government will eventually force desegregation of the public schools in any event. Should the superintendent and the board take no responsibility in the matter and leave the problem up to the federal government, or should they take the leadership in trying to change community values?

It would seem that leadership does not always involve expressing the will of the group. That is the easiest type of leadership to provide. The highest type of leadership is to raise the values and goals of the community when those values and goals are in conflict with the common good. Boards of education and school administrators who follow that policy sometimes jeopardize their positions, but they are the leaders that move the community forward.

What Options Are Available to the Superintendent When the Board Makes A Decision in Conflict with Personal Values?

Many superintendents face this problem. Before the superintendent decides the action that he or she will take, the superintendent must be sure that it is a critical value at stake, not a difference in opinion between him or her and the board. For example, let us assume that the superintendent recommends that the tax rate be increased from 10 mills to 12 mills to reduce the pupil–teacher ratio from 26 to 20 in grades K–3. The superintendent cites research showing that the early years of a child's schooling are the critical years and that reducing the pupil–teacher ratio will greatly increase the individual attention that teachers can give to pupils in those grades. The superintendent argues that this is the best investment the community can make of the additional money that can be raised by an additional two mill tax. The teachers in grades K–3 enthusiastically support the superintendent. The board however turns the request down on the grounds that in these inflationary times many people cannot afford any additional taxes and a recent article in a Sunday newspaper cited studies showing that school achievement did not necessarily increase as the pupil-teacher ratio decreased. Should the superintendent resign because the board rejected his or her recommendation? Is the superintendent's recommendation based on a critical value, or is it simply an option for spending the community's resources?

Let us take another case. Suppose that, against the opposition of the superintendent, the board has established a lay committee comprised of religious and political conservatives with the authority to censor all textbooks and all library books used in the public schools. The superintendent considers this policy a denial of freedom of thought and a violation of the First Amendment. The superintendent has attempted to change the values of the board and has failed. As a matter of fact, three members of the five-member board belong to an extreme rightist organization. Should the superintendent resign or stay on the job and continue to fight for personal beliefs?

SELECTED REFERENCES

Blau, Peter M., and W. Richard Scott, *Formal Organizations: A Comparative Approach,* Chap. 5. San Francisco: Chandler Publishing Company, 1962.

Burns, James MacGregor, *Leadership,* Chap. 15. New York: Harper & Row, Publishers, Inc. 1978.

Hoy, Wayne K., and Cecil G. Miskel, *Educational Administration, Theory, Research, and Practice,* Chaps. 9 and 10. New York: Random House, Inc., 1978.

Kimbrough, Ralph B., and Michael Y. Nunnery, *Educational Administration–An Introduction,* Chap. 2. New York: Macmillan Publishing Co., Inc., 1976.

Mailick, Sidney, and Edward H. Van Ness, eds., *Concepts and Issues in Administrative Behavior,* pp. 1–81. Englewood Cliffs, N.J.: Prentice-Hall, Inc., 1962.

7

PLANNING and EFFECTING IMPROVEMENTS in EDUCATION

The basic concepts relating to decision making and communication presented in Chapter 6 will now be applied to planning and effecting improvements in education.

Banfield stated the following concerning planning: "A plan . . . is a decision with regard to a course of action. A course of action is a sequence of acts which are mutually related as means and are therefore viewed as a unit; it is the unit which is the plan. Planning then as defined here is to be distinguished from what we may call 'opportunistic decisionmaking' which is choosing (rationally or not) actions that are not mutually related as a single means."[1]

During the Cold War hysteria in the early 1950s, planning was damned by some as being communistic. However, all successful organizations have done planning. If an organization develops a plan, it must be implemented if the organization is to be successful, and it is expected that all members of the organization follow

---

[1] Edward C. Banfield, "Ends and Means in Planning" in Sidney Mailick and Edward Van Ness, eds., *Concepts and Issues in Administrative Behavior* (Englewood Cliffs, N.J.: Prentice-Hall, Inc., 1962), p. 71.

that plan. Blau and Scott point out that this creates a dilemma.[2] There is a need for central plannning and also a need for individual initiative. The basic dilemma is the need for order and the need for freedom. In this chapter, certain suggestions are presented for resolving that dilemma.

Most people would probably agree that the schools and other educational institutions have made many significant contributions to the development of this nation. But several writers have noted that there seems to be a growing feeling of frustration—what some have called a *crisis of confidence* in public education—apparently partly because some important needs of this complex and rapidly changing society are not being met satisfactorily, and the inequities and inadequacies are being recognized more clearly than at any previous time. Many people have reached the conclusion that some major improvements in education are urgently needed and that merely continuing to increase expenditures for present provisions or programs will not resolve basic problems. In most states and communities, however, there seem to be wide differences of opinion concerning what changes should be made in education, how needed changes should be made, and whether some of the changes that have been proposed would actually result in significant improvements. Such differences in perspectives and opinions cannot be resolved either quickly or easily in a pluralistic society.

Following are some problem areas which are creating controversy at the present time:

- The school curriculum does not meet the needs of pupils in many school systems.
- Some young people are progressing through their school years without learning even to read perceptively, and many are not prepared to become productive members of society.
- The methods of financing education in most states are grossly inequitable and indefensible for many taxpayers and often result in discrimination against students in the less wealthy areas.
- Many parents and other lay citizens are seeking—but have not yet found—meaningful ways in which to participate effectively in the decision-making processes relating to education.

In terms of what is now known about social systems (see Chapter 3), leadership (see Chapter 5), provisions for relevant learning (see Chapter 15), and deficiencies and problems in education—many of which have existed for some time and cannot easily or quickly be resolved—it is evident that some major changes are urgently needed in many aspects of education. However, these changes *should be coordinated* (not made just in one aspect without considering the implications for other aspects) *and systematically planned.* They should not be made merely because they are proposed by a prestigious group or person or seem to make some minor improvements possible. In the planning process, appropriate attention will need to be given to long-range goals and priorities as well as to goals and objectives that can and should be attained within a relatively short period of time. Finally, those concerned with planning improvements in education need to recognize that compe-

[2] Peter M. Blau and W. Richard Scott, *Formal Organizations: A Comparative Approach* (San Francisco: Chandler Publishing Company, 1962), p. 247.

tent lay as well as educational leaders must be involved at least in the process of determining goals and major policies because these goals and policies must be accepted by the public before they can be utilized for guidance in effecting any significant changes in education.

RATIONALE AND BASIC CONSIDERATIONS

If educators, board members, legislators, and other concerned citizens are to cooperate effectively in planning and effecting changes that will result in significant improvements in education, appropriate processes in planning for and effecting those improvements must be utilized. Following are some basic concepts of planning that are worthy of consideration:

- Modern planning is a logical and systematic process that differs significantly from the elementary kinds of procedures utilized during earlier years.
- In a *planning society* the people cooperatively determine their goals and appropriate ways of attaining them, whereas in a *planned society* the goals are determined for the people by their rulers or government.
- The goals of a democratic society are or should be social and economic goals concerned with the welfare and progress of all citizens rather than selfish goals designed to promote or protect the concerns and privileges of special interest groups.
- Cooperation means or implies the bona fide involvement of representative and perceptive lay citizens as well as educators in studying problems and needs and in agreeing on appropriate goals and optimum ways of attaining them rather than merely accepting the goals and policies developed by a few educators or lay citizens.

Those involved in the processes of planning will find that

- Changes will occur with or without planning. However, by anticipating probable developments, we can prepare to facilitate needed changes and to avoid or mitigate some that might be harmful.
- With appropriate planning procedures it is possible to identify maladjustments or deficiencies that are causing—or are likely to cause—educational problems, and thus enable those in decision-making roles to determine in advance what adjustments are necessary.[3]

Another important concept concerning the development of a defensible rationale for planning in and for education relates to the rather common practice of reacting primarily to crisis situations. Legislation has often been enacted in an effort to deal with some acute problem or to remedy some inequitable situation; school board regulations have often been formulated for similar reasons. Obviously, changes should be made when they are needed. But when changes are made on a

[3] Adapted from Edgar L. Morphet and David L. Jesser, "The Future in the Present: Planning for Improvements in Education," in *Cooperative Planning for Education in 1980* (New York: Citation Press, Scholastic Magazines, Inc., 1968), p. 3.

piecemeal basis to deal with "crisis" situations and there is little or no recognition of the interrelationships between *present and future* needs, or the interrelatedness of the various components of the societal and educational systems are ignored, significant improvements in education are not likely to result from a long-range point of view.

In commenting in 1979 on the failure of the U.S. government to establish a long-range energy policy despite the fact that it had been recommended by three presidents, an editorial writer for *U.S. News and World Report* raised the following question: "Is there a built-in weakness of democratic government that it cannot plan beyond sundown?"[4] Many crises in financing education have resulted from "sundown planning" on the part of governors and state legislatures.

Some Important Concepts and Guidelines

Some of the important and still relevant concepts and guidelines relating to educational planning developed three decades ago by the Council of Chief State School Officers are as follows:

- The responsibility for leadership in planning educational programs properly belongs to and should be assumed by the regularly constituted educational agencies and authorities at the proper level.
- The planning procedure and process should be carefully formulated, unified, and systematically carried out.
- Educational planning should be recognized and carried out as an integral aspect of community, state, and national planning.
- Definite provision for planning must be made in educational agencies in order that planning may proceed satisfactorily and attain tangible results.
- One phase of educational planning should provide the basis for organized research; another should be built on and utilize fully the results of research.
- Educational planning must be thought of and established as a continuous process requiring constant adaptation of plans to meet emerging needs.
- Educational planning to be functional must be realistic and practical but should not be needlessly limited by existing situations.
- All educational planning should involve the active and continuing participation of interested groups and organizations.
- The planning process should result in specific recommendations which are understood and accepted by those who are participating.
- Provision for continuing evaluation of the planning process [and products] is basic.[5]

In 1949 the National Citizens Commission for the Public Schools was organized under the chairmanship of Roy E. Larsen of Time, Life and Fortune to encourage and assist lay citizens and educators throughout the nation to cooperate in im-

[4] Editorial, *U.S. News and World Report,* November 5, 1979.

[5] From report on *Planning and Developing Adequate State Programs of Education* by the Study Commission on State Educational Problems, as approved by the National Council of Chief State School Officers. Published in *Education for Victory,* December 20, 1944, pp. 15–16.

proving the schools in their communities and states. A few years later, the National Society for the Study of Education, with the cooperation of members of the National Citizens Commission and educators who had worked with the commission, published the yearbook *Citizen Cooperation for Better Public Schools*[6] that included numerous suggestions relating to cooperative procedures for improving education.

As one result of these efforts, during the decade beginning about 1950, nearly one fifth of the states and numerous local school systems utilized these or similar conceptual guidelines as a basis for conducting cooperative studies and developing plans that, in most cases, resulted in important improvements in their provisions for education.

PREPARING TO PLAN SYSTEMATICALLY

With some notable exceptions, most educational planning until recently has been of the short-range type (usually for one or two years except for population and related projections), often has been closely related to the traditional annual or biennial budgets, and has been concerned primarily with certain aspects of education. But this situation has changed significantly during the past few years as a result of several developments, including (1) many more people are interested in and understand the importance of systematic planning; (2) the kinds of information essential for effective planning can now be obtained more readily; (3) more competent personnel are available to assist with the technical as well as with the human relations aspects of planning; (4) there is a better understanding of the need for clearly stated and acceptable goals; and (5) better means are available for selecting and utilizing the best alternatives for attaining those goals.

In recent years state and local boards and administrators have been confronted with many demands and pressures for changes in the curriculum, instruction, provisions for financial support—in fact, in almost every aspect of education. Such demands by various and diverse publics obviously reflect areas of concern that must be seriously and carefully considered by administrators and board members. However, if changes are effected only in response to crisis-type situations, some of the basic problems may not be resolved. Moreover, unless serious consideration is given to organizational structures and procedures that are conducive to effective planning, these changes are not likely to result in significant long-range improvements. If constructive and lasting improvements are to be effected, it is essential that a conscious and concerted effort be made by every state and local education agency to develop (1) an organization that will facilitate bona fide planning and (2) procedures that will support effective planning processes. In other words, these agencies will need not only a properly staffed unit concerned with planning but also the resources needed to ensure effective planning.

In a changing society everyone interested in planning and effecting improvements in education must be concerned not only with current problems and needs but also with the implications for education of prospective changes in society.

[6] *Citizen Cooperation for Better Public Schools.* Fifty-third Yearbook of the National Society for the Study of Education, Part I. Edgar L. Morphet, chairman (Chicago: University of Chicago Press, 1954).

Although many aspects of the future cannot be *predicted* accurately, it is possible to utilize appropriate information and insights as a basis for *forecasting* and considering the effects of probable and alternative developments in society[7] and some of the major implications for education. For example, Harman[8] has utilized this macro view approach as a basis for considering some of the implications for education if society during the next few decades (1) merely moves into a later stage of industrialization or (2) becomes increasingly concerned with individuals and their development (as seems probable on the basis of recent developments).

Kinds of Planning

Many of the recent controversies about various aspects of education (including the limited progress made by some students, integration, and school finance) have tended to divert attention from the basic issue: *What kind and quality of education is essential to meet present and emerging needs, and how can it be provided best and most effectively?* The most promising procedure for resolving this issue seems to be through perceptive leadership and systematic, comprehensive, long-range planning *with* rather than *for* people.

Culbertson[9] has noted that there are essentially two interrelated kinds of systematic planning, each of which has different purposes: strategic planning and management planning. Each of these may be utilized for both long- and short-range planning as well as for comprehensive planning or planning concerned with some aspect of education. Moreover, each includes the concept of contingency planning (developing defensible alternatives that can be utilized if unanticipated circumstances arise).

Strategic planning, which fosters and requires productive relations and linkages with public agencies and groups other than those directly responsible for education, should receive primary attention because it involves the determination of policies and the establishment of new or revised goals and objectives. This concept should be of special interest to educational leaders who have a major responsibility for developing and implementing plans because, if properly utilized, it will help to ensure the commitment and support that is essential to facilitate needed changes.

Management planning, on the other hand, is concerned with the effective and efficient attainment of goals and objectives that have been agreed upon and accepted. It may, therefore, be conceptualized as that portion of the planning process that is implemented *after* the basic decisions relating to goals and policies have been made. Through appropriate management planning, those responsible for the implementation of these decisions maximize the chance that goals and objectives are achieved.

Strategic and management planning are interrelated in many ways and, from

[7] For example, see discussion by Richard C. Lonsdale in Edgar L. Morphet and David L. Jesser, eds. *Preparing Educators to Meet Emerging Needs* (New York: Citation Press, 1969), pp. 19–31, and the footnote references at end of the chapter.

[8] Willis W. Harman, "The Nature of Our Changing Society: Implications for Schools" (prepared for the ERIC Clearinghouse on Educational Administration, Eugene, Oregon, October 1969).

[9] Jack A. Culbertson et al., *The Simulation of an Urban School System* (Columbus, Ohio: University Council for Educational Administration, 1971).

a long-range point of view, the effectiveness and meaning of each will be determined primarily by the effectiveness and meaning of the other. Unless appropriate goals and policies are identified and accepted through strategic planning, even the most effective management planning will have limited significance. On the other hand, unless management planning ensures that the goals are achieved and policies implemented effectively, many of the potential dividends from strategic planning will be lost.

The Politics and Economics of Planning

As Bowles[10] has observed, when the problems of education are not solved within the system, they are appealed to the public and the decision is ultimately in favor of the majority—that is, it is made through the political processes. Strategic planning involves political as well as other processes that can and should provide a rational and defensible basis for major decisions and, therefore, an opportunity for everyone concerned to consider most controversies and issues from a broader and more appropriate perspective or frame of reference than might otherwise be feasible.

Strategic planning should be considered a nonpartisan—rather than a partisan—political process. For example, there must be substantial agreement among the citizens of a state or local school system that such planning is essential if adequate resources are to be provided or utilized for that purpose. However, management planning and such essential matters as the collection and analysis of data should be considered primarily technical and nonpolitical.

Planning requires funds and other resources that have seldom been available in adequate amounts to local school systems and state education agencies for that purpose. If such resources were available and utilized wisely in all school systems (1) the long-range social and economic benefits of gains in student learning and progress and in the more effective utilization of staff would probably exceed the planning costs and (2) the meaningful involvement of competent citizens in the planning and decision-making processes should result in broadening the base for the support of education in some areas.

A more extensive discussion of the politics of education is presented in Chapter 8.

Initiating the Planning Process

It is not easy to initiate comprehensive long-range strategic planning in a state or local school system in which the only experience has been with short-range planning concerned primarily with establishing or complying with minimum standards or with minor changes in one or a few aspects of education. In the first place, many people (probably including a substantial number of those involved in education) may not understand the value or importance of long-range planning.

---

[10] Frank Bowles, *Educational Opportunity and Political Reality,* Paper No. 2 (New York: Academy for Educational Development, Inc., 1965), pp.2, 11.

Moreover there may not be anyone in the system who is competent or has the insights and skills needed for successful cooperative planning. However, a number of states and local school systems, even with limited resources and many competing demands, have made substantial progress with planning.

In some states the planning has been initiated by action of the legislature or by the governor. In others, sometimes with the stimulus provided by federal funds available for planning, the state education agency has taken the initiative. In most states significant progress has been made in developing staff competency, in planning, and in helping local school systems with planning.

In any state that undertakes comprehensive, long-range strategic planning, it is important that the governor, the legislature, or preferably both the governor and the legislature, give full support. Without such support little progress is likely to be made. In local school systems the initiative may come from the administration and the board or from an influential group of interested citizens. Under optimum conditions, the proposal would have the support of the board, the staff, and leading lay citizens.

Developing an Organizational Structure

It is desirable that every state education agency, regional service agency, or intermediate unit and local school system include in its organizational design appropriate provisions for planning and other related services. Unless this is done there probably will be little or no attention to long-range planning.

If a state or local system has not been involved in strategic planning, or if plans developed earlier have not recently been revised and updated, several alternatives are available. For example, the agency or school system may (1) employ some organization or group of consultants to develop the plans, (2) organize its own staff to do the planning with or without the assistance of consultants, or (3) arrange or help to arrange for the organization of a competent committee that —with the assistance of well-qualified staff members provided by the agency or school system and of consultants as needed—will determine the basic policies for the study, analyze the materials and information, and agree on the conclusions and the details of the comprehensive plan.

In view of the previous discussion and what is known about cooperative procedures, it would seem that in many school systems the third alternative listed, with appropriate adaptations, would have many advantages over the others.[11] Many states, and a number of the larger local school systems, have utilized this approach.

The committee or group responsible for policy determination should be composed of well-qualified lay citizens and educators. Membership may be determined in a variety of ways. At the state level, appointment may be made by the governor, a legislative committee, or the state board of education. At the local level, appointment is usually made by the school board or by the board and the superintendent.

---

[11] For a more detailed discussion of this and related topics, see Chaps. 3, 4, and 5 in Edgar L. Morphet, David L. Jesser, and Arthur P. Ludka, *Planning and Providing for Excellence in Education* (New York: Citation Press, Scholastic Magazines, Inc., 1971).

At the state or local level, the policy committee should be responsible for appointing a director, staff members, consultants, and perhaps special study committees, as explained in a later section. In most states and local school systems that have planning and other related specialists on the staff, continuing studies are conducted to provide a basis for determining when revisions in the basic plans are needed. All decisions concerning basic policies are or should be made by the board rather than by the specialists.

THE NATURE AND PROCESSES OF PLANNING

As has been indicated there are wide differences in opinions about what the term "planning" means or implies. Howsam has observed that, "There is much semantic looseness among educators where change is concerned."[12] There seems to be as much or perhaps more "semantic looseness" among educators and lay citizens about what planning means. Among educators it is almost impossible to identify anyone who is willing to admit that he or she does not plan. However, in many instances educators plan to do tomorrow that which they did yesterday and, as a consequence, fail to give serious consideration to (1) determining what the future may or should be like and (2) selecting from various alternatives the procedures that are best designed to facilitate attainment of the future state or condition that is needed. Huefner has commented that

> Everyone plans—but not very well. Most of our actions are influenced by expectations of the future and a written—or at least a mental—"plan" of how that future can be improved. *But seldom have these plans been subjected to a critical evaluation of assumptions and objectives, or a careful coordination with other plans to which they must relate.*[13]

Some people prefer to describe or define planning as "to make plans"; that is, they emphasize the plans as the *product* of planning. In this context, planning presumably has taken place when a teacher develops lesson plans or when an administrator develops a budget which is considered a *plan* for controlling expenditures. Most, however, prefer another definition: Planning is the process that is utilized to attain some goal or goals. Perceived in this manner, planning means more than the development of plans; it is viewed as *a process* or a method that is developed to achieve some purpose and, therefore, is *future oriented*. Thus, by utilizing appropriate planning procedures and processes, it is possible to gain some control over future developments. This concept has prompted many planning projects and efforts in education during recent years and has contributed to the idea that many aspects of the future can be, in large measure, the kind of future for which we plan.

[12] Robert B. Howsam, "Effecting Needed Changes in Education," in Edgar L. Morphet and Charles O. Ryan, eds., *Planning and Effecting Needed Changes in Education* (New York: Citation Press, Scholastic Magazines, Inc., 1967), p. 71.

[13] Robert P. Huefner, "Strategies and Procedures in State and Local Planning," in Morphet and Ryan, eds., *Planning and Effecting Needed Changes in Education*, p. 16.

Some people may consider use of the word "technology" inappropriate in the context of a discussion relating to the processess or techniques of planning. This is understandable because that term is often used to refer to *products* rather than to *processes*. However, "technology" can be used to describe a process or processes and, because this section deals with some technical processes, the authors have used the phrase "technologies of planning" to describe them.

Each of the various planning technologies has its own unique characteristics but also has elements in common with other technologies. Each, when used properly, will contribute significantly to the attainment of appropriate goals pertinent to any plans that may be developed. Moreover, each in its own way will contribute to the development of a total process that makes it possible to (1) ascertain and analyze existing conditions with respect to needed conditions; (2) design, develop, and test strategies or procedures that are likely to achieve the conditions needed; and (3) implement, evaluate, and modify as needed those strategies that are developed. There are two elements or characteristics that every planning technology, regardless of its specialized approach, should have: planning, to be effective, must be systematic, and it should be comprehensive.

Systematic planning. The concept of systematic (and usually long-range) planning has been an integral component of the planning efforts of various segments of society for some time. The military, for example, has utilized the concept to solve perplexing problems since the beginning of World War II; scientists have utilized it in their quest for solutions to problems of medicine, biochemistry, and space travel. Planners in these fields have recognized the existence and interrelationship of the many microsystems or subsystems that contribute to the effective and efficient functioning of the macrosystem or total system. It has only been relatively recently, however, that many educators have begun to understand the significance of the facts (discussed in Chapter 3) that (1) education is a macrosystem with many subsystems that operates in some relationship to numerous other macrosystems, each of which also has subsystems; (2) the many important interrelationships among educational subsystems and between the educational system and other social systems must be recognized and understood; and therefore (3) educational and other planners need to utilize the concepts of systems and systematic planning, as a basis for developing more effective plans.

Comprehensive planning. Most planning in education has been concerned primarily or exclusively with one level or with some aspect of education and frequently has given little attention to other agencies and services (such as health and similar service agencies and programs) that may have many important implications for education.

Bona fide comprehensive strategic planning concerned with all levels and aspects of education is complex and difficult but should be undertaken in every state probably about once every decade because all levels and aspects of education are interrelated in many important, but often ignored, ways. At least periodic comprehensive planning for each major level of education should be considered essential and serious efforts made to ensure that the goals and procedures proposed are interrelated. Such questions as the following should be considered by every group involved: What will be the impact or effect of each proposed change on other aspects or levels of education? What forces and factors are likely to facilitate implementation of the desired change? To retard or prevent it?

When planning is comprehensive, it is essential that (1) values and goals be defined clearly, (2) policies relate effectively to the changes that are planned, and (3) every important and relevant factor be considered.

In addition to its systematic and comprehensive aspects, planning should relate to certain time frames. Nix[14] has identified three interrelated time frames or spans for planning:

1. *Futuristic span.* The planning group or agency looks ten or more years into the future and, from what it perceives, derives broad directions for development—that is, long-range goals.

2. *Development span.* Each unit in the agency then sets developmental goals for itself to be reached in three, four, or five years. Operational strategies and project-type endeavors are devised and implemented to bring about goal achievement. With large margins for contingencies, resources are earmarked for the endeavors and the plans provide the basic direction for the organization.

3. *Short span.* This is the mode of management by objectives. A division of project management sets down in writing what it will have accomplished six months or twelve months hence. It also identifies the operations it will undertake to produce these accomplishments and concurrently distributes, by budget, resources to the respective operations.

Specialized planning technologies. As the need for more systematic planning to effect needed changes has become increasingly apparent, a variety of specialized and interrelated (although seemingly discrete) technologies has been developed. These include the "systems approach," the planning–programming–budgeting system (PPBS), operations research (OR), the educational resources management system (ERMS), the program evaluation and review technique (PERT), the critical path method (CPM), and others that are less well known. Each technology is most useful for certain tasks or aspects of planning. Educational planners, therefore, should identify and utilize the specific technology or combination of technologies that best suits the purposes of the planning effort. These technologies have been discussed in numerous articles and books.[15]

Because experts are most familiar with and attach high value to the techniques commonly utilized in their area of specialization, one caution seems appropriate for those who are involved in educational planning: The best techniques or technologies do not necessarily solve complex problems such as many encountered in education; these problems can only be resolved by people who understand the needs and concerns of society and the role of education in a dynamic society.

[14] Charles Nix, *Planmaking Capabilities in State Education Agencies* (Denver, Colo.: Improving State Leadership in Education, 1972), p. 4.

[15] For example, see Morphet and Ryan, eds., *Planning and Effecting Needed Changes in Education,* Chap. 12, and Edgar L. Morphet and David L. Jesser, eds., *Planning for Effective Utilization of Technology in Education* (New York: Citation Press, Scholastic Magazines, Inc., 1968).

The various technologies should, therefore, be viewed as essential tools and procedures that must be used intelligently and perceptively by competent people who are responsible for attempting to solve these problems.

The Processes of Planning

As was indicated, the development of plans should always be recognized as an essential *means* to make it possible to accomplish some important purposes. The ultimate purpose of all planning in education is to help to ensure not only that the provisions, programs, and procedures will be effective and efficient in meeting the learning needs of all who can benefit from education but also that those who benefit are prepared to contribute to the orderly and wholesome development of a dynamic society.[16] It is essential for everyone who is engaged in or concerned about planning to understand that it (1) is a systematic *human* process that usually involves many kinds of people, (2) has essential technical aspects, and (3) requires a series of logical steps and procedures. The major steps and procedures are discussed briefly in the paragraphs that follow; those that have special significance for planning improvements in educational programs and learning opportunities are discussed more fully in that context in Chapter 14.

Agreement on purposes. In any cooperative effort that involves representatives of several different publics, there are likely to be divergent views about the purposes of the endeavor. If each participant perceives the purpose of the planning effort as serving primarily the ends of any group to which he or she belongs, it is probable that little or nothing will be accomplished. Thus, it is essential at the beginning that the leader and all members of the group agree on a common purpose and on major goals. Moreover, as anyone who has worked with committees or other groups knows, there may be a tendency for the group to want to move rapidly in the direction of specifics and to avoid consideration of broadly conceived goals and concepts. If this occurs—that is, if details are dealt with in the absence of any agreement on purposes and procedures—a built-in mechanism may be developed for rejection by individual members of any proposals that are not consistent with their major interests or concerns. Therefore, as preparations are made for meaningful planning efforts, it is essential that there be a commonality of understanding and acceptance of the major purposes of planning.

Organization and personnel. Some of the basic considerations relating to the development of an organizational structure for strategic planning are discussed earlier in this chapter. When an appropriate structure has been established by or for a state or local school system, the commission or agency responsible should (1) agree upon the purpose, scope, and time span, and determine the resources allotted or available and (2) decide upon the basic policies, the kinds of studies and personnel needed, and the organization and relationships considered essential. Some of the important guidelines usually observed are

---

[16] For a rather comprehensive discussion of this concept, see Morphet and Jesser, *Cooperative Planning for Education in 1980.*

- A competent executive director, who understands education as well as the planning processes, is selected to guide and coordinate all studies and activities.
- A special study committee, and perhaps a consultant, is appointed for each major aspect (such as educational programs, personnel, organization and administration, and finance) and its responsibilities and relationships are made clear.
- The sponsoring commission or agency studies all findings and recommendations of these committees and assumes the responsibility for developing (with any assistance that is needed) defensible and well-coordinated plans.

As was noted earlier, the services of a variety of technicians and other types of experts are essential in developing defensible plans. It is necessary, however, that they as well as others involved in the planning process recognize and understand that the specialists should not attempt either to develop the plans or to make the basic policy decisions. On the other hand it is essential that those responsible for developing policies and plans carefully consider all suggestions, findings, and conclusions of these specialists.

Needs and goals. The determination of needs and the formulation of goals, from one point of view, are separate steps. In reality, however, they are interrelated in so many ways that they cannot be completely separated in practice. Few of the broad statements of goals that are based on the long-accepted beliefs and value judgments of the citizens about the place and role of education in each state and in the nation are likely to be changed significantly; in fact, many of them have not yet been attained in most parts of the nation as shown by studies of needs. On the other hand, systematic studies will provide empirical evidence regarding unsolved problems and unmet needs and will help to direct attention to previously unrecognized—or at least unstated—goals relating to provisions for organization, financial support, and other matters as well as to educational programs and instructional procedures. Identification of and agreement on appropriate goals not only makes it possible to devise and implement optimum ways of achieving them, but it also provides a sound basis for establishing accountability as noted in other chapters.

Any realistic identification and assessment of needs is a complex and difficult undertaking in a state or large local school system. Although much information can be obtained through an adequate management information system, if one has been developed, considerable supplementary data will almost always have to be obtained and carefully analyzed if all needs are to be determined.

Priorities. Some goals are more important and certain needs are more serious than others. Because it will be impossible to attain all goals and, in the process, to meet all needs in a relatively short period of time, it will be necessary for every group involved in planning to agree on short- and long-range priorities. Appropriate criteria for determining priorities should be identified and accepted as a basis for making the necessary decisions. In all situations the basic criterion should probably be the following: The highest priority should be given to those goals which, when achieved, will result in the maximum educational benefits for students at a reasonable cost. In some states this might mean that reorganizing districts, revising provisions for support of schools, or removing restrictive provisions in the constitution or laws should have highest priority. In some local school systems, improving the curriculum, instructional procedures, or even the administrative organization and policies might receive high priority.

Alternatives. Frequently there are several feasible ways of achieving a desired goal or a series of related goals and of meeting certain needs in the process. After needs have been determined and goals agreed upon it is essential to (1) identify these alternatives and (2) ascertain the advantages and disadvantages—the probable implications or consequences—of each as a basis for selecting on a rational basis one that seems to be the most promising and defensible. (See Chapter 15 for a more detailed discussion relating to educational programs and Chapter 6 for processes of decision making.)

Implementation, evaluation, and revision. The development of plans has little meaning unless the plans are implemented—that is, are utilized as a basis for effecting improvements. As was indicated, the strategic planning process should be designed to facilitate implementation. The plans will (or should) specify what is to be done and provide some indications as to how certain things can best be accomplished, but they should not attempt to specify the policies and details that will be required for effective implementation. The management planning team should be expected to assume this essential but difficult responsibility. It can most effectively do so when (1) some of the members have been involved in the entire planning process and (2) those who will be most affected by the policies and procedures have an opportunity to participate in the development of these plans.

Regardless of the approach utilized, all plans are likely to include some proposals that, for one reason or another, do not work out satisfactorily. Provisions should therefore be made for continuous study and monitoring to determine the extent to which goals are being met, whether any conflicts or disharmonies are encountered, and so on, to provide a basis for needed revisions. The process of monitoring and modification may be conceived as a series of "feedback loops" that provide for the recycling of any modification that may be found necessary, either for the discrete steps or for the overall planning endeavor.[17]

SOME IMPORTANT PROBLEMS AND ISSUES

Although most people probably would agree that many changes in education are needed urgently, there are sharp disagreements about what changes should be made as well as about how and by whom they should be made. In this country, the decisions relating to major educational policies have always been determined

[17] For a more detailed discussion of this concept, see Donald W. Johnson and Donald R. Miller, "A System Approach to Planning for the Utilization of Technology in Education" in Edgar L. Morphet and David L. Jesser, eds., *Planning for Effective Utilization of Technology in Education* (New York: Citation Press, Scholastic Magazines, Inc., 1968), p. 207–211.

by the citizens or their representatives. Moreover, unless a majority of the citizens in a state or community understands the need for making major changes in education and are convinced that these changes will result in improvements, they are not likely to be made.

How Can the Kinds of Cooperation Needed for Strategic Planning be Facilitated?

In any group, and perhaps especially in a group concerned with educational planning that includes both lay citizens and educators, there may be some people who insist that others cooperate with them—that is, help them to get their own proposals adopted. When this happens, sharp controversies may develop or some of the decisions may be based on extraneous factors rather than on serious consideration of the evidence, or on what would best meet the needs of education in a changing society. What should the leader or members of the group do to help to ensure bona fide cooperation in developing constructive and defensible proposals for improving education? Some suggested guidelines relating to cooperative procedures are as follows:

- All cooperative efforts to improve education should utilize and observe the basic concepts or principles pertaining to satisfactory human relations, including (1) respect for each individual, yet continuing recognition of the fact that the common good must always be considered, (2) consideration of the talents and abilities of all persons who can make a contribution should be utilized, and (3) recognition that the thinking and conclusions of two or more persons with a good understanding of the problems and issues are likely, in most cases, to be more reliable than are the conclusions of one individual.
- The procedures used in any cooperative effort should be designed to ensure that conclusions will be reached on the basis of pertinent evidence and desirable goals.
- The leaders understand and believe in cooperative procedures.[18]

Are any of these guidelines inappropriate? If so, which ones? What are some others that should be helpful?

What Are Some of the Major Problems in Effecting Improvements in Education?

Although most people apparently agree that major improvements are needed, many seem to underestimate the need and pressures for change. On the other hand, some educators and lay citizens either seek to continue traditional programs and procedures with minor changes or tend to support what seem to be promising

[18] Adapted from Edgar L. Morphet, *Cooperative Procedures in Education* (Hong Kong: Hong Kong University Press, 1957), pp. 5–9, and Edgar L. Morphet, chairman, *Citizen Cooperation for Better Schools* (Chicago: National Society for the Study of Education, Fifty-third Yearbook, Part I, 1954), Chap. 10.

proposals for change in some aspect of education without considering either the implications for other aspects or feasible alternatives. If they become involved in planning, they may assume that the problems in the future will be essentially the same as those encountered in the past, except perhaps that more effort may be required to resolve them. In fact, they may find themselves in the position of planning for education in the kind of society in which they have been living rather than for education to meet the needs of a dynamic and rapidly changing society. What are some of the other problems and hazards or pitfalls in planning improvements in education? How can they be avoided or minimized?

Under What Conditions, If Any, Should Changes in Education be Mandated?

It may be fortunate that some people involved in organizations, agencies, and institutions tend to resist some proposals for change. If they sought change indiscriminately, life and society could soon become chaotic. When changes in education come too slowly to meet the needs, however, many people become critical and may either react in ways that would tend to handicap the students in a school system or seek to have the legislature or the board mandate the changes they consider desirable. Some people seem to think that when a law has been passed or a regulation adopted the problem has been solved. But many legal mandates (for example, those relating to equality of educational opportunity and integration) have resulted only in superficial changes, or the mandate has sometimes been ignored. Some standards or requirements seem to be essential, but most people apparently believe the emphasis in education should be on helping and encouraging staff, students, and lay citizens to seek to achieve excellence rather than on relying on laws or standards.

Should some changes in education be mandated by law or board policy? If so, what kinds of changes and under what conditions? How can undesirable kinds of mandates best be avoided?

What Is Implied by the Term "Cooperation"?

Although the term "cooperation" means to work or associate with others for mutual benefit, some "leaders" seem to think it can be interpreted to mean manipulation of other people for their own benefit—that is, helping the leaders achieve their own purposes and goals. From this distorted perspective there seem to be three kinds of "cooperation": authoritarian, controlled, and voluntary.

- *Authoritarian* cooperation is essentially the master-slave concept of human relations. The leader or leaders do all the thinking and give all the instructions. The followers or workers cooperate by carrying out all instructions.
- *Controlled* or pseudodemocratic cooperation is the same in principle as authoritarian cooperation. The leader decides what he or she wants done and uses subtle and clever means to ensure that the "right" decisions are made by the group. The "leader" may attempt to manipulate a group into agreeing

with previously determined conclusions by using any or all of the following devices: (1) encouraging the appointment of members who agree with personal purposes and goals; (2) appearing to encourage bona fide thinking and discussion, but attempting to limit or slant the information to which they have access; or (3) commending certain suggestions, and ignoring or passing lightly over others. A leader of this kind must be very clever because most members would be resentful if they realized the administrator was attempting to control their thinking and conclusions. It is surprising, however, how often the techniques of attempting to secure controlled cooperation are used in the United States by authoritarian leaders who insist that they are using democratic processes.

- *Voluntary* cooperation tends to be facilitated when people are not only free to think for themselves but are encouraged to do so. It is the opposite of the master-slave relationship, because all citizens are recognized as peers. People are not manipulated and each person is encouraged to contribute to the thinking of the group.

How can the schools and colleges prepare citizens who not only understand and support bona fide cooperative procedures but who also can detect and discredit the kinds of leaders who attempt to manipulate the thinking of members of a group? How can members of a group best cope with a leader who seems to be attempting to control their decisions?

How Can Leaders Facilitate
Needed Changes in Education?

One of the characteristics of an effective leader is that of helping to establish and facilitate the attainment of appropriate goals. This often means that the leader must help people prepare to effect needed changes. Argyris has observed that "effective change occurs when the changes are long lasting, when they are self-monitoring, and when they are reinforcing of system competence and lead to further system development."[19] As he has noted, some people believe that change may be more effective when attention is centered first on structural changes; others believe it should begin with interpersonal relationships. What criteria should leaders concerned with improvements in education use to determine when and under what conditions a proposed change (1) would be likely to meet the tests listed in the quotation above and (2) should be initially concerned with structure or with people?

Significant changes in a social system such as education usually are not made easily. Careful planning can help to minimize, but will not eliminate, the inevitable feeling of insecurity on the part of many people, some of whom may become resentful or antagonistic. Some perceptive "interventionists" may be necessary to facilitate stability and ensure progress. The purpose of any such intervention should be to find ways of utilizing the tensions to motivate individuals to seek more information, to design appropriate procedures, and to develop a commitment

---

[19] Chris Argyris, *Management and Organizational Development* (New York: McGraw-Hill Book Company, 1970), p. 164.

to the goals as well as to procedures. In education, who should play the role of interventionist? How? Should the interventionists be authoritative or authoritarian? What criteria should they utilize to facilitate cooperation in attaining the goals and, in the process, effecting the needed changes?

How Can the Best Alternatives for Improving Education Be Determined?

Whether or not the educational provisions and procedures throughout a state will be more adequate and effective within ten years than they are at present will be determined by many factors including decisions that are made in the meantime. If most changes result from pressures or haphazard developments, some may be beneficial, and others may have little significance or could actually be harmful from a long-range point of view. If, however, changes are planned systematically—utilizing the most competent leaders and the best information, insights, and procedures available—the prospects for improving all aspects of education for everyone who could benefit should be greatly enhanced. The kind of systematic cooperative planning needed, however, is not likely to occur unless it is given high priority by political and other lay and educational leaders and is strongly supported by most citizens. What steps should be taken to help to ensure that this is done?

In this complex process many important and difficult decisions will need to be made at every stage and for every aspect. The matter of selecting the best and most defensible alternatives, for example, is vital but has often been given inadequate attention. Although agreement on goals is essential, it may have little practical meaning unless the best or most defensible procedures for attaining each goal and effective ways of measuring progress are agreed upon and utilized. To be more specific, let us assume that in a certain state one goal is to ensure that during the first three years in school every normal student will have learned to read sufficiently well that, with minimum assistance thereafter, that student will not be seriously handicapped by reading difficulties. Is this goal desirable and feasible, as some authorities contend? Is this proposal based on value judgments or on valid evidence? If on the latter, what is the evidence?

SELECTED REFERENCES

Argyris, Chris, *Interpersonal Competence and Organizational Effectiveness.* Homewood, Ill.: Richard W. Irwin, Inc., 1962.

——, *Intervention Theory and Method: A Behavioral Science View.* Reading, Mass.: Addison-Wesley Publishing Company, 1970.

Bennis, Warren G., Kenneth D. Benne, and **Robert Chin,** eds., *The Planning of Change* (2nd ed.). New York: Holt, Rinehart and Winston, Inc., 1969.

Burns, James MacGregor, *Leadership.* New York: Harper and Row, Publishers, Inc., 1978.

Elam, Stanley, and **Gordon I. Swanson,** eds., *Educational Planning in the United States.* Itasca, Ill.: F. E. Peacock Publishers, Inc., 1969.

English, Fenwick W., *School Organization and Management,* Chap. 6. Worthington, Ohio: Charles A. Jones Publishing Company, 1975.

Hack, Walter, et. al., *Educational Futurism 1985: Challenges for Schools and Their Administrators.* Berkeley, Calif.: McCutchan Publishing Corporation, 1971.

Marien, Michael, and Warren L. Ziegler, eds., *The Potential of Educational Futures.* Worthington, Ohio: Charles A. Jones Publishing Company, 1972.

Morphet, Edgar L., and Charles O. Ryan, eds., *Planning and Effecting Needed Changes in Education.* Denver, Colo.: Designing Education for the future, 1967. Republished by Citation Press, Scholastic Magazines, Inc., New York.

——, and David L. Jesser, eds., *Cooperative Planning for Education in 1980,* and *Planning for Effective Utilization of Technology in Education.* Denver, Colo.: Designing Education for the Future, 1968. Republished by Citation Press, Scholastic Magazines, Inc., New York.

——, David L. Jesser, and Arthur P. Ludka, *Planning and Providing for Excellence in Education.* Denver, Colo.: Improving State Leadership in Education, 1971. Republished by Citation Press, Scholastic Magazines, Inc., New York.

Ravitch, Diane, *The Revisionists Revised.* New York: Basic Books, Inc., Publishers, 1978.

Thompson, John Thomas, *Policymaking in American Public Education.* Englewood Cliffs, N.J.: Prentice-Hall, Inc., 1976.

8

THE POLITICS
of EDUCATION

According to Simon, as was pointed out in Chapter 4, "Two persons, given the same possible alternatives, the same values, the same knowledge, can rationally reach only the same decision." In the real world, however, it is almost impossible to find two persons with the same values and the same knowledge or two persons who give the same priority to each value. Furthermore, all decisions of any consequence in the school social system affect many persons in the different subsystems of the school social system. Those persons differ widely in their goals and values. How can decisions be made when different groups in the school social system differ in their choices of policy alternatives? In a monolithic dictatorship such as that in the Soviet Union, there is no problem. The decision is made at the top of the hierarchy, and, if a group opposes the decision, it is charged with the crime of subversion.

In a democracy, such as that in the United States, the decision is made by the political process which provides the opportunity for groups and individuals to make inputs into the decision-making process. Supporters of public education have frequently urged that "politics should be kept out of the schools." But political scientists have long pointed out that public schools are political institutions and that decisions on education must necessarily be made by political processes.

Those who have urged that politics should be kept out of the schools have never meant that all educational decisions should be made by educational experts or by duly elected boards of education acting in closed sessions. What is really meant is that graft, political patronage, bribery, and other undesirable practices should be kept out of the public schools. These practices are undesirable politics and should be kept out of all kinds of government as well as the public schools. Sometimes the public school system and administrators and teachers are the victims of vicious, untruthful charges. That is unethical politics.

It has also been argued that boards of education should be elected on a nonpartisan basis. That policy is not to remove the schools from politics but rather to open the school social system to inputs from the total community.

Some school superintendents and principals have interpreted "keeping the politics out of the schools" to mean that they should make all of the decisions. Superintendents of that belief expect the board to "rubber stamp" all their decisions without question, and principals of like belief have not wanted their teachers or their school patrons to question their decisions or to participate in making decisions. That type of decision-making model does not keep politics out of the schools; it simply provides that all political decisions be made by a dictator. That type of political leadership is no longer acceptable in most communities.

All public school administrators must deal with the politics of education. Therefore, it is desirable that they be aware of the political systems with which they must deal and the political processes involved in decision making. The purpose of this chapter is to present, in a nontechnical fashion, some of the basic elements of the politics of education in elementary and secondary education with which practicing school administrators must deal.

Private schools are also involved in politics. Space does not permit an adequate discussion of the politics of private education. Suffice it to say that it is just as legitimate for private schools to be involved in politics as the public schools. Many states pass laws or regulations affecting the private schools in such matters as school curriculum, certification of teachers, school accreditation, health and safety standards of the school plant, school transportation, tax exemption, and other matters. Private schools are involved in the financing of the school lunch program in all states and the financing of school transportation and school textbooks in some states. Some leaders of private education are advocating general financial aid for private schools through the use of vouchers or tax credits on state and federal income taxes. Private schools are politically active at all governmental levels—local, state, and federal. Some of the discussions presented in the pages following are as applicable to private education as they are to public education.

SOME BASIC CONCEPTS OF POLITICS

In the following paragraphs, some basic concepts of the nature of politics are presented.

Definition of Politics

What is politics? A realistic definition of politics was presented by Lasswell, who defined politics as "who gets what, when and how."[1] This broad definition covers all types of politics both desirable and undesirable.

Easton has defined politics in education as "the authoritative allocation of values for a society."[2] His definition seems to exclude undesirable politics because his definition is concerned only with legitimate political activity. Easton enumerated the following three main types of values which were allocated differentially in the public schools: (1) Social mobility. Some schools provide curricula and learning experiences which provide more social mobility for their clients than do other schools. (2) Norms. Schools differ in the societal norms concerning racism, sexism, citizenship, cooperation, individual effort, and many other matters. (3) Business allocation. The schools are big business, spending many billions of dollars annually. The allocation of those resources involves many value choices.

Another definition of politics is that it is "the process of exercising power and influence in formulating and legitimizing policies."[3] Kimbrough and Nunnery state that, when administrators attempt to influence the formulation of policies, they are exercising political leadership and that collective bargaining is a political process because it involves the use of power in decision making.[4]

Social Systems Theory and Politics

As was pointed out in Chapter 3, any social system such as a school system is comprised of a number of subsystems and suprasystems. These systems all interact with each other and with the environment. For example, subsystems attempt to influence suprasystems, suprasystems control and influence subsystems, the community controls and influences the school system, and the school system influences the community.

A school system can be conceptualized as being comprised of the following subsystems: (1) pupils, (2) teachers and other nonadministrative employees (3) administrators, (4) the board of education, and (5) the community. Each of these systems has goals in addition to the legitimized goals of the school system. Each of these systems attempts to influence or control the actions and beliefs of the other systems to the extent necessary to satisfy its own needs. These are legitimate political activities in a democratic, open, social system. However, the governing authorities of a school system must always be concerned that the political activities of the subsystems of the school might prevent the school system from maximizing the attainment of its goals. The Getzels model discussed in Chapter 3 accurately depicts the

[1] Harold Lasswell, *Politics: Who Gets What, When, How* (New York: McGraw-Hill Book Company, 1936).
[2] David Easton, *A Framework for Political Analysis* (Englewood Cliffs, N.J.: Prentice-Hall, Inc. 1965), p. 50.
[3] See Ralph B. Kimbrough and Michael Y. Nunnery, *Educational Administration—An Introduction* (New York: Macmillan Publishing Co., Inc., 1976), p. 333.
[4] *Ibid.*, pp. 333–334.

dilemma of the administrator. The administrator must not only permit but must also encourage the political activities of subsystems in the school system to meet the needs of the members of the organization, but the administrator is also held accountable for the attainment of organizational goals.

Politics as Conflict Resolution

School administrators and boards of education in general try to avoid conflict. This is understandable because conflict makes administrators and board members feel uncomfortable, and excessive conflict may cause a breakdown (entropy) in the school system. Some conflict in a school system such as personal enmity between individuals is destructive and should be avoided if possible. However, most conflict in school decision making is necessary and in some cases may be quite beneficial.

The board must allocate financial resources because financial resources always seem to be scarce. Different interest groups compete for these scarce resources. For example, the teachers may want a 10 percent increase in salary and school patrons want a 10 percent decrease in the pupil–teacher ratio. The board does not have sufficient funds to satisfy both requests. The board must make choices. This is the normal process of budget making, and a good budget cannot be made unless competing interests are politically active in presenting their needs to the board.

Institutions of higher education and the public schools compete for revenue at the federal level and sometimes at the state level. Both compete with all other governmental functions for the allocation of resources. This competition is natural and healthy except in cases in which the public schools and institutions of higher education engage in open conflict and cast doubt on the validity of the financial needs of each. In such situations both the public schools and the institutions of higher education are likely to lose in the competition with other functions of government for resources.

As was pointed out in Chapter 3, sometimes a social system attains a static equilibrium and does not change with the needs of the times. That sometimes happens to a school system that does not change its curriculum in accordance with the changing demands of the community. If the school system does not satisfy the needs of the community, conflict results and the voters of the community may take political action to change the board and its administration. School systems in a state of dynamic equilibrium will change in accordance with the needs of the times and avoid destructive conflict.

Desirable educational innovations are frequently sparked by conflict. Interactions among the different elements of a living social system frequently accompanied by conflict are the political activities that keep a school system in a state of dynamic equilibrium. A state of dynamic equilibrium facilitates the attainment of desirable organizational goals and also the satisfaction of the needs of the members of the system. Therefore, conflict in a social system may be beneficial as well as disruptive.

Political activities involving education are found at the school system level, the state level, the federal level, and in the education bureaucracy at all levels. These activities are discussed in the paragraphs that follow.

SCHOOL POLITICS AT THE LOCAL LEVEL

Local political activities occur at the local school center level and at the school system level. The most important policy decisions are made by the board of education at the school system level. However, as has been noted already, the board in making its decisions is influenced by the superintendent, the principals, the teachers and other school employees, formal and informal interest groups, the state government, and the federal government. In this section, the politics of education at the local level is discussed.

Special Interest Groups

Special interest groups both within the formal school organization and in its environment try to affect the decisions of boards by the use of influence and sometimes by the use of power. Frequently, these groups oppose each other. For example, teachers and other school employees in many school systems are organized into unions, and they engage in collective barganing with the board to increase salaries and fringe benefits. If these requests are granted, additional financing may be required, and this involves increased taxes. On the other hand taxpayer groups bring pressure on the board of education to hold the line on taxes or even cut taxes.

Pressure is being brought on many boards of education by the NAACP for affirmative action for increasing the number of blacks in administrative positions. Activist women groups are also urging boards of education to increase the number of women in administrative positions. But white males in some school systems argue that affirmative action discriminates against them.

Boards of education are sometimes pressured by religious sects, veterans groups, patriotic societies, extreme rightist groups, extreme leftist groups, and others to change the school curriculum and to censure textbooks and library books. Some of these groups vehemently oppose each other. Some groups of parents insist that the board go back to basics and give almost exclusive emphasis in the elementary school to the "three R's." Other parents want an enriched curriculum in the elementary school including art, music, literature, and other learning experiences that develop the "whole child."

These conflicts frequently place the superintendent of schools and the board of education in dilemmas. But such is the price of democracy. The alternative is to operate a closed school system with no inputs from interest groups. But such a system will not be tolerated very long in the American democracy. The alternative available to the public is to change the board and the administration. Therefore the board must receive all these inputs but it obviously cannot satisfy all groups. As was pointed out in Chapter 6, the board sometimes "satisfices" rather than satisfies. But, if a critical value is involved, the board must have the courage to make the necessary decision even though it is unpopular with some group or groups. If it does not do so, it is not fit to govern the school system, and in time it will be discredited and discontinued in office.

School principals are also frequently involved in the politics of education. Most principals have a parent–teacher organization of some kind. Some states are experimenting with school-based management, the purpose being to move considerable decision making from the district level to the local school level. Local school advisory committees have been established by law in some states. The greater the authority given to the principal and staff to make decisions, the greater the amount of school politics at the local level. In the long run, this may be beneficial to the school system. It greatly increases the inputs of the school patrons into the school system. In large school systems, it is difficult for the patrons of an individual school to communicate with the board of education. Furthermore, in a large school system, there is no reason why every school of the same grade level should have exactly the same program. Input and political activity at the local school level increases the probability that the school program will be adapted to the needs of the pupils of individual schools. Increasing political activity at the local school level will also increase the amount of conflict at the local school level. But conflict is not always destructive. Sometimes conflict can result in needed innovations.[5]

Community Power Structures

It has long been recognized that some people in every community have more influence than have other people. The systematic study of community power structures began in the 1950s.[6] The pioneer in that movement was Floyd Hunter.[7] He made a case study of Regional City using the "reputational technique."[8] He found a monopolistic power structure comprised of a small number of elites who effectively controlled most of the significant decisions made in that city. Many social scientists generalized from that study and other studies that the power structure of most cities and towns was monopolistic.

Dahl in 1961 made a case study of the power structure of New Haven, Connecticut using the decision analysis technique and found a pluralistic power structure.[9] Dahl's study and numerous subsequent studies have shown that the anatomies of power structures differ in different communities.

Johns and Kimbrough made an extensive study of community power structure and its relationship to decision making on school finance in twenty-four districts in four states.[10] Six districts of 20,000 population and above were selected from

---

[5] See Fenwick W. English, *School Organization and Management* (Worthington, Ohio: Charles A. Jones Publishing Company, 1975), Chap. 5.

[6] Previous studies of community power influence had been reported by William Warner et al. in *Democracy in Jonesville* (New York: Harper & Row Publishers, Inc., 1949) and Robert S. and Helen M. Lynd in *Middletown in Transition* (New York: Harcourt Brace Jovanovich, 1937) but these studies did not deal extensively with the structure of community power.

[7] Floyd Hunter, *Community Power Structure* (Chapel Hill: University of North Carolina, 1953).

[8] The reputational technique involves requesting influential people of a community to identify the persons who they believe have the most power and influence in the community. The decision analysis technique consists of an analysis of the persons in the community who have been active in supporting or opposing decisions being made by the governing authorities or by popular vote.

[9] Robert A. Dahl, *Who Governs?* (New Haven, Conn.: Yale University Press, 1961).

[10] Roe L. Johns and Ralph B. Kimbrough, *The Relationship of Socioeconomic Factors, Educational Leadership Patterns and Elements of Community Power Structure to Local School Fiscal Policy*, Final Report, Office of Education, Cooperative Research Project No. 1324 (Gainesville: University of Florida, 1968).

each state, three of which were high-effort districts and three of which were low-effort districts. Four types of power structures were found in those twenty-four districts: (1) monopolistic elite, (2) multigroup noncompetitive, (3) competitive elite, and (4) segmented pluralism. Table 8.1 presents a tabulation of districts in these four categories.[11]

The monopolistic elite structure is similar to that found by Hunter in Regional City. In that model a few powerful influentials controlled the decision making on matters in which they were concerned.

(2) The multigroup noncompetitive structure is found in school systems in which two or more groups of powerful influentials exist but have approximately the same values, goals, and beliefs. Therefore, they are in general agreement on most issues.

(3) The competitive elite structure is found in a district in which two or more elite groups compete with each other for power.

(4) A segmented pluralism structure is found in districts in which many groups compete and there is wide citizen participation in decision making. No one group dominates and the influence of different groups changes from time to time. An open school system is demanded in districts with a segmented pluralism structure. Johns and Kimbrough found very few school board members or superintendents of schools who were members of the community power structure.

The data presented in Table 8.1 show clearly that school districts vary greatly in the typology of their power structures. Segmented pluralism structures and competitive elite structures are both competitive structures. Monopolistic elite and multigroup noncompetitive structures are both noncompetitive structures. Table 8.2 shows that districts with competitive power structures tend to be high-financial-effort districts and that districts with noncompetitive structures tend to be low-financial-effort districts. However, the data presented in Tables 8.1 and 8.2 show that districts with the same power structure differ in the decisions made on school finance. Therefore, school administrators should be knowledgeable of the power structures existing in their communities and keep the channels of communication between the school system and community influentials open. Usually the influentials in community power structures are solid citizens interested in the quality of life in the community as well as their economic interests. It is good politics for school administrators to keep the channels of communication open not only with

TABLE 8.1 Distribution of Power System Typologies Among Selected Districts

	MONOPOLISTIC ELITE	MULTIGROUP NON-COMPETITIVE	COMPETITIVE ELITE	SEGMENTED PLURALISM	TOTAL
High effort	3	2	5	2	12
Low effort	3	7	1	1	12
Total	6	9	6	3	24
Percentage of the 24 districts in each category	25.0%	37.5%	25.0%	12.5%	100.0%

[11] *Ibid.*, p. 112, adapted.

TABLE 8.2 Distribution of Competitive and Noncompetitive Structures by High- and Low-Effort Districts

EFFORT	NONCOMPETITIVE	COMPETITIVE	TOTAL
High effort	5	7	12
Low effort	10	2	12
Total	15	9	24

community influentials but also with the general public and all subsystems of the total school system.

Boards of education and superintendents of schools would be well advised to keep the lines of communication open with the community power structure before attempting to raise the tax rate or float a bond issue. In most school districts, it is impossible to increase taxes or float a bond issue by referendum if the community power structure disapproves the measures proposed.

Johns and Kimbrough concluded the following from their studies:

> The effective leaders of public education in the future will need to know a great deal about the politics of educational decision-making. With the passing of the years, it is becoming evident that an increasing percent of the gross national product will be expended in the public economy. The allocation of that part of the gross national product consumed by the government economy is accomplished by political processes and not by the market. Furthermore, the allocation of that portion of government expenditures devoted to public education is also accomplished by political processes.
>
> There are some who dream that government budgets, including educational budgets will sometime be determined by scientific, rational methods based on planning, programming, budgeting systems utilizing systems analysis for determining the priorities to establish for optimizing returns from alternative inputs. The researchers on this project found no evidence that these methods are being used to determine the desired level of local school financing. The evidence produced in this study indicates that the level of local effort is determined largely by political decisions resulting from the interactions of power systems with each other, conditioned by the beliefs and value systems of the components of their environment and affected only occasionally at the present time by the activities of superintendents of schools. The educational leader of the future who desires to participate effectively in political decision-making on school finance and other educational policies will be well advised to become cognizant of the interrelationships of the many forces and factors affecting political decision-making on educational policies and programs.[12]

SCHOOL POLITICS AT THE STATE LEVEL

School politics at the state level has become relatively more important during the past fifty years. Seventeen percent of public school revenues was derived from state sources in 1930, 40 percent in 1950, and 48 percent in 1979–1980. Many decisions

[12] *Ibid.*, pp. 192–193.

concerning the public schools are made at the state level including such matters as school financing, school curriculum, teacher certification, minimum standards for school accreditation, collective bargaining, school bus standards, school building standards, length of school term, and many other matters. But decisions on school financing involve more school politics at the state level than at any other decision-making area. The amount of state funds provided and the method of distribution become critical areas of decision making when almost half the school budget is provided from state sources.

It has been argued that the percentage of revenue provided from state sources does not necessarily determine the amount of state control exercised over the public schools. This may be true; but the greater the percentage of school revenue provided from state sources, the greater the potential power of state control. Simply increasing or decreasing the amount of state revenue and changing the method of state distribution are critical areas of decision making for local school districts in the states that provide a substantial percentage of school revenue from state sources. The most important decisions involving the public schools made at the state level are made through the political process.

The principal actors in the decision-making process at the state level are the governor, the legislature, the chief state school officer, the state board of education (when one is provided), and the state department of education. These officials and agencies are subject to the same pressures from special interest groups as are local boards of education. In fact, boards of education in urban districts, rural districts, wealthy districts, and districts with little wealth sometimes form special interest groups.

Prior to the middle of the 1950s, the educational power structure was monolithic in dealing with state-level decision making in many states. That is, the school administrators' organization, the school boards' organization, the teachers' organization, the parent-teacher organization, and the chief state school officer all agreed upon the same program. This monolithic group developed a powerful educational lobby that was very influential with the legislature in many states. During recent years, however, the unified action of these groups no longer exists in most states. Teachers in many states have long insisted that administrators have had too much influence in determining the financial program to be presented to the governor and the legislature. Two different statewide teachers' associations with different programs exist in many states. There is no longer a consensus on the educational program to be advocated in most states. Teachers, administrators, school boards, parent-teacher associations, the state board of education, and the chief state school officer frequently differ widely on both the educational program and the financial program needed. This development has no doubt greatly weakened the influence of the educational power structure.

Inflation began to have a powerful effect on the economy in the late 1970s. Millions of people, both employed and retired, began to experience a decline in their standards of living due to inflation. This naturally brought about a resistance to taxes and a demand for the reduction of taxes. In California, this resulted in the adoption of a constitutional amendment known as Proposition 13, which called for a major reduction of property taxes for all local governments including the public schools. At this writing, most state legislatures are more interested in tax reform and tax reduction than in improving the educational program. The influence of special antitax groups has greatly increased in recent years. This is in contrast to the years immediately following World War II, during which time there was great public support for improving the educational program and great progress was made. Current expense per pupil more than doubled between 1940 and 1960 in dollars of the same purchasing power. There was practically no increase in current expenditures per pupil between 1977 and 1980 in terms of dollars of the same purchasing power. The political success of the educational power structure in the future will no doubt be determined largely by the extent to which leaders in the system are able to form a more effective coalition of education interest groups and the economic climate of the times.

In the following paragraphs a brief discussion is presented of the political influence on the determination of educational policy of the state education agency, the governor, and the legislature.

The State Education Agency

The state education agency is comprised of the state board of education,[13] the chief state school officer, and the state department of education. Plenary authority is given to governors and state legislatures in all states to set educational policy. Campbell and Mazzoni made an extensive study of state policy making for the public schools in a sample of ten states.[14] They found that state boards of education were minor participants in setting educational policy in the states they studied and that some chief state school officers had considerable influence with governors and legislatures and others, little influence. Without exception, however, they found that the chief state school officer exerted great influence on the state board of education and the state department of education. These are important areas of influence because frequently state legislatures enact laws giving the state board of education the authority to enact regulations to implement the laws enacted. These regulations are generally administered or supervised by the state department of education.

The state department of education collects statistics on the public schools and the possession of information is a source of political power. Governors and legislatures must rely on the statistics gathered by the state department for much of their information. The same is true of state teachers' associations, superintendents' associations, school boards' associations, and the general public. Presenting information concerning the public schools is an important responsibility. The governor, the legislature, and the general public need to know the truth but the whole truth. The media including the press, television, and radio tend to emphasize the sensational. Much more attention is given to school crises, school difficulties, and school controversies than to school achievements. Therefore, school officials should present a more balanced picture of public education by emphasizing school achievements as well as school difficulties.

A more extensive discussion of the state education agency is presented in Chapter 11.

---

[13] One state, Wisconsin, did not have a state board of education at this writing.

[14] Roald F. Campbell and Tim L. Mazzoni, Jr., *State Policy Making for the Public Schools* (Berkeley, Calif.: McCutchan Publishing Corporation, 1976).

The Governor

Experienced leaders in state school politics have long contended that "If you have the governor with you, the battle is half won and if he is against you, the battle is half lost." The power of the governor to influence school legislation is undisputed. The governor has the power to veto legislation and with his or her staff, has important resources available for promoting the educational policies that he or she supports. In many states the governor has a well-qualified staff that can supply information concerning education as well as all other functions of government. In those states, the governor is not compelled to rely exclusively on the state education agency for information concerning the public schools.

Campbell and Mazzoni made an analysis of the influence of governors on state policy making in a sample of twelve states and among their conclusions were the following:

1. Governors have become involved in educational policy-making.
2. Governors varied in the extent of their involvement in educational policy-making.
3. Governors differed in the nature of their involvement in educational policy-making.
4. Governors were crucial in the formulation and initiation of fiscal legislation affecting school finance and tax reform.[15]

Governors, like legislatures and boards of education, are influenced by special interest groups. Despite the fact that public education is not usually considered to be a partisan matter, a governor has more potential influence on educational policy in a state in which he or she belongs to the same political party as the majority of legislators.

During recent years, state teachers' organizations have become much more politically active than formerly. If the teachers' association is active in its support of a candidate for governor and that person is elected to office, the teachers' association has an enhanced influence with the governor on educational policy. On the other hand, if the association supports the unsuccessful candidate, it is likely to have a negative political influence with the newly elected governor.

The State Legislature

State legislatures play the most important role in determining educational policy. Governors can veto a bill, but they cannot enact a bill into law. The legislature first deals with educational policy matters through a committee structure. The names of the committees differ from state to state. Usually, however, there will be education committees in both the upper and lower houses of the legislature, a finance committee, a ways and means or committee on taxation, and an appropriations committee. Educational interest groups must present the matters in which they are interested to these committees and must lobby individual legislators if they are successful in their political activities.

[15]*Ibid.*, pp. 169–171.

Campbell and Mazzoni requested legislators in twelve states to list certain education interest groups in the order of their influence with the legislature.[16] All states listed teachers' associations as having more influence with the legislature than any other education interest group. The state legislators differed some in their relative rank of the school administrators' association and the school boards' association. However, a majority of the legislators ranked the school boards' association second and the administrators' association third. School boards' associations and superintendents' associations usually work closely with each other. But teachers' associations sometimes differ widely from other educational interest groups. As was pointed out, in some states there are two teachers' associations, one affiliated with the NEA and the other with the AFL–CIO, each purporting to speak for the teachers. Chaos in the education power structure reduces its influence on educational policy. This conflict may have both good and bad results. It is desirable that the legislature consider all reasonable alternatives when it considers educational policy, and it may not consider those alternatives if its inputs are received exclusively from a monolithic education power structure. On the other hand, controversy in the education power structure may confuse the legislature and create a situation in which the opponents of educational progress are successful in retarding progress.

A number of state legislatures have established a qualified staff for each of its major committees. The professional staff for the education committees evaluates proposals from the education power structure and proposes alternatives for the consideration of those committees. The Education Commission of the States furnishes much important information on education to governors and state legislatures. There is no longer much danger that a monolithic education power structure will have exclusive control of policy alternatives proposed to the legislature.

SCHOOL POLITICS AT THE FEDERAL LEVEL

School politics at the federal level has become relatively more important in recent years. The percentage of public school revenue derived from federal sources increased from 3 percent in 1950 to almost 9 percent in 1980. It is true that the percentage of revenue derived from federal sources is still not very high, but influential national organizations, such as the National Education Association and the American Association of School Administrators, have recently been advocating that the federal government provide 30 percent or more of school revenue. Federal laws, regulations, and court rulings on such matters as civil rights, racial segregation, the rights of minorities, and the handicapped have deeply involved the public schools in educational policy making at the federal level.

In 1979 the Congress withdrew education from the Department of Health, Education, and Welfare and established a new cabinet-level Department of Education. The National Education Association and the American Association of School Administrators had lobbied actively for years for this action. In 1976, the National Education Association for the first time actively supported the successful candidate for president of the United States. Upon taking office, he actively supported the establishment of the new Department of Education. This activity of education in-

[16] *Ibid.*

terest groups is illustrative of the political activity of education interest groups which will likely occur in the future. Many education interest groups will no longer be just professional associations because they will have to become involved in political activity to attain their goals. Political parties in the future are likely to include planks on education in their platforms. Education interest groups will no doubt use their influence to get planks favorable to federal assistance in the financing of education.

Congress has, as have state legislatures, established committees on education. Education interest groups as well as other interest groups lobby those committees and individual members of Congress in support of their goals.

Keppel has identified nearly 1,000 interest groups who attempt to influence federal educational policies.[17] Those organizations were as follows: more than 500 national and regional educational associations, almost 150 college professional societies, 50 religious educational associations, and 15 international associations.

The main education interest groups that represent elementary and secondary education at the federal level are the National Education Association, the American Association of School Administrators, the National School Boards Association, the National Congress of Parents and Teachers, and the American Federation of Teachers. The United States Catholic Conference represents Catholic private schools.

The federal government has long followed the policy of providing categorical grants for the public schools. This policy has created an education interest group for each categorical grant, and each categorical aid interest group usually lobbies only for its own appropriation. An illustration of this is the lobby backing the impact aid appropriation. This lobby is so strong that it has resisted the efforts of three presidents to reduce it. Strong lobbies also back the earmarked federal appropriations for education of the disadvantaged (ESEA Title I), for education for the handicapped, and for occupational, vocational, and adult education. Although experts on school finance and other educational leaders have generally called for general federal aid for education, the political activities of the lobbies for categorical grants have greatly reduced the probability of obtaining general federal aid. Federal activities in education are discussed more fully in Chapter 10.

SOME IMPORTANT PROBLEMS AND ISSUES

Following are some important problems and issues in the politics of education.

How Does the Administrator Deal with Politics in the Education Bureaucracy?

Political activities are found in all bureaucracies in the private sector of the economy as well as in the public sector. Usually the larger the bureaucracy, the greater the amount of politics in the bureaucracy. Politics exist in education bureaucracies at the local level, at the regional level, at the state level, and at the federal level. In fact, politics exist in all education bureaucracies with the possible

[17]Francis Keppel, "Education Lobbies and Federal Legislation," in *Challenge and Change in American Education,* eds. Seymour Harris and Alan Levensohn (Berkeley, Calif.: McCutchan Publishing Corporation, 1965), p. 63.

exception of a school system so small that it does not have either a superintendent or a principal.

Every school administrator would like to have a smoothly running organization with a minimum of politics in the bureaucracy of his or her organization. But all organizations, including educational organizations, divide labor and tend to be hierarchical.

Division of labor itself tends to create separate education interest groups. Individual elementary, middle, junior high, and senior high schools are established. Different departments and instructional services are established in all schools except elementary schools and even in some large elementary schools. Each school, each department, and each service competes for resources. This competition for resources is natural and is to be expected in a school system which is an open social system. The goal of the competent administrator is to develop a balanced educational program. This cannot be accomplished unless the administrator is cognizant of the needs of all parts of the system. The administrator cannot have that knowledge unless all subsystems present their needs to the central office. Therefore, the political activity of the school system necessary to advise the superintendent of the needs of the subsystem is beneficial to the school system.

Some subsystems, such as a teachers' union, may present its needs so successfully that it bankrupts the school system or deprives other subsystems of their minimum needs. Boards of education have the responsibility of reconciling competing claims and developing a balanced educational program. If the board of education and the administration do their homework and develop evidence showing that it is impossible to provide the educational program needed and desired by the community on the funds available, they are in a much more favorable political position to ask for an increase in taxes.

There is another type of political activity in the educational bureaucracy that is usually not beneficial to the educational enterprise. As has been pointed out, the educational bureaucracy is usually a hierarchical structure with different levels of authority and responsibility. Most human beings treasure all or one or more of the following: power, status, money, prestige, and influence. The higher the person rises in the educational hierarchy (as well as all other hierarchies), the more of these treasures he or she will gain. Therefore, people compete for higher places in the hierarchy and sometimes use political methods to attain their goals. Some undesirable political activity within the bureaucracy can be eliminated if the administration develops a well-defined policy for promotions within the organization. However, all of it cannot be eliminated. Let us assume that an assistant superintendent in a large school system is plotting against the superintendent and is undermining the superintendent. The assistant superintendent is trying to get the superintendent dismissed and acquire that position. The superintendent becomes aware of these political activities. What alternative courses of action are available to the superintendent?

Should School Administrators Be Active in Partisan Politics?

School administrators generally belong to a political party. They have the same rights to participate in partisan politics as do other citizens. However, most citizens believe that the schools should not be "mixed up" in partisan politics. Boards of education are generally nonpartisan in their composition. Let us assume that the superintendent very strongly believes in one of the two major political parties. Would it be good school politics for the superintendent to openly endorse the candidate of his or her favorite party for governor? It has already been pointed out that teachers' associations in a number of states are endorsing candidates for governor and the legislature. Is it good politics for administrators' associations to endorse candidates for public office?

Local teachers' associations frequently endorse school board candidates. Superintendents of schools have also frequently been involved in the selection of school board members. This is especially true when the superintendent has a split board.[18] Should the superintendent attempt to get citizens who are favorable to him or her to seek membership on the board?

SELECTED REFERENCES

Campbell, Roald F., and Tim L. Mazzoni, Jr., *State Policy Making for the Public Schools.* Berkeley, Calif.: McCutchan Publishing Corporation, 1976.

Iannaccone, Laurence, and Frank W. Lutz. *Politics, Power and Policy, The Governing of School Districts.* Columbus, Ohio: Charles E. Merrill Publishing Company, 1970.

Kimbrough, Ralph B. *Political Power and Educational Decision-Making.* Chicago: Rand McNally & Company, 1964.

——, and Michael Y. Nunnery. *Educational Administration, An Introduction*, Chaps. 12, 13, 14. New York: Macmillan Publishing Co., Inc., 1976.

Masters, Nicholas A., et al. *State Politics and the Public Schools.* New York: Alfred A. Knopf, Inc., 1964.

Nunnery, Michael Y., and Ralph B. Kimbrough. *Politics, Power, Polls and School Elections.* Berkeley, Calif.: McCutchan Publishing Corporation, 1971.

Thompson, John Thomas. *Policymaking in American Public Education.* Englewood Cliffs, N.J.: Prentice-Hall, Inc., 1976.

[18] See Laurence Iannaccone and Frank W. Lutz, *Politics, Power and Policy, The Governing of Local School Districts* (Columbus, Ohio: Charles E. Merrill Publishing Company, 1970), Chap. 4.

9

THE ENVIRONMENT
and the SCHOOLS

Throughout history, the relation of the school to the community it serves has been a matter of major significance. To what extent may a faculty teach what it is committed to teach without regard to the wishes of the people? How much support can a school or school system expect if it is pursuing values not accepted with enthusiasm by the community?[1] The historic gown-versus-town conflicts regarding the university have some parallels in every active school community today. The problems have grown more difficult to understand as the nature of the community has grown more vague and the problems of education have become infinitely more difficult.

The rising expectations regarding education which have been noted in many countries of the world add to the problem. The expectations may be so high that they cannot be fulfilled, or at least not as rapidly as desired. Frustration, alienation, and antagonism may then result. Education has become the nation's and the

---

[1] Jon Schaffarzick and Gary Sykes, eds., *Value Conflicts and Curriculum Issues: Lessons from Research and Experience* (Berkeley, Calif.: McCutchan Publishing Corporation, 1979).

world's most important business; therefore, everyone tends to be involved in it and desires in some manner to contribute to it. Many have rather simple solutions to propose for complex problems. The problem in our society is accentuated by the tendency of many to equate schooling with education.

These rising expectations have been accompanied by a demand for quick action and even quicker solutions. The demand is understandable because of past inequalities and continued problems such as prejudice and racism and because childhood is experienced only once and passes quickly. While the school, like most institutions, tends to respond much too slowly, the complexity of the problem suggests that a "solution" is not to be found quickly and not without extended research and planning. There is therefore the probability that further alienation may result and that conflict may become endemic—that the energies of even those committed to the educational enterprise may contribute little that is constructive.

Some educators who have sought the participation of the "people" in education (school affairs) and who might indeed be elated over developments have recently at times tended to draw back. The implications of many current developments are difficult to assess, and the road ahead is somewhat unclear. Confronted by an almost incomprehensible power to chart their own destiny—to build or destroy—people may tend to withdraw or to seek quick and "certain" solutions. In such an uneasy world, schools may expect to feel the impact of uncertainty and changes in the society. They must also reexamine their relation to and their impact upon the society. Of this vast arena of the school or school system and its environment, a few issues will be examined as one way of getting a better understanding of the problem which confronts the educator and the citizen interested in education today.

SOME BACKGROUND CONSIDERATIONS

Education in our society has been influenced significantly by beliefs, understandings, commitments, ambiguities, and tendencies.

A Great Belief in the Efficacy of Schooling

The people of the United States have long viewed the school as the most important agency of social and economic mobility for the individual. They have assumed that if schools were provided and made accessible, children and youth would avail themselves of the opportunity. To a rather remarkable extent, this has indeed occurred. The mobility which has characterized our society has been highly related to educational provisions. The children of immigrant groups have thus in the second or third generation achieved a status to which they could scarcely have aspired in the countries from which they came. This mobility in our society was, of course, the product of other factors also. However, the point to be noted here is that this concept came to be so widely accepted that there was too little recognition of the extent to which it was not operative, of the individuals and groups which were not involved, of the considerable numbers who did not "see" the opportunity and were not "motivated" to achieve. The society and even many teachers may thus have placed the burden of failure to achieve on the student. Only reluctantly and slowly has the society started to recognize that schooling which does not lead to a job is rather hollow.

Recent studies and related controversies regarding *the impact of schooling* have challenged this naïve belief in and possibly the myths regarding the influence of schools.[2] The drive for deschooling and for alternate schools also relates to the search for a more meaningful educational experience. In part because of the previous easy acceptance of the value of schooling confusion has been widespread concerning this matter. An adequate response has not occurred. A period of years may be both necessary and desirable to sort out the available data and claims regarding various studies, to conduct additional ones, and to permit educators and the public to arrive at a more valid position regarding this highly significant issue. Few, if any, problems call more stridently for effective leadership by the educational profession.

In recent years there have been various indicators, including polls and voting on tax proposals, that the public does not hold the public sector services and those involved in them in high esteem. While this may be somewhat less true of education than of some other governmental areas, it is nevertheless a cause for genuine concern and serious planning and action.

A Tendency to Regard Schooling and Education as One

In the commitment of our society to equal educational opportunity, attention has been given largely to the provision of rather formally established opportunities in schools. This concept of equality of educational opportunity has been challenged sharply by the civil rights movement in recent years and by the attack on poverty. Teachers in many instances accepted the achievement of black children and other "disadvantaged" children as being in accord with their potential to a much greater degree than was justified. They found it difficult to think of the kinds of experiences which children had in their homes and communities in the preschool years and while in school as an important aspect of education. They assumed that the formal school opportunity could overcome the home and community inequalities which preceded and accompanied it. Actually, of course, in many cases it overcame much, for their faith in education (schooling) was an important element in the strength of the school. However, this faith was also a factor which may have prevented educators from seeing the problem of the education of the culturally different in more valid terms. In recent years the society has called for a redefinition of education—one which sees the growth of an individual in light of many factors and forces, only one of which is the school. Thus there is the growing concern about poverty, housing, the community, and the attitudes and aspirations of parents as matters of large importance for the education of the child.

[2] Studies, for example, such as James S. Coleman et al., *Equality of Educational Opportunity* (Washington, D.C.: U.S. Government Printing Office, 1966) and Christopher Jencks et al., *Equality: A Reassessment of the Effect of Family and Schooling in America* (New York: Basic Books, Inc., Publishers, 1972).

The people of the United States have seen the school as a unique institution in their society. Here, long before most other societies, they have attached great importance to the school and have wished to ensure conditions for it which would be strongly supportive. Thus, out of philosophical considerations and as a result of the widespread corruption that characterized city government in the last half of the nineteenth century, they moved toward *ad hoc* boards of education. These boards of education enjoyed a very considerable measure of independence from city government and from the political machines that controlled city government. This development was facilitated by the acceptance of the view that education was a function of the state and thus not the proper concern of the city government.

Very probably, the schools advanced much more rapidly in the United States because of the fact that they were thus isolated from other activities of city government. They enjoyed greater support and lived with higher expectations than did other governmental agencies. This removal of schools from the usual political controls gave them a special political position and support of importance. They were removed from politics thus only in the sense of being removed from manipulation by the political bosses. However, the view developed that they were nonpolitical. This and other factors caused them to develop somewhat in isolation from other local governmental agencies and services which were more responsive to political party controls. Teachers and administrators supported the view that they should be independent and that thus they would contribute most to the development of citizens of independence and the advancement of the society.

While, as has been suggested, there were large gains made as a result of this independence, it must also be noted that this was done at certain costs. Among the gains were the more rapid advancement of education (schooling) than would probably have occurred otherwise, the development of merit plans for appointment of teachers and administrators prior to such developments in other governmental services, the strengthening of the responsibilities of the administrator, and the establishment of a plan through which the people could center attention upon the schools and seek their improvement.

On the other hand, this independence led to a lack of responsiveness on the part of boards of education to the changing needs of the society; a concern on the part of teachers and administrators with academic learning rather than with the total situation in which the child lived and which had a large impact on his or her education; an inability of educators and others engaged in public services such as housing, public health, libraries, juvenile courts, and social welfare to work together with understanding; and a belief that educational services were removed from politics (not recognizing the politics of the nonpolitical), a view which in the long run may have hindered rather than advanced the quality of educational services. This tendency to regard schools as separate from the home and from other agencies remains and is difficult to overcome. Thus even today most studies of the development of less privileged children center most of their attention upon the school—for presumably it is through the school that change is to be effected. This same tendency may be found in other nations also—though in England, for example, the gulf may be less wide. Studies such as that reported in *From Birth to Seven*,[3] which centers attention not only upon the school but upon the birth and health history, the housing and home experience, the community, the parents and their attitudes and aspirations, ability and attainment, behavior and adjustment, are less likely to be conducted in the United States. Interestingly this comprehensive, longitudinal study involving all children born in one week in March 1958 was conducted by the National Children's Bureau in collaboration with various health and educational institutes and research organizations and associations of educational and medical officers.

This "isolation" may have indeed been justified in the late nineteenth and early twentieth centuries. In rural areas and small towns it was readily understandable because of the limits of local government, child, and health services. However, it must be noted that the growing complexity of the society, with its enormous concentrations of population and expanding programs of governmental services, calls for a thorough reexamination of this question. So also does the theory of government which requires a less naïve, less simple, and quite possibly a less satisfying concept of how decision making is and probably will be carried on in our democracy.

A Commitment to Equality of Educational Opportunity with Relatively Little Understanding or Agreement Regarding Its Meaning

The expansion and improvement of educational services in our society has long been related to a verbal commitment to equality of opportunity. Although equality has at times been confused with identity of opportunity, it has been used effectively as a guiding principle which united the society and in light of which advances have been secured. During this century definitions of it have changed in marked fashion. In recent years substantial changes in meaning have occurred and continue to occur. A major change has been from the definition which held that educational opportunities should be provided for all in accord with their ability to the definition which holds that not only must the opportunity be provided but also that the society has the responsibility for ensuring that children and youth can (and will) avail themselves effectively of the opportunity. Possibly there is sharper disagreement in our society regarding the meaning of this concept than there has been for some decades. Some clarification is essential as a base for moving forward in educational services. The search for a new definition—for an adequate one for our times—constitutes a major challenge to the established educational service and the forces in the society related to it.

Ambiguity Regarding Goals Related to the Diversity and Changing Values in Society

Society in the last decade has been deeply troubled in its search for new values. Many have felt that the values of the past have been inadequate and that techno-

[3] Ronald Davie, Neville Butler, and Harvey Goldstein, *National Children's Bureau* (London: Longmans, 1972).

logical and other developments offer new opportunities for men and women to build a substantially different world with less competition, tension, uniformity, institutionalization, inequality, and economic, racial, and social stratification and differences. This search in society has been paralleled by ambiguity regarding goals in the schools. The question of what knowledge is of most worth is considered in "What Are Schools For?"[4] There are calls for the schools to guide youth in learning useful knowledge; to "prophesy urgently, magnetically, and then fulfill these prophecies," an aspect of futurism;[5] "to adopt the affective domain—socialization, democratization, values in education, morality"; or to recognize that "it's the side effects that count." The public and the schools are ambiguous. There are strident calls for accountability. Can sufficient agreement be achieved—and tolerance for diversity—to enable communities and society to move forward effectively?

The future development of public education may relate significantly to the development of greater consensus regarding the basic purposes. There appears to be an increasing recognition of this need. A pluralistic society without common threads may be counterproductive even to those it seeks to assist. However, there are serious and difficult barriers to overcome. There may be an increasing number who do not believe a satisfactory consensus can be achieved and who therefore go their separate ways rather than attempt to reconstruct public education.

A Former Tendency Toward Uniformity
Challenged by a Concept of "Pluralism"

Public education in the United States was one of the important institutions through which a nation was built out of diverse people. While the melting pot theory is not defensible, it is true that a nation was built with many important and relatively common commitments. In this process and because of the vastness of the continent, limited educational provisions, and the limited supply of prepared teachers, certain procedures such as statewide control of textbooks developed. Later the mobility of the general population and of teachers and administrators as well as ease of communication resulted in a remarkable general similarity of educational provisions in spite of the large number of school districts and the number of states. Many of these arrangements and views have persisted even though challenged by knowledge of individual differences and related matters. In recent years the efforts of minorities to find a reasonable and adequate role in our society and the diversity of values among our people have resulted in a new commitment to pluralism. The more exact delineation of pluralism remains to be worked out—but it is a force challenging the old uniformity. The growing recognition of the legal rights of the individual student also challenges the traditional view.

The present situation may be viewed positively or negatively. It could result in a hardening of pluralistic lines and a reduction in commitment to or provision of more effective educational services. On the other hand it may be a large oppor-

[4]*Phi Delta Kappan*, 54, no. 1 (September 1972), 1-17.
[5]Walter A. Hack et al., *Educational Futurism 1985* (Berkeley, Calif.: McCutchan Publishing Corporation, 1972).

tunity for a society, through struggle, to achieve a more equal and adequate provision of education services—and of more vitalized and effective schools.

A Traditional Insecurity of the Professional Educator and a Search for Power by the Professional

The teacher has long had an image marked by insecurity in the United States. This however may be over; teacher groups may find that they have much more power than they believed. They are far from agreed on how or for what ends to use this power. They may become defenders of conservative approaches to educational problems. As they negotiate with the board of education and/or top administration, and especially at the state level, they may become more rigid in positions. Such negotiations may also result in the organization of the principals and other middle groups to protect their positions and exert some power. This search for power by professionals is increasingly noticed at the local or district level. As the state becomes more deeply and directly involved in educational practice this power will also be exercised to a much greater degree at the state level. It will not be a return to the 1950s when legislatures frequently followed education associations but a period marked by greater controversy. New power relationships will be developing, and this will result almost inevitably in considerable conflict. An important issue will be whether teachers, administrators, and others involved directly can develop the essential common commitments without which they self-destruct. The effective management of conflict thus has become of critical importance.

A Somewhat Simplistic Belief in "the People" and a Failure to Analyze and Affirm This Belief in Relation to the Rights of Minorities or the Individual

At various times, but especially in recent decades, there has been a considerable effort to involve more people in educational decision making. Citizens advisory committees were recommended widely. Generally they brought together representatives of various influential groups and encouraged them to join in securing educational improvements. Commonly they did not include those who tended to be little represented in decision-making processes, such as the poor and minorities. Recent demands for community power are not conceptually unrelated to the earlier views regarding people involvement. However they meet other strong power positions including the traditional legal authority of the board of education, the bureaucracy, and the profession. Further, their programs are frequently poorly thought through and lacking competent leadership. Basically no one can seriously oppose the involvement of more people—especially considering the increasing educational influence of forces such as TV outside of the school. However, the issue is an extremely complex one which calls for serious study and careful formulation, development of procedures, and appraisal. The development of site councils, as discussed later in this chapter, may be most significant.

A Belief That Conflict Should (Always) Be
Avoided and That It Is the Result of Lack
of Communication or Understanding

The former optimism and affluence and commitments of our society have at least in part been the basis for a belief that conflicts on public issues should be avoided at nearly all costs. Thus the board of education election in which the incumbents were reelected with little or no discussion of issues and no serious competitor was not uncommon or unfavorably regarded. There has also been the view that if there is conflict it is the result of inadequate communication. These views are now rejected or at least looked at much more critically. In a pluralistic society—a society in which groups hold sharply different values, a society in the process of change, a painful experience even for our change-oriented society—it is increasingly recognized that differences are inevitable and may indeed offer opportunities for development. This view assumes that attention is not being given to personal conflicts. It also assumes that our society is sufficiently mature to engage in conflict within limits relating to goals, to the common welfare, and with mutual respect for the right of other individuals and groups to hold different views. It is further based on the understanding that there are worthwhile alternative "solutions" to most problems and that they should receive serious consideration. Clearly the probable inevitability of conflict must be recognized and preparations made for avoiding its quite possible highly destructive features.

The Tendency Toward Single Issue
Politics and Categorical Programs

Many students of government are concerned about what they believe to be single-issue politics with little regard for the common or central matters which ensure the health of a society. Thus, for example, the "right to life" movement is said to urge choices among candidates with little or no regard for their general competence in government. Too frequently board of education members are elected on a single issue. Categorical programs and their supporters are feared by some because of what is believed to be their singleness of concern. Conceivably it is much easier to build a program and secure funds for a politically powerful single-issue program than to win support for general education. Many more people attend school board meetings or lobby at the state and federal level for single issues than for that general education program which should be the base of the categorical programs and without which categorical programs may struggle among themselves with too little regard for the best program for the student. If this is to be avoided it may need to be done at the local level—at the school site and system level.

The achievement of greater equality of opportunity in recent decades through the great expansion of categorical programs, with their rules, regulations, guidelines, and relations need not be debated. How this movement legitimated increased state and federal centralization and how this centralization will be employed in the future and by whom must give concern. At what point do local administrators and teachers see themselves as *functionaries* carrying out specific, defined tasks and living by regulations while lacking the initiative, the creativity, and the power to educate. Or do (or may) regulations (or some types) constitute but the framework for the exercise of creative learning facilitation?

CHANGED LOCAL CONDITIONS

While the concepts discussed here briefly have persisted, the world in which schools and school systems have existed has been in a process of extremely rapid change. Among the more important of the changes are those that follow.

From a Rural to an Urban to a Metropolitan Nation

Until relatively recently, the United States has been a predominantly rural nation. From the twenty-four urban places of 2,500 population or more in 1790, there was a steady population growth in rural and urban areas for more than a century. Although the urban growth at times exceeded the rural, it did not make spectacular gains until the early decades of the present century. By 1960 the urban population was approximately 73.5 percent and it continues to grow far more rapidly than other areas.

Much more striking than the change from rural to urban has been the transformation of the nation from urban to metropolitan. The people became metropolitan before realizing their change from rural to urban. In 1900 approximately one third of the population lived in "metropolitan areas." By 1970 approximately 68.6 percent were metropolitan dwellers and the expansion was expected to continue, though more slowly. This percentage is slightly smaller than the urban percentage because, by definition, the urban figure includes many towns and small cities which are not part of a metropolitan area.

In the early 1970s many people came to understand that the health of the various communities in the metropolitan area was dependent upon the health of the whole. The ecology movement provided more appreciation of the interrelationships of various forces and factors and of the interdependence of components. It constituted another important challenge and opportunity to the educational service.

Local Governments in Great Number and Variety

During the last fifty years, the legal boundaries of cities have not been extended as the city or metropolitan area has grown. In fact there has been very strong resistance to permitting the growth of the city through annexation. As a result, very strong municipal (some suburban, others cities) governments have frequently grown up around the city. They have been committed to preventing the expansion of the city. Further, many small municipal governments have either continued or have been established in the metropolitan areas. They have frequently been viewed as a means of avoiding the high taxes of the city and of keeping out "undesirable" developments such as factories and low-cost housing. The boundaries of these local government units are too frequently the result of "cherry-stemming" or similar procedures through which more powerful authorities secure wealthy or otherwise desirable areas. They are not logical, planned, or necessarily in accord with existing community-of-interest patterns.

In addition to the general local governments which are found in the metropolitan area there has been an increasing number of *ad hoc* authorities. Some of these exist to meet areawide problems, such as water, sewage, transportation, smog. Others serve to meet special needs or desires of the people in a given area, such as mosquito control or recreation. School districts also continue to be found in large numbers.

For the school administrator, the situation with reference to municipal governments and special districts other than for schools is of utmost important. Most metropolitan residents are served by at least four separate local governments. It is with a multitude of districts that the school administrator must work if schools are to be integrated into and developed in light of the life of the metropolitan area of which they are a part. There can be little doubt that in these highly interdependent metropolitan areas there is large need for the coordination of governmental services and great difficulty in achieving it. Further, this proliferation almost certainly has a debilitating effect upon all the local governments involved and tends to reduce the accountability to the public, which has been traditionally regarded as one of the values of local government. Financial disparities and a wide range in standards of service also result. And only in a rather reluctant and stumbling manner do citizens tend to accept the fact that they are indeed citizens of a metropolitan area as well as, probably, of a municipal government and several special districts. If it is true that participation in local government itself is an important educational experience, it would appear that not much progress has been made in making this experience realizable and satisfying.

CHANGES IN FEDERAL AND STATE ACTIVITY

The most recent decades have seen a major shift in the environment regarding education at the state and federal levels. This shift might indeed suggest that education has become more than a federal concern and that the states have been reexamining their concepts of education as a legal function of the state and of their administrative responsibility. The activity at the federal and state levels may reflect a growing realization in the society of the significance of the educational service with the resultant increasing attention to it through established political processes.

Among the major activities, actions, or programs during these decades which are considered in more detail in other chapters are the Elementary and Secondary Education Act of 1965; the Higher Education Act of 1972; the Economic Opportunity or Poverty Act of 1964; the extended federal curriculum reform efforts (their rise and fall) through the National Science Foundation, the National Institute of Education, and the federally sponsored educational laboratories; civil rights and affirmative action legislation; the law on educating all handicapped children (P.L. 94-142); the court decisions on finance such as *Rodriguez* in Texas and *Serrano* in California; and the act establishing a Department of Education in 1979.

The changes resulting from these laws have had a major impact on the educational service. They have been aimed directly at the curriculum and at the organization of schools—with a strong commitment to categorical programs. They have brought extended guidelines, regulations, and staffs identified with specific programs. These changes have had a profound effect at the school site level and at the local district level. The long-range effects of many of these developments—however laudable their goals—are unclear. However, they seem to assure the nation of very substantial changes in the educational system. And, as with any such major changes, there are almost certain to be important consequences, unanticipated by their proponents.

Although our major attention in this chapter is centered upon the local environment, it must be noted that those concerned about the education service are not generally well organized at the state and federal levels. Rather, the lack of common goals among teachers, school board members, administrators, parents, interested citizens, and classified personnel and between general education and a range of categorical programs frequently provides an opportunity for action by those with less knowledge of and commitment to public education.

OTHER ORGANIZATIONS AND AGENCIES

The great expectations regarding education also had an important stimulating effect on agencies other than public schools. While many others could be identified, such as parent–teacher associations, political parties, research and testing services, taxpayers' associations, associations of school boards, labor unions, business and professional groups, attention will be given here to only three groups.

The Foundations

The number of foundations and the wealth in the hands of the foundations has increased greatly in recent decades. Probably it is also true that the foundations increased their interest in education. The largest of the foundations, the Ford Foundation, centered attention on educational developments. A considerable part of the federal action previously described was based at least in part upon programs sponsored in part by foundations. The foundations, being free from the need to support mass programs, were able to exert an influence far beyond that which the dollars they provided would suggest. For theirs was the "venture" money so frequently not forthcoming from the public authorities. While an actual assessment of the influence exerted by the foundations is difficult to make, it is noteworthy that in recent years it has been sufficient to be the subject of considerable controversy. Some educators have felt that the foundations have not been interested in advancing money to make possible the appraisal of an idea but, rather, only to advance an idea to which a commitment existed. The American Association of School Administrators conducted a study of the influence of the foundations because of the concern found among some of its members.[6] Congressional concerns resulted in further regulation and some taxation of foundations in the early 1970s.

Educational Organizations

In recent decades, educational agencies and individuals involved in the educational process have become increasingly organized. Through their organizations, they have sought greatly increased influence in regard to educational matters.

The colleges and universities, for example, have played an increasing role in public education in the last decades. They have had important influence in such areas as curriculum, achievement testing, and accreditation. Through their own admission policies and their concern for the gifted student, they have also influenced secondary schools. The development of research programs in the field of education and the growing interest of psychologists, sociologists, and political scientists in education and the school as an institution suggest that the influence of higher educational institutions and their staff on public education will continue to be felt.

The growth of organizations of the professional staff of the schools has also been marked in recent years. Related to this growth has been a notable increase in their activity and influence. In this area, reference may well be made to organizations of administrators, curriculum and supervisory staff, guidance personnel, and teachers. The large number of different organizations has reduced the influence which these groups might have had; however, they increasingly accept the view that it is only through organization that they can be effective and correspondingly reject the idea that they should not be a militant group working toward goals which they formulate. Especially noticeable is the growth of militancy among teachers' associations and teachers' unions. They have gained a substantial increase of influence in recent years not only in salary matters but in a wide range of curricular and instructional matters. While teachers and teachers groups have had large influence in many schools and school systems, they are now gaining a new image in this regard and in the public expectations that they have a more explicit and direct role in decision making. The establishment of the Department of Education in 1979 was substantially the result of the work of the National Education Association.

Private and Parochial Schools

Recent decades have been marked by continued action on the part of certain private school groups, notably the Roman Catholic, to which attention is given here, for greater public recognition and for support in one form or another. They have been ably represented by their spokespersons in state legislatures, in the federal Congress, and in the core cities of the metropolitan areas where enrollments in their schools have become quite substantial. During recent years, they have won

[6] American Association of School Administrators, *Private Philanthropy and Public Purposes* (Washington, D.C.: The Association, 1963).

certain gains in terms of legislation for their students. They have been concerned about the limitations on such aid as have been stipulated or implied by the Supreme Court decisions and are seeking alternative solutions.

More than formerly, the religious schools and their supporters also are troubled, both financially and philosophically. They are far less sure that it would be desirable to have all children of their faith in a separate school system. The results are not conclusive in terms of values achieved. Further, they are in some disagreement regarding the causes of the decline in the 1970s in their enrollments. They have not met the problems of the culturally different or of the gifted any more effectively than have the public schools. Many had claimed that all aspects (subjects and textbooks) of instruction should be permeated by the special values of the faith. And each step toward public support must be made at some cost to the values of being private and separate. Fair employment practice acts do not suggest that religious tests may be employed in selection of teachers, principals, or other staff if there is any public support. The minority status and feeling of being discriminated against which was long a force for the religious school is losing its meaning as change in status occurs. The church also is seeking a new relation to the world outside, and some of its members are unsure that the separate school contributes in this direction. Then, too, its problems are so great with the expansion of educational services, the technological advances in education, and the decline in the availability of members of orders to meet teaching needs that it is reexamining its position regarding many educational problems and the relation of education to other religious issues.

In the decade of the 1970s there has been a sharp increase in the number of Christian academies. Many of them are small. However, their growth would appear significant and the result of various factors. While some of them may appeal as an escape from diverse aims and the confusion (including that related to desegregation) of public schools, it is clear that they have a positive goal—the provision of an education more precisely in accord with and designed to teach a fixed, traditional Christian philosophy and view of life.

Thus it would appear that we may be in a new period of "openness" regarding the relationship of public schools and some of the private agencies which have experienced problems somewhat similar to those of the public schools—while other groups tend to seek new solutions, believing that the public school does not and probably will not serve their goals. Possibly also we are beginning to reexamine the question of religious pluralism in our society, the form of it we wish to attain, and its relation to the education question.

POWER IN THE LOCAL SCHOOL DISTRICT AREA

The school administrator is in a position of leadership in a district which is but a segment of an area, metropolitan or otherwise. It is not truly a separate unit except legally, and frequently its nature is to be explained by tradition rather than logic. The administrator has responsibilities for a single service, which, however, is expanding and is increasingly linked to a great number of other services that are administered by other bodies. What is done in this unit and service is highly related to what is done in other units providing a similar service and to what is done by local authorities providing related services.

The Power Structures

The power structure of this unit is not always the same or clearly established. Depending upon the nature of the population, the traditions and wealth of the unit, and its relation to the metropolitan or other area, it may appear to be of the Hunter power-elite type. More likely, however, it is somewhat of the process-pluralist type, where power and influence on most occasions are dispersed and where decision making involves a measure of bargaining, compromise, conflict, and agreement. If an elite once ruled educational decision making, it is perhaps less likely to do so now because of the growing interest in education on the part of various groups.

The manner in which the power structure in one school district may relate to that in other school districts of the area is unclear. The question of the nature of the metropolitan area power structure and its relation to educational developments in various school districts remains relatively unexplored. This is a matter of importance both because of the fact that a metropolitan or other area is a reality and because many educational services and developments must be conceived in larger terms. The usual school district is greatly handicapped or with extremely limited resources for the development of educational TV, programmed learning, research and development, technical education, adult education, and community college education needed for the area. It may also be extremely limited in its capacity to engage in professional negotiation or bargaining, as it is dealing with agents of groups representing the resources of the whole area.

Impact of Federal and State Activities

In this situation, it is also important to note that the state and federal agencies have been playing an increasingly important role. They have already played a more important one than is generally recognized. For example, the past system of state grants-in-aid to many suburban school districts has made it possible for them to remain independent of the core city or industrial areas of which they are a part. Without such grants, probably the integration of outside areas into a single government unit would have proceeded much more rapidly. But the federal programs in education, court actions, and related matters, previously referred to, will be of far greater significance in determining the decisions made. Federal and state regulations regarding various categorical programs have a large impact not only on those in the target group but upon the education of all children and upon the vitality of the local system as well.

This development of federal-state programs has also furthered the influence of the professionals and has necessitated increasing cooperation among the districts of an area. This is not to deny the fact that members of boards of education and other legislative bodies will have a role in decision making; however, they will be dependent upon the comprehensive information and data development which must occur in the increasingly complex metropolitan and other areas. And it is the bureaucracies of the local, state, and federal governments that will be responsible for the development of these data and for their interpretation and communication regarding them.

BUILDING AN INTEGRATED SCHOOL COMMUNITY

The educational administrator and the local board of education are thus confronted with the problem of building an integrated school system and community. The people of a school district or of a school system cannot achieve the desired educational program without some cohesion and a measure of *community*. The people must be held together at least in the educational world by some mutual ties that provide a feeling of identity, belonging, involvement, and achievement. Because we may well begin with school communities that are quite heterogeneous and lacking in *community* or integration, this may be among the most important tasks facing the schools.

As a first step in this process, study of factors related to integration may well be essential. Jacob and Teune have suggested that some elements to consider as a possible base for developing an integrated political community are proximity, homogeneity, transactions, mutual knowledge, functional interest, communal character, political structure, sovereignty, governmental effectiveness, and integrative experience.[7]

Studies of this type may provide the understanding in light of which steps can be taken to develop ties among the people regarding educational issues and goals. Only with some development of this type is the local system likely to be effective, in relation to the larger immediate area of which it is a part, in dealing with the growing organizations of the area, and in working with the stronger state and federal agencies. Unless some *community* is achieved, the district is likely to be pushed along by single-purpose or external forces. Without clear-cut goals, it cannot be a strong unit which melds various pressures and considerations into a constructive organization.

The educator should be aware of facts such as the following regarding the community.

Society is characterized by large power organizations. In a community, for example, at least the following power groups of special interest to education will usually be found: the school power structure; governmental structures other than schools (some of which are directly related to political organizations); organizations of business executives, professional groups, and labor; mass media of communication; and power leaders who may function informally or through recognized organizations.

The term "power" is not used here in the sense that it is something undesirable. Rather, "power" is a word that will be used to describe the "acts of men going about the business of moving other men to act in relation to themselves or in rela-

[7]Philip E. Jacob and Henry Teune, "The Integrative Process—Guidelines for Analysis of the Basis of Political Community," in *The Integration of Political Communities,* ed. Philip E. Jacob and James V. Toscano (Philadelphia: J. B. Lippincott Company, 1964).

tion to organic or inorganic things."[8] The power of the individual is extremely limited unless structured through an organization or association. Such structuring may be provided for by statute. It may be highly formal or quite informal.

The school system itself may be viewed as a power structure. It coordinates the efforts of the board of education, administration, teaching, and other staff members in the provision and advancement of education. It generally is supported by such groups as the parent-teacher association and the school site council, which may be regarded as a part of the power structure that exists to further education.

Some other power structures in the community may oppose the school system. But it should be noted that the opportunity that groups have to organize themselves to be effective is a fundamental right that a free society must guarantee. In fact, the existence of such groups may be regarded as one measure of the level of maturity of the democratic community.

Many of the power organizations have been consciously created and have a definite purpose. The written statement of purposes, if one exists, may or may not be complete. Possibly it will not reveal some of the purposes. Informal organizations may have greater power than many that are formally organized.

Many organizations are nationally oriented. Their members think and act more like members of similar organizations in other communities than like other citizens of their own community. This situation is related to the stratification found in the community. It raises the question of whether or not the geographic community is a social community.

Individuals are frequently associated with organizations that have contradictory purposes. The professional organization to which they belong may oppose the interest individuals have in the education of children and which they demonstrate through work in an association of parents. This lack of consistency suggests the need for involvement of people in an organization if their support is to be secured.

The community existing or to be developed has important values, ideals, and concepts that can be significant levers of action. The concept of equality of educational opportunity and the understanding that it does not mean identity of opportunity, for example, is extremely powerful. Too little attention is given to such fundamental concepts in many communities, although they also have important implications for education in the state and nation as well as in the community.

The community will not act in accord with its own ideals, values, and concepts unless it knows the facts and is challenged. It is easy to profess interest in equality of educational opportunity and to behave in ways that deny it. The challenge of facts may be helpful in causing the people of a community to act in accord with their professed values.

The school district is but a part of a larger community. The district cannot and should not expect to move alone. It must be aware of the larger community (both

[8] Floyd Hunter, *Community Power Structure. A Study of Decision Makers* (Chapel Hill: University of North Carolina Press, 1953), p. 2.

in terms of its own geographical area and with reference to the metropolitan or similar area) and accept a constructive role in it.

Demographic and economic changes may have a powerful impact on schooling. Does a society of older people care less about children? Is an educative society more or less committed to schooling—to what concepts of schooling?

STUDIES OF THE COMMUNITY

Methods of Study

An effective, planned program for developing an integrated school community must be based upon the study of the community.

Many methods may be employed to study the complexities of the community and its institutions including the schools. Important methods to be employed are the following:

The historical method. This method, which is too little employed, may reveal how the community has grown, what the nature of population change has been, how the community has been organized, what educational values and issues have been prominent in it, the reasons for the existing school organization, and the relation of community education to other governmental services.

Analysis of laws and records. Statutes, minutes of boards of education and of other organizations, press treatment of education, census reports, population data, economic reports, success of high school graduates in college and in employment, and records of dropouts are samples of the large quantities of data pertaining to the community that await analysis. The amount of data available suggests the need for careful definition of purpose and study over a period of time, if a comprehensive picture of the community is to be secured.

Surveys of status and practice. What are the existing conditions? Does social stratification mark the community and the school? What have been the objectives, the programs, and the practices of the schools? What is the nature of home life? What is the place of youth, and how are their problems being met? What are the power organizations in the community, who are their members, and how do they operate? Who are the power leaders? Who controls the mass media of communication, and what is the audience and impact of each? How does the school system function as a power organization? What are the community practices and norms? These are a few of the many aspects of status and practice that might be studied as the base for the advancement of the educational system. An approach to these problems will involve the use of many techniques such as observation, interviews, analysis of records, questionnaires, and maintenance of logs and diaries.

Studies of values. These could be regarded as one phase of surveys of status in the sense that one aspect of status would be the values held. They are listed separately, however, because of their significance and because they are not generally thought of as an aspect of current status. The values held are largely ascertained through interviews, but records of elections and previous community actions, and the establishment of new private schools, may also be highly informative.

Case studies. Case studies are suggested as a method of assessing a community because they make it possible to visualize the interaction of various forces and to view the community or any of its organizations or groups as societies in action. They reveal organizations as dynamic structures. This concept of community life must be accepted if one is to be prepared to work with the forces that shape education.

Studies of the area. The school district must be informed regarding the larger geographical area of which it is a part. Therefore, in cooperation with other districts, it must provide for studies of the larger community and of other school districts. Only in this manner can essential cooperative effort be achieved and programs developed which are beyond the resources of any one district.

Studies of state and federal programs and their influence. Too often districts make little or no attempt to determine the influence of federal programs. In fact many districts are small and understaffed to such a degree that they are not prepared to plan effective utilization of the opportunities opened through federal programs. The districts of an area might well plan to attack this problem through a cooperative effort with a staff jointly employed or through the intermediate unit.

Procedure in Community Study

Equally as important as the methodological approaches used in the study of the community are the procedures by which the study is conducted. Although certain of the suggested methods would need to be carried on individually by highly trained specialists, this would not be true in the great majority of instances. Competent specialists or consultants would, of course, need to participate in planning, formulating hypotheses, constructing the instruments used, preparing research workers, analyzing data, and formulating findings. But many people residing within the community could participate in the work. Local personnel need to do much of the work, not only for reasons of greater economy and a consequent expansion of the program, but because the knowledge gained would more likely result in action.

It would, therefore, be desirable to plan considerable action research. This would involve using available resources under competent leadership. It means systematically collecting and using many data that presently go unused. It would involve many teachers, parents, older students, and other citizens of the community interested in any organization that impinges on education.

In organizing such a program no one form is to be preferred in all situations. Provision should generally be made to involve the following:

1. both laypersons and teachers
2. lay leaders of status and laypersons representative of a wide variety of groups
3. consultants

4. resource people and assistants to carry out the routine and data collecting and analysis operations, and to relate data to community values
5. research and development staff to design and appraise the work undertaken and to advise regarding implementation

Consultants and research and development staffs may be supplied by a metropolitan or other intermediate or areawide unit.

Implications of Community Study

Frequently, questions are raised regarding the use of data pertaining to the community. For example, does the administrator become subservient to the power structure when elements of it are known? Or is the administrator then in the position to become a manipulator? Or in a better position to provide constructive leadership?

The administrator, board of education, and others are in a position to act with intelligence and with reference to accepted values only when the power structure is known to them. Certainly the administrator and the board of education need to avoid becoming the tools of any single power group that may or may not have knowledge of and belief in the potential of education. At times, permitting such a group to make decisions may appear to be the easy road, but it would scarcely be consistent with the purposes of public education in a democracy.

If being a manipulator is interpreted to mean concealing facts, seeking personal power, controlling or making decisions for others, this concept or role must be rejected. However, if by being a manipulator reference is made to providing leadership and helping the community determine what its status is, how status differs from values held, and how the community can achieve what it seeks for its children and youth, the role should be welcomed. The role of manipulator might well be sought if it means helping a community reconsider and clarify its purposes. In reality, this is leadership, not manipulation.

In serving in a leadership role the school administrator needs also to recognize the power of the leader in relation to the decision-making process and the effect of the values held upon the processes and action to be taken. Too frequently, the leader may see personal views (values) as objective and the only defensible ones.

ACTION BASED ON COMMUNITY STUDY

A knowledge of the community is an essential background of action in school-community relations. Without this knowledge, any program developed must be based upon various assumptions regarding the community—assumptions that may or may not be sound.

A knowledge of the community includes a knowledge of the school, for the school is one of the institutions of the community. It can be understood only by considering various other conditions existing in the community. Without a thorough knowledge of the school and its relations to the community, the development of a program cannot be carried on in an effective manner.

The study of the community, including the school, should supply answers to such questions as What have been the media of communication between school and community? What are the areas of ignorance between the school and community? What "publics" exist in the community? What resources are available for use in the program? How competent are school personnel to participate in the program? What mass media of communication service the community and what contribution can they be expected to make? What power structures and what organizations exist in the community? What are the major limitations of the public education power structure in the community? What are the values of the community? What are the major strengths and weaknesses of the schools?

When data of the types suggested are available, it becomes possible to give careful, considered thought to the development of a program for achieving an integrated school community. In developing the program, it should be recognized that a most difficult task is being undertaken. Fundamentally, the problem is one of communication and of education. It is a matter of assisting the community in gaining knowledge of the schools, of the schools' potential, and of the procedures through which the potential may be realized. Given the diversity of backgrounds, interests, and activities of citizens, however, and the variety of media that may be employed, the problem of communication is an exceedingly complex one. A good medium of communication with a few people may have no value with many others. It must be remembered that in communication what is heard may be very different from what is spoken. And, of course, behavioristic communication may be much more effective than verbalistic.

The inevitability of communications in the school–community relations area must be recognized. A visit to a school, a meeting with children going to school, a child's report regarding events in school, the role of teachers in community organizations, a school building—an infinite number of situations exist through which some type of communication occurs. The problem is whether a sufficient number of media of high validity can be utilized to improve the understanding of school and community and enable them to progress together. If this can be achieved, a substantial benefit will result for the school and community and for education itself, as much of it goes on in the home and in the community outside the school. Thus, although the best school program is central in any school-community relations program, it also must be remembered that education is most likely to achieve significant goals through a high level of school–community understanding and action. The parent or community organization for youth with little understanding of the school is not prepared to contribute in a highly effective manner to the education of youth. But the parent and the youth groups are inevitably "educating" youth.

Suggestions Regarding School-Community Action

In developing a program to promote school–community cooperation the following guidelines should be kept in mind.

Multidirectional communication is essential and must be both the basis of the program and one of its purposes. Two-way communication is mentioned frequently. It is necessary but not likely to be effective unless accompanied by communication within the school staff and within various other agencies.

A policy statement regarding school-community interaction should be adopted by the board of education, making clear the purposes of the program and the role of school personnel. Failure to establish adequate policies in this area sharply reduces the opportunity for effective leadership by school administrators.

The program must be planned. The difficulty of the task as well as the variety of possible ends and media demand careful planning. Without such planning, achievement will probably be extremely limited. A committee of laypersons familiar with the organizational life of the community and with the media of communication within it can be of great assistance in this planning. Studies to determine the extent of information about and attitudes toward various aspects of the educational program are an essential base for planning.

An effective program can only be designed with clearly defined goals. Are there particular problems to be met, groups to be communicated with, or areas of ignorance on the part of the school or community? A planned program can be integrated with the more routine work in the field of school-community relations that is established with reference to legal requirements, events in the school calendar, and seasonal opportunities regarding aspects of the total educational program. While the vision must be large, steps toward it should permit observable progress.

Reporting is an essential element of the total program and needs to be developed in an effective manner with reference to the variety of groups to be reached. It may involve report cards or conferences with parents; press relations; the preparation of brief, attractive, and well-illustrated annual or special reports; and reports on achievements and needs of the schools. Above all it must offer satisfaction through achievement by participants.

Involvement of many citizens is desirable. It facilitates a higher level of understanding and more action than is likely to result from reporting. It avoids the tendency of school people to have the "answer" to the problem and then to attempt to win acceptance for it. Rather, it places the problem in the hands of many more people for consideration and the formulation of tentative solutions. It reveals large, unused personnel resources. It should lead to more sound solutions and to earlier implementation. It is likely to be developed effectively only if the board has adopted policies encouraging it.

A wide variety of media should be employed. The error of utilizing only one medium, such as the press or the parent-teacher association, should be avoided. This is not to underestimate the significance of such media but, rather, to suggest that consideration should be given to the many that are available. Different media may involve or reach different groups or may have a different impact.

The significance of the individual school in school-community relations should be recognized. The most impressive contact that parents will have with the school system will be at the school that their children are attending. They will inevitably think of the system in terms of their personal experiences with teachers and principal at the school they know. If many are going to be involved in working through problems and policies, it is likely to be done at the individual school level. The communities or neighborhoods served by schools vary widely in many systems, and consequently the programs at the school level need to be characterized by variation. The movement toward decentralization should substantially increase the contribution of the individual school in this program.

The central office should take responsibility for a few systemwide school-community relations activities and should concentrate its energies on the development of a staff for more effective participation in the work. Principals need help in developing programs for their schools. Teachers need assistance in developing competency for utilizing parent-teacher conferences effectively. Many staff members need to develop more competency in working as a member of a lay-professional committee or in serving on a panel. Staff members are frequently lacking in group process skills, which are most important if problems are to be worked through cooperatively. Many groups in the community remain relatively uninvolved.

Responsibility for coordination and leadership in school-community relations should be fixed upon some one person. Formerly, this person probably would have been drawn from the press. With the broader concept of the work, however, the need is to have a person with much more than press experience, although this would still be desirable in terms of mass media of communication. Today, however, skill is needed in techniques of community analysis and in communication, ability to help others develop competency in working with laypersons in a wide variety of ways, and knowledge in the field of education. The person must be an expert in public participation and involvement.

Evaluation of the program and of its various aspects is of vital importance. Many activities are carried on without any systematic attempt at collecting available data and at evaluating the work done. Many parent-teacher associations carry on programs for years without critically constructive evaluations being made. A citizens' committee is formed, operates for several months or a year, submits a report, and dissolves without anyone's studying its procedures and its strengths and limitations. When another committee is formed, there is too little knowledge available as a result of past experience. What are the results of the program of reporting through the press, or through special reports? What coverage of vital issues is offered? Various people have judgments regarding the effectiveness of various techniques and procedures, but all too rarely are they based upon a planned evaluation. Just how is desirable educational change effected?

THE COMMUNITY AND ITS SCHOOLS

In concluding this section, attention is called to the fact that the community (the local school system or the area served by the individual school) substantially determines the quantity and quality of educational provisions. Its understandings, values, and ability to organize its efforts and to act are central elements in the decisions that it inevitably makes.

In making these decisions the community must have concern for children and youth and also for various staff members connected with the schools. It must be aware of the organizational structure of the community and of the schools. It must be familiar with legal structure pertaining to schools and function in accord with it, effecting changes when needed. It must constantly seek facts so that it may make sound decisions. It must periodically reexamine its philosophical commitments and use them as standards for evaluating its practices.

In all these activities the community should be able to regard the school administrative staff as its agent, providing leadership in its relentless search for a more adequate educational program—a program involving the aspirations and practices of schools, community, and parents. The community must have an understanding of the conditions under which leadership can function effectively, and it must scrupulously protect those conditions. The leader must no less scrupulously respect the competency of the community to make decisions.

Under these circumstances, the community and its educational leaders cooperate in planning, in formulating policy, in implementing programs, and in evaluating. School-community relations are not then essentially matters of reporting or interpreting. Rather, they are carrying forward a public enterprise with laypersons and educators playing the respective roles that are most rewarding in terms of the education of people. Action now builds mutual understanding in depth.

The community must recognize that it has direct responsibility for its schools—but, perhaps equally important, indirect responsibility through the role it plays in the state and federal governmental processes. If overregulation is a reality—if "legislated learning" is to be avoided—this will result most probably because enough communities are deeply involved with schooling and are prepared to seek appropriate action regarding it.

SOME IMPORTANT PROBLEMS AND ISSUES

In the following pages, consideration is given to a few of the major issues pertaining to the community and its schools.

May Public Opinion or a Pressure Group Be Too Large a Determiner of Educational Practice?

There is danger that uninformed public opinion or perhaps a small but highly vocal group will have too large an influence on educational practice. Occasionally, a meeting is reported where a vote is taken on a rather technical subject about which the voters are uninformed. The individual or group with the greatest pressure potential does not necessarily have the sound answer.

The school administrator should not abdicate leadership responsibility, a responsibility that includes presenting the facts and the results of studies that have been carried on regarding the problem, presenting proposals for a more thorough study, and presenting suggestions for essential research. The administrator must assist groups in recognizing that there are important ways to get information regarding a matter other than asking opinions about it. Public interest in an issue needs to be seen as an opportunity for its fuller study—an opportunity for many to learn more about the issue.

This is not to suggest that public opinion should be ignored on many issues. It is an important factor in many situations and must be considered. However, this interest may be of more value in suggesting communication, clarifying goals and practices, or reexamining values than in pointing the way in regard to practice. If public opinion differs widely from the views or understandings of school personnel, an excellent opportunity would appear to exist for some planned research and a cooperative study of the problem.

The development of sound educational practices demands that there be recognition of the limitations of the expert. Often the expert may be so deeply immersed in the subject that some of the broader implications are missed. It also requires that the contribution of the expert be recognized and capitalized upon. Closer attention to many educational problems will increase the awareness of laypersons regarding the complexity of the issues. It will reduce the demand for simple solutions—especially those involving a return to some practice that may have worked reasonably well in a far simpler and quite different society. It may also result in the development of a more soundly based public opinion that could be a most important element in controlling the influence of groups not seeking constructive ends.

What are the strengths and limitations of the expert? How can a community best use the expert? What types of issues require research rather than a survey of public opinion to arrive at sound solutions?

Does the Closeness of the School to the Community Subject the School to the Narrowness of the Community?

Will not the school merely reflect the prejudices of the community if it works closely with it? Will not community lack of concern for human values limit the school in the attention it can give to them? Will the administrator become a part of the business group with which he or she associates, largely a reflector of its concepts? or the captive of a pressure group?

In response to these queries, a number of observations may be made. The community may of course contain a wide variety of groups and individuals, some of whom may have better vision regarding educational objectives than the administrator and the teaching staff. Then, too, it is assumed that the administrator has the competence to work with groups without being enveloped by them. The administrator's own values and commitments with reference to society and education are an important source of strength. Although leadership is recognized as having a relationship to various situational forces, the assumption must not be made that the administrator is without influence, adrift in a nondescript public opinion or pressure group sea. Rather, knowledge of the complexity of the leadership role enables the administrator to be more effective.

The community also has values that if brought to public attention may be important levers through which it can raise its vision and activities. The administrator has responsibilities in this sphere.

Finally, in the case of the community that does not seek or attain even desirable minimum levels of educational provision, whether in terms of what is taught or how it is taught, there is recourse to the state and to constitutional rights. In general, the state should be seen as a stimulating agency, an agency of cross-fertilization challenging communities with the pollen gathered over the nation. Regrettably, however, there will also be times when the state must make attempts at enforcing minimum standards. This role of the state should remain a minor one, one that is exercised less and less frequently as competent communities seriously contemplate and act upon educational problems. Therefore, there would seem to be much reason for seeking the close integration of the community and the school, recognizing, however, that neither local community nor the local school system will always take a sound position. The interaction of the two, with contributions to thought and practice from school and community leaders and at times from the outside, offers much promise.

Can the schools rise above the community? How can the administrator avoid becoming the instrument of the more reactionary forces in the community? of a militant, pressure group?

What Is the Promise of the PTA? the Site Council? a New Partner?

If public understanding and involvement with the education service is essential, it is clear that it is to be accomplished most fundamentally at the site level. Here the foundations are established upon which sound district, state, and federal action can be taken. Here involvement in the educational process can be educative for many. Here the impact of local district, state, and federal action must be determined. Here the effective partnership in the educational process between home and school must be forged.

In some communities the parent-teacher organization is one of the more important parts of the power structure devoted to the advancement of education. Some people hold that in too many instances the parents' group or citizens' group may become merely a mouthpiece of professional educators. Some "educators" may desire to have parents' groups play this role.

It is surely proper and desirable that the parents associated with the school should be part of the organization of the total forces devoted to education. It must be recognized, however, that the total structure related to education will be better and stronger if various parts of it enjoy a very real measure of independence and initiative. The parent group that does not think for itself is not one of great strength. Neither is it, in the long run, one that contributes significantly to education.

Educators and other citizens need to develop stronger belief in the desirability of honest differences in judgment, in the expression of different points of view. The submissive power structure is not one that will grapple effectively with large issues. Groups motivated by common purposes can gain much through the utilization of all the capacity found in them—and by developing their potential capacity through attacking important issues.

The decade of the 1970s was characterized by the establishment of many site councils—in the case of federal and state programs and in the case of many local authorities. The efforts along these lines have frequently left much to be desired.

However, this does not suggest that movement in this direction is undesirable or inevitably unproductive. Too frequently these developments have not made clear the composition of the council, its powers, its relation to the board of education, its manner of operation, or its relation to other somewhat similar bodies on the same site. And many administrators have been unready for such a body and finding several of them—each with its own specific goals, with power shifting within the council, with frequent changes in federal and state regulations—have not worked with them in an effective manner. A part of the problem, of course, related to the lack of preparation for and lack of competence of the site administrator to deal with this issue.

There has now been enough experience with such councils that a more effective arrangement should be developed. In this regard local school districts and the state and federal governments need to reexamine carefully and to clean up their policies and requirements. An effective arrangement would probably need to provide a *single* site council that can serve the needs of the school and community, the special programs, and the base program

- with representation from parents, other citizens, teachers, the administration, and students (in the secondary schools)
- with carefully defined significant powers and responsibilities
- with established procedures for appointment and term of service of members and for the organization of the council and its functioning
- with defined relationships to the principal, programs, and the local school system

A Committee on Enquiry[9] (in England and Wales) has studied this issue. It noted commitment to the "variety and individuality" of schools and the concern to ensure a high quality of education to *all* children. It favored the recognition of the "special character of the individual school" within the framework of national and local policies and provision of a single body with "an equal partnership of all those with a legitimate concern."

What Are the Limits of Involvement as a Practice Designed to Improve Educational Services?

There are limits to involvement in terms of available time, in terms of the contribution of those involved, and in terms of the abilities of the various parties to work together in a satisfactory manner.

Development of plans for and working with large numbers of laypersons is time consuming for the educator. Work with too many groups at once may result in neglecting other responsibilities. This may be remedied in part as more members of the professional staff develop competency in working with lay groups. Laypersons also have many demands upon their time, and, unless adequate resources are available to facilitate the collection of essential data, committees either fail

---

[9]Committee on Enquiry, Department of Education and Science, *A New Partnership for Our Schools* (London: Her Majesty's Stationery Office, 1977).

to do the job or do it without adequate knowledge. The limits of time for involvement therefore need to be considered carefully.

Limitations may also exist in terms of the competency of various people to work together and to contribute to the specific issue under consideration. Laypersons may be profitably involved in a consideration of the uses to which the school buildings will be put in evenings and for which provision should be made in the plans, but there would be little point in having them consider details of structural safety. Various factors have to be considered when determining whether or not there will be involvement and what the nature of the involvement will be.

Finally, it should be noted that participation must be carried on in such a manner as not to hamper the operation of the organization. Many decisions need to be made in the operation of a school or school system. Involvement is essential in broad policy and procedural determination but scarcely in the details of administration resulting from the application of the policy. Citizens may, however, be involved in preliminary screening for a principalship provided the limits of their role are clearly established in guidelines.

Unless there is a realization of the limits of involvement, it is conceivable that it will result in increasing the insecurity of the teacher and administrator and in reducing the effectiveness of the educational program. On the other hand, its possible contribution to the teacher, to the administrator, and to the education of children and young people is large. With careful consideration the dangers should be largely avoided while the benefits are secured. Fruitful utilization of involvement requires time and analyzed experience.

Why must much of the participation occur at the school level? How can staff and citizens be prepared for participation in the school–community relations activity? Are teachers prepared to work on studies in cooperation with citizens? What are the practical limits of involvement?

SELECTED REFERENCES

Bollens, John C., and Henry J. Schmandt, *The Metropolis: Its People, Politics and Economic Life,* 3d ed. New York: Harper & Row, Publishers, Inc., 1975.

Campbell, Roald F., Luvern L. Cunningham, and Roderick F. McPhee, *The Organization and Control of American Schools.* Columbus, Ohio: Charles E. Merrill Publishing Company, 1965.

——, and John A. Ramseyer, *School-Community Relationships.* Boston: Allyn & Bacon, Inc., 1955.

Dahl, Robert, *Who Governs?* New Haven, Conn.: Yale University Press, 1961.

Havighurst, Robert J. and Bernice L. Neugarten, *Society and Education,* 3rd ed. Boston: Allyn & Bacon, Inc., 1967.

Hawley, Willis D. and Frederick M. Wirt, eds., *The Search for Community Power.* Englewood Cliffs, N.J.: Prentice-Hall, Inc., 1968.

Hunter, Floyd, *Community Power Structure. A Study of Decision Makers.* Chapel Hill: University of North Carolina Press, 1953.

Kaufman, Herbert, *Politics and Policies in State and Local Governments.* Englewood Cliffs, N.J.: Prentice-Hall, Inc., 1963.

Kimbrough, Ralph B., *Political Power and Educational Decision Making.* Chicago: Rand McNally & Company, 1964.

Kirst, Michael W., ed., *The Politics of Education*. Berkeley, Calif.: McCutchan Publishing Corporation, 1970.

Rose, Arnold M., *The Power Structure: Political Processes in American Society*. New York: Oxford University Press, 1967.

Schaffarzick, Jon, and Gary Sykes, eds., *Value Conflicts and Curriculum Issues: Lessons from Research and Experience*. Berkeley, Calif.: McCutchan Publishing Corporation, 1979.

Walberg, Herbert J. *Educational Environments and Effects: Evaluation, Policy and Productivity*. Berkeley, Calif.: McCutchan Publishing Corporation, 1979.

Part 2

THE ORGANIZATION
for EDUCATION

10

THE
FEDERAL GOVERNMENT
and EDUCATION

As was pointed out in Chapter 2, under the Tenth Amendment to the Constitution of the United States, the provision for and the control of public education is considered generally to be one of the powers reserved to the states. Despite this fact, the federal government, especially in recent years, has been deeply involved in education. A 748-page volume was required to publish eighty-eight federal statutes relating to education[1] in the *Compilation of Federal Education Laws* prepared for the Committee on Education and Labor of the House of Representatives in 1971. The National Center for Education Statistics[2] listed chronologically 87 selected federal acts providing for federal programs for education and related activities.

[1] Committee on Education and Labor, House of Representatives, *A Compilation of Federal Educational Laws* (Washington, D.C.: U.S. Government Printing Office, 1971).

[2] W. Vance Grant and C. George Lind, *Digest of Education Statistics 1979,* U.S. Department of Health, Education, and Welfare, Education Division, National Center for Education Statistics (Washington, D.C.: U.S. Government Printing Office, 1979), pp. 157–162.

Fifteen of these laws were enacted between 1787 and 1940, eighteen from 1941 to 1957, and fifty-four between 1958 and 1978.

The United States Office of Education listed 114 programs administered by the office in a publication entitled *1980 Guide to Office of Education Programs.* This list does not include all the educational programs financed in whole or in part by the federal government. The National Center for Education Statistics reported thirty-two different federal departments and agencies administering federal funds appropriated for education in 1979.[3] However, approximately 77 percent of the federal funds for elementary and secondary education (excluding federal funds for pupil nutrition) was administered by the U.S. Office of Education in 1979. Federal funds for the public schools have increased from 1.4 percent of the total of federal, state, and local revenue receipts for the public schools in 1942 to approximately 9.0 percent in 1979. Federal funds for higher education have also been greatly increased during that period. In this chapter we will present a brief history of federal relations to education, describe some of the major issues, and analyze some of the recent major changes in federal educational policy.

The relationship of the federal government to public education has become the battleground for testing many important principles of law, theories of government, and philosophical values. Issues concerning states' rights, the general welfare, the police power, federalism, freedom of speech and press, freedom of religion, separation of church and state, impairing the obligation of contracts, equal protection of the laws, civil rights, the due process of the law, the power of Congress to tax and spend, and other vital matters have become involved in this problem. Decisions on public education made by the federal government serve as precedents defining the relationship of the federal government to the states and to the people on many other important issues. Fundamental changes in the economy of the nation and in international relationships are bringing about many changes in the respective roles of the federal government and the states. Changes and proposals for changes naturally become political issues in a democracy. Therefore, it is not surprising that interest in the relationship of the federal government to public education is increasing.

A comprehensive treatment of this problem would require a formidable volume. Therefore, this chapter presents only some of the more important facts and issues that will serve as a basis for the further study of the relationship of the federal government to public education.

FEDERAL CONSTITUTIONAL AUTHORITY[4]

The powers of the government of the United States are delegated rather than inherent. The Tenth Amendment provides that "The powers not delegated to the United States by the Constitution, nor prohibited by it to the States, are reserved to the States respectively or to the people." The federal government, therefore, has no powers other than those specifically conferred on it by the Constitution or such as can reasonably be implied from those specifically granted.[5] On the other hand, the

[3] *Ibid.,* p. 164.
[4] The authors are indebted to Newton Edwards, *The Courts and the Public Schools* (Chicago: University of Chicago Press, 1955), for many of the concepts set forth in this section.
[5] *Ibid.,* p. 1.

governmental powers of the states are plenary except for the powers that have been delegated to the federal government or withheld from the states by some specific provision of the Constitution.

The Constitution of the United States makes no reference to education. Therefore, under the Tenth Amendment the states have assumed the basic responsibility for public education. Any authority of the federal government to finance, to control, or to regulate education must be found in the implied powers delegated to the central government in one or more clauses of the Constitution. But the Constitution is a very broad statement of principles, and numerous judicial interpretations of these principles have greatly extended the application of the implied powers of the federal government since the adoption of the Constitution.

The General Welfare Clause

Clause 1 of Section 8 of Article I of the Constitution provides that "The Congress shall have the power to lay and collect taxes, duties, imposts and excises, to pay the debts and provide for the common defense and general welfare of the United States." This clause of the Constitution, although it deals with many other important matters, is commonly known as the "general welfare clause." It has been one of the most controversial provisions of the Constitution since the very beginning. It was the center of the famous controversy between Alexander Hamilton and James Madison. It was argued by Madison that this clause conferred no additional powers on the Congress to tax and spend, and therefore it was meant only to be a reference to powers that were specifically granted to Congress by the Constitution. Hamilton held, however, that this clause conferred upon Congress the power to tax and spend for purposes in addition to those specifically enumerated by the Constitution and in fact conferred on Congress the power to tax and spend for any purpose that it deemed to be for the general welfare.

This controversy has continued for more than 180 years, but the battleground has shifted from constitutional authority to wisdom of policy. The Supreme Court, in ruling upon the Agricultural Adjustment Act, declared that "the power of Congress to authorize expenditures of public money for public purposes is not limited by the direct grants of legislative power found in the Constitution."[6] The Supreme Court, in an opinion relating to the Social Security Act, held that the descretion of determining whether some purpose of federal expenditure was for the general welfare laid with the Congress and not the court, provided that it was not clearly a display of arbitrary power. The court further declared that the concept of general welfare is not static because what is critical or urgent changes with the times.[7]

It seems clear that the constitutional authority of the Congress to appropriate money for public education has been clearly established by the principles of law enumerated by the Supreme Court in other cases before it. Therefore, the controversy now centers on whether it is good public policy for the federal government to take positive action with respect to public education and what the nature and extent of such action should be rather than on the constitutional authority of Congress to act.

[6] *United States* v. *Butler*, 297 U.S. 1, 56 Sup. Ct. 312.
[7] *Helvering* v. *Davis*, 301 Dr. S. 619, 57 Sup. Ct. 904.

Opposition to federal control of education is widespread in the United States. The term "federal control" is interpreted in various ways by different people. Actually, the federal government from the beginning of the nation has exercised substantial control over certain aspects of the educational activities of the states, as will be explained later. Many of these controls are so well accepted that the people have seldom thought of them as controls. Actually, if a movement were started to eliminate them, there would be as much opposition as there is to more federal control of education. Such is the force of custom and propaganda.

The educational policies and activities of the states are profoundly affected by limitations on the powers of the states contained in the Constitution. Some of these limitations are discussed in the following paragraphs.

Separation of church and state. The power of the federal government to control the relationship of the public schools to religion was clearly established by the First and Fourteenth Amendments. The First Amendment provides: "Congress shall make no law respecting an establishment of religion, or prohibiting the free exercise thereof. "The Fourteenth Amendment provides in part that "No state shall make or enforce any law which shall abridge the privileges or immunities of citizens of the United States." The Supreme Court has held that this amendment makes the First Amendment applicable to the states in defining the relationship between church and state. In the case of *Illinois ex rel. McCollum* v. *Board of Education*[8] and in *Everson* v. *Board of Education*[9] the court declared the First Amendment was intended to erect a "wall of separation between church and state." The court has made it clear in these two opinions and in other opinions that tax-supported property cannot be used for religious instruction and that neither a state nor the federal government can set up a church or levy a tax, large or small, to support any religious activities or institutions.

In recent years, a number of states have attempted to give financial assistance to parochial schools from public funds. Up to the present time, the U.S. Supreme Court has declared these measures to be a violation of the First Amendment.[10]

A case involving Bible reading in the public schools was brought before the Supreme Court in October 1962. The court ruled in 1963 that Bible reading in the public schools was a violation of the First Amendment.[11]

Equal protection of the laws. Neither a state nor an agency of the state, such as a board of education, can deny a citizen of the United States equal protection of the law. The Supreme Court on May 17, 1954, in dealing with five cases before it, ruled that segregation in the public schools was unconstitutional because it denied equal protection of the laws. The court stated

---

[8] 333 U.S. 203.

[9] 330 U.S. 1.

[10] Examples of such cases are *Lemon* v. *Kurtzman,* 403 U.S. 602; 91 Sup. Ct. 2105, 1971; and *Leeman* v. *Sloan* 340 F. Supp. 1356, 1972.

[11] *School District of Abington Township* v. *Schempp,* 374 U.S. 203.

We conclude that in the field of public education the doctrine of "separate but equal" has no place. Separate educational facilities are inherently unequal. Therefore, we hold that the plaintiffs and others similarly situated for whom the actions are brought are, by reason of the segregation complained of, deprived of the equal protection of the laws guaranteed by the Fourteenth Amendment.[12]

This ruling reversed the position of the court on *Plessy* v. *Ferguson* in 1896, when it ruled in a transportation case that separate but equal facilities were constitutional.[13] The educational policies of seventeen states and the District of Columbia were vitally affected by this decision. The *de facto* segregation by race in the large cities of many other states has also been affected by this decision. It will be noted that this decision controls not only the educational policies of the states with respect to segregation by race but also the policies of boards of education wherever situated. The states' rights theory, insofar as it applies to segregation of the races, was also overthrown by this decision.

Since 1954, numerous orders have been issued by federal courts requiring boards of education to take measures to desegregate the school systems under their control. Up to the present time, all such orders providing for the implementation of *Brown* v. *Board of Education,* when appealed, have been upheld by the U.S. Supreme Court.

The Civil Rights Act of 1964 greatly increased the power of the federal government to eliminate discrimination in public education. Title VI of this act states that "No person in the United States shall on the ground of race, color, or national origin, be excluded from participation in, be denied the benefits of, or be subject to discrimination, under any program or activity receiving Federal financial assistance." This act gives any federal agency disbursing federal funds the power to withhold such funds if the recipient agency or institution violates this act. The Office of Education has used this act in recent years to force racial integration by withholding federal funds from both public and private schools and colleges that fail to comply with the provisions of the act. Since federal grants are now quite substantial, this is a powerful control designed to force racial integration. The enforcement of the Civil Rights Act has greatly speeded up this movement.

Contractual obligations. The Supreme Court in a large number of cases has ruled that neither a state nor a board of education could take action "impairing the obligations of contracts" as provided in Section 10 of Article I of the Constitution. This provision of the Constitution has been applied frequently to settling controversies between states and colleges or universities over contractual provisions of charters and to controversies between teachers and governing authorities over tenure and retirement rights. The Supreme Court has held that "a legislative enactment may contain provisions which, when accepted as a basis of action by individuals, become contracts between them and the state or its subdivision."[14] Thus,

---

[12] *Brown* v. *Board of Education,* 347 U.S. 483, 74 Sup. Ct. 686.

[13] 163 U.S. 537, 16 Sup. Ct. 1138.

[14] *State ex rel. Anderson* v. *Brand,* 313 U.S. 95.

the federal Constitution itself provides substantial control over the actions of the states and boards of education, insofar as those actions involve the impairment of obligations under contract.

The due process of law and the police power. The Fourteenth Amendment provides in part "Nor shall any state deprive any person of life, liberty, or property, without due process of law." But the police power is inherent in every state, and this power frequently must be balanced against the due-process-of law clause that protects an individual. Edwards states that "The police power is that power of the state to limit individual rights in the interest of the social group."[15] The limits of the states in exercising the police power are continually being redefined by the courts. Prior to 1860 the Supreme Court placed almost no restrictions on the states in the exercise of this police power except those restrictions specifically set forth in the Constitution. Since the adoption of the Fourteenth Amendment with its due-process-of-law clause, the Supreme Court has had much greater authority to restrict the police power of the states, but it did not begin to exercise that power until after the case of *Muller v. Oregon*[16] in 1908. In that case the court took cognizance of physiological and social facts bearing on the employment of women. This case set the precedent for considering psychological and social facts in the five segregation cases ruled on in 1954.

Space does not permit adequate illustration of these limitations on the educational powers of the states and their subdivisions. Attention has already been directed to the case of *Brown v. Board of Education* in which it was ruled that segregation itself was unequal.[17] Psychological and social facts and not abstract legal concepts were the bases for the decision.

On the other hand, the Supreme Court has upheld the constitutionality of the Smith Act.[18] This act makes it a crime punishable by fine and imprisonment to advocate the overthrow of the government by force. This act clearly comes within the police power of the federal government. It is definitely a federal control over one aspect of what may be taught in a public or even a private school. Therefore, those who insist that the federal government should have no control whatsoever over the curriculum of the public schools seem to be unaware of the inherent police power of the federal government relating to matters of national concern.

Other Aspects of Federal Controls over Education

Alexander states that federal controls over education emanate from three sources: "(1) acquiescence by states in accepting federal grants which are provided under the authority given Congress under the general welfare clause; (2) public schools may come under certain standards or regulations which the Congress has authorized under the commerce clause; and (3) courts may constrain public school actions where they come in conflict with federal constitutional provisions protecting individual rights and freedoms."[19]

[15] Edwards, *The Courts and the Public Schools,* p. 12.

[16] 208 U.S. 412.

[17] 347 U.S. 483.

[18] *Dennis et al.* v. *United States,* 341 U.S. 494.

[19] Kern Alexander, *School Law* (St. Paul, Minn.: West Publishing Company, 1980), p. 44.

Constitutional controls over the educational activities of the states and local boards of education have been discussed briefly. Also of great importance at the present time is the authority given federal agencies to withhold federal funds from states and local school districts that do not follow federal regulations in the expenditure of the funds being allocated. It is assumed that the state and local school districts assent to these controls when they accept the federal grant. All federal grants to the public schools are categorical grants, and all these grants, with the exception of the federal impact aid grants, must be expended in accordance with regulations promulgated by federal agencies. This control is made even more pervasive under the provisions of Title VI of the federal Civil Rights Act of 1964. This statute authorizes the withholding of federal funds from any agency which violates the provisions of the statute.

Title VII of the Civil Rights Act of 1964 as amended provides in part the following: "(A). It shall be an unlawful employment practice for an employer (1) to fail or refuse to hire or to discharge any individual, or otherwise to discriminate against any individual with respect to his compensation, terms, conditions, or privileges of employment, because of such individual's race, color, religion, sex or national origin." This statute provides a powerful federal control over the employment policies of the public schools and institutions of higher learning. This statute has been the basis for numerous lawsuits in which "affirmative action" is sought to redress unequal employment practices.

Title IX of the Education Amendments of 1972 forbids discrimination on the basis of sex in any educational program or activity that receives financial aid. The law gives the Department of Health, Education, and Welfare the authority to withhold federal funds from any institution that does not comply with the provisions of the act.

It is interesting to note that the Civil Rights Act of 1871 (42 U.S.C., Sec. 1983) has been used recently as a basis for action at law to obtain damages from school officials and even teachers. This act provides that if anyone causes or causes to be subjected "any citizen of the United States or other person within the jurisdiction thereof to the deprivation of any rights, privileges, or immunities secured by the Constitution and laws" they are subject to an action in equity. A number of states are now providing teachers and administrators with liability insurance to protect them from judgments based on this statute.

The due process clause of the Constitution and provisions of the Civil Rights Acts are now being used to protect the rights of students, teachers, and other school employees.[20]

It has been "conventional wisdom" in some quarters to assert that, if all federal aid to education were abolished, there would be no federal control over education. It is now evident that we will continue to have substantial federal control over education with or without federal aid. However, most of the federal controls over education are for the purpose of protecting the constitutional and statutory rights, privileges, immunities, and civil rights of citizens of the United States. This is "positive liberty" rather than "negative liberty." An example of this policy is federal statute 94-142, called the Education of the Handicapped Act, which requires boards of education to provide educational programs and facilities appropriate to the needs of all handicapped pupils. If a board of education fails to provide appro-

---

[20] For a comprehensive discussion of these issues, see Alexander, *School Law.*

priately for the needs of these pupils, it can be held liable by legal processes. It may seem to the reader from the discussion of federal controls presented in this chapter that the United States exercises more central control over education than do most other nations. The reverse is true. No other nation in the world exercises fewer central controls over education than does the United States. No other nation gives more decision-making authority over education to its major subdivisions, such as states or provinces or to local school agencies, than does the United States.

The U.S. Supreme Court in ruling on cases involving education is frequently forced to decide whether the issue is a power reserved to the states under the Tenth Amendment or whether it is a right guaranteed to the individual under the First and Fourteenth Amendments. For example, the Supreme Court in *Rodriquez* refused by a five-to-four vote to find the Texas plan of school financing unconstitutional primarily because the court held that education was not a "fundamental interest" guaranteed by the Constitution.[21] Also, the Supreme Court held that federal statutes establishing minimum wage and maximum hour requirements could not be applied to the states or to political subdivisions within the states, such as boards of education, because such requirements violated the Tenth Amendment.[22]

On the other hand, as has been pointed out, the Supreme Court in numerous cases has held the acts and policies of states and political subdivisions thereof to be unconstitutional when the rights of individuals guaranteed by the First and Fourteenth Amendments are violated.

HISTORICAL RELATIONSHIPS

Despite wide differences of opinion concerning the role that should be played by the federal govenment in public education, it has shown an interest in and has participated in the support of public education since before the adoption of the Constitution in 1789. The educational activities of the federal government include (1) financing and administering its own educational programs and (2) aiding the states and territories and institutions and agencies therein in financing and otherwise promoting education. A brief review of some of those activities is presented in the following paragraphs.

Land Grants for the Public Schools

The Ordinance of 1785 provided that "There shall be reserved the lot number 16 of every township for the maintenance of public schools in each township." This provision was repeated in the Ordinance of 1787 providing for the government of the Northwest Territory. The interest of the federal government in public education was clearly demonstrated in these words contained in the Ordinance of 1787: "Religion, morality, and knowledge being necessary to good government and the happiness of mankind, schools and the means of education shall be forever encouraged."

Ohio was the first state admitted to the Union under the Ordinance of 1787. The Ohio policy of setting aside the sixteenth section of each township for the

[21] *San Antonio Independent School District et al.* v. *Demetrio Rodriquez et al.,* 411 U.S. 1, 93 Sup. Ct. 1278 (1973).
[22] *National League of Cities* v. *Usery,* 426 U.S. 833, 96 Sup. Ct. 2465 (1976).

public schools was followed for states admitted to the Union up to 1848. Congress set aside two sections in every township for public education when the Oregon Territory was established in 1848. This policy was followed until 1896, when Utah was granted four sections in every township. Similar grants were given to Arizona and New Mexico when they were admitted to the Union in 1912.

The federal government made many other types of early grants for the benefit of the public schools. Some of those were as follows: (1) grants of funds in lieu of land grants in Indian territory, (2) additional land grants under the Internal Improvement Act of 1841, (3) grants of saline lands, (4) grants of 5 percent of the funds received by the federal government from sale of public lands in the states, (5) payment to the states of 25 percent of the income from national forests and 37.5 percent of the income received from the extraction of nonmetallic minerals for the benefit of roads and public schools, and (6) allocation of surplus federal revenues to the states in 1836.

Swift has estimated that the early grants of land given by Congress to the thirty public land states aggregated an area ten times as large as Maryland and that grants given to the states in whole or in part for the public schools totaled more than 76 million acres.[23]

Most of the states did not handle these grants very wisely. The land in many states was sold at very low prices. In other states much land was settled by private parties without the states' protesting, and title to the land was lost to the state. In still other states, funds derived from the sale of school lands were lost owing to fiscal mismanagement or misappropriation. However, the income derived from these early land grants is still an important source of revenue in a few states.

Opponents of federal aid for public education almost invariably argue that it is impossible to have federal aid for education without federal control. Nevertheless, the federal government has never exercised any control over these land grants. Perhaps if the federal government had exercised enough control over the land grants to protect them from waste and misappropriation, these grants would have been of greater benefit to the public schools. Such protection could have been given these funds without any interference by the federal government with the prerogatives of the states to determine the school curriculum, organize and administer schools, and exercise all other legitimate powers with respect to education.

The activities of the federal government in administering the territories and making land grants had other important effects on the public schools. The federal government itself organized school systems in each territory, and, when the territory became a state, the federally established school system was taken over by the state. The funds arising from land grants served as precedents for state aid for the public schools.

The Land Grant Colleges

The Morrill Act passed by Congress in 1862 granted 30,000 acres to each state for each representative and senator then in Congress or when a state was admitted to the Union. Provision was made for compulsory military training in the colleges established. The proceeds from the sale of the land grants were required to be used

[23] Fletcher Harper Swift, *Federal and State Policies in Public School Finance in the United States* (Boston: Ginn and Company, 1931), p. 59.

for "the endowment, maintenance and support of at least one college where the leading object shall be, without excluding other scientific and classical studies and including military tactics, to teach such branches of learning as are related to agriculture and mechanic arts." This act also had as one of its purposes "to promote the liberal and practical education of the industrial classes in the several pursuits and professions of life."

This act is of great significance, because it has demonstrated (1) that the federal government, when it deemed it necessary to do so for the common defense or the general welfare, could and would take positive action with respect to education and (2) that the federal government could and would take positive action with respect to vital areas of education that were neglected by the states. Prior to 1862, most institutions of higher learning catered primarily to the sons and daughters of the wealthy. Cultural and classical education was emphasized. Education in agriculture and engineering was not considered a proper activity for an institution of higher learning. This was a carry-over from European traditions concerning higher education. The Morrill Act might therefore be considered a layperson's revolt from the prevailing educational leadership of that day.

The Smith-Lever Act

The Smith-Lever Act in 1914 provided for extension services by county agricultural agents, home demonstrators, 4-H leaders, and specialists in agriculture and homemaking and for the professional training of teachers in these subjects. The Coffee-Ketchum Act of 1928, the Bankhead–Jones Act of 1935, the Bankhead-Flannagan Act of 1945, and subsequent amendments have broadened the scope and increased the funds provided by the Smith-Lever Act. The Smith-Lever Act for the first time required the states to match educational funds provided by the federal government.

The extension workers provided by the Smith-Lever Act have made a significant contribution to the education of farmers and housewives. The agricultural agents have been particularly effective in bringing the findings of the experimental farms to the farmers. The extension workers have also made significant contributions to the lives of rural youth. Field demonstrations and the "group process" were first used extensively by these workers. The extension workers were among the first educators to experiment with the techniques of group dynamics and the dynamics of change. They have clearly demonstrated the value of the role of "change agents."

The extension service provided under the Smith-Lever Act is not an integral part of the system of public education. The act is administered on the federal level by the Department of Agriculture. The extension workers are employed by the governing bodies of counties. The state director of extension services is almost always associated with a land grant institution of higher learning, but this is about the only connection between the extension program and the program of public education.

The Smith-Hughes Act

The Smith-Hughes Act of 1917 was the first federal act providing funds for vocational education below college level. This act provided a continuing appropriation for vocational education in agriculture, trades and industry, and homemaking and for teacher training in those fields. The original act required that the states and local school units match the federal appropriation on a dollar-for-dollar basis. Federal assistance for vocational education was further extended by the following acts: the George-Reed Act of 1929, the George-Ellzey Act of 1935, the George-Deen Act of 1937, the George-Barden Act of 1946, the Vocational Education Act of 1963, and the Vocational Education Amendments of 1968 and 1972.

Public interest in vocational education increased rapidly with the beginning of the twentieth century. By 1909, some 500 agricultural high schools had been established. By 1911, forty-four of the forty-seven states offered instruction in home economics in some high schools. A number of trade schools had been established in city school systems. Nevertheless, comprehensive vocational education opportunities were not available to most high school pupils. Lay organizations such as the American Federation of Labor, the Grange, the National Association of Manufacturers, and the Chamber of Commerce of the United States all urged the expansion of vocational education in high schools. The National Education Association made certain studies of vocational education but did not play a very active role in promoting the development of vocational education. The educational leadership administering the high schools in the early part of the twentieth century was concerned much more with college preparatory education than with education to meet the needs of all pupils of secondary school age. Therefore, the federal acts providing financial support for vocational education represented, in actuality, a lay revolt against prevailing educational policies.

The Smith-Hughes Act provided some federal control of vocational education, but in practice much of the control was delegated to the states. The Smith-Hughes Act and subsequent acts provided a great stimulus for vocational education. All states now spend from state and local taxes far more for vocational education than the amount provided by the federal government, despite the fact that federal funds for vocational education have been greatly increased in recent years.

Relief Measures Affecting Education

The nation was deep in its greatest financial depression by 1933. Franklin D. Roosevelt was inaugurated president in March 1933 and almost immediately he started his New Deal to break the depression. The New Deal included a large number of new and experimental measures that had as their principal purpose the improvement of the economic condition of the people. Many of these measures affected education, but they were designed primarily as relief measures. All the federal agencies established in the 1930s to administer the relief programs affecting education were abolished in the early 1940s. However, the school food assistance provided by the Federal Surplus Commodities Corporation was superseded by the National School Lunch Act of 1946, which is administered by the Department of Agriculture.

Federal Educational Activities for Defense and War Prior to 1958

It would require a formidable volume to describe all federal educational activities for defense and war. The federal government has sometimes operated elementary schools, high schools, institutions of college grade, and various other types of educational programs. Some are on service posts, some are in territories, and some are abroad. In fact, all these activities are still being carried on by the federal government. Furthermore, the federal government has carried on many types of war and defense educational activities through state and local agencies and institutions. Space will permit only a few examples.

The armed forces. The Military Academy was established at West Point in 1802, the Naval Academy at Annapolis in 1845, and the Air Force Academy at Colorado Springs in 1954. The Army Medical School was established in 1893, the Army War College in 1902 (superseded by the National War College in 1946) and the Air University in 1947.

The educational system for enlisted men began with an act of Congress in 1866 which provides that "Whenever troops are serving at any post, garrison, or permanent camp, there shall be established a school where all men may be provided with instruction in the common English branches of education, and especially in the history of the United States." Thousands of men have been taught to read and write and also have been given much additional postschool education under this program. The act of 1866 probably set the precedent for the development of the Armed Forces Institute in 1945. This institute now provides very extensive programs of educational opportunities for all career and active duty personnel. It is a voluntary off-duty program.

In summary, the educational activities of Army, the Navy, the Air Force, the Marines, and the Coast Guard now make it possible for all personnel to obtain a wide range of educational opportunities that will not only benefit the armed services but will be of great benefit to the service personnel in civilian life.

Federal impact areas. The Lanham Act of 1941 provided federal financial assistance to local governments for the construction, maintenance, and operation of community facilities in areas where war-incurred federal activities created financial burdens that the local governments could not bear. Federal authorities worked through the Office of Education in administering this act insofar as it applied to public education. This act was superseded in 1950 by P.L. 815 and P.L. 874, which continued approximately the same type of federal benefits to areas adversely affected by federal activities.

Aid for veterans. Certain postwar but war-related educational activities of the federal government are deserving of mention. The Congress in 1918 provided for the vocational education of disabled veterans of World War I, and the Vocational Rehabilitation Act of 1943 made similar provisions for disabled veterans of World War II.

The most important of the veterans' education acts was P.L. 346 of 1944, popularly known as the G.I. Bill. This act provided training for all veterans of World War II, the length of training depending upon the length of service. The educational provisions of this act were very liberal, covering almost every kind of training desired by the veteran from ballroom dancing to advanced graduate research. Approximately 8 million veterans had received some training under this act by 1954. Several millions of veterans were enabled to attend college by this act, and college enrollments more than doubled following World War II. Public Law 550 of 1952 provided educational training for the veterans of the Korean conflict. More than a million veterans of the Korean conflict have received the benefits of this act. In 1966, the Congress extended the benefits of the G.I. Bill to veterans of the Cold War. The Veterans Educational Assistance Act made educational aid for service veterans a permanent federal policy for all veterans who have served 180 days or more since January 31, 1955. The recent veterans' education acts have been administered by the Veterans Administration.

The various veterans' education and vocational rehabilitation acts have made educational opportunities available to millions of persons who otherwise would not have had those opportunities. Some studies have shown that the increased income taxes paid by veterans and vocationally rehabilitated persons resulting from increased earning power more than reimburse the federal government for the funds expended on their education.

Federal Educational Activities Since 1958

The year 1958 marked the beginning of a new era in the relationship of the federal government to education. The scientific success of the Russians in launching the first earth satellite in 1957 jarred the people of the United States out of their complacency. We were carrying on the Cold War with Russia, fully confident of our superiority in science and technology. With the launching of Sputnik I came the realization that our potential antagonist might be gaining on us rapidly. This fear triggered the passage of the National Defense Education Act in 1958, which was the beginning of a large number of subsequent federal acts relating to education.

The basic federal policies toward education have not changed since 1958. All federal funds provided for education since that date have been earmarked for special purposes. Therefore, the federal government has continued its long-time policy of providing special-purpose grants rather than grants for general purposes. However, the amounts of these grants have been increased enormously since 1958. The federal government no longer takes a *laissez-faire* attitude toward education. Education is now considered by the federal government as an important means to implement its policies of providing for the common defense, eliminating poverty, promoting economic growth, reducing unemployment, and promoting the general welfare in many other ways.

A few of the more important federal laws relating to education which have been enacted since 1958 are treated briefly in the following paragraphs.

The National Defense Education Act of 1958—Public Law 85-864. Congress defined a new role of education as follows in this act:

> that the security of the nation requires the fullest development of the mental resources and technical skills of its young men and women. The present emergency demands that additional and more adequate educational opportunities be made available. The defense of this Nation depends upon the mastery of modern techniques developed from complex scientific principles. It depends as well upon the discovery and development of new principles, new techniques, and new knowledge.

The ten titles of this act authorized grants and loans assisting both public and private education from the elementary school through graduate school. The original act provided financial aid primarily for science, mathematics, modern foreign languages, technical and vocational education, and counseling and guidance. This act was amended and broadened in 1964 by authorizing financial assistance for instruction in history, geography, civics, English, and reading. The grants, loans, fellowships, and other forms of financial aid provided under this act have had a significant impact on education in this nation.

Manpower Development and Training Act of 1962—Public Law 84-415. The basic objective of this act is to reduce the hard core of unemployment by retraining workers whose skills had become obsolete. The costs of training and training allowances for the unemployed were financed under this act. Although the primary purposes of this act were to provide occupational training for unemployed adult workers and to encourage personnel planning based on research, it also provided for "the testing, counseling, and selection of youths, 16 years of age or older, for occupational training and further schooling."

The Vocational Education Act of 1963—Public Law 88-210. This act more than quadrupled the federal appropriations for vocational and technical education. It has much broader purposes than did the original Smith–Hughes Act for vocational education. The major purposes of the 1963 act are to provide occupational training for persons of all ages and achievement levels in any occupational field that does not require a baccalaureate degree, to provide for related services which will help to ensure quality programs, to assist in the construction of area vocational facilities, and to promote and to provide financial assistance for work–study programs and residential schools. The federal provisions for vocational education were greatly extended by the amendments to the 1963 act in subsequent years.

The Economic Opportunity Act of 1964—Public Law 88-452. The major purpose of this act was "to mobilize the human and financial resources of the Nation to fight poverty in the United States." Section 2 of the act declares "that it is the policy of the United States to eliminate the paradox of poverty in the midst of plenty in this Nation by opening to everyone opportunities for education, training, work, and a life of decency and dignity, and the purpose of the act is to strengthen, supplement, and coordinate efforts in furtherance of that policy." This act, probably more than any other act of Congress, clearly recognized the social value of education as well as its economic value. Education was recognized not only for its value to the individual but also for its contribution to production and to the distribution of the fruits of production.

The Elementary and Secondary Education Act of 1965—Public Law 89-10. This was the most important federal act affecting the elementary and secondary schools passed by Congress up to 1965. It provided, at that time, approximately $1.3 billion annually to support the programs included in the act. It doubled the federal aid available for elementary and secondary schools, increasing the total revenue receipts provided by the federal government for public elementary and secondary schools in 1966 from 4 percent to 8 percent.

There are five major titles of this act. The financial aid under the first three titles is allocated to the elementary and secondary schools and under Titles IV and V to institutions of higher learning and state departments of education. Of the appropriations, 90 percent is earmarked for elementary and secondary schools.

Title I provides financial assistance for educational programs especially designed to benefit the children from families with an income below a specified level per year or who are receiving welfare aid for dependent children; Title II provides funds for libraries, textbooks, and audiovisual materials; Title III provides funds for supplementary education centers for students in both public and private schools; Title IV provides funds for regional educational research and training laboratories; and Title V provides funds for strengthening state departments of education.

The Higher Education Act of 1965—Public Law 83-333. This act contained twelve titles dealing with such matters as community service, library assistance, strengthening developing institutions, student assistance with loans and fellowships, improvement of undergraduate instruction, improvement of facilities, networks for knowledge, education for public service, improvement of graduate programs, and other programs. This act was substantially amended in 1966, 1968, and 1972.

Education of the Handicapped Act—Public Law 94-142. This act greatly increased the federal appropriations for the education of the handicapped. It has been of great assistance to the states and boards of education in meeting court requirements that handicapped pupils be given educational opportunities appropriate to their needs. The purpose of the act is to assist in initiation, expansion, and improvement of programs and projects for the handicapped at preschool, elementary, and secondary levels through grants to states and outlying territories.

Analysis of Recent Developments

Practically every important statute dealing with education enacted by Congress since 1958 has been amended in each succeeding session of Congress. For example the Ninety-second Congress in 1972 enacted P.L. 92-318 which substantially amended the Higher Education Act of 1965, the Vocational Education Act of 1963, the Elementary and Secondary Education Act of 1965, P.L. 874, the General Education Provisions Act, and related acts. Therefore, federal provisions for education are in a very fluid state.

Space does not permit a discussion of all the important federal acts involving education. Fortunately, the National Center of Education Statistics, now a section of the newly established department, annually publishes a *Digest of Education Statistics* that includes detailed information on practically all federal programs and related activities.

Attention has already been directed to the fact that there has been considerable objection to federal controls over education. The objections to federal constitutional controls over education based on the First and Fourteenth Amendments cannot be satisfied unless the Constitution is amended so as to repeal the First and Fourteenth Amendments. There would be little support for that approach. However, objections to federal controls over education caused by the administration of numerous federally earmarked appropriations are legitimate and could be satisfied by consolidating many of the special appropriations into a few large block grants. The *1980 Guide to Office of Education Programs* listed 114 separate appropriations administered by the Office of Education. This list includes only the appropriations administered by the Office of Education (now the Department of Education). As was pointed out previously in this chapter, a number of education appropriations are administered by other federal agencies.

The administration of these numerous federal appropriations greatly increases the cost of administration at both the state and local levels. The frustration caused by numerous bureaucratic controls does not promote support for financial assistance of education. Furthermore, many small school systems do not have the expertise to make application for many of the grants to which the school system is entitled. The inclusion of the many special federal appropriations in the school budget greatly increases the difficulty of developing an equitable school budget. Earmarking special appropriations at both the state and federal levels tends relatively to cause boards of education to oversupport educational functions for which appropriations are earmarked and to undersupport functions for which there are no earmarked appropriations. This is particularly true if nonearmarked local funds must be used to match earmarked appropriations from either the state or federal level. Although numerous educational leaders for many years have advocated that the numerous earmarked federal appropriations for education be consolidated into a few large block grants and that these grants be supplemented by a substantial, nonearmarked general-purpose federal grant for the public schools, at this writing Congress does not seem to be willing to change its present policy.

Although educational leaders are generally critical of the congressional policy of earmarking for special programs all educational appropriations except the appropriation for federal impact areas, a case can be made for that policy. Generally these special appropriations have been made for educational programs which have been neglected by the states and local governing bodies. Congress has considered the support of those programs to be in the national interest. Examples are programs supported by the Morrill Act, the Smith-Hughes Act, the Economic Opportunity Act, the Elementary and Secondary Education Act of 1965, the Education of the Handicapped Act, and many other acts. Federal support for these special areas no doubt stimulated innovation and development in many needed educational programs that had been neglected by the states and their local subdivisions. Most of these special federal appropriations tend to equalize to a limited extent the intrastate support of education because the states of less wealth generally receive more funds per capita from almost any type of federal appropriation than the per capita payment of federal taxes made by those states.

Recent trends in federal funds for education. There are so many different federal funds for education and related activities that different authorities seldom agree on total federal funds for education. The reason for this is that some researchers classify an appropriation for a related activity as a federal fund for education and others do not so classify it. Furthermore, there are three different ways to classify federal funds as follows: (1) budget authority, (2) actual appropriation, and (3) actual federal outlay or disbursement. The student of trends in federal financing

TABLE 10.1 Federal Outlays for Elementary and Secondary Education for 1965 and 1979 (millions of dollars)

PROGRAM	1965	1979*
Office of Education		
Compensatory education (Title I)	—	$2,580
Education for the handicapped	—	560
Emergency school aid	—	305
Bilingual education	—	130
Impact aid	349	781
Vocational education	95	458
Other	104	429
Total	$ 548	$5,243
Head Start	5	566
Other	320	956
Total, excluding food	$ 873	$6,765
School milk and child nutrition	263	2,699
Grand total	$1,136	$9,464

*Estimated.

SOURCE: Adapted from Joseph A. Peckman, ed., *Setting National Priorities, The 1979 Budget* (Washington, D.C.: The Brookings Institution, 1978), p. 92.

of education must exercise care in using the same classification in comparing federal funds for one fiscal year with another year.

The Brookings Institution[24] has made a meaningful analysis of trends in federal funds for elementary and secondary and postsecondary education. Table 10.1 shows trends in federal funds for elementary and secondary education for the years 1965 and 1979 as shown by that study. It is noted that federal funds for elementary and secondary education for 1979, including school food, totaled more than eight times the amount available in 1965. It shows the total federal outlays for elementary and secondary education to have been an estimated $6,765,000,000 in 1979, excluding food, and $9,464,000,000 including food. Conflicting reports of total federal funds for elementary and secondary education for a given year are sometimes due to one report's including federal assistance for food and another report's excluding it.

Table 10.2 shows trends in federal outlays for postsecondary education. This table properly separates payments to students from payments to institutions. Federal support for students rose from about 0.5 billion in 1965 to a little over $8 billion in 1979, or an increase of over 1,500 percent. Federal funds paid to post-

[24] Joseph A. Peckman, ed., *Setting National Priorities, The 1979 Budget* (Washington, D.C.: The Brookings Institution, 1978).

TABLE 10.2 Federal Outlays for Postsecondary Education for 1965 and 1979 (millions of dollars)

PROGRAM	1965	1979*
Payments to students		
Basic educational opportunity grants	–	2,094
Campus-based aid	131	1,099
Guaranteed loans	27	628
Health training and other HEW aid	206	309
Social Security student benefits	–	1,505
Veterans education benefits	43	2,009
Reserve Officer Training Corps and		
other military training	42	349
Other	53	104
Total to students	$ 502	$ 8,097
Payments to institutions		
Research and development conducted at		
colleges and universities	934	3,339
Programs for disadvantaged students and		
aid to developing institutions	–	226
Vocational education	57	193
Special institutions	20	126
Grants and loans for facilities (except		
health)	225	54
Health facilities and resources and		
other HEW aid	58	683
Service academies and other defense education	117	366
Other	57	119
Total to institutions	$1,467	$ 8,097
Total outlays	$1,969	$13,203

*Estimated.

SOURCE: Adapted from Joseph A. Peckman, ed., *Setting National Priorities, The 1979 Budget* (Washington, D.C.: The Brookings Institution, 1978), pp. 106–107.

secondary institutions increased from $1,467 million in 1965 to $5,106 million in 1979, or an increase of 248 percent. These trends indicate that Congress has given a higher priority to postsecondary student support than to support of postsecondary institutions. The intent of this policy no doubt has been to open the opportunity for postsecondary education to students who otherwise would not be financially able to attend postsecondary institutions.

Early in 1981 the administration brought great pressure on Congress to reduce federal appropriations to education by 20 to 25 percent on the grounds that education is a state responsibility and that federal expenditure for education contributes to the federal deficit, which in turn contributes to inflation.

THE FEDERAL EDUCATION AGENCY

Legislation was enacted by Congress in 1979 and approved by the President which established the new Department of Education with a secretary in the President's Cabinet. This action has been supported by many educational leaders and organizations for many years. But, first, let us take a look at the history of the federal education agency.

The present Department of Education had its origins in an act of Congress in 1867 that established a federal department of education headed by a commissioner. The department of education established in 1867 was made a bureau in the Department of Interior in 1868.[25]

The 1867 act stated that the federal education agency was established "for the purpose of collecting such statistics and facts as shall show the progress of education in the several states and territories and of diffusing such information respecting the organization and management of schools and school systems and methods of teaching as shall aid the people of the United States in the establishment and maintenance of efficient school systems, and otherwise promote the cause of education throughout the United States."

In 1869 Congress changed the title of the agency to Office of Education; in 1870 it was changed to Bureau of Education, and in 1929 it was changed back to Office of Education. The Office of Education remained in the Department of Interior until 1939 when it was transferred to the Federal Security Agency. It was transferred to the Department of Health, Education, and Welfare in 1953 and remained in that department until 1979 when the new Department of Education was created.

The federal education agency continues to serve the same purposes provided in 1867 act, plus additional purposes that have been provided by Congress from time to time. Those additional purposes include administration of many federal funds for education and the promotion of educational research. As has been noted, the administration of federal funds for education has involved the federal education agency in exercising substantial federal controls over local educational policies by withholding federal funds if those policies are in violation of civil rights and liberties guaranteed by the Constitution and federal statutes.

Some 152 programs from a number of different federal agencies were brought together into the new Department of Education. The department in 1980 is headed by a secretary and an under secretary and an assistant secretary for each of the following programs: (1) civil rights, (2) elementary and secondary education, (3) postsecondary education, (4) educational research and improvement, (5) vocational and adult education, and (6) special education and rehabilitative services. In addition, there is an administrator for overseas dependents, an office of private education, and an office of bilingual education and minority languages affairs. Whether this organization will provide for the needed integration of the 152 programs administered by the department remains to be seen. An intergovernmental advisory council on education and an interagency committee on education have been established to assist in promoting needed integration of services.

[25] Thirty-ninth Congress, 2nd sess.; 14 Stat. L., p. 434.

The 1979 act creating the department specifically provides that its formation shall not increase federal control of education. However, increasing the status of the federal education agency from an Office of Education in HEW to a full-fledged Department of Education with a secretary in the president's cabinet will no doubt increase the capacity of the agency to provide leadership in "otherwise promoting the cause of education throughout the country." However, there has been some political opposition to the establishment of a department of education and at this writing its future is uncertain.

SOME IMPORTANT PROBLEMS AND ISSUES

Many problems and issues relating to federal relationships to education remain to be solved. Some national issues relating to civil rights, taxation, states' rights, the general welfare, central controls, and other important matters are interwoven with educational issues. A number of these issues have been discussed; two others are discussed in the following paragraphs.

Should the Public Schools Be Used to Solve National Social Problems?

There are some who believe that the public schools should not be used to solve national social problems, such as integration of the races and the elimination of poverty. They insist that the function of the public schools is to provide "basic education" and that other agencies should solve the nation's social problems. Opponents of busing pupils to eliminate *de facto* segregation due to segregation in housing argue that this is a housing problem and not a school problem. Jenks and others argue that although education does provide opportunities for "upward mobility," it will not eliminate poverty.[26] There was much concern in the late 1970s about the decline of students' scores on standardized tests. Special federal appropriations for the public schools which have involved the schools in solving social issues have been blamed for part of this decline. What are the pros and cons of this issue?

Should the Federal Government Equalize Educational Opportunity Nationwide?

The equalizing effect of ten federal categorical appropriations combined was studied by researchers for the National Educational Finance Project.[27] It was found that federal categorical appropriations for the public schools had only a slight equalizing effect.

Although the differences in the per capita income of the states are declining,

[26] Christopher Jenks et al., *Who Gets Ahead? The Determinants of Economic Success in America?* (New York: Basic Books, Inc., Publishers, 1979).

[27] Roe L. Johns, Kern Alexander, and Dewey H. Stollar, eds., *Status and Impact of Educational Finance Programs* (Gainesville, Fla.: The National Educational Finance Project, 1971), p. 266.

considerable differences still remain. As of this writing, the personal income per pupil in average daily attendance in the state of greatest wealth was approximately twice that of the state of least wealth. Furthermore, the current expenditure per pupil in the highest-expenditure state (excluding Alaska) was approximately twice the expenditure per pupil in the lowest-expenditure state. The states with the lowest expenditure per pupil are in general the states with the lowest personal income per pupil. Should all categorical federal appropriations for the public schools be apportioned among the states in inverse relationship to personal income per pupil? Should the present categorical appropriations be apportioned as now provided by law but be accompanied by a substantial general-purpose federal appropriation provided by Congress with the requirement that it be apportioned among the states in inverse relationship to personal income per pupil?

SELECTED REFERENCES

Alexander, Kern, *School Law,* Chap. 3. St. Paul, Minn.: West Publishing Company, 1980.

Johns, Roe L., and Kern Alexander, eds., *Alternative Programs for Financing Education,* Vol. 5, Chap. 8. Gainesville, Fla.: National Educational Finance Project, 1971.

Kimbrough, Ralph B., and Michael Y. Nunnery, *Educational Administration, An Introduction,* Chap. 7. New York: Macmillan Publishing Co., Inc., 1976.

Kursh, Harry, *The United States Office of Education: A Century of Service.* New York: Chilion, 1965.

National Center for Education Statistics, U.S. Department of Education, *Digest of Education Statistics.* Washington, D.C.: U.S. Government Printing Office, Published annually.

Office of Management and Budget, *Special Analyses, Budget of the United States Government* (each fiscal year). Washington, D.C.: U.S. Government Printing Office, published annually.

Peckman, Joseph A., ed., *Setting National Priorities for 1979,* Chap. 4. Washington, D.C.: The Brookings Institution, 1978.

Tied, Sidney, "Historical Development of Federal Aid Programs," in Chap. 7 of *Status and Impact of Educational Finance Programs,* eds. Roe L. Johns, Kern Alexander, and Dewey H. Stollar, Vol. 4. Gainesville, Fla.: National Educational Finance Project, 1971.

Vieira, Norman, *Civil Rights in a Nutshell.* St. Paul, Minn.: West Publishing Company, 1978.

11

STATE ORGANIZATION
and RESPONSIBILITIES
for EDUCATION

As has been pointed out elsewhere in this book, provision for public education is considered one of the powers reserved to the states under the Tenth Amendment to the federal Constitution. However, as was noted in Chapter 10, the federal government has had an interest in education from the beginning of the nation and that interest has increased in recent years.

Under provisions of state constitutions and numerous superior court rulings, public education has been made a state responsibility. Early in our history, the states did very little, especially in the South, to discharge that responsibility. At the present time, provision for public education is seen as a major responsibility in all fifty states. Early in our history, public education was seen primarily as a matter of local concern in an agrarian society. This is no longer possible. Most people today spend most of their lives in different school districts and even different states from those in which they went to school. Education is more important for the individual and for society than it was in 1800. We are now living in a "brain-intensive" society. Education is now necessary for the economic survival of the individual and the political survival of the nation.

The state can no longer take a *laissez-faire* attitude toward public education. As shown in Chapter 19, school revenues from both state and local sources have been greatly increased in recent years, but the greatest percentage increase has been from state sources. In 1930 only 17 percent of state and local revenue for the public schools was derived from state sources but 53 percent of state and local revenue was provided in 1980 from state sources.

The increasing percentage of school revenue provided from state sources is only one symptom of an increase in state concern about public education. It is not unusual for 200 to 400 bills concerning education to be introduced in each session of the legislatures of many states. Most of these bills are not enacted into law, but the fact that they are introduced is evidence of state interest in education.

All fifty states have established state education agencies to implement state educational policies for the public schools. The state education agency is comprised of a chief state school officer, a state department of education, and, in all but one state, a state board of education. Governors and state legislatures also play major roles in the governance and support of education. These roles are discussed in Chapters 8 and 19. This chapter is devoted primarily to the role of the state education agency, particularly in its relationship to the public schools.

EVOLUTION OF STATE SYSTEMS OF EDUCATION

It is beyond the scope of this book to present a history of the development of public education in the United States. Briefly, public education in America began with laws passed by the Massachusetts Colony in 1642 and 1647 that required that all children be taught to read and that towns of fifty families or more must establish schools.[1] This precedent no doubt greatly influenced the states early in our history to consider the financing of education primarily a local responsibility. All thirteen of the original colonies, with the exception of Rhode Island, had constitutional or statutory provisions bearing on education.[2] These varied from authorization of pauper schools in Pennsylvania and low-cost schools in North Carolina to a strong mandate directing the legislature to encourage public schools and colleges in Massachusetts. These provisions tended to reflect the early attitudes toward education in the different colonies.[3] Soon, however, both Congress and the people began to insist that each new state make some definite provisions for education. Early in the nineteenth century, this concept became accepted as policy. States that adopted new constitutions or made revisions in their original constitutions tended to include stronger and more clear-cut provisions relating to the state responsibility for education. Unfortunately, the legislatures of many states failed to make adequate provisions to implement such directives.

The first state board of education was established in New York in 1784 but was given responsibility only for the colleges and academies authorized during

---

[1] Elwood P. Cubberley, *Public Education in the United States,* rev. ed. (Boston: Houghton Mifflin Company, 1934), pp. 17–18.

[2] Elwood P. Cubberley and Edward C. Elliot, *State and County School Administration* (New York: Macmillan Publishing Co., Inc., 1915), pp. 12–15.

[3] Elwood P. Cubberley, *State School Administration* (Boston: Houghton Mifflin Company, 1927), Chaps. 1, 5.

colonial days. Not until 1904 was this board made responsible for the public schools. It was only after Massachusetts established a state board for elementary and secondary schools in 1837 that the movement made any significant headway. By 1870, most states had established baords of education but, among the older states, Georgia, Pennsylvania, and Maine did not do so until after the beginning of the present century.[4]

Before 1830 only three states—New York, Maryland, and Michigan—had provided for the position now known generally as chief state school officer. During the ensuing twenty years, however, another twenty-one states authorized a position of this type, and by the beginning of the present century all states had provided for a state superintendent or commissioner of education. In many, however, the first state school officers were designated on an *ex officio* basis; that is, some state official serving in another capacity was given the additional responsibility of serving as superintendent. The movement to provide a chief state school officer in every state was given considerable impetus in the second quarter of the nineteenth century by three developments: (1) the significant contributions of Horace Mann, the first state superintendent in Massachusetts, who was appointed in 1837; (2) the need for some state official to keep a record of the school lands and account for the funds derived therefrom in each of the states; and (3) the growing awareness of the need for someone representing the state to collect information, make reports, and answer inquiries regarding the common schools that were being organized in most communities.[5]

Recognition of the responsibility of the people of each state for devising an adequate and effective system of education has developed slowly in most states but much more slowly in some than in others. There was no pattern to follow and no design that had been agreed upon. Although the people in each state had to develop their own policies and provisions for education, in many cases they were greatly influenced by what had happened in leading states such as Massachusetts. However, society has changed and continues to change more rapidly than do the provisions for education and the practices in most schools and other educational institutions. It should be apparent that state systems of education in this country are still in the process of evolution and that this process now urgently needs to be accelerated.

STATE PROVISIONS FOR EDUCATION

In some states the constitutional provisions, the laws, and the leadership provided by the people contributed to the development and operation of programs of education that were reasonably adequate and more or less consistent with the ideals, purposes, and goals generally accepted in this country at that time. In others, so many handicaps were inherent in certain policies and legal provisions that some of the stated or implied goals could not be attained.

[4] Ward W. Keesecker, *State Boards of Education and Chief State School Officers,* U.S. Office of Education Bulletin No. 12 (Washington, D.C.: U.S. Government Printing Office, 1950), p. 8.
[5] *Ibid.,* p. 25.

The State Constitution

The basic provisions for education are found in the constitution of each state, as explained in Chapter 2. Although the phraseology varies considerably, the constitution in most states includes a mandate or directive requiring the legislature to provide an effective system of public education, free of tuition charges and open equally to all who can benefit from education. Other sections in the constitution incorporate additional policies considered essential in the state.

The people of each state, therefore, determine—within limits established by the federal constitution and court decisions—the basic policies for or relating to the operation and support of education within the state. These policies may be sound and future oriented, vague and indefinite, or narrowly restrictive in some respects.

A good criterion that could be used in evaluating state constitutional provisions relating to education may be stated as follows: *The constitution should set forth the basic policies for the organization, administration, and support of adequate programs of public education; should empower and direct the legislature to establish the basic guidelines for implementing these policies; and should be free from detailed or restrictive provisions that may handicap or prevent the development of adequate provisions for or programs of education.*[6]

State Legislation

The people in each state expect their legislature to enact statutes (commonly referred to as "laws") that provide for the implementation of the basic policies and provisions incorporated in their constitution. The legislature may act wisely or unwisely and may thus facilitate or handicap the development of the educational program. Serious problems have developed in some states as a result of the tendency of the legislature to incorporate restrictive details into the law and to preempt a number of functions that should be assigned to the state or local boards of education. An adequate criterion for evaluating legislative policy may be stated as follows: *The legislature should make a serious effort to implement the constitutional directives by establishing the basic framework for the educational system and the major principles, goals, and policies to be observed in operating that system; the responsibility for developing more specific goals, minimum standards, and the technical requirements consistent with those policies, and for measuring progress, should be delegated to the state agency for education.*[7]

The provisions for the organization of education—that is, the framework within which education operates in any state—are of great importance. Although some good schools and educational institutions can be found in a state with inadequate or limiting provisions, it is likely that even these will be handicapped. Any plan of organization that creates overlapping functions, facilitates the introduction of partisan politics into any aspect of the educational program, discourages meaning-

[6] Adapted from Edgar L. Morphet, ed., *Building a Better Southern Region Through Education* (Tallahassee, Fla.: Southern States Work-Conference on Educational Problems, 1945), p. 173.
[7] *Ibid.*, p. 174.

ful local initiative and responsibility, rewards inefficient organization and operation, or makes appropriate organization and coordination difficult obviously needs
to be improved.

The legislature of each state presumably is elected to represent the people. If
many of the people are not seriously concerned about the kind and quality of
education provided, if powerful pressure groups are more interested in low taxes
than in good schools and institutions of higher learning, if people in the wealthy
communities are not concerned about education in the less wealthy areas, or if
other similar attitudes and conditions exist, the state design and provisions for
education are likely to be defective in certain respects. Moreover, if the educators
themselves are divided sharply regarding the purposes and goals of education
or means for achieving them, the people and the legislature may tend to become
confused and fail to provide for an effective program. Only when a majority of
the citizens agrees on the goals and the best means for attaining them can significant and continuing progress in improving the design and provisions for education
be expected.

THE STATE EDUCATION AGENCY

As was noted previously, every state has developed some kind of *system* of education. In reality, however, most states have established two or more systems, each
of which is primarily responsible for some level or major aspect of education (for
example, elementary and secondary education and institutions of higher learning).
These systems tend to function independently in many states with little coordination except that provided by the governor and the legislature. Many people have
become convinced that appropriate provisions designed to ensure more adequate
coordination are essential in every state if emerging needs are to be met. Some
believe this coordination can best be achieved through a properly constituted
coordinating council; others believe an agency that is responsible for all levels and
aspects of education should be established in every state.

States vary greatly in the ways they are organized for educational governance.
Harris[8] presents the following outline of those variations.

1. A few states have one agency for all levels of education. Examples: New
   York, Rhode Island, Florida.
2. Several states have an agency for elementary and secondary schools, including vocational education, and a legal coordinating or governing agency for
   higher education. Examples: Georgia, Nevada, North Dakota.
3. Some states have an agency for elementary and secondary schools, an agency
   for vocational education, and a legal state coordinating or governing agency
   for higher education. Examples: Colorado, Oklahoma, Washington.
4. Still others have an agency for elementary and secondary schools, including
   vocational education and governing boards for individual institutions, but
   no legal statewide agency for higher education. Examples: Delaware, Nebraska, Vermont.

[8] Adapted from Sam P. Harris, *State Departments of Education, State Boards of Education
and Chief State School Officers,* Department of Health, Education, and Welfare Publication
No. (OE)73-07400 (Washington, D.C.: U.S. Government Printing Office, 1973), p. 19.

It is beyond the scope of this book to evaluate the advantages and disadvantages of each alternative state plan for the governance of education. Adequate research is not available to determine the "best plan" for the state governance of education. Campbell and Mazzoni[9] made an extensive analysis of state policy making for the public schools in a sample of twelve states and did not recommend any one ideal plan. Those researchers studied only state governance of the public schools.

Basically there are two schools of thought concerning the structure of the state education agency. Many political scientists advocate that state executive power for the governance of education be concentrated in the governor. Under that concept, the preferred model is for the governor to appoint both the chief state school officer and the state board of education. Many educational leaders object to that model on the grounds that it concentrates too much power in the hands of the governor and that it injects partisan politics in the state governance of education.[10]

A number of educational leaders advocate an independent state agency for the governance of education. Under that model either the people or the elected representatives of the people elect the state board of education and the board appoints the chief state school officer. Some political scientists object to this model, claiming that it divides responsibility for the state governance of education.

A combination model is for the governor to appoint the state board members, subject to the approval of the senate and the board appoints the chief state school officer.

Most educational leaders of the public schools seem to prefer a model under which the chief state school officer is appointed by the state board of education and the state board is either appointed by the governor or is elected by the people or by the elected representatives of the people.

Because of space limitations only state governance of the public schools is discussed.

The State Board of Education

Because education is concerned with helping every individual to develop his or her full potential and provides the foundation for many of the beliefs, aspirations, and actions of the people, American citizens have always insisted that the control of education be kept primarily in their hands. To that end, they usually have insisted on and established predominantly lay state and local boards of education that are responsible to them for determining policies, goals, and basic procedures subject to the provisions in the constitution and the laws of the state.

Number and composition. The number of states having state boards of education for the public schools increased from thirty in 1900 to forty-nine in 1972. Although Wisconsin has had a state board for vocational education for some years, it has not yet established a board for elementary and secondary schools. There

[9]Roald F. Campbell and Tim L. Mazzoni, Jr., *State Policy Making for the Public Schools* (Berkeley, Calif.: McCutchan Publishing Corporation, 1976).

[10]*Ibid.,* pp. 314–366. Campbell and Mazzoni present an interesting analysis of "Alternatives for School Governance."

has been a definite tendency to eliminate *ex officio* state boards of education. In 1890, twenty of the twenty-nine state boards of education were of the *ex officio* type. By 1940 the number had decreased to eight out of thirty-nine and by 1973 to two (Florida and Mississippi). Not only the *ex officio* board but also *ex officio* board members have tended to disappear.

Partly because of the provisions of the Smith–Hughes Act, most states provided for a state board for vocational education shortly after 1920. In a number of states that had already established a state board of education, the two boards were, in effect, merged because the membership was identical. Thus, the state board of education also served as the state board for vocational education. By 1973, only four states still had a separate or independent board for vocational education.

State residential schools for the blind and deaf are under the state board of education in nearly half the states, under some other state agency in a few, and have their own governing board or boards in the remainder of the states that have such schools. In six states (Florida, Idaho, Maine, Montana, New York, and Rhode Island) the state colleges and universities come under the state board of education (or regents). In a few others the state colleges but not the state universities are under the state board. Various other combinations are found in the remaining states.

Selection of members. When the number of *ex officio* boards began to decrease some years ago, appointment by the governor became the favored method of selecting members for the state board of education. During the past fifteen years several states have changed to popular election of state board members or to selection in some other manner than appointment by the governor. The governor now appoints at least a majority of the members of the board in thirty-two states. In New York the state board is selected by the legislature; in South Carolina one member is selected by the legislators from each judicial circuit; and in Washington the members are selected by local school boards. In five states (Nebraska, Nevada— except two who are appointed by the other members—Ohio, Texas, and Utah) the board members are elected on a nonpartisan ballot. In seven states (Alabama, Colorado, Hawaii, Kansas, Louisiana, Michigan, and New Mexico) they are elected on a partisan ballot.

Size and term. The state boards for public schools range from three *ex officio* members in Mississippi to twenty-one popularly elected members in Texas and twenty-three in Ohio. Only eight states have fewer than seven members and only four more than thirteen. The length of term for appointment or election of state board members ranges from four years or less in sixteen states to nine years in three states. The tendency has been to increase the length of term to seven or nine years and to provide for overlapping terms so as to assure some continuity in service of experienced persons.

Responsibilities. In some states the differences between the functions of the chief state school officer and those of the state board of education have not been made clear. In most cases an attempt has been made to designate the state board as the body responsible for policies and regulations and the state superintendent as executive officer of the board. Where the state superintendent is appointed by the board this differentiation seems to work out satisfactorily. In most states where the state superintendent is responsible to the people because he or she is elected by popular vote, there have been, and probably will continue to be, conflicts and uncertainties from time to time.

It is generally recognized that the state board of education should have the legal responsibility for the general supervision and management of all aspects of the public school program of the state. However the board would not only be ill advised but would be inviting difficulties for itself and the educational programs if it did not expect the chief state school officer and his or her staff to make studies, prepare reports, and submit recommendations for its consideration in arriving at decisions regarding policies and standards. The major functions of most state boards of education may be listed as follows:

- To appoint and fix the compensation of a competent chief state school officer who should serve as its secretary and executive officer.
- To determine areas of service, establish qualifications, and appoint the necessary personnel for the state department of education.
- To adopt and administer a budget for the operation of the state education agency.
- To authorize needed studies and, with the assistance of appropriate committees and consultants, to develop and submit to the governor and legislature proposals for improving the organization, administration, financing, accountability, and other aspects of education in the state.
- To adopt policies and minimum standards for the administration and supervision of the state educational enterprise.
- To represent the state in determining policies on all matters pertaining to education that involve relationships with other state agencies and the federal government.
- When authorized to do so, to adopt policies for the operation of institutions of higher learning and other educational institutions and programs operated by the state or to approve major policies recommended by the board or boards of control for such institutions.

The Chief State School Officer

Potentially the most important educational position in any state is that of a chief state school officer. However, in some states this position has been one of relatively minor significance as contrasted to those occupied by superintendents of some of the larger school districts or presidents of state institutions of higher learning.

Although a few states, primarily in New England, adopted from the beginning the concept that the chief state school officer should be selected by and responsible to a state board of education, many states for one reason or another assumed that the chief school officer should be elected by popular vote, appointed by the governor, or selected in some other manner. In 1896 the chief school officer was appointed by the state board of education in only three states; in thirty-one states the chief school officer was elected by popular vote and, in most cases, on a partisan political ballot along with the other officials; in nine the governor appointed the state superintendent and in three the state superintendent was appointed by the general assembly.[11] Since that time many significant changes have occurred.

In 1973 the chief state school officer was appointed by the state board of education in twenty-seven states and appointed by the governor in five (Maine, New Jersey, Pennsylvania, Tennessee, and Virginia). The number of states requiring election by popular vote had decreased to eighteen. In four of these (North Dakota, Oregon, Washington, and Wisconsin) the election was by nonpartisan ballot. It is interesting that in about one third of the states the chief state school officer serves *ex officio* as a member, and in some states as chair, of the state board of education. This seems to place the chief school officer in an anomalous position, since as a superintendent he or she would recommend policies and standards to the board, as a board member would vote on them, and as a superintendent would implement those that are approved.

Two factors that have handicapped the development of the position of chief state school officer in several states have been the low compensation provided and failure to recognize that special qualifications are needed. Generally, as states have changed from popular election to appointment by the state board, salaries have been improved and higher qualifications have been recognized as necessary. Most people in some states now recognize that the person selected for the position as chief state school officer should be the most competent educator who can be found and that the compensation must be adequate to attract such a person.

The duties and responsibilities of the chief state school officer vary considerably from state to state. In the more progressive states they usually include the following:

- To serve as secretary and executive officer of the state board of education.
- To serve as executive officer of any board or council that may be established to facilitate coordination of all aspects of the educational program.
- To select competent personnel for, and serve as the administrative head and professional leader of, the state department of education to the end that it will contribute maximally to the improvement of education.
- To arrange for studies and organize committees and task forces as deemed necessary to identify problems and to recommend plans and provisions for effecting improvements in education.
- To recommend to the state board of education needed policies, standards, and regulations relating to public education in the state.
- To recommend improvements in educational legislation and in provisions for financing the educational program.
- To explain and interpret the school laws of the state and the policies and regulations of the state board of education.
- To prepare reports for the public, the state board, the governor, and the legislature that provide pertinent information about the accomplishments, conditions, and needs of the schools.

[11] Adapted from Fred F. Beach and Robert F. Will, *The State and Education,* Office of Education, Miscellaneous No. 23 (Washington, D.C.: U.S. Government Printing Office, 1955), p. 30, and Robert F. Will, *State Education, Structure and Organization,* Office of Education, Miscellaneous No. 46 (Washington, D.C.: U.S. Government Printing Office, 1964), p. 26.

The duties and responsibilities of all state departments of education have expanded greatly during the past quarter of a century. For many years these responsibilities were assumed by the state superintendent with the assistance of a secretary or two. In 1900, there were only 177 professional and other staff members in all state departments of education. This number increased to 3,718 in 1940[12] and to approximately 15,000 by 1972 and has increased considerably since that time.

Increases in the number of staff members have been associated with the major stages in the development of state departments of education. At first, these departments were concerned chiefly with accounting and reporting functions. The second stage of development placed considerable emphasis on regulation and inspection. At present, increasing emphasis is being placed on leadership in planning and effecting improvements in education and developing procedures for accountability. As a result of these changes, much more attention is being devoted to the selection of competent professional personnel who can assist educators in the field; organize conferences; plan and conduct studies; lead in facilitating improvements in the state educational program as well as in local programs; and work effectively with the governor, the legislature, and representatives of other state and federal agencies.

In a study of state departments of education, Beach identified three major types of functions, which he classified as leadership, regulatory, and operational responsibilities.[13] The need for greater emphasis on leadership functions in many state departments of education is evident to all who study educational problems. If this need is to be met satisfactorily, it seems apparent that (1) the chief state school officer who administers the department should be selected because of the ability to provide professional leadership in improving the state provisions for education; (2) the professional members of the department staff should be carefully selected on a basis which will assure that they not only are leaders in their respective areas of specialization but also can work effectively with others in studying and solving educational problems; (3) the department should be so organized and administered that effective functioning is facilitated; and (4) the people and the legislature should insist on and support the kind of services that can be provided through competent and creative leadership in the state department of education.

EMERGING STATE RESPONSIBILITIES AND RELATIONS

Various authorities have directed attention to such basic concepts as the following: education is in the public domain; it is "political" in a broad sense because it is operated by an agency of the formal political government; its nature and functioning are affected by the political and social climate in which it operates; and, as a formal, specialized structure and organization, education is a subsystem of a

[12] Fred F. Beach and Andrew H. Gibbs, *Personnel of State Departments of Education,* Office of Education, Miscellaneous No. 16 (Washington, D.C.: U.S. Government Printing Office, 1952), p. 6.

[13] Fred F. Beach, *The Functions of State Departments of Education,* Office of Education, Miscellaneous No. 12 (Washington, D.C.: U.S. Government Printing Office, 1950), pp. 3–17.

complex system concerned with the broader processes of acculturation and socialization in the nation.[14]

To understand why a system of education, or an agency for education, is organized and operated in certain ways, it is necessary to identify and understand the beliefs, values, and aspirations of the people and the forces operating in the state as well as those in the national setting. But these have changed in many important respects during recent years and will undoubtedly continue to change. As one result, some of the traditional roles, functions, and priorities of educational agencies and institutions are no longer considered appropriate under modern conditions and are currently being modified in most states in an effort to meet emerging as well as many current needs that have been ignored previously. Some of these modifications have been planned carefully on the basis of systematic studies; others have been haphazard or inadequate.

The most important responsibility of every state education agency in the future will be to provide the leadership and services needed to improve continuously the quality of education in a major effort to achieve excellence in every aspect of education throughout the state. If this effort is to be successful, the agency will need to find effective ways of cooperating with—and obtaining the cooperation of—the governor, the legislature, other state agencies, institutions of higher learning, major organizations, local school systems, and many others, including appropriate representatives from the federal level and perhaps from other states.

The quest for excellence in education will require systematic and comprehensive long-range planning, the utilization of appropriate strategies for effecting needed changes, continuous monitoring and appraisal of progress, and the periodic revision of plans to deal with new or unrecognized problems and needs (see Chapter 7). It will also necessitate, in many states, a different plan of organization, new attitudes and approaches, and different roles for most members of the state department staff.

The major responsibilities of the state education agency, in addition to developing and maintaining an appropriate structure and operating procedures for the staff, will include services and procedures designed to

1. increase the adequacy and effectiveness of educational policies in the state as authorized or required by existing laws, regulations, and professional standards, and
2. identify, develop, and encourage promising new or improved policies, procedures, and practices in the organization, administration, operation, and support of education (encourage continuous educational renewal).

Relations with Other State and Federal Agencies

State agencies. In a number of states, responsibilities for certain functions or services involving or related to the public schools have been assigned to agencies other than the state agency for education. Some of these assignments have been

---

[14] See, for example, J. K. Galbraith, *The Affluent Society* (Boston: Houghton Mifflin Company, 1958), p. 355; and Howard Dean, "The Political Setting of American Education," in *The Social Sciences View School Administration* (Englewood Cliffs, N.J.: Prentice-Hall, Inc., 1965), pp. 213–217.

made capriciously and unwisely. In such cases, local school officials have often become involved in red tape and delay because they were required to attempt to work with a variety of state agencies whose roles and services were not coordinated satisfactorily.

The following criteria are generally recognized as desirable for guidance in planning state services and developing coordination in education:

1. Services primarily educational in nature should be provided by the state agency for education, and those chiefly noneducational should be provided by other state agencies.

2. The state education agency or some other appropriate educational agency established by the state should be charged with the responsibility of co-ordinating the entire state program of education. It should work in close cooperation with other appropriate agencies of state and local governments in planning and providing services in areas of joint concern.

3. When two state agencies are concerned with policy matters involving the schools, any minimum standards or regulations that are found to be neces-sary should be approved and adopted jointly by both agencies. For example, in matters involving school health the standards should be approved jointly by the state board of education and the state board of health.

4. The state department of education should serve as a coordinating agency and clearing house for matters involving formal relations or contracts with—or applications from local school systems to—other state or federal agencies. For example, in the school plant field, the state department of education should be able to save local school systems much confusion and delay if it has the responsibility for obtaining approval of plans by the state fire mar-shal, the state health department, and any other state agency that is responsi-ble for approving any aspect of the plant program.[15]

Federal agencies. Many agencies of the federal government have been concerned with one or another aspect of education for some years (see Chapter 10). Important problems of federal-state-local relations have been encountered from time to time. Although the increased national interest in education and the additional funds for education provided by Congress during the past few years have helped to stimulate all states to make important changes in their provisions for certain aspects of education, some of these developments have resulted in serious problems and concerns. Because most of the federal funds have been categorical (that is, they can be utilized only for the purpose designated), the requirements for partici-pation result in considerable detailed work in preparing applications and reports, the state's provisions for financing schools have been largely ignored, and the funding has often been so late or uncertain that realistic planning is often impossi-ble, *state priorities in some cases have been seriously distorted.* Fortunately there are many indications that at least some of the most indefensible federal policies will be abandoned in the near future and that a bona fide federal–state partnership will emerge.

Many people are seriously concerned that an increasing number of important

[15] Adapted from National Council of Chief State School Officers, *The State Department of Education* (Washington, D.C.: The Council 1952), pp. 25-26; and Beach, *The Functions of State Departments of Education* (Washington, D.C.: Office of Education, U.S. Government Printing Office) pp. 7-8.

decisions regarding education may continue to be made at the federal level. Some realignment is probably inevitable, but this does not mean that the concept of state responsibility for education is outdated. What it does mean is that *all states must face up to their responsibilities and prepare promptly to meet them realistically*. The people in every state will need to reevaluate their existing policies and procedures as a basis for developing better ways of meeting their responsibilities for education in the future. Such improvements will not only provide needed safeguards against inappropriate federal encroachments but will also establish a basis for constructive cooperation that should assure more adequate programs of education.

State Policies and Standards

Since the legislature should not attempt to prescribe by law all details of policies and standards that may be needed for education, an important question that arises is, How much responsibility or discretion should be delegated to state or local boards of education? A generally recognized principle of law provides that *limits or boundaries should be established for any discretionary authority that is granted*. Thus, the legislature should prescribe only the basic state policies, goals, and standards and should authorize the development of more specific policies, goals, and standards by an appropriate administrative agency, such as the state board of education.

Some minimum standards have been found necessary in every state as a means of helping to ensure adequate educational opportunities. However, states have learned by experience that the establishment of minimum standards alone will not solve the problem. Those standards cannot substitute for adequate state and local leadership and planning, nor can they result in satisfactory programs of education unless the state plan ensures that sufficient funds will be available to finance these programs.

Among the important criteria relating to standards and regulations that have generally been accepted by authorities are the following:

1. Although a major responsibility of the state should be to provide adequate leadership and services, it should, when necessary, establish those minimum standards and only those that are universally applicable, that are designed primarily to assure adequate educational opportunities for all children and youth, and that in no way limit the freedom of local school systems to go beyond the established standards.

2. In making decisions regarding the desirability of minimum standards or other controls, preference should be given to retaining control locally, especially for those elements concerning which there is no certainty that central authority will provide the best long-term results.

3. The advantages of local responsibility for educational programs should be protected and promoted by avoiding inhibiting controls over local boards of education, school programs, or school funds by the state, the state education agency, or by noneducational authorities.[16]

[16] Adapted from National Education Association, Committee on Tax Education and School Finance, *Guides to the Development of State School Finance Programs* (Washington, D.C.: The Association, 1949), pp. 5–10.

State Leadership and Coordination

Among the most important functions of state leadership are planning and co-ordination. Planning, to be effective, must be based on carefully developed studies, research, and bona fide cooperation in determining purposes, goals, and objectives and agreement on steps to be used in attaining them. Improvements in the state provisions for education cannot be left to chance developments. Failure to formulate defensible plans and proposals for improving educational programs may result in unfortunate changes sponsored by groups with vested interests, perpetuation of inefficiencies that handicap the entire program, or even failure to obtain the support of the people and the legislature in providing funds to meet emerging school needs. Cooperatively developed and well-formulated plans should, on the other hand, result in constantly improving programs that are strongly supported by the people.

Few people realize the amount and extent of coordination needed in any state if education is to be developed satisfactorily. In addition to coordination involving state agencies and institutions, there must be coordination and cooperation *within* the state department of education. No member of the staff can operate satisfactorily without relating his or her work to what others are doing. No bureau or division can function in isolation. Most educational problems are interrelated. Finance is not merely a matter of money; it also relates to the provision of necessary services and facilities. Curriculum improvement requires consideration not only of subject matter but also of students and their needs and the relationship of each aspect of learning to other aspects. The need for coordination in research and planning should be obvious. Without coordination, there is likely to be much duplication of effort and failure to give appropriate attention to matters of considerable importance. Competition and rivalry may be disastrous when there is no effective coordination.

Many services provided by the federal government are not well coordinated and result in some confusion for state and local school systems unless these agencies and groups agree upon a plan and provide the leadership needed to ensure effective coordination. In most situations the state education agency is necessarily involved in developing plans for such coordination.

SOME IMPORTANT PROBLEMS AND ISSUES

A few of the problems and issues relating to state educational organization, administration, and responsibilities are discussed briefly on the following pages.

How Should the Staff of the State Education Agency Be Organized and Function?

Procedures for selecting and appointing professional personnel for state education agencies (which may include social scientists, economists, systems analysts, computer programmers, and similar kinds of specialists as well as leaders and specialists in many aspects of education) are usually influenced or restricted by established state policies that may be classified roughly as follows: (1) personal or political appointments made and terminated by the decision of the chief state school officer in some states in which he is elected by popular vote; (2) appointments based on legally established civil service specifications that may or may not be adapted to the competency or salary levels needed to attract competent professional personnel from any state for service in the department; or (3) the establishment of an "institutional status" for the state education agency (similar to that authorized for institutions of higher learning) that will enable the board to establish appropriate qualifications and salary levels within limits set by the authorized budget.

Traditionally, most state department staffs have been organized into semi-autonomous divisions or units, each of which was directly responsible to the chief state school officer for some level or aspect of education. Frequently there has been relatively little communication or cooperation among these units. At present many departments are being reorganized in an effort to assure maximum coordination and cooperation in planning and effecting needed changes in education. Several have established an administrative or coordinating council, reorganized existing divisions to meet modern criteria and needs, created temporary task forces for special purposes, and taken other steps designed to ensure effective communication and more rational decision making. But communication across the boundaries of a social system, such as the state education agency, is even more difficult than is communication among the units within that system. Few state or local education agencies have made satisfactory progress thus far in communicating effectively with lay citizens, many organizations, or other units of government.

What kinds of policies, provisions, and procedures will be most helpful in facilitating adequate staffing, organization, and functioning of a state department of education? in facilitating meaningful communication within the department and with other people and groups outside the department?

What Responsibilities Should the State Education Agency Have for Research?

Although research is essential to identify problems and needs and to provide a basis for assessing progress, few state education agencies have the personnel or resources needed to undertake significant research studies. The development of long-range goals and plans for achieving them will be facilitated by utilizing appropriate data and the findings from related research studies as bases for the carefully considered value judgments that must be made.

There is serious doubt as to whether state departments of education should undertake basic research, as this usually can be done better and more appropriately by universities or independent research agencies. State departments, however, should be interested in encouraging such research and seeking to identify practical implications.

The state department probably should have a research or a research and reference unit that is concerned with the development of a statewide research plan and program, with facilitating coordination and cooperation, and perhaps with undertaking certain projects on its own initiative. Many of these studies might well be concerned in one way or another with procedures and innovations designed to effect improvements in the educational program or organization. The permanent staff should probably be small, but funds should be available for extensive use of consultants and for assisting institutions and other agencies to plan and conduct special studies as needed.

The research functions of the state department of education should probably include (1) helping to create a favorable climate not only for research but also for utilizing the findings of research; (2) identifying major problems and issues concerning which research is especially needed; (3) stimulating ideas for research and the development of research projects; (4) helping to coordinate the research efforts in the state and to focus attention from time to time on certain problems that need special study; (5) assisting, or locating qualified consultants who can assist, with research design; (6) developing, organizing, and keeping up to date a "library" of research findings in areas that would be of interest and value in the state; and (7) developing a plan for ensuring that the research findings in appropriate areas are summarized, synthesized, and interpreted in such a way that they will be of maximum benefit to educational leaders in the state who should utilize them.

How can the state agency help universities and local school systems in the state to encourage and cooperate in studies that would be especially helpful to the state department and to local school systems? Would a research coordinating council be helpful?

What Procedures Should Be Utilized in Improving State Provisions for Education?

Most state education agencies are almost always under some pressure to improve certain aspects of education, such as finance, the curriculum, or the preparation and certification of teachers. Yet all aspects of education are interrelated and piecemeal changes, even though they may result in some improvements, are not likely to resolve some of the basic educational problems. Sooner or later, in almost every state the need for a systematic study of all major aspects of the state provisions for education seems essential. A comprehensive study of all provisions and programs may direct attention to imbalances and problems that might be overlooked in studying only certain aspects. (See the discussion in Chapter 7.)

Under what conditions should a comprehensive study be undertaken? What should be the respective roles of the state education agency and of lay citizens and educators in planning and conducting any studies that may be needed and in developing proposals for improvements in education? How should such studies be financed, organized, and conducted? What problems are likely to be encountered and how can these best be avoided or resolved?

SELECTED REFERENCES

Bakalis, Michael J., *A Strategy for Excellence,* Chap. 1. Hamden, Conn.: The Shoe String Press, Inc., 1974.

Campbell, Roald F., and Tim Mazzoni, Jr., *State Policy Making for the Public Schools.* Berkeley, Calif.: McCutchan Publishing Corporation, 1976.

Campbell, Roald F., Gerald E. Sroufe, and Donald H. Layton, eds., *Strengthening State Depart-*

ments of Education. Chicago, Ill.: Midwest Administration Center, University of Chicago, 1967.

Conant, James Bryant, *Shaping Educational Policy.* New York: McGraw-Hill Book Company, 1964.

Designing Education for the Future Series, especially *Implications for Education of Prospective Changes in Society* (1967); *Planning and Effecting Needed Changes in Education* (1967); *Cooperative Planning for Education in 1980* (1968); and *Emerging Designs for Education* (1968), eds. Edgar L. Morphet, David L. Jesser, and Charles O. Ryan. Denver, Colo.: Designing Education for the Future. Republished by Citation Press, Scholastic Magazines, Inc., New York.

Fuller, Edgar, and Jim B. Pearson, eds., *Education in the States: Nationwide Development Since 1900.* Washington, D.C.: National Education Association of the United States, 1969.

Harris, Sam P., *State Departments of Education, State Boards of Education, and Chief State School Officers.* Washington, D.C.: U.S. Government Printing Office, 1973.

Improving State Leadership in Education Series: *Emerging State Responsibilities for Education* (1970); *Planning and Providing for Excellence in Education* (1971), republished by Citation Press, Scholastic Magazines, Inc., New York; and *Revitalizing Education in the Big Cities* (1972), eds. Edgar L. Morphet, David L. Jesser, and Arthur P. Ludka. Denver, Colo.: Improving State Leadership in Education.

Usdan, Michael D., David W. Minar, and Emmanuel Hurwitz, Jr., *Education and State Politics.* New York: Teachers College Press, Columbia University, 1969.

12

SCHOOL DISTRICTS
and THEIR
ADMINISTRATION

Instead of directly administering and operating all schools and educational programs, every state except Hawaii[1] has established local school districts and delegated to them (within limits prescribed by the state constitution and legislature) the responsibility for organizing and operating schools and other related provisions for education. Traditionally these districts have also been responsible for providing a large part of the funds they utilized not only to operate the schools and programs but also to finance the necessary services and facilities. But these traditions have changed in a number of states and can be expected to change even more significantly in the near future. Some commonly used terms relating to state provisions for local organization and operation of schools that sometimes have been misunderstood or misinterpreted by both lay citizens and educators are discussed briefly in the paragraphs that follow.

---

[1] Although in Hawaii the state operates and finances all schools and programs, district superintendencies have been established with headquarters on the four larger islands: Oahu, Hawaii, Kauai, and Maui.

A *local school district* (local education authority) is a quasi-corporation[2] authorized or established by a state for the local organization and administration of schools. It is comprised of an area within which a single board (or officer) has the responsibility for, and commonly has considerable autonomy in, the organization and administration of all public schools and related educational programs. It has certain powers, usually including limited power to specify tax levies for school purposes, that have been delegated by the state.

A *local school* (or educational center) is any one of several places or locations in a district at which educational programs are authorized by the governing board to be conducted for children, youth, and/or adults. The term is also used to refer to the group of students and staff members participating in the educational processes at any such location, or to the facilities used for that purpose. Thus, there may be a school for early childhood, elementary, intermediate, high school, or adult education or for any authorized combination of these groups or of learning activities.

A *local school attendance area* is usually that portion of a school district whose population is served in part at least by a single school. During recent years, however, some students in many of the larger districts have been transported from beyond the customary attendance area boundaries to facilitate integration or to enable them to benefit from programs designed to meet their special needs.

An *intermediate unit* or a regional service agency is a unit or agency established by a state to provide some educational services for the state education agency and for the districts within the region or area it is expected to serve.

A *decentralized district* or school system is one in which several subunits (or subdistricts) have been established within a district—usually a large city—and authorized to assume designated responsibilities for education (but not for tax levies or financial support) in their respective areas.

LOCAL SCHOOL DISTRICTS

The early settlers and leaders in this nation could have made an assumption similar to the one made by those who went to Australia: Each state should be responsible for organizing and operating all schools and programs of education. However, the people who settled in this country made a different assumption: Each state should be responsible for the education of its citizens, but school districts should be organized as needed, and the responsibility for providing, organizing, administering, and operating schools and programs of education in accordance with state policies and requirements should be delegated to them. Each of these assumptions had many implications for the development of education. Each also has resulted in some problems. For example, in the United States many of the school districts as organized originally proved to be too small to provide an effective program of education; the people in some districts did not take their responsibilities seriously; and in many areas the local resources were so inadequate that only limited education could

[2] As defined by Newton Edwards, "A Quasi-corporation . . . is purely a political or civil division of the state; it is created as an instrumentality of the state in order to facilitate the administration of government. . . . A municipal corporation proper is a city or town incorporated primarily for purposes of local government." *The Courts and the Public Schools* (Chicago: University of Chicago Press, 1955), p. 63.

be provided. In Australia, although inequities in financial support have been minimized, some leaders have concluded that the state agencies for education have tended to become bureaucratic and inflexible, that there has been little citizen interest, and, as a result, that schools often have difficulty in adapting to modern needs.[3]

In this country, some of the units created by states for local governmental purposes (for example, cities, towns, townships, or counties) were also assigned considerable responsibility for organizing and operating schools. In most states, however, special districts (frequently with the same boundaries) were established for the local governance of education. These districts usually were not subject to control by other local governmental agencies. However, in some states a local government agency was either granted some authority over the school district or was even organized to encompass education within its framework of responsibility (as in some cities with special charters).

The provisions for the organization and operation of local school districts within each state developed out of the political philosophy and the geographic circumstances of the growing nation. Although early Massachusetts legislation placed local educational responsibility and control in the town (township), the people were not long satisfied. As the colonists spread out and new communities developed, the residents wanted their own institutions, such as churches and schools, and the towns were divided into school districts. This seemed appropriate at a time when population was sparse, when communication and transportation between communities were difficult, and when isolation was the condition of life. As the frontier moved westward, this tendency continued. The concept of "home rule" in education is historical.[4] As one result, in most states the legislatures authorized small settlements and rural areas to be organized as local school districts. Many districts in some states still have the same limited boundaries established under frontier conditions.

For many years the small district, with its school in close physical proximity to the students and controlled by residents of the community, was looked upon as the epitome of educational organization. Every community came to look upon itself as independently competent to choose its teachers, determine the conditions and program of learning, and govern and finance its school. It was this extremity of provincialism and isolationism that caused Horace Mann to refer to the Massachusetts law establishing small local school districts as "the most unfortunate law on the subject of education ever enacted by the State of Massachusetts."

Some Factors Affecting District Organization

Since frontier days, the people in each state have been attempting more or less seriously to adapt their schools and school district organization to new and changing circumstances. However, a local school system in one sense is a domesticated organization which has been slow to change. Some factors that continue to require serious consideration are discussed briefly in the following paragraphs.

[3] S. D'Urso, ed., *Counterpoints: Critical Writings on Australian Education* (Sydney: John Wiley & Sons Australasia Pty. Ltd., 1971).

[4] American Association of School Administrators, *The American School Superintendency*, Thirtieth Yearbook (Washington, D.C.: The Association, 1952), p. 103.

①**Improvements in transportation and communication.** The time and distance limitations on communication and the movements of people have been greatly extended. People now have contact with persons, places, and organizations that are much farther removed from their places of residence, and they in turn have impact on them. As one result, school districts in many areas have been expanded or reorganized to meet the needs of rapidly growing communities and other related developments in society.

②**Expanding educational programs.** The citizens have made continually increasing demands on the public schools. Most schools that offered only the rudiments of instruction to a limited number of young people have been replaced gradually by institutions that offer a broad scope of learning experiences to nearly every segment of society. Efforts to provide adequate educational opportunities, to avoid duplication of offerings, to facilitate articulation involving different grade levels and programs, and to meet many other needs have stimulated the development of larger districts.

③**Changing economic circumstances.** As long as schools remained small and the basis of economic wealth was largely the land from which the people produced their sustenance, the matter of financing education was considered to be a local problem. However, the economy and sources of income have changed greatly. Other types of wealth have come into existence or have increased in importance and consequently the economic resources are much more unevenly distributed than during pioneer days. As a result of the rapidly growing industrialization and urbanization, differences in the ability of local districts to support schools have increased significantly in many areas.

④**Changing patterns of educational leadership.** In face of the increasing complexities encountered in organizing and administering programs of education, the lay school boards in smaller districts, with increasing frequency, have either operated with evident inefficiency or have had to turn to state or other educational leaders for advice and direction. Well-prepared and competent administrative leaders and supporting staffs have been available generally only to the larger districts. Increasingly, the fact has been recognized that only districts of sufficient size and ability to attract, support, and retain competent lay and educational leadership are able to assume bona fide local responsibility in and for their school systems. The maintenance of ineffective local districts has stimulated the establishment of state direction and control.

Some Significant Trends

As early as 1837, Horace Mann advocated the abolition of the newly created common school districts and reestablishment of the town system in Massachusetts. Since then most states have been concerned from time to time with matters relating to school district reorganization including proposals for permissive legislation, compulsory reorganization, semicompulsory plans, or legislation embodying some financial incentives for reorganization. Many states have relied chiefly on educational leadership at state and county levels to facilitate reorganization. Several have created state commissions on district reorganization to provide criteria and guidelines.

Number of districts. As a result of these and other related developments, there has been a significant decrease in the total number of school districts during the last fifty years. In 1932 (the first year for which reasonably complete information was assembled), there were 127,244 local school districts in the United States; in 1942, there were 115,384 districts; in 1952, 70,933; in 1962, 26,800 (2,420 of which did not operate any schools); in 1973, approximately 17,000; and, in 1977, over 16,000. Over 75 percent of all districts in the nation, however, still have fewer than 2,500 students (25 percent have fewer than 300 students), and some do not operate any schools. On the other hand, more than 63 percent of all students in the nation are in districts that have an enrollment of more than 5,000. The evidence available indicates that from 3,000 to 5,000 properly organized districts could more adequately provide education in modern American society and encourage more meaningful local responsibility for the operation of schools than is possible under the present district structure. It is also apparent that since 1970 the number of districts has not declined significantly.

Kinds of districts. There are many kinds or types of school districts. For example, in Florida, Maryland (except the city of Baltimore), Nevada, and West Virginia, all counties are organized as school districts. In most Southern states and in Utah, all county areas are organized as school districts, but the major cities usually constitute school districts that are not included in the county units in which they may be geographically located.

Arizona, California, Illinois, Wisconsin, and a few other states have distinctly different prevailing patterns. A wide variety of districts is found within each state. Only the unified districts have a single board of education responsible for all education, kindergarten through high school. In other areas of each of these states, and in many rural areas in some other states, there are separate districts for elementary and for secondary school students with separate governing boards and administrative officers for each level. However, the separately organized elementary and high school districts are gradually being replaced by unified districts.

The basic types of school districts can be classified, for the most part, into six main categories: (1) the common school district, most frequently found in the rural areas of several states, is generally relatively small both in area and in enrollment, frequently has a single school, and usually provides education only on the elementary level; (2) county unit districts with boundaries coterminous—or nearly so—with county lines; (3) city school districts that are usually coterminous—or nearly so—with city boundaries; (4) county districts in which the cities constitute separate districts; (5) special "independent" districts organized by legislative act in some states to provide education on an elementary or high school level or both; and (6) town or township districts. To this should be added high school districts, usually encompassing two or more elementary school districts, found in several states, and separately organized junior or community college districts that have been created in some states. Most county unit, city and town or township districts, and many of the county districts in which the cities constitute separate school districts, are unified—that is, they include grades K through 12.

Organization and relations. In most instances the local school district is a relatively autonomous unit operating by authorization of the state and not responsible to other governmental units except in specified instances. Each district has a governing board that is usually elected by the people. Except in small districts and in some county districts in which the superintendent is elected, a superintendent is appointed by the governing board as its chief administrative officer and policy consultant. Under the superintendent's professional leadership the local district has the opportunity, subject to minimum requirements and increasing regulations established by the state (and for certain programs by the federal government), to develop its own program of education. This traditional but declining autonomy of the local school district is uniquely American, and the preservation of what is commonly called "local control" is a rallying issue about a variety of school problems.

Nevertheless, as has been pointed out, school districts are legally instruments of the state for the accomplishment of the state's educational function. The state legislature, subject to state and federal constitutional limitations and court decisions, has complete authority over such districts and may instruct, advise, direct, create, or abolish them in accordance with its judgment regarding the welfare of education in the state. A most significant issue is whether states will establish and assist in the development of strong local districts—which can exercise responsibility and be genuine local partners—or whether they will attempt to control through an increasing mass of detailed laws, rules, and regulations.

Characteristics of Effective School Districts and Schools

The chief function of a school district is to make it possible for the citizens of the area to provide for the organization, operation, and administration of an adequate, economical, and effective educational program for those who should be educated in and through the public schools. Any district that fails to carry out this function satisfactorily is an ineffective district. The ineffectiveness may be due to the attitude of the people, to the limited size of the area, to inadequate human or economic resources, to failure to recognize or meet emerging needs, or to any combination of these factors.

Because some of the major characteristics of a satisfactory program of education and of provisions for its organization, administration, and support are discussed elsewhere in this book, major attention will be centered here on other criteria, including size (number of students) that must be observed if a district is to be in a position to operate effectively. However, the number of students should not be the only determining factor, because an adequate number of students does not assure effectiveness; it only makes it possible when other conditions are favorable.

When an area is too small in terms of population, it cannot provide an adequate program at an economical cost. When it is too large in terms of distance or population, the citizens may have difficulty in communicating, agreeing on goals, and cooperating in developing policies and plans.

Authorities are agreed that every district should be in a position to provide an educational program that extends through at least the high school grades. Separate districts for elementary and for high schools, even though they may be fairly large, are not considered desirable because education should be a continuous process, unhampered by unnecessary complications for voters, for children, or for the educational staff.

Research shows that reasonable economies of scale cannot be attained in districts with school populations of fewer than about 10,000 students. Districts that are smaller in size are faced with higher unit costs for an adequate educational program as the number of students decreases. In districts with fewer than 1,800 the unit costs become so great that adequate opportunities can seldom be provided. Many people, therefore, believe the minimum acceptable size for a school district should be 10,000 students in all except the most sparsely settled areas where the minimum probably should be 5,000. These minimum sizes should not be confused with optimum sizes, which in many areas should probably be between 25,000 and 50,000 students.

The organization of districts that meet the criteria suggested would make it possible to resolve the small-school problem in all except isolated and sparsely populated areas where such schools may have to be continued regardless of higher costs.

School Districts and/or Local Education Agencies

In recent years there has been an increase in the use of the term LEA—local education agency or local education authority. This term, used in England for many years in referring to the local unit responsible for education, has in the last decade gained substantial acceptance in the United States. It implies a somewhat different orientation, organization, and responsibility from the traditional one. It escapes the rather narrow connotation of the local *school system* and suggests that the local education authority may indeed coordinate or provide for a much wider range of educational services. Many school systems are providing services for children, youth, and adults beyond the operation of schools, and more will probably be doing so in the future. It should be noted that the provision of schools would remain the central responsibility of the local education agency as it has been of the school district.

This wider range of educational services is indicated by many practices and proposals pertaining to education. Examples are preschool provisions, industry-based vocational or technical education, youth services, library services, child health services, performance contracts, voucher plans, placement and follow-up of youth in employment, and community-based rather than school building-based schools. A local education agency may be engaged in these or other programs which are part of the educational service but which may not be regarded specifically as a part of a school system. They, or some of them, however, would clearly be seen as appropriate areas of service by a local education authority. The development of a rather more diverse range of programs and services would appear essential in the building of an adequate public education program in the future. This change in title appears fitting as we move toward a local agency with broader powers and greater responsibility for meeting diverse educational needs in a highly complex society. This title also suggests that some educational services may be rendered by other agencies under contract, for example, or in cooperation with the local education authority. The local education authority would thus be the responsible agency for educational services in the local area though it would not directly provide all of them. It should, however, provide the essential coordination of these services and leadership in the development and evaluation of them.

It should be noted that the concept of a responsible local education agency implies a further reduction in the number of school districts in some states. Many existing districts are too small to have the resources essential for the development of or administration of adequate educational services. The states and the federal government have generally not expected initiative and innovation to be shown by most local authorities because of a lack of confidence in their competence. The belief in the significance of education in our society, as in other societies, indicates that the role of the local authority needs to expand sharply in the years immediately ahead.[5] This should occur concurrently with the increase in state and federal action in education.

The traditions and myths of our society regarding local control of education as well as present societal needs constitute an impressive base upon which to develop local school authorities of great vitality and unique characteristics.

If this is to be accomplished, it will be necessary not only to avoid restrictive state regulations but also to recognize that a local educational agency is a political and social system, closely related to external and internal traditions, needs, and forces. Provision will need to be made to facilitate change within it as a result of planning, experimentation, and research. Its own differences from other authorities and the variety within it will be greatly valued. Then it may become the instrument of its staff and its people to achieve to the fullest basic values drawn from the past struggles and experiences in the development of men and women. Whether or not the society achieves these values with the aid of education will depend upon the vision and action which is found within local authorities. There would be less reason to expect them to be achieved in a monolithic system, which would dominate a state or the nation and which was not continuously rebuilt utilizing the resources, energies, inspirations, and initiatives of the people (staff and citizens) in local units or authorities. The movement toward a local authority from a system is believed to be an essential step through which to respond to the call for greater variety in educational provisions in a constructive manner while maintaining a cohesive, vigorous local agency committed to the educational interest of all people. This view, of course, does not deprecate the essential role of the state and federal government in establishing guidelines to attain minimum standards, in ensuring the rights of all people, in providing leadership, in facilitating experimentation and local initiative, and in providing financial resources. The case for a stronger, more vital partnership appears to be unassailable.

---

[5] In this regard see Jesse Burkhead, *Public School Finance Economics and Politics* (Syracuse, N.Y.: Syracuse University Press, 1964), p. 284. "The consideration of who would lose power in such a new working arrangement—the local school board, state department of education, the professional, academic, or layman adviser—is a meaningless one because a new institutional framework for the educational process would increase the responsibility of all and would make the tasks more difficult, but surely more interesting, provocative, and meaningful. As institutions grow in size and complexity, the challenge of all concerned increases. To be sure, individuals who are unwilling to accept change or different ways of doing things are bypassed and become disgruntled. But the persons and groups accepting change and challenge usually find the new situation brings greater responsibility."

THE STATE-LOCAL PARTNERSHIP

Even though the educational system has been a state operation in accord with statute and judicial interpretation, it has also been a service characterized by partnership. In the early years of the nineteenth century the state did not exercise its interest in education vigorously. Some local areas established schools and developed them, but other communities provided little in the way of educational opportunity. Whether a community had good schools or not was probably more the result of local forces and factors than of any special activity on the part of the state. This is not to deny that general or special state laws existed with reference to education or that there were some state leaders such as Mann and Barnard who supplied much encouragement. But education actually developed as a local activity. State educational personnel was exceedingly limited and quite unable to serve the great number of local districts in a direct manner.

When the state did become more interested in the development of an educational service that would meet the needs of children and youth, it generally chose to do so through local school districts. Thus the partnership was strengthened. The state offered certain financial aid and stimulated local districts by making available trained state personnel who could work with them in meeting their problems. The direct provision and management of the schools was a responsibility of local authorities. Thus it could be said that the school system was actually a local one. It was a state system marked by variety, by wide differences in opportunity, and by excellent provisions in some cases and extremely inadequate ones in others. In later years the state became much more active and sought to guarantee all children and youth at least a minimum level of opportunity. Even this, however, was done through local districts. The system was scarcely a decentralized one, for it had never been centralized. It was rather a partnership with the state rendering much assistance and giving attention to the development of more competent and responsible local partners.

A system was achieved in which it was hoped that desirable experimentation and innovation would result from the independence of local districts in developing schools to meet needs. Many of the advances that have marked education have come from the exercise of initiative by local districts. After the worth of these practices was demonstrated in some communities, they gradually spread to many other communities. In some instances the spread of the practices was aided by the state department personnel—in other cases by the enactment of legislation supporting them financially. Our state system of education is also a local system and a partnership.

The nearness of the schools to the people has always been a distinguishing feature of the school system. In few other countries has there been such a close relationship between the schools and the people. This has had both advantages and disadvantages. It has been a major factor in the strong interest that the people have had in their schools. The development of the schools has been related closely to this interest. It has stimulated the making of adaptations in educational practice. It has resulted in a school system of remarkable vitality and excellence, though also with serious shortcomings and with relatively little exercise of rigid controls by state and federal governmental agencies.

On the other hand, it resulted in the continuance of many small school districts that did not provide reasonable, adequate educational opportunity even though their costs were high. Furthermore, the "interest" of certain pressure groups in education has at times known no bounds, and interference with the schools has harmed them. Materials have been introduced or eliminated from the curriculum as a result of pressure by some group—not always one interested in or competent to judge "what education is of most worth." Teachers also have been subjected to pressure or even discharged without adequate reason or even the opportunity to be heard. The responsibility of the trained educator has at times been seriously hampered by the unsound action of citizens.

Despite the difficulties that have been encountered, few desire to increase the distance between the schools and the people. The desire is to move in the other direction, especially in larger communities in which the distance separating them may be greater than is generally recognized. In this development, however, there is a growing awareness that some guidelines need to be established. Such guidelines should facilitate close relationship and high public interest without undesirable interference.

In recent years the people of our society have been reexamining their values to an unusual degree. Consequently they have been seeking greater diversity in educational practice and have grown sharply critical of the educational *system.* Many have come to regard it as a rather rigid bureaucracy which meets the needs of those operating it more than the needs of children; as an institution which suffers from serious hardening of the arteries and which finds innovation and change unpalatable or even impossible. One of the results of these views has been the demand for decentralization and for greater variety in schools with more parental choice regarding types of schools.

In the last decade or two we have also seen the development of much greater interest and participation in the educational service by the federal government. This has been done especially through the financing of categorical programs. These programs (as well as state categorical programs) have been aimed at specific needs or groups and accompanied by substantial rules and regulations. While their intent has been good and their contributions substantial, they have resulted in many problems for the local education authority and may not have advanced the educational service to the degree hoped for. In fact, if such programs become too numerous, too tightly regulated, and too competitive with one another and with the general education program, they may have important negative effects. If the categorical program effort continues to expand without correction of its serious flaws, it may indeed seriously undermine the possibility of developing highly innovative, responsible, and competent local authorities for the educational service.

THE BOARD OF EDUCATION

While, generally, there has been a close relationship of the citizenry to the schools, there has been a legal structure for the establishment and development of the local school authority. The legal responsibility has rested upon the education committee of the town in New England and in other sections of the country upon the board of school trustees, school directors, or board of education.

The board of education has been under considerable attack in recent years. During the 1970s, in many cities its legitimacy was questioned—critics holding that it did not adequately represent the changing composition (economic, social, racial) of the population. At that time considerable attention was given to reducing the power of the board of education through decentralization. This took a wide range of forms, though perhaps the best known was the establishment of subdistricts as in New York City and Detroit. Generally achievements under "decentralization" did not match the rhetoric of its proponents, and for a variety of reasons it lost much of its appeal.

Another aspect of the decentralization movement has been the development of school site councils. Although such councils have been known for many years, there has been considerable movement in recent years to give them legal status, to define their membership, and to increase considerably their powers.[6]

Boards of education have also experienced reduced power or authority in recent years as a result of growing federal and state rules and regulations and as a result of teacher power and legislation requiring collective negotiations regarding a significant range of matters.

Although local school districts and boards of education have been challenged in recent years, Lutz and Iannaccone find in their study of dissatisfaction theory that there is democracy in school district governance and that the local board continues to be "the primary grass-roots unit of democratic government" in the nation.[7]

Selection of Board Members

The members of boards of education are generally elected by popular vote. In the majority of instances they are not sponsored by political parties and are not elected as members of a political party. In some of the larger cities, board of education members are appointed by the mayor. In a few cases they have been appointed by another agency such as judges of common pleas courts. The appointment procedures have been employed in some cases to effect a closer relationship between the education service and local government services. In other cases appointment reflects some lack of belief in the ability of citizens to elect competent school board members. Opinion in general, however, strongly supports popular election, though it is recognized that board members of a wide range of competence are found under any plan of selection.

Formerly, many board of education members were elected as representatives of wards or areas within the district. This tended to result in board members' representing the ward from which they were elected and too largely ignoring the needs of the whole district. Consequently, there has been until recently a long-term trend toward election at large. Despite this trend some boards continue with election of members for subdistricts or areas within the school district, and a few have turned to it recently. This arrangement may be necessary where people in certain parts of the district or from certain ethnic groups feel that they will be completely over-

---

[6] See Chapter 9 for a fuller discussion of this movement.

[7] Frank W. Lutz and Laurence Iannaccone, *Public Participation in Local School Districts* (Lexington, Mass.: D. C. Heath & Co., 1978), pp. 129, 132.

shadowed by a more populous section. Election by subdistricts should be viewed as a somewhat temporary expedient to be replaced when the confidence of the people in the district as a unit has been established. It should be undertaken with an understanding of the limitations inherent in it. A promising compromise between election at large and election by subdistricts is the requirement that members be residents of specified areas but elected by vote of all of the people of the district.

Board members are generally elected for overlapping terms of three to six years. To ensure reasonable continuity, the longer term (with no more than one or two members elected in any one year or two elected every second year) appears to be preferable.

Size of Boards

The size of boards has varied greatly. Many small rural districts have had only three members. In some of the cities the boards grew as the city added territory, until late in the nineteenth century some boards had several hundred members. During the current century, with the elimination of many of the smaller districts and with an awareness of the problems resulting from extremely large boards, the trend has been toward boards of five to seven or possibly nine members.

Board Duties

The board of education is responsible for the establishment and operation of the local public school system. This usually includes responsibility for kindergartens and grades one through twelve. In some states, depending upon the size of the district, the board also makes provisions for adult education, various special education offerings, and junior college education. Statutes fix this responsibility upon local boards of education either by mandating broad and implied powers or by specifying in more detail the duties and powers of the local board of education. In either case it should be clear that the local board derives its power legally from the state. It thus is an agent of the state and also of the people of the district whom it serves. It serves the people of the district in accord with the mandate of the powers vested in it by the state. With the recognition that equality of opportunity can be achieved only through a social action program broader than the school system, it may be expected that the board of the local authority will be granted larger powers pertaining to the development of children and youth. Some federal grants have stimulated action in this direction.

Among the many powers of the board of education the following are of outstanding importance:

1. Selection of a chief administrator, the superintendent of schools.
2. Establishment of policies and procedures in accord with which the educational services are administered and a range of programs are developed.
3. Establishment of policies relating to planning improvements and to accountability.

4. Adoption of the budget and the enactment of provisions for the financing of the schools.
5. Acquisition and development of necessary property and the provision of supplies.
6. Adoption of policies regarding personnel including the establishment of essential policies and procedures for collective negotiations and the approval of agreements relating thereto.
7. Appraisal of the work of the schools and adoption of plans for development.

Board Organization and Functioning

When boards of education were large, dependence upon administrative staff was limited, and board members represented subdistricts, the practice of administering schools through the standing committee system was widespread. It was not uncommon for individual board members to get deeply involved in the details of administration. They interviewed applicants individually for teaching positions and selected instructional materials.

Today, it is agreed that board members need to recognize that they as individuals do not have powers regarding the schools. Statutes fix responsibility upon the board of education rather than upon individual members. Furthermore, the standing committee is not favored, though boards may from time to time appoint temporary committees to consider a special problem and report back to the board. The desirability of having the board recognize the establishment of policies and procedures, rather than involve itself in administrative details as a major responsibility, is increasingly clear. This, of course, assumes that the board has competent leadership and staff to develop and provide it with the data that are essential as the basis for the determination of policies and procedures. It also assumes that the board has an administrative staff that can administer the schools in accord with the policies and can report results, including the inadequacies of established policies and procedures.

Thus, the board of education is or should be a unified body devoted to the provision and advancement of the educational service with the cooperation of the teaching, administrative, and other groups of personnel and the cooperation of parents and various other agencies concerned with the development of children, youth, and adults. Its cooperative relationship with the administrative and teaching staff is especially important because of the close understanding that must exist among them if the organization is to function properly.

If the board of education is to discharge these difficult responsibilities in an effective manner, it needs to give attention to and make provision for procedures to be followed at board meetings and to records regarding board actions. Otherwise, it will spend its time in the discussion of details rather than policies, and it will frequently engage in lengthy discussions of matters about which it does not have essential data.

The successful board of education meeting is dependent upon a number of factors such as preparing the agenda and related materials effectively, planning the meeting, giving adequate hearings to individuals and groups, and reviewing the meeting.

The agenda should be prepared several days before the meeting and should be submitted to the members of the board along with various staff reports on issues and proposals containing the essential data and alternative solutions that must be studied by the board members if they are to be prepared to make decisions. At the opening of the meeting, brief consideration should be given to the plans for the meeting, with tentative allocation of time made to different matters on the agenda. The rules of the board should establish procedures for getting items on the agenda. The rules should provide that under certain circumstances brief presentations may be accepted from individuals or groups regarding matters not on the agenda. The time for such presentations, however, should be limited, and discussion and action generally should be delayed until essential related data may be gathered and presented to the board. At the conclusion of meetings, at least occasionally, the procedures followed should be reviewed. If considerable time was wasted through lack of planning, this should be recognized and plans made to avoid similar situations at later meetings. Meetings can be made fruitful and effective if adequate attention is given to the manner in which they are conducted. Attention can and should be given to important instructional issues frequently overlooked because of lack of time. Many boards in recent years have given more attention to developing plans for a consideration of these matters. Otherwise, the details of buildings, finance, and business administration will consume the total energies of the board.

The successful functioning of the board is largely a result of the assistance it has in planning the agenda and the conduct of its meetings. No other person can render as large a measure of assistance as the superintendent of schools. Partly in recognition of his or her central relation to sound board functioning many boards designate the superintendent to serve as their secretary.

The politics of confrontation and the vigorous challenge by teacher and community groups is causing many boards of education to carefully reexamine their own organization and policies. This would appear to be imperative if they are to discharge their responsibilities effectively. For the power of the board may otherwise be eroded without an awareness of what is occurring.

THE SUPERINTENDENT OF SCHOOLS

The importance of the position of the superintendent of schools has already been implied in the consideration of the work of the board of education. The position is at least equal in significance to any other position in the community. If schools are to contribute to the development of the values of the people and not just reflect the community, it will in no small part be because of the leadership furnished by the superintendent.

Although the role of the superintendent and the type of leadership needed may vary from community to community and over time, there is little reason to question the view that factors such as pluralism, teacher power, "the widespread sense of social and educational crisis," and the "waves of conflict within and without school systems" call for the best leadership talent available in society. Further, the challenge may be sufficient to attract or produce more charismatic and even prophetic leaders.[8] Later in this chapter the importance of the structure or organiza-

[8] See Jack Culbertson et al., *Preparing Educational Leaders for the Seventies* (Columbus, Ohio: University Council for Educational Administration, 1969), Section III.

tion of the educational service is emphasized. Whereas organizational development and organizational health are of large significance, it should not be assumed that they lessen the imperative need for a much greater effort to identify, select, and prepare men and women for leadership roles in the educational service. The profession of educational administration, school districts, and the universities need to respond to this challenge cooperatively.

Selection of Superintendent

No single act of the board of education is more important than its selection of a superintendent. If one is chosen who provides the needed leadership and who is an excellent administrator, the work of the board can be far more effective. An inadequate administrator will make it virtually impossible for the board to render excellent service. The board therefore should devote great care to the selection of the superintendent.

It may do this by first clarifying the role and competencies that it desires of a superintendent and then indicating the personal characteristics and educational background and experience that it believes relate significantly to this role. It may also want to assess the local school and community situation as a basis for defining the role. Many boards desire the assistance of professional educators in doing this job. The retiring superintendent, members of the state department of education, or professors in neighboring colleges or universities may be able to render valuable assistance to the board in the work of defining the position and the type of person needed and in doing at least preliminary screening of applicants.

After the position has been defined, recommendations of persons for the position should be sought from colleges, universities, and leading school administrators. The position is too important to be filled merely by receiving applications of those who by chance hear of it and apply. In the last analysis the board itself will have to choose the person—but it can do a far better job if it has followed procedures such as those suggested here and does not find its energies consumed in interviewing large numbers of persons who hold administrative certificates but vary widely in competence.

The quality of person secured will, of course, be dependent in part upon the situation. Important considerations in the local situation will be the board and its procedures and attitudes, the quality of the professional staff, the community attitudes toward education, and the nature of the contract and the salary. The initial contract should be long enough to give the superintendent the opportunity to study the situation, to develop plans, and to have a chance to test them through application. This suggests that a three- or four-year contract is a minimal one for the initial contract with provisions for extension. Preferably the contract should be performance based, setting forth mutually agreed upon goals and objectives and a plan for reviewing performance.

Responsibilities of the Superintendent

Another important factor related to the quality of superintendent who will accept the appointment is the concept of the position held by the board. Few excellent people will go into a situation in which they are denied opportunity to perform the duties they regard as those properly vested in the superintendent. In this respect, it should be noted that the duties of the superintendent are largely determined by action of the board—except in a few large cities where a charter or statute partially defines the duties. There are relatively few powers conferred on the superintendent by statute. Although some strengthening of the powers of the superintendent through statute is probably desirable, most laypersons and educators favor keeping major responsibility for defining the responsibilities of the superintendent in the hands of the board of education.

Among the important duties of the superintendent are

1. To serve as chief executive officer of the board of education and thus to be responsible for all aspects of the educational service.
2. To lead the board in the development of policies.
3. To provide leadership in the planning, management, and evaluation of all phases of the educational program.
4. To select and recommend all personnel for appointment and separation, to lead in plans and programs for staff development, and to guide (but not serve as negotiator) in collective negotiations.
5. To prepare the budget for submission to the board and to administer it after its adoption by the board.
6. To determine building needs and to administer building programs—construction, operation, maintenance, and contraction of facilities.
7. To serve as leader of the board, the staff, and the community in the improvement of the educational system.

If superintendents are to render superior service, it is important that their duties be defined clearly, but this should not be done by stating a multitude of details that tend to limit activity and produce a rigid administration lacking vision and initiative.

Again it should be noted that the role of leadership is now more "demanding and formidable" than in any previous period. Bennis in his consideration of post-bureaucratic leadership has said that it involves

four important sets of competencies: (1) knowledge of large, complex human systems; (2) practical theories of intervening and guiding these systems, theories that encompass methods for seeding, nurturing, and integrating individuals and groups; (3) interpersonal competence, particularly the sensitivity to understand the effects of one's own behavior on others and how one's own personality shapes his particular leadership style and value system; and (4) a set of values and competencies which enables one to know when to confront and attack, if necessary, and when to support and provide the psychological safety so necessary for growth.[9]

Staff Organization

The growth in responsibility and the larger size of local school systems as a result of the elimination of many of the small districts, the growth in population, the

[9]Warren G. Bennis, *American Bureaucracy* (Chicago: Aldine Publishing Company, 1970), pp. 185–186.

changing concept of what constitutes an adequate education, the increasing aspirations of the people regarding education, and the growing relations with the state and federal governments—all have led to substantial increases in size of administrative staff. These increases have at times resulted in sharp criticism of administrators and in the charge that too large a percentage of the budget is devoted to administration. Most of this criticism is probably unjustified. However, it should be recognized that the organization of staff, the determination of special competencies needed, the definition of responsibilities, and the appraisal of administrative functioning are highly essential in what is more generally becoming a large-scale organization.

Consideration of the responsibilities of the superintendent listed here suggests the importance of an administrative staff of adequate numbers and high quality. The administrative staff consists of not only the assistant superintendents, directors, and administrative assistants found in the central office but also those in area or divisional offices and the principals and assistants located in the respective schools. In small systems the superintendents will need to discharge many responsibilities with very little administrative assistance. In large systems their work may be largely the identification of needed development and leadership in stimulating it, the coordination of the work of others and the direction of the growth of other administrators in the discharge of their responsibilities.

A few decades ago, there was some question as to whether the school system should be organized on a unit or dual or even multiple basis. Fundamentally, this was a question of whether the superintendent of schools should be the chief executive of the system or whether there should be no one chief executive. It is almost universally agreed today that the organization should be a unitary one and that, because the superintendent of schools is basically concerned with instruction (the educational program), he or she should be the chief executive. It is also widely accepted that the organization should facilitate development and satisfaction of organizational expectations and individual needs.

The superintendent of schools has an important decision to make regarding the manner in which the staff is organized. A few decades ago the line-and-staff organization was generally accepted as the most desirable type. With changing concepts of the meaning of educational leadership, this concept of organization has undergone further examination. Can the school principal be effective, both as a line and a staff officer? Or is the term "officer" acceptable? Does the line-and-staff organization facilitate the cooperative effort that the school administrator seeks in the school system today? Is there some other type of organization that is more in accord with present-day concepts of leadership and that has larger potential?

To what extent should the new administrative staff be located at the central office? At the school level? At selected secondary schools which serve as centers for a number of schools? Or in large systems should there be area superintendents with an office and staff located in the area served? If so, which services shall be decentralized and which centralized?

Fundamental also is the question of the staffing pattern of the local school district. Rapid change in education demands new personnel or reassignment of those employed. An old organization is called upon to meet new challenges, to plan, to provide new services, and to coordinate services. The organization is frequently subjected to criticism by legislative committees and by teachers' organizations. The growing specialization of staff and range of services including categorical programs provided in a school system as well as the increasing rate of change emphasize the need for modifying staffing patterns and staffing ratios. Without such guidelines, essential staff provisions to facilitate planning, appraisal, contraction, and constructive change are not likely to be made.

A central question regarding the staff is whether it should be functional (traditional) or organic. Bennis has predicted that in the future, organizations

> will be adaptive, rapidly changing *temporary systems,* organized around problems to be solved by groups of relative strangers with diverse professional skills. The groups will be arranged on organic rather than mechanical models; they will evolve in response to problems rather than programmed expectations. . . . Organizational charts will consist of project groups rather than stratified functional groups, as is now the case. Adaptive, problem-solving, temporary systems of diverse specialists, linked together by coordinating executives in an organic flux—this is the organizational form that will gradually replace bureaucracy.[10]

The matrix organization has many commendable features. Its introduction and utilization, however, must be accompanied by great sensitivity to and ability to deal with problems which may result.

Probably the most important and difficult of the chief administrator's responsibilities is that of selecting and stimulating the development of the members of the administrative team. If the staff in the central and area (site) offices are highly competent in their respective fields and if they can work effectively as a team and with other people, the superintendent's burdens are greatly reduced. If the principals of the schools are competent and provide leadership in the study of children and youth, the development of the educational program, the stimulation of student growth, and home–school coordination, then a superior school system should result. In a large system the superintendent cannot hope to work directly with large numbers of the teaching staff, but he or she can influence them greatly through the organization evolved and the administrative staff developed.

The Management Team

The management or administrative leadership team, as a relatively formal arrangement, developed only in the late 1960s. The concept, however, has been a part of the process of staff involvement that many successful superintendents employed in earlier years. The management team generally is comprised of all principals and assistant principals and of all districtwide supervisors and administrators, classified and credentialed.

The major role of the management team is to provide effective administration. This involves the development of sound policies for consideration and approval of the board of education; the establishment of respect and understanding between the board of education and the administration; the building of communication,

---

[10] Bennis, *American Bureaucracy,* p. 166. See also E. G. Bogue, "Disposable Organizations," *Phi Delta Kappan,* 53 no. 2 (October 1971), 94–96.

cooperation, trust, frank interaction among the administrators of the system; the achievement of that centralization essential for a "system" while enhancing the autonomy of the school which is imperative in an effective education service—building essential cooperation and trust between the central office and the individual school; and the implementation of policies, monitoring the results, and exercising accountability.

The growth of the management team concept has been greatly stimulated by the collective negotiations movement which has eliminated administrators from teacher organizations and has made the role of the site principal who wishes to be effective even more complex and difficult than formerly. It has also been stimulated by the threat of the unionization of middle management.

The major difficulties experienced with the management team have been overcoming the status or hierarchical levels felt by members of the team; developing a policy statement regarding the team—its makeup and model (single, dual, multiple), powers (limitations), appeal procedures of members; and the continued accountability of the superintendent.[11]

THE POLICY AND PROCEDURE GUIDE

As a way of summarizing this conception of the role of the board of education and the superintendent of schools, attention will be turned briefly to the significance of developing an administrative or policy and procedure guide. It should contain policy statements that guide the board, the superintendent, and other staff in the administration of schools in the system, and it should outline procedures regarding some of the more important activities. It can be of great value for the orientation of new board members and new staff. It serves to give to each party involved a better understanding of his or her responsibilities and thus lessens misunderstandings. It aids the public in understanding how the schools are operated. It facilitates getting the work of the schools done and helps center attention upon the various phases of work that need to be planned and carried through. In the development of a guide all those who are affected by it should be involved. The past practices of the board and system should be analyzed as one basis for it. In the preparation of the guide it is very important that attention be given not only to the specific duties to be discharged by each party but also to the fact that many of the activities can be effectively discharged only through the cooperative action of a number of parties.

The guide should, for example, help principals to understand the major responsibilities that are theirs—and also the extent to which they should serve as leaders of others in decision making rather than just as decision makers. The development of too detailed a code that would result in rigid organization and operation should be avoided. A rigid organization which fails to recognize that the informal organization may be as important as the formal one is not likely to result in an effective educational system.

---

[11] American Association of School Administrators, *The Administrative Leadership Team,* Superintendent Development Career Series No. 5 (Arlington, Va.: American Association of School Administrators, 1979).

Can the Local Education Agency Domesticate the Range
of Categorical Programs Which May Have a Too Limited Focus?

The local school district has the responsibility to develop an educational pro-gram which among other things should respond to the educational needs of all children and youth of the district. In recent years it has been more responsive than formerly to many demands; however, much remains to be done in terms of ex-pected attainments. In recent decades states and the federal government have estab-lished many categorical programs. Some of them have been poorly planned even to assist in the education of limited groups. Frequently they are administered by bureaucrats of the state and federal governments who are highly committed (under-standably) to the application of specific rules and regulations pertaining to the respective programs.

While the potential contribution to be made by these categorical programs should be recognized, it must also be noted that it is expecting a great deal to as-sume that they will assist in the maintenance of a balanced educational program. They are not designed to do this. Further, each program may have its own staff which may well judge results in terms of its own group rather than upon the ability of the system to meet a range of needs in a responsible manner.

As a result of some categorical programs serious morale and other personnel problems arise. Critics suggest that at times they see themselves as separate educa-tional systems. Because many children have multiple special needs, they are in more than one categorical program each of which wishes to "count" them—and to teach them. In some instances such children may spend far too little time with one competent teacher—but instead circulate among several less competent ones. Thus critics wonder if the programs pursue their self-perpetuation rather than the best education of children. Also the serious questions of costs and administration should be addressed.

If the local education authority is to make the contribution expected of it, it must tackle these problems and work to overcome some of the almost inevitable consequences of a categorically organized school system. It must in fact go beyond this and continue to provide for many needs which for a given community are of highest significance even if they have not won the endorsement of a single focused national pressure group.

How Can the Board of Education Appraise
the Results of the Educational Service?

Probably the most difficult of the responsibilities of the board of education is that of appraisal. It has selected its staff, provided resources to carry the program through, and devoted long hours to a consideration of many policies and proce-dures; now it must evaluate, for without evaluation it lacks the basis for decision making regarding future planning and development. Several steps are suggested. They assume that board members are competent.

Each board member should, with the help of the state association of school boards and that of the local staff, develop considerable knowledge about education. That member will not be an educational expert—and must avoid assuming that he or she has become one. But that member must become familiar with schools, educational practices, alternatives, problems, and issues. Otherwise, that member cannot exercise that judgment that appraisal requires on his or her part. Some of this knowledge can be acquired through planned visits to schools. For such visits some background and assistance are necessary in order to understand the significance of what is being observed.

Considerable knowledge can be gained through board of education meetings that are planned with this purpose. Materials need to be developed regarding the services or issues under consideration and distributed prior to the meeting. Various staff members may make presentations. Alternative policies and practices need to be presented. Board of education meetings that greatly increase the board members' knowledge of the educational service are not likely to occur unless the need for them is recognized, plans are made for them, and specified times are set for them.

The development of more adequate research provisions and the conducting of continuous evaluation programs are other essential steps. Too little is done in planning for a continuing evaluation program which over a period of years would collect large amounts of data about the variety of programs and services that are provided in the schools. The board that will insist upon the development of such plans has taken a long step in the direction of developing a base in the light of which appraisals can be made.

Finally, the board may periodically seek a more comprehensive appraisal. It, too, like the continuous appraisal referred to, may be carried forward under the direction of the administrative staff. It also may involve the assistance of consultants. It generally should be cooperative—involving teachers and citizens as well as personnel from outside the district selected because of their special competencies.

Board of education members and the staffs associated with them should recognize that appraisals are inevitably going to be made. Attention therefore needs to be centered upon the problem of ensuring that appraisals have a real measure of validity and avoiding the too readily available alternatives of making appraisals on the basis of few or no facts, on the spur of the moment, or in consideration of personalities.

Boards of education need also to recognize that the emphasis in recent years upon the development of a systems approach which requires a serious planning effort, the clarification of goals, the development of specific instructional and instructional support programs, the development of objectives cooperatively by staff involved, and the establishment of evaluation procedures offers an approach of significant promise.

What is the role of the superintendent of schools in assisting the board of education to appraise the educational service?

Can and Should the Work of the Board of Education and That of the Administrator Be Sharply Separated?

In an effort to assist individual board members to avoid getting involved in the details of administration, frequently it is pointed out that the individual board member, except when the board is in session, has no legal powers not possessed by all other citizens. Further, it is held that the board should see its role as that of policymaker, and the administration should administer in accord with established policy. This view may be sound enough. However, it is unrealistically simple. Consider, for example, the question of the selection of personnel.

A desirable policy would doubtless be that the most competent personnel should be secured—that personnel which can render the greatest service to children. The board however would probably wish to go well beyond such a general policy statement in discharging its responsibility in this area. It would probably wish either to adopt procedures that were judged most likely to implement the policy effectively or to ask the administration to submit to it the regulations and procedures proposed to be employed. In the consideration of the policy and especially in the consideration of procedures related to it, the board needs the assistance of the administrative staff. Studies would be required outlining various possible procedures and indicating their probable results. The administrative staff would seek the assistance of members of the instructional staff in formulating such proposals. Periodically, also, the board would wish the assistance of the executive arm in evaluating the procedures in the light of results produced and in effecting modifications. Thus, although the board would adopt the policies and the procedures through which they are to be implemented, it generally could not hope to do the job without very important assistance from its administrative staff. In a sense, therefore policy making is engaged in by board, administrator, teachers, and other interested parties. Only policies developed through cooperative effort are likely to be sound and have genuine promise of implementation.

Approaching the issue from the other side it can be observed that policy making is a part of administration. Furthermore, such actions as approval of plans, adopting the budget, fixing the tax rate, and authorizing borrowing for capital outlay purposes are important phases of administration. Regarding all these matters, the administrative staff has a highly significant role to play, though the final decision is legally that of the board. In these matters, both the board and administrators are significantly involved in reaching a decision. Other groups such as the teachers and community groups may also play important roles. With the increase in community interest in education and the growing strength of the organized educational profession, it is likely that the problem of determining "who makes the decision" may be more difficult in the future. The growing complexity of the situation, however, demands that attention be given to fixing the responsibility for initiation, for example, and clarifying the expectations of the various groups involved. What thus appeared to be a rather simple problem—the separation of the powers of the administrator and of the board—is a very complex one, one that will be satisfactorily resolved only through extended cooperative effort based upon mutual confidence and respect among the parties involved.

All this is not to suggest that the board or its members should again become involved in the details of selecting teachers. The procedures employed should outline clearly the steps to be followed by a competent professional staff in making the selection. The board would confirm the appointments, maintain an interest in the results, and receive reports regarding them. This it would need to do to meet its legal responsibility regarding the employment of personnel and to be enabled to discharge its appraisal function.

How can the essential cooperative relationship and the recognition of the respective responsibilities of the superintendent and board be attained? How can the board avoid becoming an instrument of the superintendent? of the teachers' organization?

*Is the Superintendency a Defensible Position
or Are the Expectancies of the Position Too Great?*

The superintendency which has long had a reputation for insecurity and short tenure is in one of its most troubled periods. This is a result of many factors, including the growing expectations for education, the increased role of teachers in administrative and policy decisions, and the view that educational leadership must mean community leadership. Thus *de facto* segregation, an important community problem, has become a major challenge to the school system and to the superintendent.

With the growing awareness of the great variation in the expectancies regarding the superintendency, the question has been raised whether the position is not an impossible one. Should the administrative organization be changed to reduce the varying "demands" on the superintendent? Has there been a tendency to regard the superintendent as the one who can resolve inevitable conflicts—and then to condemn him or her when they are not resolved?

Certainly the superintendency is one of the most difficult positions conceivable because of the impact of expectancies. And even boards of education and individual members, for example, may have widely varying views regarding the superintendency and may over a period of time change their expectancies. In communities in which the local superintendent is largely an administrator and not a leader, the position is a much simpler one to fill. However, it is probable that neither our society nor the administrators themselves would choose a system that might be easier for the individual but would lower the vision of the system, for out of the conflict of expectancies may come much desirable educational change.

Furthermore, the emphasis upon responding to needs and providing alternative educational programs encourages research, experimentation, and development regarding many issues in education. The superintendent should take the initiative in formulating problems for study and experimentation, in securing and utilizing research facilities, and in seeking answers through carefully planned development and evaluation. This emphasis may avoid or blunt both unsound attacks and plans and too much dependence upon past experience.

Acceptance by the superintendent of the fact that others may be equally desirous of serving youth and the society may be helpful. The superintendent must recognize that to be helpful to others—to be a leader of others—he or she must be perceived by others as one who is helpful, one who is a leader.[12] This perception on the part of others has to be earned through demonstrated ability to understand and to work with others and through demonstrated commitments to the purposes of public education.

Finally, the superintendent must recognize that in the very large difficulties of the position are to be found large opportunities. The position is a highly influential

[12] Harriet O. Ronken and Paul R. Lawrence, *Administering Changes: A Case Study of Human Relations in a Factory* (Cambridge, Mass.: Graduate School of Business Administration, Harvard University, 1952), p. 305.

one and he or she may play a negative role, as Callahan has indicated.[13] The superintendent can, however, recognize that it is not too unlike other leadership positions in a vital democracy. Kerr has written of the university presidency in terms not at all unlike the experiences of many superintendents. As Kerr has stated, the position of the leader-initiator is rarely a happy one. But there are goals beyond happiness. "Some abuse" is to be expected. "He wins few clear cut victories; . . . He must find satisfaction in being equally distasteful to each of his constituencies; he must reconcile himself to the harsh reality that successes are shrouded in silence while failures are spotlighted in notoriety." But in return for this the superintendent has the satisfaction of knowing that he or she is "in the control tower helping the real pilots make their landings without crashes even in the fog." The superintendent is in an enviable position to both guide the planning and monitor the flight.

Would it be desirable to state more fully the duties of the superintendent in statutes or in board policy? If so, what duties?

Can a "System" Be Achieved If Individual Schools or Area Subdivisions Have Large Leeway and Encouragement to Exercise Initiative?

As local school systems have developed in the United States, considerable attention has been given to the development of the system as a whole. Citizens' groups have frequently been quite vocal in demanding that similar programs be offered in all schools as a way of attempting to provide what they have regarded as equality of opportunity. Boards of education and administrators also have not been adverse to developing the central office staff so that needed data regarding the schools may be readily available and that planning may be done in any part of the system in which it is needed. The availability of information resulting from the use of modern data collecting and processing equipment has now altered this situation.

Emphasis upon the development of the system can have the unfortunate effect of reducing the significance of the school or of a small number of schools that may serve a part of the district. All schools may tend to look toward the central office for leadership rather than utilize the opportunity which is theirs either individually or in cooperation with other schools of their neighborhood. Similarly, the specialized staff may be housed largely at the central office rather than at the schools where the instruction is carried on. Such developments can lead to the view that the central office is apart from the schools and is the place where decisions are made. Complaints by school personnel regarding the "downtown" office then are not uncommon.

The view offered here is that the best system can only be achieved by fixing large responsibility upon individual schools or groups of schools serving an area and challenging them to develop the program that best meets the educational needs of the children involved. This does not mean that systemwide goals should not be established or that central purchasing is not advantageous. The adoption of the

[13] Raymond E. Callahan, *Education and the Cult of Efficiency* (Chicago: University of Chicago Press, 1962).

[14] Clark Kerr, *The Uses of the University* (Cambridge, Mass.: Harvard University Press, 1963), p. 40.

philosophy and practice which holds that the strong system is the system composed of outstanding schools, each having distinctive achievements, is strongly urged.

The great interest in the decentralization of school systems which has developed in recent years is indeed encouraging. It must be recognized however that it may not be easy to achieve. Teachers' groups may exercise their growing power to block it. Further, it is possible to have illusory decentralization[15]—deconcentration of power from the central office to divisional offices or schools—but with decision making in all important matters remaining at the central office and with little involvement of people (staff and citizens) at the division or school level. Developing and testing decentralization programs remain of great significance.

Generally teachers will support that system in which they have strong commitments to the school of which they are a part. They will have strong commitments to the school if they have been able to develop pride in the manner in which the school meets its educational problems. Thus, the unity that should characterize the strong system is developed by affording opportunity for diversity, which appears to be essential if education is to develop in consideration of the needs of children and youth.

How Should Educational Services Be Coordinated with Related Services Such as Library, Social Welfare, Public Health, Youth Agencies, Private Schools, Housing, and City Planning?

The growing concentration of population in metropolitan areas and the growing complexity of society point to the need for closer coordination of the efforts of the educational services and other public and semipublic services concerned with individual and community development.[16] This appears necessary and inevitable if education and the other services are to be administered effectively. Closer coordination among the services should lead to better understanding of children by the various agencies. It also should result in the strengthening of each agency, because greater understanding would result between and among the lay and professional personnel who are associated with the various agencies including the schools.

Decades of development have tended to separate education from other public and private services in the United States. Public education has been uniquely valued as the road to equality of opportunity and the progress of the society. Thus, it has had its own separate government in our society to a far greater degree than in most societies. Federal educational legislation and other developments, stimulated by the problems of the great cities and the recognition of inadequate achievement of goals, has called for a reexamination of the relation of public education to other agencies involved with the development of children and youth. It calls also for a rethinking of the relation of education and schooling. Research has also made increasingly clear the fact that equality of opportunity can only be achieved with a change in parental attitudes and aspirations and the contribution of all agencies which have an impact on the social and economic level of families and children.

[15] James W. Fesler, "Approaches to the Understanding of Decentralization," *Journal of Politics,* 27 (August, 1965), 536–566.

[16] Theodore L. Reller, ed., *The Public School and Other Community Services,* Annals of the American Academy of Political and Social Science, 302 (November 1955).

Fiscal independence for schools has created some misunderstanding on the part of some people concerned with other community services. Without reopening the question of fiscal dependence or independence at this time, there is little question but that much more coordination of effort could be effected. The school system having a responsibility for the development of youth and legally having a relationship with more of them than any other agency should accept responsibility for initiating and facilitating such coordination.

In a middle-sized city or other large district, some effort at coordination must be made through the central office of the school system and that of other agencies. Here the criteria for such coordination should be developed in coordination with the other agencies concerned. New patterns of coordination need to be developed and tested during the present decade.

The heart of the effort at coordination, however, must be at the secondary school attendance area or neighborhood level. The education of a child or youth is greatly influenced by the home, the community, and the school. It is essential that these parties know one another and know something of the efforts of each other. The necessity of home–school cooperation has been emphasized. There has not been a similar emphasis upon school–community cooperation, even though the school is spoken of frequently as the community school, and improved community living looms as one of the major objectives. The effort at coordination should be related to the neighborhood that may contain three or four elementary schools, a couple of junior high schools, and a senior high school. It may also contain private schools, a public library, youth clubs, state employment offices, and a public health center. The area may be larger or smaller than this, depending upon the area organization of related agencies and upon existing feelings of community or neighborhood. It needs to be large enough to involve some resources in terms of personnel from various agencies, yet small enough to make it possible to know youth and resources well.

The nature of the organization for coordination found in various sections of a large school district will vary widely because of their different needs. Although coordination of existing resources is essential, it should be noted that the identification of needs and the securing of more adequate provisions will be the major challenge to both lay and professional personnel.

What factors make it difficult for the schools to achieve the cooperation of other agencies working toward community improvement and equality of educational opportunity?

SELECTED REFERENCES

American Association of School Administrators, *Professional Administrators for America's Schools,* Thirty-eighth Yearbook. Washington, D.C.: The Association, 1960.

———, *The Administrative Leadership Teams,* Superintendent Career Development Series No. 5. Arlington, Va.: The Association, 1979.

Argyris, Chris, *Management and Organizational Development,* New York: McGraw-Hill Book Company, 1971.

Carlson, Richard O., *School Superintendents: Careers and Performance.* Columbus, Ohio: Charles E. Merrill Publishing Company, 1971.

Culbertson, Jack, Robin H. Farquhar, Alan K. Gaynor, and Mark R. Shibles, *Preparing Educational Leaders for the Seventies.* Columbus, Ohio: University Council for Educational Administration, 1969.

Cunningham, Luvern L., Walter G. Hack, and Raphael O. Nystrand, eds., *Educational Administration: The Developing Decades.* Berkeley, Calif.: McCutchan Publishing Corporation, 1977.

Griffiths, Daniel E., *The School Superintendent.* Englewood Cliffs, N.J.: Prentice-Hall, Inc., 1966.

National School Boards Association, *New Dimensions in School Board Leadership.* Evanston, Ill.: The Association, 1969.

Schmuck, Richard A., and Philip J. Runkel, *Handbook of Organization Development in Schools.* Palo Alto, Calif.: National Press Books, 1972.

Sergiovanni, Thomas J., and Fred D. Carver, *The New School Executive: A Theory of Administration* (2nd ed.). New York: Harper & Row, Publishers, Inc., 1980.

Ziegler, L. Harmon, M. Kent Jennings, and G. Wayne Peak, *Governing American Schools: Political Interaction in Local School Districts.* North Scituate, Mass.: Duxbury Press, 1974.

13

AREA SERVICE AGENCIES and ORGANIZATION and ADMINISTRATION IN METROPOLITAN AREAS

The increasing and more direct role of federal and state governments in education service constitutes a significant challenge to those who value local district administration of education. The inadequacy of many of the local districts in some states invites the state to administer education through categorical programs and through seeing local districts as arms or extensions of the state rather than as partners buttressed by the people of the district. The public opposition to the reduction of the number of local units remains very strong. Although these extensions of state action can be understood and may have genuine merit, there is also concern regarding both the immediate and long-run impact of such developments; that is, even if local "control" is regarded as a myth in substantial part, it has had an important impact on educational development in our society. In few societies have the people believed in the potential of schooling and in their part in determining its nature and scope to as great a degree. Under a state-operated system the maintenance or indeed the further development of this valued closeness of the people to the schools would probably be unlikely.

It is in the context of changing state and local district responsibilities that the question of the role, organization, administration, and financing of an intermediate unit must be examined. In this chapter consideration is given to the general problem of area educational service agencies and then to the special problem of administration in metropolitan areas.

INTERMEDIATE UNITS AND AREA SERVICE AGENCIES

The intermediate unit of school administration developed first in the Midwest when most school districts were small and communication was slow and difficult. The need for some agency to perform certain services both for the small, relatively isolated districts and for the state soon became apparent. Because counties had been established by most states as local units of government (following somewhat the pattern in England), it seemed logical for them to be designated as the intermediate units for schools in many states. However, the township was actually the first intermediate unit established in some of the Midwestern states, notably Michigan and Indiana. The need at that time seemed to be for an agency to oversee small districts, to enforce certain state regulations, to gather information for the state, to direct the distribution of state funds within the area, and to provide certain services for the districts.

The primary concern and responsibility of these intermediate units was for rural schools, although at first they were also legally responsible for some general oversight of town and small-city schools. As cities began to increase in population in many states, they tended to develop separate organizations for government and for schools, to bypass or ignore the intermediate units, and to insist on an independent status. Thus the intermediate unit in most states became predominately an organization for limited control of and service to rural schools and also for service to the state.[1] In some instances, the intermediate organization was resisted as an unwanted arm of the state; in others, it was considered at times as a protector of the local district against unwanted state-level control. But in all instances the intermediate unit, when established, was created by state action and was a political subdivision of the state, organized in part to assist in carrying out the state's educational function.[2]

Intermediate Unit Organization and Role

According to a study by Hooker and Mueller,[3] thirty states had established by 1969 some type of intermediate or regional units for education. Each of the six New England states utilized what were called "supervisory unions"; nineteen other

---

[1] William P. McLure, *The Intermediate Administrative School District in the United States* (Urbana: University of Illinois Press, 1956), p. 3.

[2] Shirley Cooper and Charles O. Fitzwater, *County School Administration* (New York: Harper & Row, Publishers, Inc., 1954), Chaps. 4, 5.

[3] Clifford P. Hooker and Van D. Mueller, *The Relationship of School District Reorganization to State Aid Distribution Systems.* Part 1. *Patterns of School District Organization* (Minneapolis: University of Minnesota, 1970), pp. 59–60.

states had established the county as the intermediate unit for some or all areas; and five had created regional service agencies that were not coterminous with county boundaries. However, five of the states in the latter two groups were in a transitional stage from county to regional units and consequently had some units of both types.

Those who have studied the evolving intermediate unit structure seem to agree that under modern conditions the county is not a logical or defensible type of intermediate unit in most situations. Many counties have a relatively small population, and the boundaries established during an earlier period are frequently not appropriate in the light of recent population developments and trends. Moreover, in many states the county superintendent is still elected by popular vote and may not be the best qualified person to direct the development of an adequate intermediate unit program. Many people are concerned that, for various reasons, the establishment of county intermediate units may tend to perpetuate small and inadequate school districts and thus delay urgently needed reorganization.

In several states the role of the intermediate unit has not been defined clearly, and, perhaps for this and other reasons, the limited financial support available has made it impossible for most of them to provide much more than rather routine services. On the other hand, the regional Boards of Cooperative Educational Services (BOCES), established in New York in 1948, have attracted generally favorable attention throughout the nation because of the kind and quality of services many of them provide. During recent years several other states have begun to develop somewhat similar regional service agencies rather than the more traditional type of intermediate unit.

In the report of a study of intermediate units and regional service agencies, Chambers[4] identified the following control and organizational patterns that are utilized singly or in some combination by states that have established such units:

- they are branch offices of the state department of education,
- they are independent locally controlled service agencies,
- all public local education agencies in the state are included in the system of regional service agencies, or
- participation in regional service agencies is voluntary and some areas and districts are not included.

Emerging Concepts and Policies

Hooker and Mueller, after observing that intermediate units are changing from primarily regulatory to service functions commented that

Coupled with this change is a restructuring of the boundaries of the intermediate units to reflect the socio-economic areas that exist irrespective of county lines. . . . The service function has reshaped the intermediate unit. The states that have not shifted to this idea have seen the intermediate unit

[4]Ernest W. Chambers, *Planning for Regional Education Services in a State* (Denver, Colo.: Improving State Leadership in Education, 1971).

[begin to] drop out of a significant place in the educational structure in their state.[5]

Unfortunately, needed changes will probably come slowly in many states. For example, the county will tend to persist as an intermediate unit in a number of states partly because of tradition but, perhaps equally important, because powerful vested interests may seek to prevent or delay the development or implementation of realistic alternatives. The changing socioeconomic situation, the elimination of small districts through reorganization, and the emergence of new concepts and points of view relating to what is required to ensure adequate educational opportunities, however, are resulting in new perspectives concerning provisions for the organization and operation of educational institutions and programs.

Even when all districts in a state have been reorganized, there will probably be a need for regional educational agencies that can provide a number of special services for component districts that could not be provided economically or effectively by the state education agency. These services would vary somewhat from state to state and among the regions in a state, but they probably would include a media and communications center, a computer and data processing center, and a center to assist with needs assessment, and perhaps some responsibilities for planning and appraisal of progress, for special projects, and for assistance with other programs and services. These agencies should probably be financed primarily by funds from state and perhaps federal sources and governed by a competent board that would be responsible for developing appropriate policies. As Haskew[6] has observed, a basic question is, "How can states use to advantage extra-district entities to achieve enhanced productivity for the schools?"

In recent decades the desirability of area educational service agencies for many states has been demonstrated—the exceptions being state-operated systems which would need regional offices and states which had a relatively small number of local units—most or all of which were large enough with essential resources to meet the growing demand for educational services.

The federal and state categorical programs almost demanded an authority other than the local unit in many states. The local unit did not have the staff to keep up with developments, assessing need, preparing proposals, establishing and monitoring programs, and submitting reports. Many, perhaps most, of the county intermediate units were also of limited competence in these areas. The Education of All Handicapped Children Act (P.L. 94-142) was especially challenging (even overpowering) to many local units and to smaller county offices.

By 1980 the need for educational service agencies in many states was clear, and some important steps had been taken to develop or establish such agencies. Confusion still existed regarding the desirable geographic boundaries, the balance of control of the agency between the state and local units, desirable financial provisions, and the powers which it should have. The agency was favored for its service functions rather than for the contribution it might make through control

[5]Hooker and Mueller, *Patterns of School District Organization,* p. 58.

[6]Lawrence D. Haskew, "Leadership Through State Systems of Service Centers: Some Strategic Considerations," Supplementary Statement in *Planning for Regional Education Services in a State,* p. 25.

(accountability). However, the growing concern regarding attempted detailed regulation by federal and state agencies suggested that the intermediate unit might have an important role in administration. If the local unit does not have the capacity (the financial stringency tends to decrease capacity) and the state or federal agency sharply reduces its effectiveness through overregulation, the intermediate unit might make an important contribution. Thus the agency which is not exclusively controlled by either the local unit or the state may itself exercise a necessary and effective type of administration. If this should occur, the intermediate unit could indeed be the part of the educational administrative structure in which greatest advance is made for a decade or more—advance in terms of service and administration (planning, development, provision, monitoring, and evaluation).

EDUCATIONAL ORGANIZATION AND ADMINISTRATION IN METROPOLITAN AREAS

This subject has not been analyzed carefully in most books dealing with the general organization and administration of elementary and secondary education. Is educational administration in metropolitan areas sufficiently different to justify special attention? It is our view that the metropolitan area and its components indeed have a uniqueness in problems and issues. Further, although the inner cities have lost the leadership role in education which they held for decades, the severity of issues confronting them may stimulate educational responses through which they may become more innovative and thus regain a significant measure of leadership.

The Inner City and the Metropolitan Area

Before analyzing the problems of the metropolitan community it is necessary to make clear some facts about the area with which we will be concerned. Until about three or four decades ago, as the population of a city increased and as housing or industry extended beyond the legal boundaries of the city, these areas were often annexed. Thus the city grew and in many instances included all or most of the population and the commercial and industrial developments which were an integral part of it. However, a few decades ago this situation changed. Greater ease of transportation enabled people and plants to be farther removed from the central city and in fact to be removed from the boundaries of the city. To a degree, then, there were economic and what appeared to be social advantages in continuing to be a part of the city for certain purposes but removed from it for others. Suburban communities then desired to maintain their independence and eventually organized into cities or townships which resisted annexation to the city and which did not work cooperatively with one another or with the central city. Thus the crazy quilts which are metropolitan America today came into existence.

More than two thirds of the population of the nation is located in metropolitan areas if the definition of the U.S. Bureau of the Census of metropolitan areas is accepted. This definition holds that each standard metropolitan statistical area must contain one city of at least 50,000 population or a population concentration of at least 50,000 (including a municipality of 25,000 or more) which constitutes for general economic and social purposes a single community.[7] Generally an SMSA includes the entire county in which the central city is located and adjacent counties if they are *metropolitan in character* and *economically and socially integrated* with the central city or county surrounding it. This definition, it will be noted, sets only approximate limits and causes some people to believe that it results in the inclusion of too much area. Others believe that the resulting population figure is too small to describe true "metropolitanism."

In 1970 the proportion of SMSAs in which the suburbs were the more populous sections of the metropolis reached 47 percent and was increasing. At that time the SMSA suburbs contained 37 percent of the people of the nation and the central cities 32 percent.[8]

The ten largest metropolitan areas in the nation include almost one fourth of the population. The growth of these areas has apparently peaked, with the central cities of most of them declining.

It must be noted that metropolitanism does not imply the same type of growth or development in different states or regions. Some metropolitan areas are spread out far more than are others. Some are characterized by far more rapid growth than are others. The artificial barriers between the central city and suburbs vary considerably as do the percentages of population found respectively in the suburbs and core city. Some are intracounty and others intercounty. Variations exist with respect to percentages of population from various ethnic groups. However, although differences among metropolitan areas should be noted, it is important to recognize that metropolitan areas have numerous characteristics in common, including population size, interdependence, decentralization, governmental fragmentation, and specialization.

In terms of the economic life of the nation, metropolitan areas are even more impressive, having a percentage in terms of almost any measure exceeding that of population. Thus this worldwide phenomenon has a significance which is difficult to appreciate—metropolitan areas tend to dominate regions and nations. In examining these facts Bollens and Schmandt state

> Metropolitan areas not only encompass most people and most jobs in the United States; they also contain the bulk of the country's public and private financial resources and a preponderance of its human talent. They are the primary centers of industry, commerce, labor, and government, as well as of education, art, music, drama, and entertainment. They provide ways of life and ideas that pervade the entire nation. They are magnets of hope, both economic and social, for millions of people. As such, they pay a price in problems and difficulties, some social or economic, others governmental. Some involve deficiencies of public services or gross inequities in financing them; others concern the capacity of people of different racial, ethnic, educational, and social backgrounds to get along with one another. Still others involve the ability of newcomers and the metropolitan community to adjust adequately to each other, and the competence of metropolitan areas to maintain a suitable living environment in the face of continued growth.[9]

[7]John C. Bollens and Henry J. Schmandt, *The Metropolis: Its People, Politics and Economic Life,* 3rd ed. (New York: Harper & Row, Publishers, Inc., 1975), p. 3.
[8]*Ibid.,* p. 18.
[9]*Ibid.,* p. 2.

"A Mosaic of Social Worlds"

The simplicity of the structure of the former town with its "other side of the tracks" is in marked contrast to the metropolitan area. It is described as

... heterogeneous, constantly changing, fragmented;

... arranged spatially in an often confused and seemingly incompatible pattern;

... numerous neighborhoods and suburban groupings of varying social, ethnic and economic characteristics scattered throughout the metropolitan complex;

... the luxury apartment casts its shadow on the tenement houses of workers. The Negro ghetto is ringed by a wall of white neighborhoods. The industrial suburb lies adjacent to the village enclave of the wealthy.[10]

Thus, the metropolitan area is balkanized. Homogeneity characterizes many neighborhoods. Some neighborhoods are affluent, others are populated heavily by refugees of a rapidly changing society. Many live where they do partly because of financial resources, others because of a type of enforced segregation. These neighborhoods have vastly different educational needs and expectations of a school system and differ in their participation. These different neighborhoods may be described by such factors as social rank, urbanization, and segregation.

In terms of social rank, the range is from the neighborhoods composed largely of broken homes, minorities, high unemployment, and unskilled workers to those made up largely of professionals, business executives, and college graduates. Urbanization refers to the family and home situations which prevail. They range from the suburban area marked by single-family units, few working mothers, and young families with small children to the rooming house and apartment areas with many single men and women, single-parent families, and married couples with no children, both of whom are working. The factor of segregation relates to the ethnic composition. The segregation may be an imposed one, as is frequently the case of the Negro, or it may result from other forces such as the tendency for a religious group to settle around a school. The tendency for segregation to increase in metropolitan areas is one of the major challenges to our society. Only recently has serious consideration been given to its fuller implications. Even today, the middle and upper economic classes of various racial groups continue to escape from the core city and to settle in a suburb, perhaps hoping to avoid the problems of the metropolitan area. Thus, in spite of the expressed desire of the society to have less segregation, it may have more. This situation poses major problems for education and its governmental structure and raises the question as to whether people are or will be citizens of a metropolitan area or only of a neighborhood.

Further analysis of the metropolitan area and of its neighborhoods can well be done regarding such matters as mobility of the people, age structure of the population, changing ethnic composition, percentage of youth in the population, fertility of the population, recreational needs and opportunities, occupational patterns, and occupational mobility. Regarding all these matters, attention must

[10] *Ibid.*, p. 66.

also be given to changes which are still occurring, for the metropolitan areas are especially characterized by rapidity of change. Further, any general description of core cities or suburban areas must be regarded as of limited validity—myths regarding them are many and generalizations cloak diversity.

In this mosaic of ethnic and social worlds, major issues and directions of the society are being determined. The desegregation struggle in the metropolitan areas poses many problems. Central issues are the questions concerning (1) how to achieve the social justice to which we are legally and ethically committed for economic and ethnic groups; (2) to what extent and in what manner should (can) the school lead or succeed in this effort; and (3) would a coordinated effort of agencies such as those related to school, welfare, housing, family-life planning and development, and employment have greater promise of achievement than thrusts by one or more of these programs alone? If so, how can such coordination be achieved? And when and by what means does desegregation (racial or socio-economic) lead to integration?

The City Versus the Surrounding Area

Any consideration of education in the metropolitan area must give attention to the core city and to the surrounding area. The central city which had been a leader in education has now lost that position in almost all cases. Its facilities and staff are no longer outstanding. Rather it is torn by strife. Its board of education, no less than its general government, is being challenged to overcome difficulties which appear almost overwhelming. Many of its citizens do not believe the board of education acts in the interest of their children and youth. The financial advantage which it formerly enjoyed has disappeared—in fact in many cases it is now financially disadvantaged, especially considering the nature and quality of educational services it must develop if it is to make a claim to being effective. The short tenure of the superintendent appears to be increasingly found also for principals. In an effort to regain creditability and effectiveness it seeks increased participation by staff and citizens. It also explores the concept of decentralization and makes attempts to move in that direction—hoping thereby to win that understanding and support which must be regained if it is to move forward. Except for a few cities it tries administrative decentralization rather than political decentralization.[11]

In the meantime the suburban areas and the small municipalities surrounding the central city struggle to remain independent of the city. Many of them are too small to develop highly effective programs. They vary widely in wealth, social composition, educational and occupational levels, life-styles, and human resources. It proves to be a myth that the suburb is the fulfillment of the middle-class dream

---

[11] Decentralization is employed here as "the generic term to describe all types of power distribution, with the adjective 'administrative' tacked on to identify instances of internal allocation and 'political' to cover the transfer of authority to officials who are responsible to a subjurisdictional electorate or clientele." This is in accord with James W. Fesler, "Centralization and Decentralization," *International Encyclopedia of the Social Sciences,* Vol. 2 (New York: Macmillan Publishing Co., Inc., 1968), pp. 370–377, as cited by Henry J. Schmandt, "Municipal Decentralization: An Overview," *Public Administration Review,* 32, Special Issue (October 1972), 572.

with low taxes, pure environment free from crime—an uncongested retreat. They discover that they are not cut off from the city to the degree they desire. The problems of youth in our culture pervade them. Still they resist the development of closer relations to the city and the thought that the metropolitan area must attack its problems in a more cooperative, planned manner. New *ad hoc* or intermediate authorities make it possible for them to provide more adequately some services such as vocational-technical and aspects of special education. In many instances however they continue to be rather insulated pockets, providing an educational service which is not well attuned to the realities of the metropolitan area of which they are a part. The intermediate unit assists them in some measure to provide for the staff development and instructional improvement which is essential.

In some instances through a council of superintendents or other staff an effort is made to bridge the gap between the districts. In many others the level of understanding and especially of cooperative effort is regrettably very limited.

Any effort to develop a metropolitan feeling or government is muted by the reluctance of the area surrounding the core city to move in that direction. In some instances this reluctance is also supported by leaders of the "minority" group or groups in the central city. They have gained some power, or at least see it in their grasp in the central city, and regard any move toward metropolitanism in government as a move to deny them that opportunity to govern which they have won so recently. They fear that a metropolitan organization would once more submerge them and destroy leadership opportunities to them. As they gain leadership roles in government in central cities, it is conceivable that a better base for metropolitan action may result.

DISTRICT STRUCTURE IN THE METROPOLITAN AREA

Serious inadequacy characterizes the district structure in metropolitan areas. This is true for local government purposes as well as for education. In 1967 the metropolitan areas in the United States had almost 21,000 local governments (including those for education) of all types. The average number of local governments per metropolitan area was over 90. The Chicago metropolitan area had 1,113; the Philadelphia area 871; and the Pittsburgh area 704.[12]

Many of the local governments in metropolitan areas are small in population and geographically. Approximately two thirds of these municipalities had a population under 5,000, and one half covered a land area of less than a single square mile. Residents of metropolitan areas are generally served by four local governments including a school district, at least one special-purpose district, a county, and a municipality or township. In addition an increasing number are served by special-purpose authorities or districts which involve a major portion of the metropolitan area such as those for water, sewage, transportation, air or smog control, and environmental development.

Many small school districts also continue to exist in metropolitan areas. They may be pockets of wealth, pockets of poverty, segregated social or economic units, or racial enclaves. Generally relatively little attention has been given to the problem

[12] *Reshaping Government in Metropolitan Areas* (New York: Committee for Economic Development, 1970), p. 13.

of school district structure in metropolitan areas. In fact policies of the state—such as state financial arrangements—frequently have encouraged the development and maintenance of quite inadequate units. Commissions on school district organization have devoted their energies largely to rural areas. They have seldom noted how different and more difficult to justify is a district of 1,000 or 5,000 population which is a part of a major metropolitan area from a district of the same size in a mountainous area with extremely sparse population. Few if any states have set up significant guidelines for school district structure in metropolitan areas.

Provisions for district organization and regional educational services in the metropolitan areas in every state need much more careful consideration than they have received thus far. Neither reorganization of existing districts nor additional funding will suffice to resolve some of the complex educational problems in these areas.

On the basis of a study of public education in the San Francisco Metropolitan Bay Area, Reller proposed that the number of school districts be reduced from 164 to 30 or 40, each of which would be prepared to meet certain basic needs more effectively.[13] He concluded that, even after reorganization, these districts would not be in a position to provide effectively for all aspects of the educational program. He, therefore, recommended the creation of a regional or metropolitan district for education that in certain respects would serve as a regional service agency for the districts in the area. This proposed metropolitan district would have its own board and administrative staff and would be responsible for financial matters, for providing educational assistance for the component districts, for special educational services for certain types of students such as the severely handicapped, perhaps for community college programs, and for the development of programs for older youth and adults.

Hooker and Mueller,[14] after studying the hodgepodge of school districts in the Kansas City and St. Louis metropolitan areas, directed attention to serious and indefensible inequities in educational opportunities and in the progress of students, in funds available for support of schools, and in other respects that resulted from existing district boundaries and financing policies. On the basis of these and other related findings, they recommended that (1) each metropolitan area be established as a district or agency for purposes of obtaining and apportioning to the component operating districts on an equitable basis all funds for support of schools, for coordination of planning, and for providing special services needed by the districts; (2) the component districts be reorganized with more realistic and defensible boundaries; and (3) each component district be primarily responsible for developing and implementing programs and policies designed to meet the needs of its students.

A variety of arrangements other than the crazy quilt pattern which is now widespread might be considered both for school and for general local government. Among them are (1) a one-tier system, (2) a one-tier system with extended administrative decentralization, (3) a two-tier system, and (4) a federation of local units.

A *one-tier system* could be achieved by having one large unit or in larger metro-

[13] Theodore L. Reller, *Problems of Public Education in the San Francisco Bay Area* (Berkeley, Calif.: Institute of Government Studies, University of California, 1963).

[14] Clifford P. Hooker and Van D. Mueller, *Equal Treatment to Equals: A New Structure for Schools in the Kansas City and St. Louis Metropolitan Areas* (report to the Missouri School District Reorganization Commission, June 1969).

politan areas several somewhat equally sized smaller ones—all of which are independent units directly responsible to the state. If the one-tier system results in an extremely large district, many people would probably favor provisions within it for extended administrative decentralization. The *two-tier system* would provide a government for education for the entire area but would probably provide limited powers for the central or first tier and place very substantial responsibility for decision making, operation, and management upon the second tier. In the plan to have a *federation of local units* covering the metropolitan area, the local units would be the basic ones and the federated unit would be granted most of its powers by the local units. In this plan it would be desirable to have the local units reasonably equivalent in size and all of such size as would facilitate or ensure substantial competence in providing and administering important services.

All these proposals suggest that the county or traditional intermediate unit may have little or no place in the metropolitan area. In fact the first tier of government in a two-tier system might indeed be a very adequate intermediate unit in a number of metropolitan areas. Such a first-tier unit might well be the regional unit for the metropolitan area if the state were divided into regions as intermediate units.

It must be recognized that a major issue related to any of these plans is the size of the unit—whether first or second tier. In larger metropolitan areas no unit can probably be justified with a minimum of less than 100,000 population—for no unit smaller than this is likely to be able to provide services extending from preschool through secondary or community college and including special education and vocational and technical education, except at an extremely high unit cost. Further, smaller units are unlikely to obtain the administrative leadership essential for staff and program development. On the other hand, there is a basis for the argument that a unit, especially a second-tier or operational one, should not be so large that citizens may have the belief or may experience a unit which eludes responsiveness to them. This same concern need not exist regarding the first-tier unit if it is a government of limited powers and if the operation and management of schools is the responsibility of the second tier.

If our society should move in the direction of having a local education authority,[15] the second-tier units would probably have full responsibility for operation of schools while the first tier might be involved more directly in some of the extra-school educational services which would serve the metropolitan area or a substantial part of it. It would also probably have significant responsibility with reference to planning, to finance (achieving greater equality of opportunity in the metropolitan area), to staff development including administrative staff, to research and development, to technical areas such as computer-assisted instruction, and to physical facilities and capital outlay.

Planning for Reorganization

The question as to how such reorganization of government for educational purposes in metropolitan areas can be achieved may properly be raised. It is unlikely

[15] As was suggested in Chapter 12.

to result from the application of procedures heretofore followed with reference to school district reorganization. It is likely to occur only if the people (including educators) of the metropolitan areas recognize how inadequately they are organized to provide essential educational services and even to make their case heard in state legislatures. No one speaks for the metropolitan area today—and frequently through silence or direct action various parts of it speak against one another. Further, a more rational governmental organization for education in metropolitan areas is likely to occur only if state legislatures recognize that the planning for and establishment of an adequate structure for the development and administration of education is one of their most fundamental responsibilities—and that the continued neglect of this responsibility can only result in having the legislature make more and more decisions regarding the details of the educational service and processes—in matters regarding which they have minimal competence.

The inadequacy of district structure must be recognized as a highly important element in the federal court decisions pertaining to the Wilmington and Detroit areas and desegregation. Whatever the final outcome of these cases, they need to be seen in this context. Further, the *Rodriguez* and *Serrano* cases pertaining to district ability to provide educational opportunity unrelated or less related to local district wealth are substantially the result of legislative inaction in terms of developing a more adequate governmental structure for education. Conceivably our society will move in the direction of state-operated systems of education and replace local government authorities with district offices of the state department of education. If we move this way, however, we should do so knowingly—with an awareness of the possible or probable costs. Given the commitments and traditions of our society, the direction here suggested is believed to be one which might well be highly preferable even though it might not be quite as tidy.

Some Encouraging Developments

In concluding this brief statement on district structure for educational government in the metropolitan area, it should be noted that a considerable number of large cities in the United States have moved in the direction of decentralization. In 1966, the New York state legislature mandated the development of a plan for decentralization in the ponderous New York City school system. On the basis of this plan, thirty-one "community" school or subdistricts were created, each of which has a board and an administrator responsible for employing staff, developing the curriculum, and preparing and administering a budget. Consultants and other resource personnel are provided by the central staff and the state department of education. In some of these districts, decentralization seems to have worked reasonably well; in others, there have been major problems. At least these developments constitute one interesting attempt to provide for decentralization.

Other approaches to decentralization, frequently involving the appointment of administrators for areas within a large district, have been developed in Atlanta, Chicago, Dade County (Florida), Detroit, Los Angeles, Montgomery County (Maryland), St. Louis, and several other large districts, but the best solutions to these problems are obviously still being sought. Many other smaller cities have also adopted some limited form of decentralization with area offices in recent years—some of these plans have been dropped while others continue.

The development of the two-tier system in Toronto should be recognized as one model of metropolitan area organization—though, as should be expected, not without problems. Finally, the effect and achievements of the English Parliament along these lines is worthy of careful study. Through the Local Government Act of 1972 the Parliament provided for a two-tier system of local government in metropolitan areas but fixed the responsibility for the operation of schools on second-tier authorities. The second-tier authorities have a minimum population of 250,000. While some consideration was given to fixing certain responsibilities for education upon the first tier, it was found to be too difficult to draw a clear line between those educational responsibilities which were to be exercised by the first- and second-tier authorities, respectively. A principle which was followed was that the small city (roughly 400,000 or under) and surrounding area should be a one single-tier local unit while the large conurbation should have two-tier government with a metropolitan county (first tier) divided into a number of boroughs (second tier) of at least a 250,000 population each. This major local government act, designed to produce strong local authorities with important taxing (rate) power, resulted in the creation of 101 local authorities in the nation with educational responsibilities. These local authorities are general purpose. However, more than half of their expenditures are for education, and the education committee is widely regarded as the most important. Further, the local authorities receive a large general grant (not specifically for education or other designated services) from the Parliament which is based upon a number of factors involving need and ability. Thus an attempt is being made to preserve and strengthen local government responsibility in one nation marked by metropolitanism.

STATE AND FEDERAL GOVERNMENTS AND THE METROPOLITAN AREA

One of the most serious group of problems pertaining to the large city (and the metropolitan area) is that of the images held regarding it and related views and practices.

Looking first at the large-city school district, it must be observed that historically it enjoyed a large independence from the state. It was in the forefront in educational matters and did not depend upon state standards or guidelines or even heavily upon state financial aids. As a result state departments of education rendered few services to it and in fact were not staffed or otherwise prepared to serve it in a substantial manner. Such state departments were involved heavily with the many small and poor districts which were below state minimum standards. The big city expected little from the state department of education, and the state department of education did not interfere with that expectation. Only during the last decade have state departments seriously considered their obligations to the big cities. A number have now made staff and other provisions to enable them to be of more assistance. However, in spite of the nature and extent of the problems confronting the big city in the last decade, the state department of education is not generally today seen as a source of substantial assistance.

Because of the traditional state–big-city relationship and because of the plight of the big cities and the power and financial resources of the federal government, there has been a strong tendency in recent decades for the big cities and the federal government to develop a special direct relationship. At times this relationship has avoided involving the state. An extremely strong statement regarding the desirability of such an arrangement is that of Shedd, who suggested *"that the federal government nationalize the big city school systems of this country:* that their operation and their funding be taken over by the government."[16]

He stated further that he sees "a national system in the big cities, totally federally funded, as the only solution" by which the nation's urban schools can be rescued from disaster. This drastic solution would separate the big city from the metropolitan area of which it is an integral part and would challenge the tradition of state responsibility for education. The fact that it has been offered, however, must be seen as an indication of the seriousness of the problem of education in the big cities and of the "failure" to meet it through local and state action.

Another important aspect of the problem of the metropolitan area is that it generally has not been seen by the people themselves as a unit with common problems and that it has not been so regarded by state and federal bodies and authorities. As was indicated, state legislatures have not generally grappled seriously with the problem of district structure in metropolitan areas. Rather, through legislation they have encouraged and facilitated the continuation of many small school districts surrounding the city. In the legislature no one speaks for the metropolitan area. Most citizens and educators see themselves as citizens of school district or village X rather than as citizens of a metropolitan area. Perhaps as the metropolitan area grows larger and more difficult to cope with, they cling more desperately to the village—except in such matters as water, sewage, air, and transportation where they cannot hold to the boundaries of an earlier day. They hope to escape the problems of the big city even though economically they are an integral part of it and even though problems related to education cannot be confined to the big-city boundaries.

When the extent to which the tone and quality of education in the nation is set in the metropolitan areas is recognized, the extremely serious implications of the inadequate governmental structure for education in these areas can be better understood.

DECENTRALIZATION IN THE METROPOLITAN AREA

No concept has received more widespread approval in the past decade than decentralization. This was partially in response to the demand for more participation by the citizenry. Other related factors were the fear of the power of the educational bureaucracy and the growth of governmental centralization or federal power in many aspects of life. The traditional American belief in local government or local autonomy was also a factor which aroused support because of the fear that it has slipped or is slipping away. Another matter of importance has been the realization

---

[16]Mark R. Shedd, *National Policy and Urban Schools* (New Haven, Conn.: Yale University, Institute for Social and Policy Studies, 1972), p. 13.

or belief that the big-city systems have been notably unresponsive to the needs of the children or the people of large sections of the city—namely the minority or culturally different.

Although Cillié[17] pointed out a considerable number of years ago that our big-city systems had indeed become highly centralized, this viewpoint has not been widely accepted. Rather, we have held fast to the belief that our system of administration of education is highly decentralized, as Kandel[18] indicated so effectively in comparing it with other systems. Both were correct. Whereas the general situation in the nation was properly characterized as one with much responsibility at the local level—because state centralization had never existed and many of the local units were very small—nevertheless, the large cities had become highly centralized in their organization and operation. When the percentage of children of the nation found in the large cities is considered, a surprising number of our children were in rather centralized units while the mythology or reality of a highly decentralized system persisted.

Any serious consideration of decentralization in the large city requires careful definition if it is to be meaningful. For it can be applied to a variety of situations or can describe widely varying practices. Further, it is possible to widen participation in various ways while increasing centralization through further strengthening central decision-making power. The illusion of decentralization can thus be achieved. The meaning of decentralization is rather different when applied to the metropolitan area, which has lacked centralization to a striking degree, from its meaning when applied to the core city, which has probably been highly centralized. If an adequate structure is achieved for the metropolitan area to enable it to function as a unit at least for major limited purposes, such development should very probably be accompanied by a carefully developed plan of political decentralization. Unless this concurrent decentralization occurs, the development or acceptance of any metropolitan authority is highly unlikely.

Decentralization is being used here to describe the movement of decision-making power to a unit nearer the place of action and the fixing of responsibility for decision making upon the people of the unit. Accordingly the establishment of divisional or field offices to represent or act for the central administration is not considered decentralization. On the other hand, if such offices become responsive to the staff and citizenry of the unit or district and if the staff and citizens of the unit share substantially in the decision making, it may properly be regarded as a decentralized system. Decentralization thus involves the attainment of a measure of centralization or ability to act in the interest of the whole area followed by the delegation of certain specified powers and responsibilities to a subunit.

La Noue and Smith have reviewed the forces related to the trend toward decentralization in the late 1960s and early 1970s. They note that the community control rhetoric which was an important force in the early years of the movement lost much of its appeal as political realities were faced and as a measure of re-

[17]F. S. Cillié, *Centralization or Decentralization* (New York: Teachers College, Columbia University, 1940).

[18]I. L. Kandel, *Types of Administration,* (Wellington: New Zealand Council for Educational Research, 1938).

sponsiveness occurred in many systems. They believe that the "decentralization movement has been neither revolutionary nor inconsequential"[19] though disappointing to those who expected profound changes and to those who viewed it as purely transitory.

There are many constraints on the achievement of a high degree of decentralization in big-city school systems. Many of these are not fully recognized by some of those who speak easily and positively of decentralization. Among them are

- *Legal barriers.* Statutes fix responsibility upon the board of education of the city and generally do not provide for subunits with significant powers.
- *Tradition.* The organization of the system has been toward a growing centralization. Economics, communication, the pursuit of efficiency, and technological advances are all seen as forces favoring the continuance of the traditional organization. In fact some of these, such as the development of more adequate information (data) systems, may make decentralization more viable.
- *Difficulty of developing a new structure.* The determination of adequate subunits and the delineation of the powers which should remain with the central body and the subunits respectively is exceedingly difficult. Subunits with a "community identity" may indeed be unacceptable because of their economic or ethnic imbalance.
- *Opposition of teacher groups.* While this is not inevitable, it is highly probable, for many teachers and teacher organizations will find less security and considerably more effort needed to maintain certain positions if they can be negotiated with subunit levels. Further, at the subunit level they may come into sharper disagreement with groups seeking "community power."
- *Difficulty of developing a responsible subunit.* While the idea of subunits is enthusiastically endorsed, few have given attention to the problems of developing leadership in a new unit or to achieving citizen participation and representativeness. Most institutions have a history which undergirds their functioning. The building of a new institution quickly is a major challenge and one for which too little provision is generally made. Thus early enthusiasm can quickly turn to disillusionment.
- *The delegation of decision making to the individual school.* This may appear to make unnecessary the establishment of an administrative unit between the central office and the school. If the individual school has large powers, the subunit must be an authority with important firmly delegated or established responsibilities or it will be seen only as an undesirable buffer for the central administration and a further bureaucratic invention to delay action.

These constraints are not offered to discourage attacks on the problem of centralization. Rather they are offered in the hope that they may be considered in the development of a strategy to achieve an effective metropolitan structure with political decentralization.

---

[19] George R. La Noue and Bruce L. R. Smith. *The Politics of School Decentralization* (Lexington, Mass.: D. C. Heath & Co., 1973), p. 239.

PLANNING AND DEVELOPMENT IN THE METROPOLITAN AREA

In recent decades there has been a sharply increased awareness of the possibilities of planning and a recognition that planning in fact is one of the major responsibilities of the educational administrator. It is suggested here that the metropolitan area offers special opportunities in this regard. The crisis which exists regarding education and other public services provides an increased willingness on the part of many who would otherwise be complacent to approve and to participate. The rapidity of change also suggests the greater field for planning educational development. Further, it is in the metropolitan area that the greatest resources for planning are found.

In examining the problem of recognition of the potential but also the limitations of planning, Reller has observed that

> We have slowly come to recognize the necessity for planning, and to understand and appreciate its possible contributions as well as its limitations. The vast, complex, interrelated changes in urban life, which continue with or without planning, urgently demand more careful study than has been common. Unless there is systematic planning for improvements, the very stability of our society is seriously threatened. In the light of the growing evidence, there has also developed a more humble expectation from planning.

Walsh has noted that

> plans that purport to be holistic grand designs, vast and comprehensive models of future society, are interesting, but usually utopian. Moreover, man is as capable of planning himself into misery and ugliness as he is of stumbling into them.[20]

Reller also noted

> However, man cannot afford to fail to use his intelligence in formulating comprehensive policies, harmonizing goals, seeking greater agreement among the many actors in the metropolitan scene, and in establishing an agenda to focus and organize debate, examining activities not only in terms of an annual budget and incremental changes but also in terms of long-range needs and resources, broadening the available base of information as the basis for decision making, identifying alternative plans and their probable results, and introducing innovation into the metropolitan government scene which may be heavily laden with inertia.[21]

Planning and development in the metropolitan area provide a number of especially inviting opportunities. They include the opportunity

[20] Annamarie Hauck Walsh, *The Urban Challenge to Government* (New York: Praeger Publishers, Inc., 1969), p. 181.

[21] Theodore L. Reller, "Developing a Revitalized Educational System," in Edgar L. Morphet, David L. Jesser, and Arthur P. Ludka, eds. *Revitalizing Education in the Big Cities* (Denver, Colo.: Improving State Leadership in Education, 1972), p. 102.

- To involve state and noneducational local planning staff in educational planning. One of the barriers to more effective work in the metropolitan area is the lack of common goals and understanding, cooperation, and mutual acceptance among professional staff engaged in various services. Planning is an area where the professionals, each with his own limited vision, may come together with less threat than in direct administration. Further, staff in a number of agencies, planning and otherwise, may be more experienced in planning than most of those directly involved in education.

- To involve those engaged in services which have a large impact on education but which may not be directly involved with schools. These include such services as land use, housing, youth programs, social welfare, health, library, and environmental development. Thus education and schooling may be advanced in a more educative society.

- To enable educators to contribute more significantly to the "quality of life" in the metropolitan area and to facilitate the improvement of the contribution of the school to this end. To examine again the question of whether environment can be controlled or whether it is the controller. While relevancy of the instructional program can be unintelligently or inappropriately pursued and with too little recognition of its limitations, it warrants serious consideration.

- To facilitate the development of an effort or a structure involving a number of governmental agencies at the state, local, and federal level to carry forward the educational program, and thus to overcome such simplistic views as "education is the province of the board of education and the administration of education in the metropolitan area is a local responsibility." Planning should ensure a more complex and potentially more promising and realistic view and structure.

- To manage educational (including schooling) costs.

As Coombs and Hallak have said

> To get at this whole problem of education change and innovation, new types of planning are needed that penetrate beneath the outer "macro" dimensions of educational systems to their internal affairs (which economists, perhaps understandably, have hesitated to grapple with). Unlike most educational planning to date, this new generation of planning, yet to be elaborated, must extend beyond the goal of linear expansion of the educational *status quo* and become a positive force for redesigning entrenched and now inappropriate educational processes. Its emphasis must be on systems design—on educational processes designed to fit relevant objectives for each place and time and learning clientele in an efficient and effective manner. To achieve that sort of "design approach" to educational planning, economic research and analysis must join hands with pedagogical and sociological research and analysis. Only then will the vital concepts of cost effectiveness and cost benefit acquire their full meaning and receive more realistic application.[22]

To achieve very much in this direction, resources (financial and human) greater than those of school districts (even those of metropolitan areas) must probably

---

[22] Philip H. Coombs and Jacques Hallak, *Managing Educational Costs* (New York: Oxford University Press, 1972), p. 270.

be involved. This could be a challenge to metropolitan area authorities with specialist staffs. They could test theories of educational change and development and regain for the metropolitan area the leadership role once held by the cities. The problems of educational processes in the metropolitan area—involving as they do issues such as unemployment and alienation of youth, low achievement and dropout, opportunities to develop positive attitudes toward the society, language and dialect problems, perceptions of the school as an institution, drug culture and violence, and staff development—constitute some of the most difficult educational issues confronting the society. Congressional concern regarding these problems has been a major stimulus to federal activity in educational research and development in recent decades. Regrettably during this period most metropolitan areas have not been organized and staffed adequately to enable them to grapple with these problems directly. Conceivably a direct attack on problems such as these by the metropolitan areas with the cooperation of universities, educational laboratories, and other resources is one of the more promising approaches. Clearly more adequate authorities must exist in metropolitan areas with responsibility for research and development if a vigorous effort is to be made to understand such issues and to plan and test proposed steps to meet them. Such metropolitan area authorities, if properly constituted, would have important advantages over existing institutions and agencies in attacking many of the major educational issues of our society.

SOME IMPORTANT PROBLEMS AND ISSUES

Should the Metropolitan Area Be Reorganized for Educational Purposes with a Two-Tier District Structure?

No definite answer has emerged to this question. However, there is much evidence available that for various matters the metropolitan area needs to be organized to enable it to meet educational needs more effectively. Provisions for technical, vocational, and special education are important cases where this is true. Adult education and community college education are also significantly dependent upon this development. If essential planning, research, and development is to be carried forward, a relatively large authority will be needed to provide the necessary staff competencies. Programs of staff development—of the middle-management group, for example—also call for resources well beyond those of the great majority of school districts in the metropolitan areas. The effective development and utilization of computer-assisted instruction also requires competencies not found in the small school district.

On the other hand, there is no doubt that many of the people desire to have an increased opportunity to participate in decision making and even in the processes of education. The apparent importance of the attitudes and aspirations of parents with reference to the educational development of children supports this desire. The impact of community alienation upon the schools also points to the need for genuine communication between the schools and the public. It would therefore appear highly desirable that there be recognition of the desirability of keeping the schools "close to the people."

These facts and judgments suggest that a structure must be developed which will facilitate planning and utilization of resources available only to a large unit while providing for more participation. This can be done through a two-tier system, a decentralized large unit, or a federation of competent local units. Basic to it, however, is the development of much more knowledge regarding decentralization, a minimum population size for local operation units, the achievement of a metropolitan citizenship.

Can a school district (second tier) of less than 100,000 population be justified in a metropolitan area of 1 million? Why or why not?

How Can a Reorganization of School District Structure Be Achieved in Metropolitan Areas?

Certainly the adequate reorganization of school districts in metropolitan areas is extremely difficult and is not likely to occur unless change takes place in a number of directions. Among needed conditions for such a development are

- A recognition that state and federal educational finance plans have been a major contributor to present structure or to the maintenance of present structure. This needs to be coupled with an awareness that new major state finance proposals need to be examined in terms of their impact on district structure and need to be formulated in such manner that they will facilitate a more adequate structure rather than the maintenance of the status quo. Regrettably many such plans, perhaps unintentionally, freeze inadequate structures.
- The development of more adequate governmental structure for general local government purposes. More adequate provisions for educational government may indeed precede those for general government. However, significant movement in regard to general government would facilitate similar developments involving education. What is reasonably adequate governmental structure in the metropolitan area has meaning both for general purposes and for education. Further, if that coordination of general government and education which is imperative is achieved, it will be substantially facilitated by somewhat parallel developments in structure. What school district will coordinate its planning or recreation or health programs through a dozen cities?
- Metropolitan educational authorities need to be developed concurrently with regional educational units throughout the state. Otherwise they are unlikely to receive general support. The regional units should either replace or become the intermediate units. The need for regional units in the parts of the state other than those that are metropolitan may not appear quite as pressing. However, they can play a highly significant role in the development of the education service and in making less likely a drift toward state operation of schools. Such regional units need to be highly responsive to adequately sized and competent local units.
- Educators of the metropolitan areas need to develop common understandings regarding the problems of education in the metropolitan area and greatly in-

creased ability to cooperate and coordinate the efforts of their respective districts. Too frequently educators of suburbs and city have little understanding of their respective problems and see no or few common metropolitan education problems. Such understanding should be expected to precede the development of cooperation among the citizens of the respective districts. The development of a high level of cooperation among the educators (administrators and teachers) is essential not only to achieve essential reorganization. It is also an important element in the operation of a reorganized metropolitan area. This has been clearly illustrated by the work of the superintendents of the respective cities which constitute metropolitan Toronto. A similar informal organization of directors of education in Greater London has been a major force in the operation of schools in that metropolitan area.

- The respective powers of the central metropolitan board of education and those of the operational units need to be defined by a commission responsible to the legislature. In general, in accord with the traditions of our society the central board should have only a few limited powers—though very important ones—and the base units (second tier) should have large and relatively untrammeled responsibility for operating the educational system. Accordingly the staff of the central unit should remain small. The second-tier authorities must be large enough to be competent to provide a wide range of educational services at a defensible cost. They and schools within them should be encouraged to develop diversity in their programs and practice.

- Public understanding and opinion must be developed in support of the more adequate, responsive, and responsible structure.

Can voting by the people of the many school districts of the metropolitan area be regarded as a viable method of achieving the essential structure for educational government? Why or why not?

In the Metropolitan Area Have the Advantages of One Type of Governmental Structure for Education over Other Types Been Demonstrated?

Although in this chapter a preference has been indicated for a two-tier system, it must be acknowledged that the case for it over other plans is not clearly established. Efforts to overcome the "failure" of schools in core cities may be made and substantial improvement may be effected through different organizations. They range from the plan whereby the metropolitan office is a field division of the state through a modified field division, a coterminous field division and local government, to a substantially independent local government.

Probably there could be agreement on such matters as the following:

- Significant parental involvement must be achieved. Parents educate and want quality schooling.
- Present structure in most metropolitan areas is inadequate and legislatures have been extremely slow in responding to the challenge.
- Schools alone cannot bear the burden of providing educational service. Many other agencies must be involved.

- Financing of schools and other educational services in most metropolitan areas, especially in core cities, has been quite inadequate.
- The resources of the metropolitan area must be utilized in the interest of the children of the area to a much greater extent than is usual.
- Accountability, more adequate management, efficiency, and effectiveness must be strengthened.
- Development and evaluation are essential areas which must receive greatly increased attention.
- Decentralization should be sought within the big city and within a metropolitan framework. In the finance area, *"the guiding principle is to allow a maximum of control over, and responsibility for, expenditures at the local or building level* while using the central or regional level for revenue raising and perhaps certain special services."[23] Somewhat similar guiding principles can be developed for areas such as curriculum and instruction.
- Considerable tension may be expected as issues are worked through regarding the roles of the central unit and its bureaucracy, the new local units, the teaching staff, and the communities which seek to participate in a substantial manner. This tension may well be the basis upon which a new and vital structure and operating system may be developed.

Is the metropolitan area governable? Can it govern itself in educational matters? If so, how?

Can That Racial and Socioeconomic Balance Essential for Successful Schools be Achieved and Maintained in Big-city Schools and Neighborhoods?

Can that racial and socioeconomic balance essential for successful schools be achieved and maintained in big-city schools and neighborhoods?

Plans for school desegregation in smaller cities and in cities with few low-status or minority students appear to be working quite satisfactorily, but desegregation plans in large cities have not been successful.

We believe that racial and socioeconomic balance can be achieved and maintained in many big city schools and neighborhoods. We also think that many families are willing to live in neighborhoods that are integrated socioeconomically and racially and to send their children to schools in these neighborhoods, if they have confidence that a good balance will be maintained in local institutions.

Socioeconomic balance appears, nevertheless, to be a prerequisite for the successful operation of many big city social institutions, including the public schools. Major national studies indicate that socioeconomic integration is more important than racial integration in affecting achievement levels, and

[23] John W. Polley, "Improving Provisions for Organization, Housing, Financial Support and Accountability," in *Revitalizing Education in the Big Cities,* p. 75.

yet desegregation plans have historically given little attention to maintaining, much less achieving, a favorable socioeconomic mixture.[24]

It would appear that the schools are not likely to be successful in inner cities unless the trend toward deterioration of neighborhoods is reversed. Concentrated poverty, youth unemployment, and social and economic disorganization create a climate in which successful schools are almost inevitably improbable. A planned attack, involving various governmental and private efforts, would appear to be essential if the problems of education are to be met in metropolitan areas. Schools can and must aid in the rebuilding of neighborhoods, and neighborhoods can and must aid in revitalizing schools.

What Form of Decentralization of the Large-City System Will Most Likely Facilitate Balancing of Roles of the Professionals with Parent and Community Participation?

Experience in recent years suggests that political decentralization is more promising than is administrative decentralization if some shift in power is sought. Some shift in power may be essential if the underlying alienation is to be countered and if participation is to have much significance. It must also be recognized that the turn to administrative decentralization may be in part an attempt to avoid the demand for political decentralization. Certainly political decentralization is generally more threatening to a bureaucracy than is administrative decentralization. Political decentralization calls for greater change, for greater mutual understanding and trust, and for a higher level of creativity. These facts also may support moves toward administrative decentralization rather than political.

If decentralization is sought which goes beyond "administrative restructuring,"[25] in what manner, to what extent, and with what community (parental) participation can this be achieved?

SELECTED REFERENCES

Altshuler, Alan A., *Community Control: The Black Demand for Participation in Large American Cities.* New York: Bobbs-Merrill Co., Inc., 1970.

Bollens, John C., and Henry J. Schmandt, *The Metropolis: Its People, Politics and Economic Life.* 3rd ed. New York: Harper & Row, Publishers, Inc., 1975.

Committee for Economic Development, *Reshaping Government in Metropolitan Areas.* New York: The Committee, 1970.

Curriculum Essays on Citizens, Politics and Administration in Urban Neighborhoods, Public Administration Review, 32, Special Issue (October 1972).

[24] Daniel V. Levine and Robert J. Havighurst, *The Future of Big City Schools: Desegregation Policies and Magnet Alternatives* (Berkeley, Calif.: McCutchan Publishing Corporation, 1977), pp. 269, 273.

[25] Marilyn Gittell, "Decentralization and Citizen Participation in Education," in *Curriculum Essays on Citizens, Politics and Administration in Urban Neighborhoods, Public Administrative Review,* 32, Special Issue (October 1972), 682.

LaNoue, George R., and Bruce L. R. Smith, *The Politics of School Decentralization.* Lexington, Mass.: D. C. Heath & Co., 1973.

Levine, Daniel V., and Robert J. Havighurst, eds., *The Future of Big City Schools: Desegregation Policies and Magnet Alternatives.* Berkeley, Calif.: McCutchan Publishing Corporation, 1977.

Meranto, Philip, *School Politics in the Metropolis.* Columbus, Ohio: Charles E. Merrill Publishing Company, 1970.

Morphet, Edgar L., David L. Jesser, and Arthur P. Ludka, eds., *Revitalizing Education in the Big Cities.* Denver, Colo.: Improving State Leadership in Education, 1972.

Ornstein, Allan C., Daniel U. Levine, and Doxey A. Wilkerson, *Reforming Metropolitan Schools.* Pacific Palisades, Calif.: Goodyear Publishing Co., Inc., 1975.

Reller, Theodore L., *Educational Administration in Metropolitan Areas.* Bloomington, Ind.: Phi Delta Kappa Foundation, 1974.

14

THE ADMINISTRATION
of the COMMUNITY
EDUCATION CENTER*

Whereas public school education seems destined to operate in a continual state of turmoil, the problems and issues inherent in that turmoil are protean and mobile. In the early 1970s, school principals were generally desperately trying to find additional facilities, more teachers, and an adequate supply of textbooks and materials for an apparently ever-expanding population of children. But, by the late 1970s, sharply declining enrollments in the public schools forced school boards and administrators to undertake the difficult task of reducing staff and closing schools. Yet, there appears to be the strong probability in the early 1980s, not that school enrollments will grow dramatically, but that there will be a shortage of qualified teachers, particularly in the large cities.

Similar dramatic reversals in direction can be seen in other areas of public education: for example, the turning away of public support, both political and financial, from educational innovation in school organization, curriculum design, and instruc-

*Prepared in large part by John P. Matlin, assistant dean, School of Education, University of California, Berkeley.

288

tional techniques. However, amidst these apparent inconsistencies, there seem to be continuing trends toward the development of the individual school as a community education center. Both federal and state laws have mandated that public education be provided to a broader segment of the population. The percentage of elementary schools in the nation providing a kindergarten increased from 49.5 percent in 1968 to 88.8 percent in 1978; enrollment in prekindergarten programs has increased steadily since 1964; and there is strong pressure to expand public education to much younger children, in the age group of from two to four years.[1] The provisions of P.L. 94-142 require local school districts not only to provide public education to handicapped children and adults to the age of twenty-one but also to seek out actively such students. Services for children have been increased steadily in such areas as day care, health, and food. And the evolving nature of the American family and the changed relationships of parents or of parent to children seem to portend ever greater reliance upon public agencies, particularly the public school, for support.[2]

The already strong participation of parents and other members of the community in various areas of public school education continues to grow. These include the assessing of the educational needs of their children; the questioning of the curricula and the instructional strategies used to meet those needs; the demand for educational options or alternatives to what some parents see as the traditional type of schools while other parents now press for a "back-to-the-basics" choice; and the active involvement in the school's activities as volunteers, paid aides, advisory council members, teachers, learners, supporters, critics, and change agents.

The future of the public school remains clouded by social forces which are potentially contradictory. As the school moves toward becoming the intellectual center of the community, it also faces profound crises that endanger its very survival. The increasing reluctance of the general public to finance to the same degree as in the past all local governmental agencies, including the public schools, and the tentative approaches to some sort of a voucher system for financing education are only a few of the more obvious manifestations of those crises. Whatever the future, there is no doubt that the community school center, as the operating unit of the school system and the critical component which produces the educational services, is in sharp public focus.

Other chapters in this book give major emphasis primarily to the suprasystems of the school center. However, the basic function of the superstructure of board of education, superintendent, and central staff is to provide the facilities, staff, and services that should facilitate the production of educational services at the school center. Both federal- and state-funding projects are increasingly focusing their efforts upon the individual school. But a study of the administration of the school center finds little agreement within or between policy or theory as judged by pre-

[1] William L. Pharis and Sally Banks Zakariya, *The Elementary School Principalship in 1978: A Research Study* (Washington, D.C.: National Association of Elementary School Principals, 1979), p. 51; Mary A. Golladay, *The Condition of Education, 1976 Edition*, Statistical Report, National Center for Education Statistics (Washington, D.C.: U.S. Government Printing Office, 1976), p. 15; National School Public Relations Association, *Education USA*, 22, no. 8 (October 22, 1979), 57.

[2] Alan Pifer, *Perceptions of Childhood and Youth*, Reprint of 1978 Annual Report (New York: Carnegie Corporation), pp. 8-11.

vailing practices and in the growing body of literature critical of the public schools. Some students of administrative theory conclude that the emphasis on theory and research in educational administration during the last two decades has little to show for its efforts,[3] whereas those who have made comprehensive surveys of the public schools conclude that there is currently even less agreement among educators on all the critical issues facing public education than in the past.[4] There are many reasons for these divergencies, including those stemming from the historical development of the public schools and those coming from the current social context.

Our schools were developed initially on an extremely decentralized basis, as was pointed out in previous chapters. Even in city systems, during the first half of the nineteenth century, the school center was usually a ward school governed by ward trustees. It was not until shortly before the middle of the nineteenth century that the practice of giving citywide boards responsibility for the schools of a city was initiated. At about this same time, these boards began the practice of employing a professional superintendent to administer the schools. By the middle of the twentieth century, the large majority of public school pupils attended schools in multiple-school districts.

The position of the school principal also changed as the schools moved from a basis of decentralization to one of centralization. One-teacher schools required no principal. As small multiple-teacher schools were formed, one teacher was named head teacher. As these multiple-teacher schools grew larger, the practice of employing nonteaching principals emerged. When school districts were small, the duties of principal and superintendent were discharged by the same person. As multiple-school districts were formed, it became necessary to employ principals for multiple-teacher schools and superintendents for multiple-school districts. Thus two major types of school executives have evolved in the American school system, the executive of the individual school and the executive of the administrative district. Of course, all schools in the United States are not organized according to this pattern, and various stages in the evolution of the organization of American education can probably still be found in existence somewhere in the nation.

The trends toward the centralization of the administration, supervision, and financing of public schools continue to the present time to some degree. But, in the late 1960s, the belief that the advantages of centralization of local school systems had been demonstrated and that we could expect this plan to continue with the same force was challenged. There is growing evidence that local school community members have seen centralization as a loss to themselves of control of their community school center, as an assumption by the professional educators of all aspects of educational decision making and instructional implementation, and as an alienation of the school and its staff from the community. There are reviews of recent literature which see the goal of federal funding of public school education in

[3] Andrew W. Halpin and Andrew E. Hayes, "The Broken Ikon, Or, What Ever Happened to Theory?", in *Educational Administration: The Developing Decades,* eds. Luvern L. Cunningham, Walter G. Hack, and Raphael O. Nystrand (Berkeley, Calif.: McCutchan Publishing Corporation, 1977), pp. 261-297.

[4] Pharis and Zakariya, *Elementary School Principalship,* p. xi.

the late 1960s to be an attempt to make schools more responsive as well as to integrate the bottom segments of the population.[5]

There has grown a thrust toward decentralization, community control, and community participation. Decentralization includes the delegation by central authority to subunits of the local school system of functional responsibility and some decision making. Community control implies the assumption by elected community representatives of decision making and responsibility concerning the educational program and the expenditure of money for a school or group of schools. Community participation implies formal and systematic methods to involve members of the school community in advising and assisting in the decision-making process on the local school level. There is evidence that many large school districts are moving in one or all of these areas[6] although there is increasing doubt that community participation is having any real influence in the operation of the public schools.

The primary purposes of this chapter are to explore and describe the decision-making role of the community school center; the relationships of the school principal to the central administration, to the school staff, to the students, and to the community; and the problems and issues which apparently are vitally affecting these relationships. This exploration and description will be conducted partially in the context of some major concepts which have been developed in the study of organization and administration, partially in the context of the organizational structure of the individual school, and partially in the context of current phenomena relating to the public schools.

THE DECISION-MAKING ROLE OF
THE COMMUNITY SCHOOL CENTER

The decision-making role of the school center is determined largely by the board of education and the superintendent, although increasingly the school staff and the community are also affecting that role. In some school systems, the area of decision-making assigned to individual schools is narrow. The rules and regulations of the board with respect to individual school administration are written in great detail. The courses of study for each grade level and the curriculum generally also are prescribed in great detail. The principal in such systems usually has little to do with the appointment of either instructional or noninstructional personnel and must seek the approval of the superintendent on all but the most trivial matters. The principal and faculty often have little opportunity for leadership.

However, there has been a pronounced shift during the 1970s in the perceptions of both elementary and secondary principals regarding their role in decision making. This is surprising because it occurs in a context of a growing loss of public support, less financial support, growing teacher militancy, and increased com-

---

[5] Lois S. Steinberg, "The Changing Role of Parent Groups in Educational Decision Making," in *Partners: Parents and Schools,* ed. by Ronald S. Brandt (Alexandria, Va.: Association for Supervision and Curriculum Development, 1979), p. 48.

[6] "Decentralization and Community Involvement in Local School Systems," National Education Association, *Research Bulletin,* 48, no. 1 (March 1970), 3-7.

munity demands for participation in school decisions. In 1971, a comprehensive study concluded that elementary principals believed that they were increasingly being isolated from involvement in group decision making that affected leadership and the operation of their schools. They believed that they had little or no opportunity to participate in districtwide decision-making processes and did not have the independence in the operation of their schools which the secondary school principals had.[7] A 1978 study of the nation's elementary school principals concluded that the typical principal felt that he or she had been given enough authority to deal with the responsibility placed on him or her and that he or she had some influence on decisions made in the district about elementary education. In this survey of all the nation's elementary school principals, the randomly selected group of 1,688 principals who responded reported, by a margin of 80 percent to 20 percent, that they believed their authority was commensurate with their responsibility.[8]

A similar study of the nation's secondary school principals yielded a usable response from 1,131 principals from a random sample of 1,600. Contrary to a similar survey done in 1965, this 1977 survey indicated that the secondary school principals felt that they had a reasonable amount of authority and participation in matters of staffing, budget, and the allocation of funds.[9] A comprehensive study also was made in 1977 of sixty senior high school principals chosen from each state on the basis of being effective leaders. Although this select group felt that it had a reasonable amount of autonomy and resources, most of the principals in it gave a low priority in terms of their activities to the areas of curriculum development, teacher in-service education, program evaluation, and community involvement.[10]

In contrast to school systems that exercise rigid control over the educational activities of individual schools, other school systems do give school centers a considerable degree of freedom in decision making. Following are some of the characteristics of the school systems that fix important responsibilities on school centers:

- Board actions with respect to the education program are expressed in terms of broad policies and objectives rather than in terms of detailed specific regulations.
- The principal and staff are expected to take the primary responsibility for the development of the educational program at the school center.
- The principal, in accordance with policies approved by the board, recommends to the superintendent for appointment all personnel, both instructional and noninstructional, employed at the school that he or she administers. This does not mean that the principal should have complete autonomy in the matter of appointments. All persons recommended for appointment by the principal should meet the qualifications set forth in board policies. Further, especially in large systems, the principal cannot possibly do all the necessary

[7] Keith Goldhammer et al., *Elementary School Principals and Their Schools* (Eugene, Ore.: University of Oregon Press, 1971), pp. 4-5.

[8] Pharis and Zakariya, *Elementary School Principalship,* pp. 71-72.

[9] David R. Byrne, Susan A. Hines, and Lloyd E. McCleary, *The Senior High School Principalship.* Volume I. *The National Survey* (Reston, Va.: National Association of Secondary School Principals, 1978), p. 24.

[10] Richard A. Gorton and Kenneth E. McIntyre, *The Senior High School Principal.* Volume II. *The Effective Principal* (Reston, Va.: National Association of Secondary School Principals, 1978), pp. 22-27.

recruiting. These systems normally establish a personnel department. This department usually conducts initial interviews, obtains records of college training and experience, writes for recommendations, and performs such other services required to provide a roster of qualified personnel available for appointment.

- Representatives from the principals, teachers, the central staff, and others advise with the superintendent concerning any regulations of systemwide application before the superintendent presents such regulations to the board for adoption.

- The budget is based on an educational plan, but that plan is not developed exclusively by the superintendent and central staff. The overall educational plan is based on an analysis of the educational needs at each individual school center. Therefore, the principal and staff at each school are given important responsibilities for participating in developing the educational plan upon which the budget is based. The principal and staff are expected to work closely with the citizens of their school community in developing the educational plan.

Elsewhere in this book attention is directed to the fact that one of the most important problems of educational administration is the determination of the appropriate level of government at which a particular decision should be made. Education is a state responsibility; therefore, the legislature has extremely broad powers with respect to public education. Sometimes legislatures exercise those powers unwisely by enacting too many specific laws regulating the curriculum. Laws or regulations of the state board of education that are too detailed and specific with respect to the curriculum sometimes handicap local school systems and individual schools. As was pointed out, boards of education sometimes handicap individual schools by rigid rules and regulations.

The development of education depends on more than adequate financing, administrative efficiency, and the elegance of organizational structure. Development implies change, but change does not always mean evolution or growth. Changes in a school system and in the school center are usually adoptions or adaptations of innovations. There is reason to be pessimistic about the innovations of the past twenty years, the theoretical framework of those innovations, and the changes initiated by central administration and by school centers. The decade of the 1960s was characterized by many innovations stimulated by federal and private funds, but there is much evidence that little change has taken place as a result of the millions of dollars invested in the school systems. Does this mean that the emerging theories of administration, organization, leadership, and cooperative action described elsewhere in this book as well as the procedures suggested have not been adequately understood or used? Does the school center only need greater freedom and the possibility of more productive initiative than now prevails in many large centralized school systems? There is still much work to be done by the organizational theorist in education. Related severe problems for the practicing educational administrator remain. For example, in the psychology of administration there are limited data on the thought processes of educational administrators and the significance of those thought processes for later decisions.[11]

[11] Louis M. Smith and Pat M. Keith, *Anatomy of Educational Innovation: An Organizational Analysis of an Elementary School* (New York: John Wiley & Sons, Inc., 1971), pp. 238–239.

THE PRINCIPAL

The possible roles for both elementary and secondary school principals are determined largely by the principal's perceptions of those roles, by the roles assigned by the central administration, and by the perceptions of the principal's role as held by the school staff and local school community. In the past twenty years, those perceptions and role assignments have been changed greatly by such forces as collective bargaining, federal and state guidelines for funding grant proposals and their implementation, legislation and court decisions, and the increasing involvement of students, parents, and other community members in public school decision making and in increased expectations of the school. Gorton concluded that the literature reveals six major roles for the principalship: "(1) manager, (2) instructional leader, (3) disciplinarian, (4) human relations facilitator, (5) change agent, and (6) conflict mediator."[12]

The principal and the staff are expected to develop and administer the educational program at the school center within the broad framework of policy established by the people through the legislature and their local board of education. Various studies have been made in the past thirty years to determine the specific competencies needed by the principal to carry out this major responsibility and the relationships of those competencies to competencies needed by superintendents and supervisors of instruction. Woodard[13] made an extensive study of the competencies needed by these three groups in the early 1950s and found that, of 203 competencies listed as essential for superintendents, principals, or supervisors, 70 percent were common to all three types of positions. Several conclusions were drawn from this and similar studies. There were some important differences between the job of the superintendent and the job of the principal, but the nature of the critical tasks performed was not greatly different. The preservice training program for principals should include many of the same features included in the preparation program for superintendents. Because principals often become superintendents or are given important executive and leadership responsibilities in large school districts, they should be given similar training to be competent in discharging those responsibilities.

The conclusions from these earlier studies seemed to focus upon the area of similarities without considering that the area of differences might be crucial to the performance competencies of the principals. A study made in the 1960s[14] gave evidence that preparatory programs for principals are inadequate, that they do not differentiate between the superintendency and the secondary and elementary school principalships, that generalized preparation programs are provided which are based upon the advance of administrators through the ranks and hence which emphasize the terminal job rather than the intermediate jobs, and that little consideration is given to experiences which might develop knowledge, skills, and critical insights in the prospective principals. Although the study cited dealt mainly

[12] Richard A. Gorton, *School Administration: Challenge and Opportunity for Leadership* (Dubuque, Iowa: William C. Brown Co., Publishers, 1976), p. 65.
[13] Prince B. Woodard, "A Study of Competencies Needed by School Administrators and Supervisors in Virginia with Implications for Pre-Service Education," (unpublished doctoral dissertation, CPEA Project, University of Virginia, 1953).
[14] Goldhammer et al., *Elementary School Principals*, p. 7.

with the elementary principalship, it included comparisons with the secondary principalship and has implications for the latter.

A study reported by Daniel E. Griffiths[15] indicated the need for considering further the competencies needed by the principal and the matters which his or her preservice training should include. Four elementary schools were selected on the basis of whether they had an open or closed organizational climate and a high or low socioeconomic setting. Each of the four principals' offices was videotaped for fourteen days, six-and-a-half hours daily. An analysis was then made of the problems recorded in terms of frequency, types, and the initiators of the problems. One startling finding was that a total of 12,062 problems, each with an initiator, was derived from the videotapes. Griffiths concluded that this sheer weight of problems indicated the need for a principal's office with a completely different form as well as the need for training which would prepare the principal for this incomprehensible task. Was this finding unique to the four elementary schools studied or to just the elementary principalship? Are the numbers of problems and initiators of problems growing, particularly in urban schools? How does the principal perform other tasks and exert educational leadership in the face of the magnitude of the problems?

Some writers in the field of secondary school administration are concerned that many secondary school administrators are projecting a low-level image of their profession because they are concerned with organizational management and maintenance rather than with educational and institutional leadership. Secondary school principals are said to be neglecting their role of instructional leadership if they spend most of their time on the relations of students and teachers, reports, schedules, athletic events, and the like. Secondary school principals are caught in the same context of reality as are the elementary principals, and the definitions of their required competencies and preservice training should reflect that reality. If the preceding is the context of reality for the principal how will educational leadership be provided in the community school center?

RELATIONSHIP OF THE PRINCIPAL TO THE CENTRAL STAFF

An executive in the line organization is in a position of potential role conflict because that person is under pressure from superordinates to attain the goals of the organization and is under pressure from subordinates to assist them in attaining their individual goals. The principal holds a position in the line organization which is vulnerable to several types of role conflict. By virtue of being closest to the teachers, the principal may be placed in a situation of role conflict which can be dysfunctional as well as personally painful, if the teachers expect the principal to express their norms, sentiments, and needs, even when they are not congruent with organizational purposes. Another potential source of conflict is lack of clear definition of the role of the principal in relation to the central staff.

The relationship of the principal to the central staff of the school system should be defined and understood clearly by all parties concerned. The nature of that

[15] Daniel E. Griffiths, "What Happens in the Principal's Office?" *UCEA Newsletter*, 14, no. 1 (October 1972), 407.

relationship varies in different school systems, as has been pointed out. In school systems that provide a considerable degree of freedom for school centers and that expect the principal to be a real rather than a nominal leader, the relationships are somewhat as follows:

- Lines of communication between the principal and the superintendent are direct rather than circuitous. District superintendents or supervising principals who serve as line officers between the superintendent and the building principal sometimes retard action rather than facilitate it. In large school systems, the superintendent will have deputy or assistant superintendents who may serve as line officers for certain matters. The operating arrangements should be so designed that these officers facilitate rather than retard the development and operation of the educational program.

- There is direct functional communication between the principal and the business office, the maintenance department, the central film library, and similar central services where the matters concerned are within the established policy or within the budget for that school. On matters outside the budget or established policy, the principal communicates with the superintendent or a designated representative and does not act without approval.

- The principal is recognized by the central staff as the executive head of the school that he or she administers.

- No one from the central staff has direct control over the employees at a school. The principal has that responsibility.

- The principal and not the supervisory staff of the central office is administratively responsible for the educational program of the school that the principal administers. The supervisory staff of the central office are staff officers and not line officers. Therefore, they act in an advisory rather than administrative capacity.

- The principal is responsible for executing board policies at the school center. If the principal does not believe that a particular policy is sound, he or she has the right and the responsibility to seek a change in policy. However, until the policy is changed the principal either executes it or resigns from his or her position.

- The board of education does not adopt a policy or educational program until it has been studied carefully. Such studies should involve principals, teachers, lay citizens, and others when appropriate.

- The relationship between the principal and the central staff is friendly and cooperative. The principal is not an isolate but rather a member of a team that has the characteristic of an effective group.

This may seem to be a somewhat formal statement of relationships, but, according to recent national surveys of elementary and secondary school principals, reported earlier in this chapter, much progress seems to have been made in implementing these relationships. Additionally, the 1978 national survey of the elementary school principals reported a new type of shared decision making at the school district level in the form of the administrative team. The 1968 survey of elementary principals did not even include questions related to the administrative team or to the areas of negotiations or strikes.

The administrative team was defined in the 1978 study as "bringing administrative and supervisory personnel together for purposes of interaction, consultation, and decision-making." Over two thirds (68 percent) of the principals reported some sort of administrative team arrangement in their district, whereas 82 percent reported that the elementary principals in their district were included on teams in a meaningful way. In districts with teams, 74 percent of the principals believed that the team had strengthened the administration of their school system. This survey also found that the administrative team dealt with labor-management problems in 74 percent of the school districts where the teachers had collective bargaining rights.[16] Similar data were not available for the secondary school principals, but, based upon past relationships between high school principals and the central administration, it is reasonable to expect a similar or even a stronger place on the administrative team for the secondary school principals.

Although showing remarkable growth in a relatively short period of time, the administrative team is still an emerging and evolving relationship. Will school principals continue to be, and to believe that they are, included on such teams in meaningful ways? What areas of education will be included in the realm of the administrative team's responsibilities? Will the principals look to the administrative team to help determine their own salaries, fringe benefits, and working conditions? Will administrative team membership align the principals even more strongly with the central administration in its collective bargaining with the teachers? If so, will this make more dysfunctional and more painful the role conflict of the principal? These and many more questions must now be considered because of this new relationship.

ORGANIZING THE SCHOOL AND THE STAFF

The organizational structure of the community school center is influenced by a number of factors, including the size of the school, the available facilities, the goals of the school, the variety of programs, the school level, the community involvement, and the organization of the program. As schools become larger the organizational structure becomes more complex and more critical in carrying out the educational functions. Elementary schools of 600 to 800 pupils, junior high or intermediate schools of 1,000 to 1,500 pupils, and senior high schools of 1,200 to 2,000 pupils have become common in urban and suburban areas. Much larger schools are found in many school systems.

Size is not the only factor creating organizational problems. A wide variety of types of grade organization is found in the public schools. A 1,000-pupil senior high school presents very different organizational problems than does a 1,000-pupil school including grades 1–12 or a 1,000-pupil school including only grades 4–6. The type of facilities available is also important in determining the organizational structure. A high school with traditional facilities has organizational possibilities different from a high school which uses its community resources and has multisized instructional spaces, instructional materials centers, learning laboratories, banks of automated instructional devices, computer outlets, or movable walls. Elementary school facilities have similar implications for organizational structure.

The local school staff can be roughly classified as follows: (1) the instructional staff, (2) the clerical and secretarial staff, (3) the custodial staff, and (4) the lunch-

[16] Pharis and Zakariya, *Elementary School Principalship*, pp. 75–77.

room staff. The instructional staff in a large elementary or high school may include the following types of instructional personnel: regular classroom teachers with many specializations, teachers of exceptional children, resource teachers, adult education teachers, itinerant teachers, assistant principals, curriculum consultants, administrative assistants, deans, counselors, librarians, psychologists, teacher and community aides, coordinators of community resources, and physiotherapists. This staff reflects the variety of programs found in the school as well as the goals of the school. It may also reflect the basic or general program and a variety of categorical programs which may or may not be integrated into the basic program.

There are a number of variations in the way in which the work may be divided for administering an elementary school. One teacher may teach children in two or three grade levels in a small school, whereas in a large school there may be a number of sections at each grade level or each teacher may have a multigraded or multiaged classroom, similar to that in the smaller school. The elementary school may be organized on a self-contained classroom basis, a departmental basis, a team teaching basis, a learning center basis, an ungraded basis, or some other basis.

Large high schools are commonly organized on a departmental basis, each subject area making up a department. This plan has the advantage of providing for vertical articulation of subject matter, but it does not facilitate interdisciplinary coordination. This type of organization has sometimes developed into a monocratic bureaucracy. There have been hopes that the high school of the future will move from rigid mass instructional practices to provisions for individual differences among learners, such as independent study, individual library research, self-instruction with autoinstructional devices, vertical and horizontal enrichment, large-group and small-group teaching, programmed materials, computer-assisted instruction, and emerging new instructional materials and media. The area of instructional strategies is discussed at length in Chapter 15.

No specific plan of organization is useful for all types of schools. The principal and the staff at each school should have the freedom to develop the particular plan of organization that best meets the needs of that school, in cooperation with the parents and community members. This freedom to organize has taken on new dimensions of importance in light of recent research that suggests organizational variables, such as the size of the school system and the individual school and the number of grade levels in the school, may influence the way in which the principal defines his or her work, making such work routinely predictable rather than innovative.[17]

WORKING WITH THE STAFF

The organizational plan lays the basis for the procedures by which the principal works with the staff, both instructional and noninstructional. Ideally, all members of the staff would participate in the development of the plan or organization. No

[17]Columbus Salley, R. Bruce McPherson, and Melany E. Baehr, "What Principals Do: A Preliminary Occupational Analysis," in *The Principal in Metropolitan Schools,* ed. Donald A. Erickson and Theodore L. Reller (Berkeley, Calif.: McCutchan Publishing Corporation, 1979), p. 35.

better method of achieving acceptance and understanding has been devised than the method of participation.

One of the major differences between a school that is a monocratic bureaucracy and a school that is characterized by collegial pluralism is observable in faculty meetings. Following are some of the characteristics of faculty meetings in the latter type:

- Faculty members and not the principal usually preside at meetings. The principal is the chief executive officer of the faculty but that responsibility does not require presiding at all meetings.
- The agenda is prepared by a committee of the faculty. The principal has the same right as other members of the faculty to place matters on the agenda.
- The major amount of time at faculty meetings is spent on program development and policy formation, and only a minor portion of time is spent on announcements and routine matters.
- *Ad hoc* study committees frequently make reports to the faculty on matters being considered.
- The principal participates in faculty discussion on a peer basis with other members of the faculty.
- The faculty strives to reach consensus before taking action.
- The faculty considers the recommendations on appropriate matters from the parent–teacher association, citizens' committees, and student groups before taking action.
- When the faculty is making decisions on matters involving noninstructional employees, those employees are involved in the decision-making process.
- The principal does not veto actions of the faculty unless the actions are in conflict with state law or with the regulations of the board. The principal should avoid having to make this type of veto by making clear to the faculty members the limits of their decision-making authority. There is nothing more frustrating to a faculty than to be invited to make a decision on a matter and then be advised later that the faculty did not have the authority to make the decision.

Yet the literature concerning faculty meetings consistently indicates that the teachers consider the effectiveness of such meetings to be a major problem. The use and effectiveness of faculty meetings has been further limited by the master contract for teachers, which sets negotiated limitations on the number and length of such meetings. Under collective bargaining, can the principal plan faculty meetings with the characteristics just described? If not, where will the decision-making process for the improvement of instruction that underlies those characteristics be found?

In addition to the faculty meeting, other major differences were described in the past of schools' moving from monocratic bureaucracy to collegial pluralism. These included the creation of a faculty senate and the provision of some type of grievance machinery, particularly for grievances involving such matters as objections to policies set by the principal, department heads, or supervisors; staff meetings; assigned duties other than those involving teaching; and methods of evaluating teachers. State laws and collective bargaining are increasingly preempting such areas, making difficult the discernment of the direction in which collegial pluralism is now moving.

Although the concept of the administrative team, as discussed in this chapter, is used primarily on the district level and was started at that level with the advent of teacher militancy and collective bargaining, it is starting to emerge as a useful mechanism at the school level.[18] It is seen as a tool to pool human resources to achieve school as well as district objectives, and it is defined to include school personnel with administrative functions or supervisory responsibilities. The composition, structure, processes, and functioning of the school administrative team should be analyzed, planned, and implemented with care.

One last painful aspect of working with the staff should be mentioned, although it may be of transitory significance. Principals who just a few years ago were expanding their teaching staffs are now experiencing the difficulties of reduction in force (RIF). Not only are many schools not hiring new teachers and are losing the benefits of new ideas and youth but they must lay off newer members of their staff and even tenured teachers. How creative and innovative can the principal and the teaching staff be when the projections indicate continued reductions? What new aspects of role conflict are thus engendered for the principal? What in-service training and what principles does the principal require and follow under RIF?

THE PRINCIPAL AS INSTRUCTIONAL LEADER

Of the major roles described for the principalship, there is an apparent dichotomy between the principal's role as an administrative manager and as an instructional leader. Typically surveys show that principals regard instructional leadership as a primary function and one on which they would like to spend the major portion of their time yet on which they tend to spend relatively little time. They tend to spend a major portion of their time in management activities. However, given the current status of project funding and financial stringencies, some boards of education are calling for principals who are more trained in business manager kinds of skills. But the principal is still regarded generally as the executive in the line organization at the scene of action and, as such, responsible for the development and implementation of the instructional program at the school.

Recurring questions include the type of instructional leadership that the principal can provide to the teachers who are more expert in their particular subject areas and whether the principal's primary concern for the attainment of established organizational objectives makes it realistic to expect the "leader" to be innovative. It was mentioned in this chapter that recent research suggested that the principal is bound in the definition of role and work by organizational variables. The survey of effective senior high school principals conducted in 1977, referred to several times in this chapter, indicated that secondary school principals required not only role clarification but also improved skills in such areas as curriculum development, teacher in-service education, and program evaluation. Elementary school principals have expressed similar needs.

[18] Gorton and McIntyre, *The Senior High School Principal,* pp. 84-97.

These questions and considerations require some review of the current knowledge in the areas of curriculum, instruction, and learning as well as an analysis of the organization of the school in terms of educational programs. These areas will be discussed in the next two chapters.

WORKING WITH STUDENTS

If the principal and his or her staff accept the collegial, pluralistic theories of administration and organization, that commitment must also include students. This commitment is reinforced by the many court decisions in the past decade which reaffirm the constitutional rights of students, their status as citizens, and the requirements of due process. The growing assertiveness of high school students and even of elementary school pupils for a voice in the planning of their educational experiences bolsters further that commitment. In a sense, democratic living has been forced upon the school.

Walton has pointed out the ambiguous organizational role of students.[19] It is not clear whether they are members of the school center or customers and clients. The students are not on the payroll; yet, unlike customers, they are required to spend much of their lives in attendance, analogous organizationally to hospital patients, prison inmates, and residents of homes for the aged. There have been questions about the rights of students to participate in academic and management affairs, with increasing evidence that students, particularly in the high schools and junior high schools, are grappling with the same questions. There is indication that students are seeking greater involvement in their school center's functioning. The principal and the staff need to make that involvement relevant and knowledgeable. The greater danger in not doing so lies not in the potential for disruption but in the massive apathy and alienation of students from school.

Often the ability of students to participate effectively in decision making is underestimated by both teachers and parents. It is often assumed that students cannot participate wisely in decision making until they are fairly mature. But skillful teachers make extensive use of pupil-teacher planning even in the kindergarten. These experiences develop the leadership competencies of students and maximize the conditions for effective learning. They also minimize discipline problems. As students grow in their ability to solve problems and make decisions, they develop competency to participate in many phases of classroom management.

Many school programs and policies affect students so directly that they should share in the development of those programs and policies. Some examples are extracurricular activities, school discipline, class and club activities, and similar activities. Many schools have had long and successful experiences with student participation in school government, student councils, student advisory committees, and similar means for student participation in decision making. Students not only participate in planning but frequently administer or participate in the administration of many activities. The basic question that the principal must face in these activities is concerned with whether they are real or contrived.

---

[19] John Walton, *Introduction to Education: A Substantive Discipline* (Waltham, Mass.: Xerox College Publishing, 1971), pp. 135–138.

The relationships of the school center to its community formed the basis for the opening paragraphs of this chapter and for the conclusion that the school center has the potential for becoming the intellectual center and educational catalyst of the community. Recent literature on the public school, the community, and community education seems to imply different, important ways in which the principal and the staff can work with the community in addition to those described traditionally if the potential for leadership is to be realized.

The way in which the principal and staff work with the community not only affects the educational program of the school but also has a major influence on the entire school system. Early studies indicated that community attitudes toward the superintendent, the board, and the central staff were affected by the working patterns of principals as well as by community attitudes toward the local school. Those working patterns were greatly affected during the 1960s and thereafter by the great growth in community involvement in the public schools.

The traditional ways in which the principal worked with the community included the concept of school public relations, the use of all forms of publicity, and the use of various cooperative procedures. More specifically, these three areas included, respectively (1) school visiting days for parents, open-house programs, sports activities, individual parent-teacher conferences, the use of the community members as resource persons, and many similar activities; (2) mass media of communication such as newspapers, radio, and TV; newsletters and school publications; and talks by the principal and staff members to community groups; and (3) cooperation with the PTA, civic groups, other community groups and governmental agencies, and private individuals.

In the 1970s many new and modified forms of parent–citizen participation in the school devolved. These forms of participation were categorized by Fantini[20] as follows: (1) for public relations; (2) for instructional and curriculum support; (3) for crisis resolution; (4) for school governance, defined further as being consultative, advisory, shared, community control, and individual or family control; (5) for applying legal resources to educational problem solving; and (6) for education through citizen-consumer lobbies. Inherent in the new forms of participation was the assumption that they would promote parent–citizen influence on educational policies and program implementation.

Studies conducted by the Institute for Responsive Education since 1974, concerning the new forms of parent-citizen participation, were reported in a 1979 Association for Supervision and Curriculum Development publication.[21] These studies were conducted on the basis that studies prior to 1970 indicated that educators defined the rules for parent participation in the schools, that most school boards endorsed those rules, and that the influence in local school policy of parents and nonparents was restricted to supportive participation. The new participatory structures which were examined were grouped under the headings of school de-

---

[20] Mario D. Fantini, *The People and Their Schools: Community Participation* (Bloomington, Ind.: Phi Delta Kappa Educational Foundation, 1975), pp. 22–26.

[21] Steinberg, "The Changing Role of Parent Groups," pp. 46–57.

centralization, government-mandated councils, state- and local-mandated councils, child advocacy groups, federally funded programs, and the "changing PTA." The conclusion on the question of whether these new participatory structures were adequate was that "the available data . . . have indicated that they have not created, in most instances, adequate opportunities for parents to have access to decision making at either the local district or federal and state levels."[22] Even more disturbing to the school principal than this conclusion should be the report's underlying premises that these new structures were devised because local school boards and administrators had neglected the educational needs of the students and that principals are generally responsible for stifling effective parent–citizen participation. The report concludes that the parents' major task is to try to find out who has the power and how parents can get a fair share of that power.

For the principal and the staff who are concerned with implementing the new participatory structures, a new leadership and a new service function in our society are indicated. In addition to examining traditional attitudes, what new understandings, skills, and capacities are required and how are these developed? Bowles spent several years studying the question of school–community relationships and reported findings which are directly relevant to the preceding question.[23] It was found that the process involved in the school–community relationship was more important than the specific activity and that the five process variables analyzed were differential in their effects upon the various possible outcomes. The process variables were identified as access, resolution (which turned out to be essentially the same as access), communication, involvement, and participation. The outcomes were in four areas: student achievement, effectiveness of school–community relations programs, support for the school, and trust in the school or institutional legitimacy. If student achievement was the outcome sought from the school–community relationship, access and resolution or real problem solving were the critical factors. Participation was *not* important and by itself was not significantly related to any of the listed outcomes. Involvement was primarily the variable enhancing school support, and the remaining two outcomes were related to effective communication. The implications of this study are significant in terms of the need for human relations and mediation skills, the organization of all school staff for problem solving, the decentralization of community relations functions to the local school, and the small influence of communication, participation, and involvement on achievement unless problem solving or conflict resolution also occurs.

Is it possible that some principals, whose attitudes toward all the desired outcomes of effective school–community relationships are, in fact, very positive, are being categorized as neglectful and resistant because of a misunderstanding and a misuse of the five school–community relations processes? If so, how can attitudes be translated into effective behaviors? What are the implications for the success of some of the newer mechanisms such as school advisory councils and needs assessment?

---

[22] *Ibid.,* p. 54.

[23] B. Dean Bowles, "Little Things Make a Difference: At Least in Community Relations," *Wisconsin R & D Center News,* (Fall 1979), 1–3.

SOME IMPORTANT PROBLEMS AND ISSUES

A concomitant of the continued turmoil in public school education has been the questioning of and attack upon virtually every phase of the local school operation. The concepts, organizational structure, and current phenomena described in this chapter have reflected, if only sketchily, what appear to be great social changes, uncertainties, and dissentions. The often optimistic applications of the limited theoretical concepts of the past have not appeared to be congruent with current realities. The projection a few years ago of the rational solution to local organizational problems through the use of research findings and derived general principles has not been validated. The principal and staff continue to face greater issues and problems.

Some of these issues and problems have been discussed in the preceding pages; others are discussed in the following pages. Many are in the process of developing; those omitted may prove to be as important as those selected, while the unforeseen effects of those discussed may prove to be quite different from how they now appear.

HOW WILL THE ROLE OF THE PRINCIPAL BE DEFINED?

Perhaps the most critical problem still faced by the principal is the general ambiguity of the position. This ambiguity goes beyond the question of whether the principal is an administrative manager or an instructional leader. A solution proposed to clear this ambiguity is that criteria be developed that will define the principal's role explicitly but not in detail which results in rigidity and loss of overall perspective, that the principal be trained to carry out that defined role, and that the principal be given the assistance needed to carry out modern, effective, instructional programs. However, this same source points out that administrators at all levels have the problem of lacking knowledge and techniques for dealing with major social issues, the complex human and organizational relationships within the school systems and the community, and the complexities of educational technology.[24] Who, then, has the knowledge and competency to define the principal's role? When it is further realized that the social issues, the complex relationships, and modern technology, themselves, are in the process of formation and emergence, it can be seen that the task of defining the principal's role is not a simple one of definition or of deciding between two general viewpoints. Rather, the principal's role is in the process of being defined by many forces, often contradictory in their potential impact.

Those forces include collective negotiations by the teachers and the gradual inclusion of the principal with the central administration on the administrative team. These areas have been discussed elsewhere in this chapter and are the focus of Chapter 18. The principal represents middle management and must interpret and carry out negotiated contractual obligations. The principal is excluded from teacher organizations in their negotiations, but some principals still look to formal collective bargaining for their own interests. What are some of the implications of these trends for the definition of the principal's role? How might they affect the tradi-

[24] Goldhammer et al., *Elementary School Principals*, pp. 17, 166–172.

tional role of the educational leader? Is the principal coming out the loser in the educational power game? How will the principal gain the skills and understandings of the grievance process to avoid becoming bogged down in a flood of petty grievances? What preparation is essential for the effective contract administrator?

What will be the effects of the movements toward accountability and competency testing? The public, with increasing translation into state laws, is asking that the students be competent in certain basic areas of learning, that the school district and each school have written educational aims, and that each teacher have behavioral objectives for the class generally and for each student specifically. How should those educational aims be developed and what leadership behavior is indicated for the principal? What is the principal's role in developing the behavioral objectives and for achieving those objectives? What improved understandings and skills will be needed by principals in the areas of curriculum, instruction, teacher in-service education, and program evaluation? Do these movements indicate a strengthening of the principal's role as educational leader?

Many schools have one or more federally funded special programs which required extensive planning at the school and which must follow detailed rules and regulations in their implementation, including the submission of comprehensive reports. Many of these programs recommend or mandate the formation of parent–citizen advisory councils. These programs and requirements are paralleled in many states by similar legislation. In some schools several programs must be accounted for individually as well as coordinated by the principal. Thus, many see principal's emerging as managers of projects and special programs. What skills and understandings are required for this function and how does it influence the definition of the role of the principal?

SELECTED REFERENCES

Anderson, Lester W., and Lauren A. Van Dyke, *Secondary School Administration* (2nd ed.). Boston: Houghton Mifflin Company, 1972.

Cunningham, Luvern L., Walter G. Hack, and Raphael O. Nystrand, eds., *Educational Administration: The Developing Decades*. Berkeley, Calif.: McCutchan Publishing Corporation, 1977.

DeVita, Joseph C., Philip Pumerantz, and Leighton B. Wilklow, *The Effective Middle School*. West Nyack, N.Y.: Parker Publishing Company, Inc., 1970.

Erickson, Donald A., and Theodore L. Reller, *The Principal in Metropolitan Schools*. Berkeley, Calif.: McCutchan Publishing Corporation, 1979.

Gorton, Richard A., *School Administration: Challenge and Opportunity for Leadership*. Dubuque, Iowa: William C. Brown Co., Publishers, 1976.

——, and Kenneth E. McIntyre, *The Senior High School Principal*. Volume II. *The Effective Principal*. Reston, Va.: National Association of Secondary School Principals, 1978.

Pharis, William L., and Sally Banks Zakariya, *The Elementary School Principalship in 1978: A Research Study*. Washington, D.C.: National Association of Elementary School Principals, 1979.

Sergiovanni, Thomas J., and Fred D. Carver, *The New School Executive: A Theory of Administration* (2nd ed.). New York: Harper & Row, Publishers, Inc., 1980.

Smith, Louis M., and Pat M. Keith, *Anatomy of Educational Innovation: An Organizational Analysis of an Elementary School*. New York: John Wiley & Sons, Inc., 1971.

Walton, John, *Introduction to Education: A Substantive Discipline*. Waltham, Mass.: Xerox College Publishing, 1971.

Part 3

D EVELOPMENT
and ADMINISTRATION
of PROGRAMS
and SERVICES

15

CURRICULUM *and* INSTRUCTION: THEORETICAL CONSIDERATIONS*

It is generally accepted that the ultimate task of the public school is the education of the learners, although it cannot also be assumed that there is a general agreement as to the main purposes of that education or how it is best effected. It is also generally accepted that the school administration is responsible for everything that goes on in the schools. Superintendents and principals, with some boards of education also taking an increasing part in administrative matters, have that responsibility as educational leaders presiding over one or more institutions.

There are differing opinions as to the relative importance of the educational administrator's responsibility for management functions as contrasted to instructional matters, with the latter often being delegated to subordinates. There has been strong criticism, especially from some boards of education, that their administrators are too little prepared in the area of management. Duties in this area have been

*Prepared in large part by John P. Matlin, assistant dean, School of Education, University of California, Berkeley.

309

incorporated increasingly into selection criteria for new administrators and into training programs for incipient administrators. Administrative duties have proliferated, while becoming vastly more complex, under the pressure of a variety of powerful forces: federal and state government rules and regulations mandated both in the general operations of the school and in connection with special programs and funded projects; the evolving legal intricacies contained in the redefinition of the rights of students, parents, teachers, and other individuals; collective negotiations, contract management, and other relationships stemming from increasing teacher militancy and teacher unionization; the increasing and changing participation of parents in the school because of mandated district and school site councils; the changing relationships with all types of public media and the strong criticisms of public education; the changing nature of the students, not only through legal redefinition but through dimly understood cultural upheavals; and a great number of political changes that enmesh the schools in a variety of issues and problems.

The place of matters of curriculum and instruction among all the functions implied in the varied forces listed is not generally agreed to or clear. Although students of educational administration seem generally to give attention to the instructional leadership role of the administrator, they vary in at least three areas in their analyses and interpretations of it: (1) the importance of that role as compared with all other important roles (2) the theoretical and conceptual information they bring to bear in their discussions, and (3) the activities they propose for administrators to carry out this role.

SOME VIEWPOINTS OF INSTRUCTIONAL LEADERSHIP

Following are some examples of those differing approaches to instructional leadership. Sergiovanni and Carver, in their analysis of the "new school executive," made a systematic presentation of administrative behavior and educational decision making, with only small reference to curricular and instructional functions. They believe that no administrator would challenge the view that the general goal of the schools is to provide learning experiences for the students and that the superintendent or principal who persists in ignoring problems of curriculum content is engaging in abdicating behavior.[1] Newell stated much more strongly that the first and foremost concern of the administration should be the curriculum of the school.[2]

Ellena, as editor of a curriculum handbook for school executives, saw as inevitable in 1973 that the superintendent take responsibility for curriculum decision making if such decisions were to be made and implemented efficiently and in a dependable manner.[3] Gorton, in analyzing the leadership responsibilities and opportunities of the school administrator, found that, although the administrator

[1] Thomas J. Sergiovanni and Fred D. Carver, *The New School Executive: A Theory of Administration* (New York: Harper & Row, Publishers, Inc., 1980), pp. 164, 269.

[2] Clarence A. Newell, *Human Behavior in Educational Administration* (Englewood Cliffs, N.J.: Prentice-Hall, Inc., 1978), p. 190.

[3] William J. Ellena, ed., *Curriculum Handbook for School Executives* (Arlington, Va.: American Association of School Administrators, 1973), p. 376.

may increasingly not be recognized as the instructional leader of the school, he or she is still the one to whom the major supervisory responsibilities are assigned at the building level. Gorton concluded that the administrator must become more proficient and knowledgeable in supervision in order to be an effective instructional leader and that the administrator's emphasis should be on curriculum improvement rather than on the administration of instruction.[4]

However, these differing interpretations of the instructional leadership role of educational administrators may derive as much from the tremendous scope of the many viewpoints involved as they do from whatever importance the writer may attach to a particular role, with the need to narrow any one approach in the study of educational administration. Thus, the real question is not the apparent dichotomy between the management and the educational leadership roles of the school administrators but how administrators will perform the many functions for which they are responsible and the knowledge and proficiencies they will seek to make that performance effective.

The discussion in this and the following chapter is based upon the assumption that school administrators are educational leaders, that this includes being instructional leaders, and that the pertinent question is not whether they will be involved in the curriculum but how they will be involved. It is further assumed that in their quest to improve the instructional programs, administrators must be knowledgeable and proficient in the areas covered by current analyses of administrative behavior and decision making, analyses which are incorporating increasingly the application of knowledge from the social sciences. There is a large and growing body of literature in these areas as well as on the various management functions of administrators. There is also a wealth of research and literature in the fields of curriculum, instruction, and learning; it will be assumed that the administrator has some familiarity with those fields.

Goodlad saw the period of the 1970s in public school education as one which was consumed with power struggles, an emphasis on the refinement of the behavioral bases of accountability, and the development of tests to measure the attainment of proficiencies and competencies. But he also speculated that this period might be "preliminary to a renaissance of interest in classic questions of curriculum, learning, and teaching." He concluded that what would now be useful would be a carefully selected body of information on the present state of learning, teaching, and educational leadership in our public schools.[5] Such a body of information, although it must still be regarded as being incipient, is becoming available.

In this and the following chapter, the attempt has been made to describe a brief, but carefully selected, sampling of that information in a search for findings and interpretations in the areas of curriculum, instruction, and learning that seem to be of particular importance to educational administrators. These findings come out of the cumulative context of past literature but with insights and conclusions that are not always in accordance with the conventional wisdom and which sometimes have significant implications for the thoughtful planning and effective ac-

[4] Richard A. Gorton, *School Administration: Challenge and Opportunity for Leadership* (Dubuque, Iowa: William C. Brown Co., Publishers, 1976), pp. 207–209, 232.

[5] John I. Goodlad, *What Schools Are For* (Bloomington, Ind.: Phi Delta Kappan Educational Foundation, 1979), pp. 44, 102.

tivities of educational administrators and school faculties. For example, how the administrator defines curriculum has a major influence on how the school is organized.

THE MANY AND VARIED MEANINGS OF "CURRICULUM"

There are almost as many definitions of "curriculum" as there are articles on that subject, and a great number of such articles have been written in the past twenty years. Not only are these definitions varied, but they cover a broad range of inclusion, from a narrow definition of curriculum as a specific course of study or even a textbook to a broad statement that includes the total educational opportunities or experiences offered in the school. Qualifying adjectives are also applied or rejected, such as whether those opportunities are planned or unplanned, hidden or not hidden, intended or not intended. Cuban has pointed out that the various meanings of curriculum have their own separate literature as developed by theorists and that, when the National Institute of Education attempted to obtain public advice on curriculum issues in 1976, the ambiguity of that term was underscored as it offered at least six different meanings of the word.[6] However, educational administrators already are personally familiar with this ambiguity from their professional education as teachers and administrators and in their administrative efforts to deal with the curriculum. But the impact on their efforts requires some analysis.

Writers justify their choice of a particular definition of curriculum on the basis of what they intend to discuss in terms of the research and other information available, the possibilities for change, and the types of interventions to be suggested. They usually settle on a moderately broad definition which starts with a statement of the need to analyze the nature of the discipline or subject, the nature of society, and the nature of the learner. They then attempt to take into account several major areas, including philosophical considerations as to the purposes of education in a democratic society; federal and state legislative and judicial impacts on curriculum; the national development of curricula, especially active in the 1960s, with the emergence of the "new" approaches and the various alphabetized projects; local school district development of curriculum, including the adoption and adaptation of national curricula and commercial materials, courses of study, textbooks, and so on; teaching strategies and techniques and how the teacher will operate in the classroom; and the various psychological approaches to the nature of the learner and what the learner does in the classroom. Thus, they tend to include theories of curriculum, instruction, and learning in their definitions, theories that are complex and, themselves, in various stages of exploration, development, and validation.

The administrator who intends to profit from the various analyses must keep in mind the variety of concepts involved as the indicated understandings, proficiencies, and operational strategies and techniques may be quite different according

---

[6] Larry Cuban, "Determinants of Curriculum Change and Stability, 1870–1970," in *Value Conflicts and Curriculum Issues: Lessons from Research and Experience,* eds. Jon Schaffarzick and Gary Sykes (Berkeley, Calif.: McCutchan Publishing Corporation, 1979), p. 141.

to the many aspects of the definitions being used. It cannot be claimed that all the definitions, no matter what the intent of the particular writer, are equally clarifying, valid, or useful to the educational administrator. The matter is made more difficult for the administrator who does not have clear, operational definitions for his or her own use, who is not certain of what he or she is trying to do in the area of curriculum, and who does not know what the probability is that he or she is having or will have any degree of influence with what he or she is doing.

DIFFICULTIES INHERENT IN "CURRICULUM" AS USUALLY DEFINED

The definitions usually employed in discussions of curriculum, as described, may be useful to educational administrators in reminding them of the number of forces at work, their complexity, and the variety of theoretical approaches which are being used in trying to understand their relationships. But such definitions may also be detrimental if administrators try to operate in a general accordance with the vast concepts involved. There are several major difficulties inherent in the usual discussions of curriculum that have implications for administration.

Differing Operational Activities Involved

First, even if the field of curriculum were a unified endeavor of interrelated areas, it would still be necessary for the administrator to regard separately each major area as each area calls for a different kind of operational activity. For example, the role and actions of the educational administrator in the area of the development of national curricula are quite different from the role in developing the specific curriculum for the school. Or the role in developing the specific curriculum for the school is quite different from the role involved in working with an individual teacher and the teaching–learning situation in a specific classroom. The administrator's understandings, proficiencies, and operational actions are very different in each major area, as are the types or effectiveness of any influence the administrator may have. There is also much evidence that the most important role, concerning classroom implementation of the curriculum, has been the most neglected.

The Absence of Assumed Relationships

However, it has become increasingly apparent that the interrelationships assumed between and among the major areas of curriculum are not really present and that what is being described is a statement of what should be rather than what is. This is not necessarily an undesirable description unless the two states of being are confused. The nationally developed curricula, for example, as finally presented in outlines, materials, and prescriptive behaviors as to usage, have been found to be very different from the curriculum which has been finally implemented in the individual classroom. The inquiring administrator will find that his work and influence in one phase of the curriculum is almost totally unrelated to the other phases and, ultimately perhaps, not even remotely connected to the curriculum of a specific classroom.

During the decade of the 1960s, it was believed that a considerable number of innovations, national curricula, and new concepts were being developed and introduced into the public schools. Surveys of the actual operations in the elementary public schools did not indicate the realization of those expectations. One such survey was made of 158 classrooms of sixty-seven schools in twenty-six school districts in the major cities of thirteen states in a nationwide geographic spread. Classrooms were observed and teachers interviewed on the K–3 level in schools that were considered to be average, special, or innovative, with some schools having a large proportion of environmentally disadvantaged children. In general, the data for the three different types of schools presented the same configurations. The study found that almost all the schools observed a course of bland uniformity, regardless of the school setting or pupil population.[7]

This nonimplementation in the classroom of innovative projects was substantiated by a later, large, systematic study by Rand Corporation of federally supported innovative programs. The Rand researchers surveyed 293 innovative projects and found that nonimplementation was common and that "the most that could be hoped for was a process of *mutual adaptation* in which both the practices in a given school and the innovative project being attempted were modified by one another."[8] Thus, at a time when curriculum defined as the national development of curricula and new approaches was going through a tremendous development and greatly influencing commercial materials, textbooks, and courses of study, curriculum defined as instructional practices in the classroom was undergoing very little change. Are individual classrooms similarly not related to the ongoing educational policies of their local boards of education or to the programs which the local principal may believe are being implemented? What is the curriculum of any specific classroom?

The Great Reliance on Rationality

A third difficulty with the broad definitions of curriculum as usually developed is related to the assumption of interrelationships that are not really present and has to do with the technical, rational approach that has marked most of curriculum development to date as well as much of the other theoretical work in curriculum generally. Hampson discussed the emerging questioning of the technical conception of curriculum as a process of ends and means.[9] Various critics of the technical conception have pointed out its quasi-scientific nature, with its theorists tending to leap from descriptions to prescriptions for classroom instruction on

[7] John I. Goodlad, M. Frances Klein, and associates, *Behind the Classroom Door* (Worthington, Ohio: Charles A. Jones Publishing Company, 1970), pp. 33–34, 39, 86–87.

[8] William Lowe Boyd, "The Changing Politics of Curriculum Policy Making for American Schools," in *Value Conflicts and Curriculum Issues,* pp. 106–107.

[9] David H. Hampson, "Perspectives on Curriculum Development," in *Strategies for Curriculum Development,* eds. Jon Schaffarzick and David H. Hampson (Berkeley, Calif.: McCutchan Publishing Corporation, 1975), pp. 1–3.

the basis of possibility rather than on any known probability of validity or relevance to instruction; the serious limitations of the behavioral objectives approach; and the fact that theory is inadequate to curriculum tasks even where it is appropriate and that ". . . we should, consequently, divert our energies to the practical, the quasi-practical, and the eclectic."

Lindblom and Cohen helped to place the discussion of what curriculum is and the limitations of broad definitions and rational, technical approaches in a useful perspective for educational administrators. They sought to determine the parameters of usable knowledge in the social sciences and in social problem solving, which seems to include curriculum theory, development, and usage, insofar as it is relevant to administration. In their search for usable knowledge, they developed the concepts of ordinary knowledge, interactive problem solving, social learning, analytical problem solving, and authoritativeness.

By "ordinary knowledge" they meant ". . . knowledge that does not owe its origin, testing, degree of verification, truth status, or currency to distinctive PSI (Professional Social Inquiry) techniques but rather to common sense, casual empiricism, or thoughtful speculation and analysis." They called it knowledge even if it was false and suggested that people always depended heavily on ordinary knowledge while the social scientists refined ordinary knowledge to a greater degree than they created new knowledge.

In "interactive problem solving," "the preferred outcome comes about without anyone's having analyzed the given problem or having achieved an analyzed solution to it." Rather, a solution or preferred situation comes about by what the participants do rather than what they think or understand. "Social learning" describes the different behavior that certain groups of people must learn before problems can be solved. For example, the energy crisis will probably be solved not by information concerning fuel shortages or fuel alternatives but because of the changed behavior of automobile drivers resulting from waiting in long lines at gasoline stations or from paying increasingly high prices for gasoline.

"Analytical problem solving" describes the approach which is usually thought of as the scientific approach that focuses on causal explanations of social phenomena, or PSI, and which is only one of several equally important routes to social problem solving. Furthermore, even if PSI comes out with a scientifically highly verified proposition, it will not be accepted as "authoritative," that is, to be acted upon, unless it is somehow congruent with ordinary knowledge, interactive problem solving, social learning, or the many conflicting influences from which policy often emerges.[10]

The concepts just described appear to have much relevance to the search for usable knowledge in the area of curriculum. There is much ordinary knowledge in education that everyone possesses but that is possessed unequally in terms of its reliability, probable truth, and general quality. This is as true among professional educators as it is among legislators, parents, and the general public. Policies are being decided, actions are being taken, and educational problems are being attacked, if not solved, through interactive problem solving and social learning, which may lead the public schools into profoundly different directions from those

[10] Charles E. Lindblom and David K. Cohen, *Usable Knowledge: Social Science and Social Problem Solving* (New Haven, Conn.: Yale University Press, 1979), pp. 12, 16–20, 34, 42.

regarded as traditional in the past. For example, what is the social learning and what are the implications of that learning for the public school curriculum involved in the collective bargaining relationship of teachers to school districts and the development of binding contracts?

Some of these new directions, in the opinion of many thoughtful educators, include a serious popular questioning of the role of public schools as the common school and the beginning of the dismantling of the public school system. Yet a large group of educators and researchers who are involved in the investigation of curriculum and the implications of those investigations for practices in the schools claim that research results are now available that could have a profound constructive influence, if used, upon the educational effectiveness of teachers, administrators, and schools. What information does the instructional leader extract from this analytical problem solving, how does he or she determine its usefulness in a specific situation, and how is it used effectively in light of the other forces just described? Is the information being presented, even if scientifically verified, "authoritative"? That is, can the administrator act on it?

SOME USEFUL PERSPECTIVES OF CURRICULUM

In examining determinants of classroom learning environments, Talmage and Eash narrowed the focus of curriculum to three variables, which seems to be an appropriate focus for educational administrators also. They used curriculum to mean that which is taught, instruction to include the planning and implementation of the teaching-learning transactions, and instructional materials as the physical media through which the curriculum as mediated by the instructional program is experienced. They acknowledged that there is not a clear-cut distinction among these three components but proposed a method to look at each component separately as well as their interactions.[11]

Goodlad and his associates gave a preliminary report of a massive study of schooling, in which five perspectives of curriculum were developed as part of a carefully drawn framework that was considered to have an atheoretical orientation.[12] In discussing the assumptions that guided their research, they did not use what they regarded as the "production" or factory model of schooling, where schooling is veiwed as inputs and outputs. They doubted the utility of this model in seeking to describe or improve schools. Rather, their perspective was a contextual one and ecological theory became increasingly appealing to them in seeking to make sense out of their data, although they were very careful to state that their goal was not to develop an alternative theory of schooling and that their research was of an exploratory rather than a confirmatory nature. They also believed that it is probably premature to do longitudinal studies concerning relationships with achievement indicators until the contextual domain is better described.[13] Thus,

[11] Harriet Talmage and Maurice J. Eash, "Curriculum, Instruction, and Materials," in *Research on Teaching* (Berkeley, Calif.: McCutchan Publishing Corporation, 1979), pp. 161–162.

[12] "A Study of Schooling," reported in four issues of the *Phi Delta Kappan,* November 1979–February, 1980.

[13] John I. Goodlad, Kenneth A. Sirotnik, and Bette C. Overman, "An Overview of 'A Study of Schooling,'" *Phi Delta Kappan,* 61, no. 3 (November 1979), 174–178.

their concerns about the conceptualization of schooling are related to the previous discussion in this chapter and the traditional reliance on analytical problem solving as the only important route to social problem solving.

They described the five perspectives of curriculum as follows:

1. The *ideal* curriculum or the abstraction obtained by reviewing the literature and defined as "beliefs, opinions, and values of scholars in the disciplines and in schooling regarding what ought to be included in the curriculum and how it ought to be developed."

2. The *formal* curriculum or the expectations for what should be done, which are "derived from sources outside the classroom and consist of such things as state or district guidelines, school department syllabi, listings of course offerings, legislative decrees, national curriculum projects (e.g., BSCS or PSSC), commercially prepared learning materials, school board policies, district statements of philosophy, and even demands by community groups or parents for the inclusion or exclusion of specific content."

3. The *instructional* curriculum where the teachers "bring their own values, beliefs, and competencies to bear as they plan their teaching" and adapt or do not adapt the formal curriculum to their classrooms and the individual differences of their students.

4. The *operational* curriculum or that which actually goes on in the classroom and "takes into account the alterations made in the instructional curriculum as teachers actually engage with students in the teaching–learning process."

5. The *experiential* curriculum or "1) student perceptions of the curriculum that is offered to them and 2) what is actually learned—student outcomes."[14]

They concluded that the picture resulting from their analysis of the curriculum data would probably be a complex one and that the school curriculum would turn out to include several of the perspectives described: formal, instructional, operational, and experiential. These perspectives could be useful to the educational administrator in exploring the role as instructional leader and the knowledge required for different aspects of that role and the possibilities of influencing the various aspects of the curriculum, with the ultimate goal of improving learning. The role of the instructional leader now can be divided into two major categories, each calling for different types of knowledge and proficiencies and each allowing for different kinds and degrees of influence by the administrator on the instructional program and on learning. The remainder of this chapter will consider these two categories under the general headings of curriculum development and curriculum implementation.

CURRICULUM DEVELOPMENT

However "curriculum" is defined, there is an underlying pattern to the many approaches used in curriculum development, a pattern which some writers believe has not changed substantially in about the last twenty years, although there are

[14] M. Frances Klein, Kenneth A. Tye, and Joyce E. Wright, "A Study of Schooling: Curriculum," *Phi Delta Kappan*, 61, no. 4 (December 1979), 244–245.

signs that it may now be changing. Walker[15] believed that at least three separate categories of endeavor were included under curriculum development, a distinction which may be helpful to educational leaders. These categories are related closely to the first two perspectives of curriculum, namely, the ideal and the formal. The three categories consisted of (1) curriculum policy making or "the establishment of limits, criteria, guidelines, and the like with which curricula must comply, without developing actual plans and materials for use by students and teachers"; (2) generic curriculum development, which includes "the preparation of curriculum plans and materials for use potentially by *any* students or teachers of a given description"; and (3) site-specific curriculum development or "the many measures taken in a particular school or district to bring about curriculum change there." These distinctions are not generally seen in discussions of curriculum development; all three aspects are part of an overall process which might lead to changes in the school and classroom if successful, but the requirements for effective functioning in the three different areas are different in important ways.

Curriculum policy making and generic curriculum development are critical components of the overall process of curriculum development but are not determined directly by school administrators in their role of instructional leaders of the district or the school. They must know about and take into account these two categories and can try to influence them in their general role of professional educators and as citizens and parents. The wide literature on curriculum and its development seems most applicable to these two categories, in their theoretical approaches and in their general guidelines, even though they often are directed toward local curriculum developers and users.

Site-Specific Curriculum Development

The third category, that of site-specific curriculum development, is of direct relevance to the educational administrator. This category is seen as involving four basic tasks for which the administrator has a major responsibility:

1. *The need for a curriculum change at the site must be established* to the satisfaction of those involved;
2. *Available generic plans and materials must be examined* for their suitability to the local situation;
3. *Generic materials must be adapted to site-specific conditions,* or, if suitable generic materials are not available, *site-specific plans and materials must be developed;* and
4. *Steps must be taken to implement the new program* as standard operating procedure at the site.[16]

Walker specified some basic considerations and concerns of which administrators should be aware in site-specific curriculum development: Funds are often scarce for those activities not essential for ongoing school functioning, with the

[15] Decker F. Walker, "Approaches to Curriculum Development," in *Value Conflicts and Curriculum Issues,* pp. 267–277.
[16] *Ibid.,* p. 270.

likelihood that such funds will become even more scarce in the future; the concentration of time, money, and effort is usually on the implementation stage; local problems and needs are usually identified through an informal, unfunded process; a priority is placed upon smoothly functioning day-to-day operations; generic expertise in subject matter, psychology, and evaluation may be quite limited since the local teachers and administrators are usually the sole participants; and major publishers are relied upon for suitable materials. However, the local participants know vital site-specific information, such as community attitudes, available resources, student achievement levels, interests, and aspirations, and the distinctive characteristics of the local teachers.

Guidelines to Selecting and Organizing Curriculum

It may be useful to reiterate briefly some of the basic priorities which are generally agreed upon by curriculum developers in selecting and organizing curriculum and which the educational administrator can use as guidelines when examining generic materials or developing site-specific materials. Some of these priorities are including only the most valid and significant content, knowledge of fundamental underlying structure that is accessible to exploration, and content according to the extent that it reveals the characteristic spirit and method of inquiry within the fundamental discipline; giving preference to content which promotes the learners' continuing intellectual development, develops a perspective of the world today, and contributes to an understanding of the phenomenon of change; and choosing content which offers a wide range of intellectual challenge, develops a sequential continuity of learning, and maintains consistency with a central curriculum focus. There are other equally important guidelines that the administrator will want to develop and consider.

Minimum Competency Testing Programs

The formal curriculum, as part of curriculum development, is being greatly influenced by legislative decrees and state guidelines in the form of minimum competency testing legislation. The educational administrator in a state which has adopted such legislation is aware both of the complexities which it brings and the potential impact on the curriculum as, for example, in focusing attention on the basic skills. Over half the states now have legislation for some type of assessment of their elementary and secondary students in terms of competencies, and many states require the demonstration of some minimum level of competency in certain areas as a prerequisite for a high school diploma.

In a recent book, Jaeger and Tittle presented a series of papers which they believed would be useful to school administrators not only in some of the technical aspects of the design of competency testing programs but also how those programs "are likely to affect their curricula, the psychological well-being of their students and teachers, and some of the most important policies that determine their authority in running the schools." In a summary chapter, they concluded that "competency testing is social and political dynamite" and that with the "state controlling the extrinsic rewards of schooling, control of instructional content and process cannot long remain in local hands."[17]

This brief reference to the book by Jaeger and Tittle in no way attempts to summarize its contents or to substitute for a careful reading of the various papers. Rather, it is included because state legislation, and the public demand behind it, is such a powerful force in the public schools. It is clear that state-mandated competency testing will grow both geographically and in its uniformity. Most of the research to be reviewed in the next section of this chapter indicates a growing body of usable results in the area of basic skills, and basic skills are the integral concern of minimum competency testing programs. There is both a challenge and an opportunity for the instructional leader to take into account the results of the research while attempting to influence the carrying out of the state's mandates in a constructive manner and in the best interests of the students.

CURRICULUM IMPLEMENTATION

Of the five perspectives of curriculum discussed earlier in this chapter, two perspectives—the ideal and the formal—dealt with that phase of curriculum, broadly defined, which may be regarded as the development of curriculum to the point of actual classroom instruction. It also has become clear that what happens after the teacher closes the classroom door is the implementation of the instructional program for the students, which is not always related in significant fashion to the first two perspectives. The last three perspectives—the instructional, the operational, and the experiential curricula—have finally to do with the teaching–learning act and with student outcomes. Included are the "whole" teacher, how the teacher chooses to adapt the formal curriculum, what the teacher does in the moment-to-moment teaching act, and how the students perceive their instruction and the curriculum. What influence does the educational administrator have upon these three curricula? What knowledge is required? And what proficiencies should be used?

"The Quiet Revolution"

A large and growing number of educational researchers, research reviewers, and analysts of massive surveys of research reviews are claiming that there has been a "quiet revolution" in educational research in the last decade. They claim that this research has produced an understanding of some of the variables or factors that directly influence learning in the classroom and has yielded a number of consistent, positive results on the relationship of learning outcomes to instructional conditions. As the 1960s produced a considerable number of curriculum innovations, national curricula, and "new" approaches to the disciplines, so the 1970s may have produced usable descriptions of effective instructional conditions that

[17]Richard M. Jaeger and Carol Kehr Tittle, eds., *Minimum Competency Achievement Testing: Motives, Models, Measures, and Consequences* (Berkeley, Calif.: McCutchan Publishing Corporation, 1980), pp. vi, 367, 484–487.

have definite policy and administrative implications for the educational leader. To back their claims, the educational researchers have analyzed, methodically and carefully, literally hundreds of research studies.

The effort was made in this chapter to describe some of the major findings of this burgeoning research, especially those findings which seem to have operational significance for educational administrators. Obviously, only a very limited reporting of the research is possible and many important reports and conclusions will not be included here. However, a limited set of themes and interpretations, often in contradiction to each other, have emerged, and these can be reported with some degree of thoroughness.

This research has focused on teacher effectiveness, and the researchers indicated that the focus has evolved, or at least changed, in its direction. Earlier studies sought for effectiveness in the personality traits or characteristics of teachers, until both the complexity of the lists and the lack of usable results turned attention to the methods of teaching being used. It then shifted to the effects on learning of the classroom climate created and maintained by the teacher. More recently, it has focused upon the mastery of a set of competencies by the teacher and the ability to use those competencies appropriately or on professional decision making in a context of professional knowledge and proficiencies.[18]

There also have been changes in the research methodologies used in analyzing teacher effectiveness and a continuing disagreement as to the methodologies that are the most appropriate. The nonresearcher, educational administrator, who seeks as a practitioner to learn from the research studies, will find this to be a sharp but bewildering argument. There are discussions of conventional research with its factorial design and randomization procedures, process–product approaches, clinical inquiry, ecological theory, and variations of these methodologies. It will be up to other writers to describe the nature of this argument and to attempt its resolution; the limited goal here is to seek from documented sources that which appears to be usable to the administrator, with the knowledge that there is also a great danger of being simplistic.

Research-Documented Significant Instructional Components

In an article which provided the caption for the previous section of this chapter, Walberg, Schiller, and Haertel reported the results of their careful review of a systematic collection of research reviews.[19] These reviews included those published from January 1969 to the time of the report and included research on all levels of schooling in instructional and related areas. They also made available to the reader a comprehensive three-page appendix listing the reviews that were the basis of their report.

They concluded that certain instructional conditions consistently produced

[18] Donald M. Medley, "The Effectiveness of Teachers," in *Research on Teaching: Concepts, Findings, and Implications,* eds. Penelope L. Peterson and Herbert J. Walberg (Berkeley, Calif.: McCutchan Publishing Corporation, 1979), pp. 12–16.

[19] Herbert J. Walberg, Diane Schiller, and Geneva D. Haertel, "The Quiet Revolution in Educational Research," *Phi Delta Kappan,* 61, no. 3 (November 1979), 179–183.

favorable learning outcomes, that other conditions were plausible but less confidence could be placed in their effects, that certain conditions still required much more research, and that there was no set of conditions that was superior on all outcomes. They found that the following methods or conditions have a consistent positive effect on learning outcomes: time allocated for instruction or used for learning, for cognitive learning; smaller class size for significant learning benefits; mastery learning for superior results in achievement, retention and attitudes; programmed instruction for more favorable effects on achievement and interest; direct instruction for achievement gains, though they believed that the results should be interpreted cautiously; the use of adjunct questions, advance organizers, and the analytic revisions of instruction; and the impact of innovative curricula on tests that reflect the intent of those curricula. They described a number of other instructional conditions and also concluded that much research was still required in outcomes on such traits as creativity, self-concept, independence, and ethical maturity.

Brophy reviewed several recent, large-scale field correlational studies at the elementary school level and concluded that there was strong support for generalizations about teacher behavior and student learning.[20] Included were generalizations of significance to administrators, such as certain teachers, more successful in bringing about student learning than are other teachers, exhibit a consistent difference in their teaching behavior; specific teaching behaviors are rarely appropriate in all situations, but several patterns of behavior consistently produce learning gains; teachers who believe and act as though their basic role is to instruct students in the curriculum are more successful than are teachers who do not; "effective teachers know how to organize and maintain a classroom learning environment that maximizes the time spent engaged in productive activities and minimizes the time lost during transitions, periods of confusion, or disruptions that require disciplinary action"; the various elements of direct instruction are supported as being effective and include a structured curriculum, direct instruction from the teacher working with the whole class, a teacher-maintained academic focus, and high success rates in answering teacher questions; and all the specific findings vary to some extent with the ability level of the pupils, the context, and the grade level.

Brophy also reviewed studies at the junior and senior high school levels and found that, while everything was not directly applicable from the described findings concerning direct instruction, certain aspects were similar. For example, at the secondary level growth in reading skills was associated with "maximizing time on task, instructing the total group most of the time, directing questions to specific students (rather than to volunteers), regularly providing feedback, controlling negative behavior, encouraging positive behavior, and using guides and probing questions when students do not know the answer." Similar correlations were found in various mathematics and algebra studies. However, this similarity was found only to the extent that the primary goal was basic skills mastery; there was not a similar relationship between direct instruction in English classes and student learning, for example.

[20] Jere E. Brophy, "Teacher Behavior and Student Learning," *Educational Leadership,* 37, no. 1 (October 1979), 33–38.

Direct Instruction

Rosenshine focused on the research dealing with the opportunity to learn or the content which is covered, the number of minutes the student paid attention to the instructional activity or was academically engaged, and on direct instruction. His review was limited to instruction in reading and mathematics achievement of elementary students, and he cautioned against implementing the findings into evaluative checklists for teachers. Under direct instruction, the results of recent studies were grouped under "academic focus, grouping students for instruction, whether the teacher or the students select classroom activities, questioning, and management." In the studies reviewed the effective or successful teachers were those who spent less time on nonacademic activities and maintained a strong academic focus, were strong leaders and directed instructional activities rather than the students doing so, provided supervision and adult monitoring of the students' activities, and used factual questions and controlled practice on materials where the student error rate was low.

Rosenshine was concerned that there might be something grim about the implications of direct instruction for the formal classroom as a cold, regimented, humorless place. However, he found that the research data to now did not show negative side effects of direct instruction and that teachers of formal classrooms could be warm and flexible and could permit much freedom of movement. But the "worst situation with respect both to students' engaged time and to gain in achievement, was found when teachers were high in affect but low in cognitive emphasis."[21]

Peterson, however, cautioned that the strong suggestions that direct instruction is the most effective way of teaching, in the recent reviews of research on teaching, could be simplistic. She believed that only several of the many studies comparing traditional and open teaching had been considered and that questions should still be explored as to what educational outcomes were considered, for what kinds of students, and where direct or indirect ways of teaching were the most effective. Her conclusion, after a review of the research, indicated that, for increased student achievement, the direct approach might be, on the average, slightly better than an open approach. But the open approach appeared to be better "for increasing students' creativity, independence, curiosity, and favorable attitudes toward school and learning." Also the research suggested that the open approach could be more effective for some students, while other students could do better in a more direct approach. Some general implications for educational leaders are obvious: They must consider what educational objectives are to be met and what the students' needs are, and neither approach is sufficient by itself.[22]

Time as Related to Academic Achievement

Berliner added significant information in the area of time devoted to academic activities in a report of the Beginning Teacher Evaluation Study (BTES) in California. This research project has been conducted since the early 1970s and ultimately

[21] Barak V. Rosenshine, "Content, Time, and Direct Instruction," in *Research on Teaching,* pp. 28–56.

[22] Penelope L. Peterson, "Direct Instruction Reconsidered," in Penelope L. Peterson and Herbert J. Walberg, eds., *Research on Teaching: Concepts, Findings, and Implications* (Berkeley, Calif.: McCutchan Publishing Corporation, 1979), pp. 57–69.

focused on three measures of time: allocated time, engaged time, and academic learning time (ALT). These include the time provided for instruction in a particular area of content, the time a student is actually attending to instruction in that area, and the time a student is working with instructional activities or materials that are at an easy level of difficulty.

Allocated time varied widely among classrooms; for example, one class spent 400 minutes on linear measurement in mathematics while another class spent only 29 minutes in the same area. Engaged time in reading or mathematics instruction also varied dramatically. For example, in fifth grade reading there was a range of engaged time per day in the classes studied of between 48 and 119 minutes per day. Differences in academic learning time were similarly large.

Berliner raised the question of whether it was fair to the students and their parents to allow teachers such latitude in what is taught and whether it would be desirable to have a tighter control of the functional curriculum of the classroom.[23] These are, of course, important questions for educational administrators and should lead them to consider further the relationship of student achievement to a few classroom procedures which are highly susceptible to change.

Alterable Variables

Bloom stressed the importance of the methodological shift in educational research from considering stable or static variables to considering variables that are alterable. He considered this shift to be the most important change and central to the major revolution that has taken place in educational research in the last decade. He believed that the number of alterable variables was still small but that their consideration could greatly improve student learning. Among these important alterable variables he included time on task; cognitive entry characteristics or the "specific knowledge, abilities, or skills that are essential prerequisites for the learning of a particular school subject or a particular learning task"; the use of formative testing rather than only summative testing; qualities of teaching rather than of teachers; and some home environmental factors.[24] This perspective raises some interesting questions for the educational leader: How alterable is teacher behavior? How can that behavior be altered? What influence does the instructional leader have in promoting such altered behavior? Does the way in which the school is organized have an influence on alterable variables?

Teacher Effectiveness in Classrooms of Disadvantaged Pupils

Medley made a careful analysis of 289 empirical studies of teacher effectiveness, using four criteria of quality to screen those studies. The four criteria were a definition of effective teaching, a description of competent teacher behavior, evidence for the generalizability of the findings, and process–product relationships

---

[23] David C. Berliner, "Tempus Educare," in *Research on Teaching*, pp. 120–135.

[24] Benjamin S. Bloom, "The New Direction in Educational Research: Alterable Variables," *Phi Delta Kappan*, 61, no. 6 (February 1980), 382–385.

that had a practical importance. Only fourteen studies met the criteria but they yielded 613 relationships, many of which were verified in more than one study and so could be referred to as being dependable.

The findings of this report are similar to those just discussed and to many similar reports not discussed in this chapter. However, Medley focused on the behaviors of teachers in the primary grades with pupils of low socioeconomic status. He concluded that the research provided detailed information about the behavior of teachers who were effective in such situations. These successful teachers maintained a supportive and orderly classroom climate, devoted more time to academic activities in whole-class grouping rather than small-group activities or independent seatwork, and used more low-level questions and fewer pupil-initiated questions. The first type of behavior, maintaining an orderly classroom, tends to fit in with the ordinary knowledge of administrators. However, the remaining two, dealing with groupings and method of instruction, do not fit into the usual fund of ordinary knowledge.

Medley concluded that the chance that the findings he reported might be altered by future research are negligible and that, therefore, the implications of the findings for teacher in-service education, evaluation, and accountability could almost be regarded as imperatives. He believed that the research strongly indicated "a substantial, if not dramatic, improvement in achievement, in attitudes toward school, and of disadvantaged pupils' self-images would result" if teachers were held accountable for their teaching behaviors in the three areas described and if "these qualities were used as the basis of selection, retention, merit pay, and so forth." These are strong words from a researcher and particularly challenging ones for instructional leaders.[25]

Changes in Teacher Behavior

Joyce reported on an extensive, ten-year, research project to develop methods for teachers to expand their repertoire of models of teaching. Models of teaching were divided into four categories and consisted of teaching strategies based upon theories of learning and development designed to promote certain kinds of learning. The last four years of the project to the time of the report included a series of studies to determine whether teachers "could practice models of teaching that required patterns of behavior considerably different from those that are normally observed in the classroom." The various studies included in this research project showed that teacher candidates could learn a variety of models and use them at will. These teachers generally used their old style of teaching when they did not choose to use a learned model of teaching, and the researchers came to the belief that trying to modify the general teaching style of teachers was not as fruitful as was the acquisition of a repertory that could be used at will and when it seemed to be appropriate to the teacher.

Other studies showed that in-service teachers could acquire models of teaching at about the same rate as preservice teachers. Subsequent work demonstrated that the capability to use a considerable variety of models could be acquired by

[25] Medley, "Effectiveness of Teachers," in *Research on Teaching,* pp. 16–26.

teachers if the following factors were present: adequate time, demonstrations on videotape and with actual children, practice with small groups of children, the provision of feedback, and help to determine where the teaching approaches were appropriate within the curriculum.[26]

The research seems clear in demonstrating that teachers can acquire new and different teaching behaviors which they can use at will. Other research indicates various types of teaching behaviors that could produce learning results in specific situations and for specific educational objectives. The actions that educational administrators take to try to influence the behavior of others is not within the realm of this chapter. Some specific implications of the literature will be discussed in the next chapter, but the processes of leadership, administrative behavior, and decision making are topics for other approaches to educational administration.

SOME IMPORTANT PROBLEMS AND ISSUES

Educational researchers are considering a number of problems and issues in the areas of curriculum, instruction, and learning, within the new viewpoint of bringing the results to bear on the real world of the public schools. Every report seems to end with more questions than were considered originally. It is more appropriate that the type of questions and answers that would stem from the discussion in this chapter be reserved for the following chapter concerning the operational implications. However, there is the great danger that the various research reports, both those reported here and the many more that were not, could lead to mistaken actions unless several cautions are kept in mind. These cautions, in themselves, contain a myriad of problems and issues and can be described somewhat as follows:

1. Useful data and insights have been derived from scholars in education with different viewpoints and perceptions and from research following different methodologies. There appears to be a continuing controversy among the scholars and the researchers as to how rational the complex area of schooling is and which methodology gives the more valid results.
2. Any method of research, even that based upon the assumption that the process is nonrational, proceeds in a rational fashion and is reported similarly. This could lead the users of the results into mistaken action if they confuse the rationality of the reporting for the nature of the process being researched.
3. The research reports will not be seen for what they are—reports with great significance for educational administrators but, nevertheless, limited in scope. They give insights into parts of the educational process but should not be confused with the whole process. On the other hand, even though they may only explore a small part of the process, the administrators cannot wait until the whole context is surveyed and understood. That may take generations, but school starts tomorrow.
4. Although the researchers are starting to claim some operational significance for their results, they also point out the limitations of those results. Each

[26] Bruce R. Joyce, *Selecting Learning Experiences: Linking Theory and Practice* (Washington, D.C.: Association for Supervision and Curriculum Development, 1978), pp. 4, 35–39.

real situation must be analyzed carefully to see what information is pertinent.

5. The results must not be oversold or overinterpreted. There are no panaceas and no operational procedures that do not call for thoughtful planning and pragmatic implementation.

6. There are at least three limitations of the literature and the research, even if their implications have great validity: (a) the findings represent only a small part of factors relevant to increasing teacher effectiveness, (b) the quality of instruction has not really had much attention from the researchers as has the process of instruction, and (c) the research has essentially concentrated on making the status quo in education more effective and has said little or nothing about basic changes in schooling.

SELECTED REFERENCES

Alfonso, Robert J., Gerald R. Firth, and Richard F. Neville, *Instructional Supervision: A Behavior System.* Boston: Allyn & Bacon, Inc., 1975.

Ellena, William J., ed., *Curriculum Handbook for School Executives.* Arlington, Va.: American Association of School Administrators, 1973.

Goodlad, John I., *What Schools Are For.* (Bloomington, Ind.: Phi Delta Kappan Educational Foundation, 1979.

Gorton, Richard A., *School Administration: Challenge and Opportunity for Leadership.* Dubuque, Iowa: William C. Brown Co., Publishers, 1976.

Jaeger, Richard M., and Carol Kehr Tittle, eds., *Minimum Competency Achievement Testing: Motives, Models, Measures, and Consequences.* Berkeley, Calif.: McCutchan Publishing Corporation, 1980.

Joyce, Bruce R., *Selecting Learning Experiences: Linking Theory and Practice.* Washington, D.C.: Association for Supervision and Curriculum Development, 1978.

——, and Marsha Weil, *Models of Teaching* (2nd ed.). Englewood Cliffs, N.J.: Prentice-Hall, Inc., 1980.

Lindblom, Charles E., and David K. Cohen, *Usable Knowledge: Social Science and Social Problem Solving.* New Haven, Conn.: Yale University Press, 1979.

Michaelis, John U., Ruth H. Grossman, and Lloyd F. Scott, *New Designs for Elementary Curriculum and Instruction* (2nd ed.). New York: McGraw-Hill Book Company, 1975.

Peterson, Penelope L., and Herbert J. Walberg, eds., *Research on Teaching: Concepts, Findings, and Implications.* Berkeley, Calif.: McCutchan Publishing Corporation, 1979.

Schaffarzick, Jon, and David H. Hampson, eds., *Strategies for Curriculum Development.* Berkeley, Calif.: McCutchan Publishing Corporation, 1975.

——, and Gary Sykes, *Value Conflicts and Curriculum Issues: Lessons from Research and Experience.* Berkeley, Calif.: McCutchan Publishing Corporation, 1979.

16

CURRICULUM
and INSTRUCTION:
OPERATIONAL
IMPLICATIONS*

If the literature of the last decade in the areas of curriculum and instruction is considered with care, a number of significant implications emerge as guidelines for administrative behavior in those areas. The previous chapter included a brief overview of that literature and some of its important themes and interpretations. This chapter will explore some of the implications for administrative planning and activities. It must be acknowledged that this exploration has many limitations, that other interpretations are possible, that new insights will emerge as the literature grows, and that the administrator must keep in mind the cautions listed at the end of the last chapter. However, it must also be acknowledged that a sufficient base of information is now available to make constructive suggestions for more effective instructional leadership. Some educational administrators already seem to be utilizing that information.

*Prepared in large part by John P. Matlin, assistant dean, School of Education, University of California, Berkeley.

Following are some of the more critical generalizations derived from the literature on curriculum and instruction which seem to have important operational implications:

- In the last two decades, a considerable number of curriculum innovations, national curricula, and new approaches to the various disciplines or subjects have been developed.
- School districts and individual schools have undergone great stress and significant institutional change as a result of many powerful societal forces as well as the educational developments just summarized.
- The individual classroom has appeared to be little influenced in its instructional operations by either the educational developments or the societal forces noted, except for scattered exceptions.
- Research in curriculum and instruction has focused in the past decade on factors that bring about more effective teaching behaviors in the classroom within the general, current orientation toward public schooling; there seems to have been at least a temporary cessation of major efforts to bring about radical changes in the system of schooling itself.
- The current interpretations of educational research have indicated that, in accordance with ordinary knowledge but contrary to some of the previous interpretations of past research, the behavior of teachers in the classrooms is an extremely significant variable in terms of the learning that takes place in the individual classrooms.
- Various specific aspects of teaching behavior have been found to be significant in terms of criteria used in research; some aspects are congruent with ordinary knowledge, but others seem to be contrary to such knowledge.
- Much of the current knowledge about effective teaching behaviors seems to be particularly relevant for improved learning by children of low socioeconomic status.
- Some of the more significant aspects of instructional conditions generally and teaching behavior specifically that are consistently related to favorable learning outcomes include academic learning time, mastery learning, academic focus, whole class grouping, strong teacher leadership, classroom management, questioning strategies used, high success ratio in the answering of questions, and smaller class size. These are alterable variables.
- However, specific teaching behaviors or sets of instructional conditions are not superior on all outcomes or appropriate for all situations. The behaviors listed seem to have consistently positive effects on achievement in the basic skills, particularly in reading and mathematics. But some researchers and educational practitioners are finding those behaviors to be effective in other subject areas and for other outcomes.
- Teachers can and will learn different models of teaching or teaching styles. These different models or styles are acquired in addition to the old style of teaching and can be used at will when considered appropriate by the teacher.
- The conditions of in-service education needed to acquire the new teaching styles have been researched and include the factors of adequate time to learn, demonstrations, practice with small groups, feedback, and help in determining the appropriateness within the curriculum of the new teaching approaches.
- However, school districts are not tightly knit educational organizations, and there are only mildly responsive relationships between the various elements

of the school system; those elements include school boards and superintendents, principals, and teachers. In instructional matters, the various levels are characterized by autonomy, with a "loose coupling" among the principal, teacher, curriculum, and the student.

Other equally important generalizations may be derived from the current literature, but those listed are sufficient to serve as guidelines for possible lines of action by boards of education and by educational administrators. These guidelines include general implications for policy making in public education at all levels of government, general implications for the actions of school boards of education and school administrators, and specific implications in the areas of curriculum development and curriculum implementation by school districts, schools, and classrooms.

SOME GENERAL IMPLICATIONS

The improvement of public school education has been one of the major concerns and bases for action on all levels of government in the United States. There has been a steady growth in legislation, judicial decisions, specially funded projects, and governmental agencies to monitor the various policies and regulations which have been designed to meet that concern. More recently, there seem to be indications of federal and state retrenchment in the financing of public school education, a continued diminution of public support, falling public school enrollments, and a growing emphasis upon accountability and efficient management.

Students of public school education discern a great vulnerability on the part of school systems and schools to the various forces listed. But, as summarized at the beginning of this chapter, there is considerable evidence that past policies and actions have had relatively little impact upon the individual classroom, with the considerable work in curriculum and instruction showing a similar lack of impact. This resistance to outside influence on the classroom has been regarded by some educators as a safeguard against bureaucratic interference at the same time that it may have been a barrier to more effective instructional practices. There now appears to be a danger that policymakers will attempt to use the current knowledge of the nature of curriculum development and implementation to design new policies, rules, and regulations.

Some cautions in using the current knowledge concerning curriculum and instruction were summarized at the end of the last chapter. The various research reports and interpretations of the general knowledge in those areas stress the limited nature of the findings, the efforts to use research methodologies that take into account and take place within the context of the individual school, and the great concern that the school not be seen as a factory subject to rational, technical interventions to improve educational productivity. The emerging understanding of curriculum and instruction does not point toward the further assumption by legislatures and courts of the problems of low academic achievement or indicate the kinds of policy interventions that would correct poor teaching or bolster student learning. If anything has become apparent, it is the great harm to educational functioning that can result from such an assumption.

Unfortunately, a compelling argument has been made that governmental policy-makers are using research models prematurely as a basis for designing accountability and assessment programs. Wise[1] theorized that the rationalistic approach of some researchers in studying the schools leads policymakers to believe that schools are rationalistic and to use this belief as a basis for making their decisions. He saw an inevitable movement toward "incremental bureaucratic centralization" of the educational system if the preceding approach and other forces in our society continue, with each policy intervention contributing to the further bureaucratization and centralization of education. He believed that "To the extent that educators accept the bureaucratic conception of the school, the more bureaucratic will the schools become *in fact*." He concluded further that policy intervention generally cannot solve problems of low productivity in education; that teachers' organizations may contribute to excessive rationalization of the role of the teacher, even as teachers as individuals resist that conception of their role; and that centralization and hyperrationalization will increase to the extent that demands for improvement of the educational system are addressed to policymakers rather than to the educational system.

Wise proposed that "*schools and colleges should be held responsible for the production of education, while other levels and branches of government should be held responsible for ensuring equity within schools and colleges.*" This seems to be a far cry from the traditional calls in the past for leadership from the federal government and from state educational agencies. However, the reports of research in curriculum and instruction in the last decade seem to present some easy solutions for intervention by the governmental policymakers and thus the implications of that research may have some profoundly negative consequences. For example, it may be attractive for a federal project manager to impose a rigid standard for academic learning time (ALT) in reading and arithmetic for all recipients of federal grant money without regard for the many factors which make each classroom unique in the teaching-learning transaction. This requirement could be further compounded by the massive movement toward competency-based education and growing state legislation to restrict promotion and the granting of high school diplomas to those students who can pass minimum competency tests in designated areas.

The operational implications of the knowledge regarding curriculum and instruction for governmental policymakers seem to become clearer in terms of the actions those policymakers should *not* take. However, a review of their emerging actions appears to indicate that they are taking such actions and will continue to do so with much support from the public. The possibilities for negative policy making are many and can be met, if not withstood, by educational leaders with a firm foundation in curriculum and an understanding of the complexities of the instructional process. Of even greater importance, can the educational administrator give constructive leadership to meeting the growing governmental mandates while utilizing in a

[1] Arthur E. Wise, *Legislated Learning: The Bureaucratization of the American Classroom* (Berkeley, Calif.: University of California Press, 1979), pp. xi, 94, 199–207.

particular school district or school the knowledge and understandings now available in curriculum and instruction?

Local School Boards of Education

If the basic function of the school district is the education of the learner, then matters of curriculum and instruction should be the focus of the basic policy-making and administrative decisions made by the local boards. There has been a strong pressure to make political instead of educational decisions in light of powerful forces, including retrenchment because of declining enrollments and shrinking financial support, the demands of collective bargaining, legislative mandates, and the continuing demand for improved achievement scores for minority children. This focus implies that boards must ask their administration for plans that outline the curriculum and instructional programs, seek information about the educational functioning of the classrooms, give help to teachers and administrators in the improvement of the instructional program, assess the progress of student and staff performance, and provide the necessary resources for staff development and for the longitudinal implementation of the plans.

There are some encouraging outcomes where such an orientation toward curriculum and instruction is used as a basis for policy making. Talmage and Eash reported a five-year study of desegregation of a school district whose focus was on the variables of curriculum and instruction within a specified improvement effort.[2] The plan called for the help of a nearby university to set up an "evaluation research design to provide information that could be used by the school board to formulate policy and by the administrative staff to help in developing the curriculum and instruction program." The plan was carried out over a five-year period, a data base was established on the learning environments and achievement, and it very soon became apparent that curriculum and instruction required considerable attention. In the first three years achievement gains were limited and an intensive study showed grave deficiencies in the instructional practices as well as a curriculum that was limited in subject matter.

An in-service program was introduced for principals on the monitoring of classroom instruction; principals became aware of curricular deficiencies and the fact that teacher performance varied widely. A commitment was called for to meet specific objectives in instruction and curriculum, with the result that several teachers, who were the lowest performing, resigned rather than meet those commitments. The study reported that "Substantial achievement gains have since been made at each grade level for both races. These gains date from direct attention to curricular and instructional concerns and their interaction." The study concluded that "attention to the variables of curriculum and instruction within a specified improvement effort pays greater dividends than working on the more nebulous interpersonal variables that are the focus of many organizational development projects." They also reported increased personal satisfaction of the students, a

[2] Harriet Talmage and Maurice J. Eash, "Curriculum, Instruction, and Materials," in *Research on Teaching: Concepts, Findings, and Implications*, eds., Penelope L. Peterson and Herbert J. Walberg (Berkeley, Calif.: McCutchan Publishing Corporation, 1979), pp. 172–174.

stabilized school district, greater parental satisfaction with the schools, and a movement toward integration from desegregation. A necessary first step to successful desegregation was attention to curriculum, instruction, and classroom interaction.

Educational Administrators

The general implications for superintendents and principals from the current literature on curriculum and instruction can be summarized briefly. Although educational administrators must be knowledgeable in matters of school management, their basic focus must be on educational leadership. Their key contribution to education is not that of efficient management but an effective instructional program. Goodlad has indicated some of the consequences of this viewpoint. Superintendents have tended to delegate the wrong things. They may delegate management functions as well as the demanding detail for administering the instructional program to the associate superintendent, but they must not delegate the responsibility for the educational program. They must work directly with the principals, as the school is the key unit for change, while building in discretionary time for themselves to think, to plan, and to lead.

Principals must not only be knowledgeable and proficient in matters of curriculum and instruction but must also develop a comprehensive educational plan for their schools and provide the teachers with support, encouragement, and the necessary resources. The principal must expect each teacher to "develop and use a guiding framework of concepts, principles, and methods that appear to influence the learning process positively" and work actively with each teacher to accomplish this task. To be effective, the principal must know the various aspects of democratic working relations with the faculty and also must be able to recognize what such a "guiding framework" entails. The administrator must understand the significance of the statement that "it lies within the capability and is the responsibility of every teacher to develop a comprehensive grasp of those basic elements that comprise the process of instruction." Finally, the principal must develop an agenda based upon local school needs, using that agenda to compare the current instructional program in his or her school with various alternatives, and then plan and project the steps which must be taken toward an improved alternative.[3]

A painful but critical observation should be expressed at this point. The discussion undertaken in the preceding and this chapter has attempted to find the significance, if any, of the current literature on curriculum and instruction for the behavior of the educational administrator. However, another theme has also been discerned in this literature but has not yet been stated. Put simply, in report after report the researchers in curriculum and the interpreters of that research look upon the traditional behavior of educational administrators as one of the greatest stumbling blocks to the improvement of curriculum. In a sense, "the enemy is us," with some scholars in curriculum development also concluding that the currently dominant theory of management is not conducive to the implementation of effective curriculum improvement and must somehow be confronted.

[3] John I. Goodlad, *What Schools Are For* (Bloomington, Ind.: Phi Delta Kappan Educational Foundation, 1979), pp. 89–102.

English is the most recent to articulate the latter conclusion:

> The current management model of schooling has frozen the curriculum. It is preoccupied with time and activities within self-contained units. Uneven learning curves, pupil boredom, excitement, discovery, joy, creativity, are continually "smoothed out" in order to maintain the existing organization design decision. While doing so may be anachronistic to learning, it is *compatible* with the definition of schooling."[4]

SOME SPECIFIC OPERATIONAL IMPLICATIONS

Some specific, operational inferences may be drawn from the literature in the areas of curriculum development and implementation by school districts, local schools, and individual classrooms. The subjective act of inference should be recognized within any statement of implication. Thus, the suggested specificity is not to be interpreted to mean a detailed plan of action for a specific school district or school or to deny the interrelatedness of the various areas to be discussed. Each institution must, of course, draw its own inferences and chart its own course of action in light of the myriad of variables and the dynamics of human relationships in its own community.

A few selected topics within the general scope of curriculum and instruction will be considered in the remainder of this chapter. These topics include the development of curriculum guides or courses of study, selection and usage of instructional materials, selection and usage of instructional technology, standards of achievement and minimum competency testing, instructional strategies and instructional techniques, mainstreaming of handicapped children, and implementation of federal categorical programs. No doubt there are other equally important topics that should be considered, and the discussion of the chosen topics will not be comprehensive.

In considering these various topics, the effort will not be made to reconstruct the massive literature available in each of them. Nor will the importance and power of the many other forces which govern the actual functioning of the public schools be denied. Rather, a limited exploration of the relevance of the current literature on curriculum for educational leadership will be the goal.

The Development of Curriculum Guides or Courses of Study

It is assumed that all activity in the area of curriculum and instruction, on any level of the school district, is aimed toward an ultimate impact on classroom instruction and student learning. Otherwise, all such activity becomes essentially meaningless in the context of the basic function of public school education. Although Goodlad differentiated among the five perspectives of curriculum, the first four perspectives (ideal, formal, instructional, operational) are without purpose if they do not lead to the last perspective (experiential). The development of a course

---

[4] Fenwick W. English, "Curriculum Development Within the School System," in *Considered Action for Curriculum Improvement*, ed. Arthur W. Foshay (Alexandria, Va.: Association for Supervision and Curriculum Development, 1980), p. 152.

of study or curriculum guide within a school district is a common venture and one which can be considered broadly enough to touch all five curriculum perspectives and to be subject to scrutiny from many of the findings of the current literature on curriculum and instruction.

The following discussion will be narrowed to a certain type of curriculum guide development but will be explored in much greater detail than subsequent topics. This was done both because the topic includes many of the other topics by implication and to set a context for the discussion of the other topics and for those not covered in this chapter. A brief description of guidelines and procedures usually followed in developing a districtwide course of study or curriculum guide is offered first; then some emerging concerns derived from the current literature on curriculum and instruction are considered as they apply to the usual procedures and to educational leadership.

Guidelines and procedures usually followed. The local school board, in formal session, instructs the superintendent that a course of study or curriculum guide must be developed in a certain area or that a course of study in that area must be revised completely and improved. The reason or reasons that the board calls for the course of study, the subject or area involved, and the grade level or levels for which it is to be designed will have a great deal to do with how the development of the course of study proceeds. These factors will also help to determine the nature of community involvement, the types of task forces or committees established by the superintendent, the scope of involvement of teachers and administrators from the various schools for which the course of study is being planned, and the type of outside help and consultant service that is employed.

The leadership of the endeavor, partially dependent upon the size of the school district, will usually be delegated to the curriculum director, subject supervisors, building principals, or department chairs, the delegation depending upon whether the curriculum guide is for the whole district, a particular school, or a single subject offering within a school.

The specific situation will also determine the form in which the particular course of study will include the components of curriculum construction as agreed to by theorists and practitioners: "identification of educational goals and objectives; selection and organization of content, learning activities, and teaching processes; and evaluation of student outcomes and the effectiveness of the design process."[5] It would also be expected that the guidelines for selecting and organizing content, as discussed in the previous chapter, would be used.

Surveys will probably be made of commercially available teaching and learning materials, particularly textbooks, under whatever regulations are established by the particular state for such materials and under the policies of the local board of education. Materials will be recommended for purchase and incorporated into the course of study. The materials may be used as purchased, adapted to local needs, or augmented if they are weak in specific areas.

What will probably result will be a curriculum guide or course of study, either broadly or narrowly designed, depending upon the original charge by the board of

[5] Geneva Gay, "Conceptual Models of the Curriculum-Planning Process," in *Considered Action for Curriculum Improvement*, p. 120.

education. Further, as asserted in a treatment of secondary school teaching methods, the teacher today "is more likely to be given a curriculum guide or resource unit which provides him with suggestions and aids which he adapts and uses as he sees fit."[6] Many sources confirm the validity of the latter observation not only for the secondary but also for the elementary schools and teachers.

Emerging concerns regarding the usual procedures. Although the usual procedures for developing an area of curriculum within a school district were described only briefly, they are considered to be basically sound procedures and represent a fairly accurate picture of what generally occurs. The usual outcome, in light of past experience, can also be predicted for most of such curriculum development:

> Most school district personnel in curriculum have no idea of the extent to which any given curriculum spelled out in a guide is being followed; nor do they know, if it were followed, the degree of variation from teacher to teacher, department to department, school to school, or subdistrict to subdistrict of the total system. Drawing together a group of representative personnel who write a new curriculum guide is moving from one hypothetical curriculum to another.[7]

English pointed out further that curriculum guides tend to be global kinds of guides which set up topics and their sequence in a particular K–12 system but that leave it up to the teachers to decide the pacing, emphasis, repetition, or even the amount of time. In a recent newspaper article a principal of a school with a large proportion of socioeconomically disadvantaged children who were doing poorly on the basic skills was quoted as saying that in his school the teachers use their time as they see fit; he did not know how long they spent on skills each day. Other districts were quoted regarding how long teachers *were supposed* to spend on reading, language, and mathematics.

Yet there is a rather massive research that is claimed to show conclusively that the most powerful variable associated with student achievement, particularly in the basic skills and for socioeconomically disadvantaged children, is time on task and academic learning time. Are there many principals who do not believe that it is part of instructional leadership to know at least how much time their teachers allocate to the basic skills each day? Is the number even greater of those principals who do not include also the time devoted to the task or the materials and methods used in instruction? What is the role of the superintendent as the instructional leader of the district regarding those principals?

Curriculum development on a districtwide basis will tend to have greater similarity to generic curriculum development than to site-specific curriculum development. It will be designed to be used potentially by any type of students or teachers and consequently will probably be used little by any specific teachers or students. Site-specific curriculum development criteria must be incorporated as a phase of districtwide efforts if there is to be any expectation that the new program will become

[6] Leonard H. Clark and Irving S. Starr, *Secondary School Teaching Methods*, 3rd ed. (New York: Macmillan Publishing Co., Inc., 1976), p. 40.
[7] English, "Curriculum Development," in *Considered Action for Curriculum Improvement*, p. 149.

standard operating procedure in the specific classroom. The documented research on the lack of introduction into the classroom of curriculum innovations strongly corroborates the preceding generalization.

The research explored in curriculum and instruction, the amounts of money which have been expended in school districts for the development of districtwide curriculum guides, and the documented small impact of curriculum innovations upon the classroom all point to a probable ineffective usage of school resources in terms of money, time, and effort. Some suggestions and recommendations are emerging from the current literature that are directly relevant for educational administrators in the more effective use of available resources.

Some specific suggestions for curriculum development. Several specific suggestions made by Czajkowski and Patterson to curriculum workers and administrators, as derived from their theoretical analysis of curriculum change, are relevant to this discussion. The district administrator has significant impact on program improvement by a perceived expression of interest and by providing adequate support in terms of resources. The principal must give active, strong support to the program and create a school climate that fosters the program. The new curriculum must be "reinvented" in each school by the teachers and the administrators; it cannot be transferred as an entity to any new situation but must go through the complex interactions which are necessary to make it "their" curriculum. The process of learning the new curriculum is a long, nonlinear process and requires different kinds of support at different phases. An ongoing part of any school curriculum change must include continuous staff development. And, finally, program improvement at the school should include coordination of curriculum activities, the staff development activities, and the program evaluation activities.[8]

Patterson and Czajkowski gave some additional suggestions to educational administrators to achieve successful implementation of new curriculum. These suggestions include extensive planning for the implementation, provision of sufficient resources for the period of time necessary for implementation, planning for the involvement of the teachers who will use the curriculum, consideration of the importance of communication while implementation is going on, consideration of the culture of the school as it affects how and what change will actually occur, and the provision of adequate staff development opportunities which should include the competencies required not only to implement the curriculum but for resocialization or the changing of certain interactive skills, attitudes, and habits.[9] Their last suggestion seems to parallel the discussion in the previous chapter of interactive problem solving and social learning and gives some indication of going beyond rational or analytical problem solving as the only method to work on social problem solving. For a creative instructional leader, it may represent a breakthrough in having an impact within the classroom on instruction.

For instructional leaders who are concerned with time on task and who are convinced that attention to this variable would increase learning in their school, English

---

[8] Theodore J. Czajkowski and Jerry L. Patterson, "Curriculum Change and the School," in *Considered Action for Curriculum Improvement*, pp. 171-175.

[9] Jerry L. Patterson and Theodore J. Czajowski, "Implimentation: Neglected Phase in Curriculum Change, "*Educational Leadership*, 37, no. 3 (December 1979), 204-206.

described an analytical procedure, called "curriculum mapping," to be used to study the real time and task dimensions encountered by the learner. This technique can be used to get at the significant variation in time spent on the particular learning task and in the content taught among classrooms. It aids in providing a base line of actual time and task emphasis as well as providing a focus for instructional and curricular adjustments.[10]

These specific suggestions can be summarized as follows:

1. Districtwide curriculum development should be limited to basic guides and recommended instructional materials as well as to the provision of consultant aid to the schools. Limited resources should be spent in such endeavors.

2. Curriculum to be implemented in the classroom should go through the process of site-specific curriculum development.

3. There should be a recognition of and provision for the staff development over an extended period of time necessary for ongoing curriculum implementation, and adequate resources should be part of any such efforts.

4. There should be a great reluctance to jump from innovation to innovation; conversely, any innovation or change to be undertaken should be planned with care.

5. Instructional leadership by the superintendent to the principals, and by the principals to their faculties, is an essential part of curriculum improvement.

6. Teachers can and will learn new styles of teaching, given adequate support. Staff development must be planned and financed as carefully as the curriculum project; it must include provisions for interactive problem solving and social learning.

7. Any new curriculum must be adaptable to the specific school and must be adapted by the faculty of that school. A stable faculty is essential in this process; new teachers to the faculty must be continuously brought up to the levels of knowledge and understanding of the other teachers.

8. The principal must use methods to compare the desired curriculum design with what is actually going on in the classroom both so that the design may be adjusted for greater effectiveness and so that instructional staff can receive notice in advance if student performance is falling off because time on task or content taught is not in accord with that necessary for effective instruction.

Other suggestions can be added to this list. However, the educational administrator who has not dealt with curriculum or instructional matters may already be completely discouraged. It should be remembered that these suggestions can be interpreted and implemented variously; that each institution must chart its own course of action; and, as described earlier in this chapter, that the orientation of educational administrators toward curriculum, instruction, and classroom interaction is a long-range commitment. A three-year period just to discover the deficiencies in the instructional practices and design an in-service program for principals is not unreasonable. If there is discouragement with this complex approach and the commitment involved in it, then the question may be asked, What is proposed to improve the curricular program, the instructional program, and student learning?

[10] English, "Curriculum Development," in *Considered Action for Curriculum Improvement*, pp. 153–156.

Discussion of the role of educational administrators in the selection and usage of instructional materials in the context of this chapter will be limited and focused narrowly. A survey of the literature and research in curriculum and instruction reveals at least two areas of limitation: (1) in the availability of research on instructional materials and dependable results that can be used as guidelines for administrative actions and (2) in the emergence of constructive operational implications for educational leadership in the results and interpretations that are available; the operational implications seem to include severe limitations on the effectiveness of instructional leadership. The nature of those limitations as well as more constructive possibilities will be explored.

However, the reason for a narrow focus should be considered first. Explication of the variable of instructional materials by professional curriculum developers generally is broad in scope. For example, in the previous chapter it was defined to include the physical media through which the curriculum as mediated by the instructional program is experienced. In a comprehensive treatment of the analysis, planning, and evaluation of curriculum and current principles of curriculum development, Michaelis, Grossman, and Scott developed the concept of "instructional media." They included within this concept three categories: (1) printed materials, which included a range of materials from textbooks to simulation games; (2) audiovisual materials, which included sound and film resources, realia, pictorial resources, graphic materials and equipment, and so on; and (3) community resources, which included actual trips into the community, the mass media, and locally available printed resources. They also reported specific criteria and procedures for selecting instructional media.[11]

Such comprehensive definitions are necessary for a complete approach to curriculum analysis and for those who specialize in curriculum development. But the current literature and research indicate a different reality for the educational administrator as instructional leader and indicate a much more limited range for constructive action. In 1970 it could be concluded from the research that conventional instructional media (teacher, books, blackboard, maps, pictures, and charts) accounted for about 99 percent of the time of the students in the public school classroom. This was summarized in the statement, "Teacher, books, and a chalkboard sum up the basic technology used with children in virtually all public school classrooms." Instuctional television was used in less than 3 percent of total classroom hours in a study of the sixteen largest school districts.[12]

Ten years later, in a massive study of schooling that was in progress, it was reported that in the schools studied and in the only subject analyzed to that point, it appeared that in the high school English–language arts classes only the traditional kinds of printed materials were in use by more than half of the students. Innovative materials "films, filmstrips, slides, tapes and records, simulations, learning kits,

---

[11] John U. Michaelis, Ruth H. Grossman, and Lloyd F. Scott, *New Designs for Elementary Curriculum and Instruction*, 2nd ed. (New York: McGraw-Hill Book Company, 1975), pp. 123–127.

[12] Larry Cuban, "Determinants of Curriculum Change and Stability, 1870–1970," in *Value Conflicts and Curriculum Issues: Lessons from Research and Experience*, eds. Jon Schaffarzick and Gary Sykes (Berkeley, Calif.: McCutchan Publishing Corporation, 1979), p. 160.

teaching machines, television" were used by less than half the students. The percentage of students using television was less than 4 percent.[13]

An interesting contradiction appears to be present in the different interpretations concerning the usage of instructional materials. One study reported a recent national survey that indicated students spent more than 90 percent of their time with instructional materials when they were engaged in learning activities.[14] However, the study on schooling surprisingly found that teachers perceived commercially prepared materials and even textbooks as having a relatively low level of influence on what they taught within a given subject.[15] The study speculated that "Perhaps the amount of time and money spent on such sources is questionable."

At least two major observations may be made from this information. First, the busy educational administrator should probably give a priority of time and resources to the selection of the conventional instructional materials, because available information shows that they are mainly used by teachers. Second, the instructional leader should be concerned with trying to influence teaching behaviors both in the use of conventional materials and in expanding the usage of "innovative" materials. What are some specific observations or guidelines which are relevant to the selection and usage of the conventional materials, particularly of textbooks?

Specific observations concerning the selection of materials are the following:

1. The options for the selection of textbooks and similar materials are very limited. The researchers report not only overt censorship of books but also prior censorship in that certain types of materials and approaches are never published because commercial publishers must appeal to a wide market. Two states, Texas and California, because of their methods of state adoption of textbooks, effectively inhibit the content of textbooks which are distributed nationally.

2. No textbooks are value free or neutral in terms of values. Communities and parents are increasingly questioning the values contained within the adopted materials. The educational administrator must know the local community as well as when to confront that community's pressures to carry out educational programs with the necessary materials.

3. The local production of basic or supplementary materials should be considered, and such production would ameliorate the consequences of the preceding two observations. However, this is a costly process and one for which additional expertise is required, so it is not a feasible alternative for most school districts.

4. Communication may be an important cause of the perceptions of teachers concerning materials. At times, it becomes the simple matter that the sources of materials are not made available and useful to teachers. In other words, resources must be made available and planning very carefully done for the process of *how* materials are to be selected. It is surprising to find how often the latter process is poorly handled by educational administrators.

5. There is limited research concerning the nature of different approaches to, for example, reading by different textbook series and the consequences for

[13] Barbara J. Benham, Phil Giesen, and Jeannie Oakes, "A Study of Schooling: Students' Experiences in Schools," *Phi Delta Kappan,* 61, no. 5 (January 1980), 338–339.

[14] Talmage and Eash, "Curriculum, Instruction, and Materials," in *Research on Teaching,* p. 165.

[15] M. Frances Klein, Kenneth A. Tye, and Joyce E. Wright, "A Study of Schooling: Curriculum," *Phi Delta Kappan,* 61, no. 4 (December 1979), 246.

the learning environment. This information is useful for schools with differing goals and which seek a particular kind of classroom climate. There are also available detailed treatments of well-considered practices in the selection of materials.[16]

6. District administrators, particularly of the larger school districts, should be aware of the emergence of computer-guided manufacturing of books. It may be possible to meet the needs of local districts with tailored texts.

7. The selection of "free" materials should be given attention by instructional leaders. There is considerable indication that such materials need to be balanced with other types of information, interpretations, and viewpoints.

8. The selection of instructional materials should be as closely related as possible to their usage. Districtwide selection of a single textbook, for example, may be extremely costly in terms of its lack of usage within the individual classroom. Selection of materials should be part of the site-specific curriculum development process, with the district's providing a basic framework, recommendations, and articulation between levels and schools.

Specific observations concerning the usage of materials are the following:

1. The use of a wide variety and range of materials within a classroom may tend to be counterproductive in regard to some instructional strategies, such as learning for mastery or a concern for academic learning time. The teacher may become a manager of materials and not be able also to carry out teaching behaviors which have been found to be effective.

2. Sheer logistical problems may be a factor in the nonusage of some materials. For example, the science curricula of the 1960s were often thwarted by the inability to keep materials in supply and available for delivery at the time needed. If such supplies and materials are to be used, the administrator must provide adequate support, not only in terms of the materials but for the maintenance and delivery of them.

3. Class size becomes an important factor in the use of materials. A large number of students in a crowded space provides problems of control and leads teachers to use limited materials, as a textbook, as a way of helping to maintain order. If teachers are asked to individualize instruction, part of the support needed is a smaller number of students.

4. If teachers are to use conventional materials more effectively and to move toward using innovative materials, the need for effective in-service procedures becomes critical. Staff development must be planned carefully with the teachers, directed toward the development of specific teaching styles or models of teaching, and conducted over long periods of time. School administrators need to participate in similar types of staff development.

Selection and Usage of Instructional Technology

The observations and suggestions made in the preceding section, in the discussion of instructional materials, have been relatively modest if the emerging technology is considered in terms of its implications for schooling. Instructional media

---

[16] For example, see Jack Frymier and associates, *Annehurst Curriculum Classification System: A Practical Way to Individualize Instruction* (West Lafayette, Ind.: Kappa Delta Pi Press, 1977), for a comprehensive system of classifying curriculum materials in terms of individual learners.

can be regarded in three categories for the purposes of educational leadership: (1) the conventional instructional materials as discussed, (2) the "innovative" instructional materials as referred to, and (3) the emerging technology.

It may be inferred that teachers generally are still in the area of using conventional materials and need assistance in that use. That is not a firm inference as surveys in this area are still pending; also, there are probably greater numbers of teachers and schools whose usage of the innovative instructional materials is effective and sophisticated than was true ten years ago. The experiences of students outside of the school, as well as the entrance into teaching of teachers who themselves have been reared with the "innovative" materials, may have led to great progress in the usage of a wider variety of instructional materials. Balancing such a thrust, the movement toward a "return to the basics," the cutback in school financing, and the movement toward accountability and competency testing may be counterforces leading toward a restriction in the use of instructional materials. All that is available now as guidance in this area is informed speculation.

However, there is a small but growing speculation as to the significance of the emerging technology, for example "microprocessor" technology and the related development of microcomputers. The use of memory devices, such as the "floppy disks," with the capability of making local disks as well as buying commercially prepared ones, is already possible. Electronic equipment is evolving at a tremendous pace, opening up all types of usage. For example, by telephone the local computer can tie into huge data banks such as that of *The New York Times.* To the non-computer expert the language and the possibilities of the new technology are bewildering.

Some knowledgeable educators see staggering implications for public schooling in the emerging technology. The "software" or the actual programs of instruction are in no way at the same advanced level as the "hardware" or the technology. Computer programmers are scarce and highly paid. However, commercial companies may risk the finances required to combine the technology with the work of computer programmers and the consultation of educational curriculum specialists to develop educational programs that may well function outside of the traditional institution of public schooling. Goodlad in his works seems to believe that, in fact, many of the basic teaching skills that have been or are again becoming the major province of the schools could be done more effectively and efficiently outside of the school system.

It would be unprofitable to speculate further or to try to derive implications for instructional leadership from these emerging technological developments. However, the educational leader surely must at least make the effort to assure as effective a usage as is possible of the conventional and the innovative instructional materials that are currently available.

Standards of Achievement and Minimum Competency Testing

The two general areas in this section are interrelated in their interpretation and implementation, are extremely complex in terms of their possible implications for public schooling, and in their recent historical background are inextricably interwoven with the national effort to make certain that every person in the United

States has "an equal opportunity to receive an education of high quality regardless of his race, color, religion, sex, national origin, or social class."[17] To this law have been added further categories of persons, such as handicapped children in P.L. 94-142. Some observers see a further trend by both the federal and state governments to mandate that learning occur or to assure that education will be effective.

The most obvious implication for educational administrators is that they must have a knowledge and understanding not only of the policies and regulations concerning standards and competencies that come from the policymakers at the federal, state, and local levels, but also some awareness of what is implied by those policies and possible courses of action for constructive implementation of them. A limited effort will be made in this section to provide a few specific observations in regard to standards and competencies, and the reader is then referred to the more comprehensive works that are available in these areas.

Standards of achievement. Gay provided a clarifying context for different interpretations of standards of achievement in differentiating between four different conceptual models of curriculum planning.[18] The four models were identified as academic, experiential, technical, and pragmatic. The *academic* model is based upon a viewpoint of curriculum development as governed by academic rationality and theoretical logic; its standards have to do with the development of intellectual abilities that can be used in any learning context, not with the acquisition of knowledge and factual information *per se*.

The *experiential* model is based upon a learner-centered, activity-oriented approach to teaching and learning; its standards have to do with person- and process-oriented objectives, such as learning how to learn and think autonomously, valuing, developing positive self-concepts and individual creativity, and similar objectives. The *technical* model is based upon an analytical approach and sees planning in terms of "systems," "management," and "production"; its standards are similar to those of the academic model, but it uses "the logic of 'systems analysis,' empiricism, scientific objectivity, and managerial efficiency." It relies upon the use of "needs assessment" and the translation of the educational needs into observable, measurable, and behavioral terms.

The *pragmatic* model is the way in which actual curriculum planning occurs; it draws from the other theoretical models, from the conventional wisdom, and from common sense. Because curriculum practitioners are concerned with practical realities, they must take into account various pressure points. The various pressures in society have made a single issue a focal point; it has to do with the current concern for a return to the basics and for minimum competency testing.

Standards of achievement can be derived from any of the models just listed, with the pragmatic model being seen as a way of implementing any of the theoretical models. Instructional leaders, when they are involved in helping to define standards, can determine the potentialities of various options, from what sources they are being derived, and the possible consequences in terms of types of programs and the methods of evaluation that are indicated. Defined standards of achievement are

---

[17]Public Law 92-318, Sec. 405.

[18]Gay, "Conceptual Models," in *Considered Action for Curriculum Improvement*, pp. 120-143.

generally identified with the technical model, and the educational leader will need to understand the components of systems analysis.

There is much literature in the area of systems analysis, and it can only be touched upon in this section. However, the first component of the systems framework consists of an empirical analysis of needs or a "needs assessment," which has much to do with defining standards of achievement. English and Kaufman have outlined the process of needs assessment and its place in the action taken to fulfill the desired educational goals. Educational administrators are called on frequently to conduct needs assessments and often fall into the trap of using a "felt needs" approach in which the participants express their pet solutions rather than obtaining a list of outcomes or skills, knowledges, and attitudes that the students should acquire. Other undesirable practices include the definition of needs from the results of standardized tests or extensive development of philosophical statements of education which tend to lead to the same type of confusion as the felt needs approach.[19]

The preceding discussion is meant to illustrate the complexity of the technical model and the constructive leadership which the educational leader can give if knowledgeable and proficient in its components. This leadership is especially needed in carrying out the mandates in a growing number of states concerning minimum competency testing for grade promotions and for obtaining high school diplomas.

Minimum competency testing. "A minimum competency test is designed to determine whether an examinee has reached a *prespecified level* of performance relative to *each* competency being tested."[20] Competency tests introduce standards to interpret the performance of the examinees and are a type of criterion-referenced test. Where the educational leader has an influence on the development of competency tests, he or she can help to derive competencies from the various models discussed in the preceding section; that is, the skills to be measured can be school skills or life skills.

But it is in the impact on classroom instruction that the importance of minimum competency testing will be felt. Teachers must teach the competencies as defined; therefore the development of the competency test is of great importance. The basic reference cited in footnote 20 includes reports which cover thoroughly various aspects of competency testing, such as how to specify competencies, establish minimum standards, and develop measuring instruments. The administrator will need to have consultant help to work with the group that develops the competency tests.

English also pointed out an important implication of competency testing for time and content variance. Curriculum guides tend to allocate specified periods of time to complete an area and so have a low time variance but have only general

---

[19] Fenwick W. English and Roger A. Kaufman, *Needs Assessment: A Focus for Curriculum Development* (Washington, D.C.: Association for Supervision and Curriculum Development, 1975).

[20] Ronald K. Hambleton and Daniel R. Eignor, "Competency Test Development, Validation, and Standard Setting," in *Minimum Competency Achievement Testing: Motives, Models, Measures, and Consequences*, eds. Richard M. Jaeger and Carol Kehr Tittle (Berkeley, Calif.: McCutchan Publishing Corporation, 1980), p. 369.

references regarding content, pacing, and sequence for decisions by teachers. The latter indicates a large degree of content varience. It may be that a minimum competency approach will require the content variance to be reduced but the time variance to be greater. Thus the adoption of minimum competency tests indicates the need to change curriculum and instruction and will not, in itself, produce the desired results. There will not be a constructive implementation of competency testing and little impact upon the classroom unless the curriculum is also changed.

Instructional Strategies and Instructional Techniques

Of all the areas included in curriculum, instruction, and learning, the major focus in the research has been on instructional strategies and techniques. Although the focus may seem narrow, there are now not only a number of research reports and many interpretations of that research available but also reports of the experiences of school districts and schools that have put into practice some of the operational suggestions concerning teaching behaviors in the classroom. With the quantity of literature now available and with such clear implications for the educational leader, little needs to be added.

The questions facing the instructional leader in this area are not so much what instructional activities are effective but for what goals they are appropriate, whether or not they are relevant for the specific situation, and ways in which the instructional leader can work with the faculty to attain the indicated teaching behaviors. These are questions which call upon the various approaches to administrative behavior, such as decisionmaking, leadership, or change theory.

The comments in the preceding two paragraphs can be illustrated in one area in which there is much research. Benjamin Bloom is recognized as the educator who brought together the various components that make up learning for mastery about a decade ago. Briefly, LFM (learning for mastery) contends that almost all students can learn excellently under certain instructional conditions. These conditions include a systematic approach, help for the students when and where they have difficulties in learning, enough time for each student to achieve mastery, clear criteria of what mastery is, and the use of diagnostic tests and the indicated necessary corrective work.

A recent issue of *Educational Leadership*[21] was given mainly to various articles concerning LFM. In the fourteen articles included in this issue reports were given on reviews of the research, a longitudinal research project that included work in 3,000 schools, the experiences of various school districts from small districts to the Chicago public schools, a conversation with Benjamin Bloom, and two articles which pointed out concerns and problems with LFM. With the articles there are a series of references, related both to theory and practice, for further detailed information. The superintendent of the Chicago public schools gave a short overview of how the idea of mastery learning involved the entire school system, ". . . from board chambers to classroom, in a unified program of curriculum, instruction, evaluation, and management." This program included a continuous progress curriculum,

---

[21] *Educational Leadership*, 37, no. 2 (November 1979).

criterion-referenced testing programs, administrative goals, mastery learning instructional materials, and a competency-based promotion policy.[22]

A reading of these articles and of whatever further references are necessary can give the instructional leader much help in terms of specific operational suggestions. There are specific suggestions for the training of principals and teachers in LFM which are congruent not only with the research on LFM but with the research discussed in Chapter 15 concerning models of teaching and in-service education. If the concept of LFM does not seem to be appropriate to the needs of a particular school or school district, the literature on instructional strategies and techniques contains other areas of specific operational suggestions.

Mainstreaming of Handicapped Children

Public Law 94-142, the Education for All Handicapped Children Act of 1975, obligates the public schools to place each child in the "least restrictive environment" and to develop and implement an "individualized education program" (IEP). Interpretation of the least restrictive environment requires that handicapped children be mainstreamed or educated with children in the regular schools and classes except where the nature or severity of the handicap does not make this effective educationally.

The purpose of this legislation, and that of the individual states in the same area, is to assure an effective education for all handicapped children. All the literature and the discussion of it in the previous sections of this chapter would indicate overwhelmingly that the legislation is not a sufficient condition to assure the more effective education. What must be changed are classroom conditions and the adoption of more effective instructional strategies and techniques. Educators generally find that this mandate is grossly underfunded. There are also many questions as to the soundness and feasibility of implementing this legislation, particularly in regard to the IEPs.

For the instructional leader who attempts to bring about a constructive implementation in this area, in spite of the lack of proper funding and the many other problems involved, there are several operational implications inherent in the areas already discussed. For example, the major implications of LFM, as summarized, seem especially applicable to the mainstreaming of handicapped children. However, the teachers will also need greater administrative support in terms of smaller class size, additional instructional materials, and very focused in-service education to carry out the components of LFM in a reasonable manner. Teachers will need to develop and use new teaching behaviors in mainstreaming, but they will require assistance in determining what those new behaviors should be and in acquiring those behaviors in their repertory of teaching skills. Assistance in these latter areas will be needed from institutions of higher learning, especially from teacher educators, and from the professionals in special education.

---

[22]*Ibid.*, pp. 120–122.

Implementation of Federal Categorical Programs

For many years the federal government has provided money for schools to stimulate specific educational activities in the form of categorical grants. Some states have also used the categorical-funding approach to help school districts meet the greater cost of special education programs. There are many problems and concerns with this type of public school funding that are considered in texts on school finance. The concern of this section is for the significance of such federal programs in terms of the curriculum and instructional programs of the school. It is especially concerned with those school districts and schools, attended in large numbers by socioeconomically disadvantaged children, in which several different programs are present in the same school. The educational administrator has the responsibility for the overall supervision of programs that must maintain their identity for funding yet which draw on the same pupil population.

At times some particular projects are funded as autonomous units, outside of the usual administrative channels and not supported by any local district tax funds. Such programs receive only the general surveillance of the administrators and move outside of the regular school programs. Recent opinions of some educators contend that the school district might be wise not to seek the various funded programs because of the bureaucratic regulations which must be followed, the types of assessment that are used, the loss of autonomy by the local school board, and the disruption created within the school and the classroom. These contentions are countered, of course, with political and financial considerations.

However, insofar as these programs are considered in terms of the implications of the research on curriculum and instruction, the literature may be helpful. The research in such areas as LFM, direct instruction, and academic learning time is even more significant and dependable when the instructional conditions for socioeconomically disadvantaged children are involved. Schools using these instructional methods in categorical programs have reported increased learning by their pupils. For example, in a study of a Follow-Through program, children who ranked at the top in reading achievement spent 50 percent more time in academically engaged minutes than did the children who were ranked the lowest in reading achievement gains.[23] There has been consistent evidence that Title I programs have become more effective in improving the education of disadvantaged children in many local schools. However, this has occurred only after simplistic solutions, such as adding teachers or teacher aides, or purchasing more audiovisual materials and equipment, were discarded and attention was paid to the learning problems of the children and instructional strategies that addressed them.[24]

But the literature also points to some negative results that may stem from implementing several federal programs within a school. The need for classroom control, the advantages of large-group instruction for certain areas of learning, the need for time on task, and the need for direct supervision of learning by the teacher

[23] Barak V. Rosenshine, "Content, Time, and Direct Instruction," in *Research on Teaching*, p. 34.
[24] Ralph W. Tyler, "Educational Improvements Best Served by Curriculum Development," in *Research on Teaching*, p. 251.

may all be victims if programs are allowed to be conducted without some coordination centrally in the school. Or there is the danger that a teacher may be forced into undesirable instructional procedures for that teacher under the pressure of too many monitors. For example, a teacher operating in a more flexible setting but with enough allocated time to permit sufficient academically engaged minutes may be forced to become more inflexible if the allocated time is reduced because of the pressure of too many programs and the dispersion of children outside of the classroom.

Programs and instructional strategies which are imposed from the outside or from the top down have little chance of constructive impact upon classroom behavior. The need for in-service education is apparent. The discontinuance of federal funding may also be felt drastically if the changed classroom behaviors have not become part of the regular repertory of the teacher.

SOME IMPORTANT PROBLEMS AND ISSUES

This chapter on the operational implications of the research and literature in curriculum and instruction has presented several important problems and issues. It is in the nature of the current turbulence in public education that almost any changes proposed in the behavior of people will raise problems and issues according to the intensity of the changes proposed. Only a relatively few such areas could be presented in a short report, and the discussions were more illustrative than comprehensive. There remain a number of areas of problems and issues, a few of which will be described briefly.

What are the implications of the literature in curriculum and instruction for the instructional leader regarding:

1. Bilingual education? There are several philosophies and a variety of instructional strategies contending in this area for control and for resources. What dependable research results are available for guidance to action for the educational leader?

2. Guidance and youth services? Many young adults leave the schools and are either unemployed or unemployable. What are the implications in the area of learning of the basic skills that could help produce more effective services? Are instructional strategies, such as learning for mastery, applicable?

3. The new instructional strategies? Do they constitute a threat to the academic freedom of teachers, and is the curriculum in danger of being controlled excessively? Or is academic freedom even a relevant issue in this area?

4. The forces of social learning and interactive problem solving in the context of collective bargaining? What will such learning mean for the instructional behavior of the teacher in the classroom? Is there danger that an artisan attitude will bring about unforeseeable changes in the classroom and in relationships with the instructional leader?

5. Radical changes in schooling or school programs? Will the public school system face greater challenges even as it begins to show improvement in the basic skills? For example, will the new educational technology make much of what has been discussed obsolete in the next several decades?

6. Pre- and in-service programs for administrators? Is a proper balance of attention being given to instructional matters? Will the actual duties of the administrator permit instructional leadership?

7. Current improvement in schools? Why do innovative curriculum and improved instructional strategies flourish in some schools and school districts, and not in others? How will or should the public react to the wide variations in performance by teachers and administrators?

SELECTED REFERENCES*

Clark, Leonard H., and Irving S. Starr, *Secondary School Teaching Methods* (3rd ed.). New York: Macmillan Publishing Co., Inc., 1976.

Edelfelt, Roy A., and E. Brooks Smith, eds., *Breakaway to Multidimensional Approaches: Integrating Curriculum Development and Inservice Education.* Washington, D.C.: Association of Teacher Educators, 1978.

English, Fenwick W., and Roger A. Kaufman, *Needs Assessment: A Focus for Curriculum Development.* Washington, D.C.: Association for Supervision and Curriculum Development, 1975.

Foshay, Arthur W., ed., *Considered Action for Curriculum Improvement.* Alexandria, Va.: Association for Supervision and Curriculum Development, 1980.

Frymier, Jack, et al., *Annehurst Curriculum Classification System: A Practical Way to Individualize Instruction.* West Lafayette, Ind.: Kappa Delta Pi Press, 1977.

Walberg, Herbert J., ed., *Educational Environments and Effects: Evaluation, Policy, and Productivity.* Berkeley, Calif.: McCutchan Publishing Corporation, 1979.

Waterman, Floyd T., et al., *Designing Short-Term Instructional Programs.* Washington, D.C.: Association of Teacher Educators, 1979.

Wise, Arthur E., *Legislated Learning: The Bureaucratization of The American Classroom.* Berkeley, Calif.: University of California Press, 1979.

*See also references in Chapter 15.

17

HUMAN RESOURCES
and ADMINISTRATION*

The general aim of educational administration is to ensure that school systems function properly, that is, according to preconceived purposes and plans of action. Administrators are needed to convert a variety of resources, such as human resources, funds, facilities, and plans, into an effective enterprise capable of achieving the system's mission. Administrators are the activating element in the transformation process.

Of the several major plans which administrators develop for the operation of an educational institution (such as the organization structure, educational program, logistics, human resources, and external relations), none is as critical to the success of the undertaking as are those affecting the people responsible for their implementation. Human resources are the life blood of an institution. They help to conceive the kind of service the schools can render, to develop and implement plans needed to achieve the goals, and to make adjustments between plans and reality. Formal

*Prepared in large part by William B. Castetter, professor of education, University of Pennsylvania.

structure, rules and regulations, courses of study, position guides, and policies may be developed, but they take on significance only as people make use of them.

Administrative activities relating to personnel in the employ of an organization are referred to as the *personnel function.* Plans for and decisions about personnel flow from institutional purposes. Positions evolve from purposes; positions form the organization structure. Personnel decisions, including the quality and quantity of human resources needed, recruitment, selection, induction, union relationships, compensation, development, security, and information have a significant impact on the budget as well as on the attainment of organizational purposes and require considerable thought, planning time, and effort of all administrative personnel to maintain system stability and viability. The general intent of personnel administration is to develop and maintain a highly motivated and effective school staff.

In the past decade we have witnessed significant changes in concepts about, cognizance of the need for, approaches to, and increasing complexity of the personnel function in school systems. Contemporary efforts in the area of personnel are directed primarily to its continuing evolution. Most organizations accept the fact that personnel administration is an essential activity. As illustrated in Chart 17.1, contemporary concerns of those involved in personnel administration are twofold: (1) how to cope with the human problems emerging in organizations and (2) how to incorporate into personnel administration the most promising ideas from the rising stream of conceptual developments to resolve personnel problems more effectively. In the text which follows we shall examine in turn the nature and importance of the personnel function as well as organizational designs for its administration which are being brought about by societal, economic, political, and organizational pressures.

STRUCTURING THE PERSONNEL FUNCTION

Chart 17.2 illustrates the general functions of the superintendency and the homogeneous activities related to each function. Analysis of Chart 17.2 indicates that the main function of a school organization (instruction) is a *line* function. *Supporting functions,* such as logistics, planning, personnel, and external relations are staff functions. While it is true that there is no universal model for structuring the personnel function in any and all school districts, there is considerable agreement in both theory and practice as to the underlying assumptions involved in organizing the personnel unit. The following assumptions illustrate such points of agreement.

- The major components (minifunctions) of the general personnel function generally fall into the following categories: human resources planning, compensation, recruitment, selection, induction, appraisal, development, maintaining and improving performance, security, union relations, and information. Each of these major components is subdivided into processes. This type of specialization escalates as the size and complexity of the organization increases.
- While all personnel assigned to administrative roles engage in activities related to the personnel function, it is generally conceded that the personnel function is a staff function. This is to say that personnel is both a responsibility of the

Emerging Problems in School Systems with Implications for Personnel Administration	Conceptual Developments Applicable to Resolution of Personnel Problems
Social Behavioral factors such as increased emphasis on self-realization, freedom, meeting individual needs, new life-styles, superior-subordinate relationships, psychological reality, social mobility Legal-political factors Government regulations **Economic** Higher standard of living Higher cost of living Higher salaries, wages, benefits Rising financial expectations Employment mobility Emphasis on personal security Imbalances in personnel supply and demand **Organizational** Union ascendancy Larger systems Institutional complexity Changes in staff size Position specialization Increasing professionalization Decentalization Individual-organization conflict Responding appropriately to social change Organization renewal to meet individual needs and organizational goals Sharing of power	Development of new theoretical systems applicable to personnel administration Emergence of a variety of contemporary schools of administrative thought Contributions of behavioral science concepts, such as satisfaction of human needs, motivation, informal organization, the role of the individual and the group in organizations, participation, power equalization, executive behavior Technological developments, including quantitive analysis, application of computer to staffing process, PERT, personnel practices, human resources planning New techniques and methods in recruitment, selection, development, performance appraisal

CHART 17.1   Emerging Human Problems in School Systems and Conceptual Developments Applicable to Their Resolution

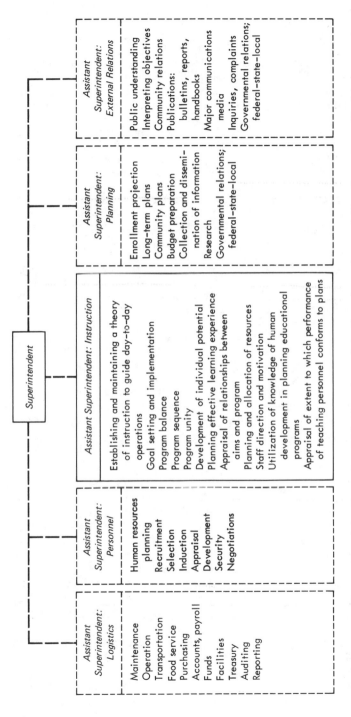

Superintendent

Assistant Superintendent: Logistics

Maintenance
Operation
Transportation
Food service
Purchasing
Accounts, payroll
Funds
Facilities
Treasury
Auditing
Reporting

Assistant Superintendent: Personnel

Human resources planning
Recruitment
Selection
Induction
Appraisal
Development
Security
Negotiations

Assistant Superintendent: Instruction

Establishing and maintaining a theory of instruction to guide day-to-day operations
Goal setting and implementation
Program balance
Program sequence
Program unity
Development of individual potential
Planning effective learning experience
Appraisal of relationships between aims and program
Planning and allocation of resources
Staff direction and motivation
Utilization of knowledge of human development in planning educational programs
Appraisal of extent to which performance of teaching personnel conforms to plans

Assistant Superintendent: Planning

Enrollment projection
Long-term plans
Community plans
Budget preparation
Collection and dissemination of information
Research
Governmental relations; federal–state–local

Assistant Superintendent: External Relations

Public understanding
Interpreting objectives
Community relations
Publications:
 bulletins, reports, handbooks
Major communications media
Inquiries, complaints
Governmental relations; federal–state–local

CHART 17.2 Illustration of the General and Minifunctions of the Superintendency: A Five-Component Model

entire organization and a special group or department within the central administration. A staff function is usually concerned with activities auxiliary to or supportive of the main function of instruction. There is seldom operating or line authority delegated to personnel involved in administering the personnel function as it is organized in the model illustrated in Chart 17.2.

- Another way of analyzing the personnel function is to separate it into decision-making and decision-implementing activities. Personnel decision making, such as those involving basic courses of action affecting the structuring of the function, or broad personnel plans affecting the system's budget, are generally the province of the superintendency, acting in concert with the board of education. Decision-implementing activities are concerned with the essential steps in carrying out major personnel plans developed by upper levels and usually delegated to lower levels of the administrative hierarchy. Recruitment, for example, may be established as a centralized staff function; selection of personnel, however, may be decentralized. This concept conceives both line and staff personnel to be involved in certain aspects of the general personnel function.

- Resolution of modern personnel problems in school organizations is of such crucial importance that the organization structure should include an administrator primarily responsible for the personnel area. This means that the personnel function is formed into a central unit, administered by an assistant superintendent, to aid the chief executive as well as line and staff units, in solving personnel problems with which they are confronted. The personnel unit in the central administration is related to and dependent upon other organizational units such as logistics, instruction, planning, and external relations.

In summary, a systematically developed and defensible organization can contribute materially to linking together the elements of the personnel function and to integrating these elements with other functions so that they facilitate effective goal achievement.

PLANNING THE PERSONNEL FUNCTION

The impact of the administration of the personnel function on the effectiveness of an organization depends to a considerable extent upon the *plans* and *planning capability* it develops. Types of personnel plans needed, who makes them, how they are made, and the manner in which the who and how are integrated become basic considerations in administering the personnel function.

Planning taxonomy classifies plans into two general categories: *standing* and *single use*. Standing plans include missions, long-range strategies, goals, purposes, policies, programs, procedures, processes, systems, structures, and rules. Such plans provide consistent arrangements by which schools decide to solve problems in carrying out the district mission. Standing plans are relatively permanent and are used to guide and control the multifaceted functions which characterize a school system. They are especially applicable in dealing with recurring work, activities, problems, and decisions. Single-use plans, on the other hand, are of limited duration. Projects, annual budgets, or plans whose lives are of limited duration and are designed to accomplish a short-run objective exemplify the single-use plan. Regardless of the plan used, it represents a predetermined course of action.

Types of plans involved in the administration of the personnel function are illustrated in Chart 17.3. The plans shown are grouped into three types—pertaining to the *aims structure,* the *organization structure,* and *personnel processes.* Plans within the aims structure are those designed primarily to establish and maintain *instructional* and *instructional support programs.* Plans contained in the organization structure are especially concerned with *positions* generated by the aims structure. Plans relating to the personnel processes are those designed to attract, develop, and retain *personnel* needed in the human resources system generated by the aims structure.

The personnel processes in operating plans designed to administer the personnel function include human resources planning, recruitment, selection, induction, appraisal, development, compensation, maintaining and improving performance, security, union relations, and information.

Each of the foregoing personnel operating processes, it should be noted, is

CHART 17.3   Types of Plans Involved in the Administration of the Personnel Function

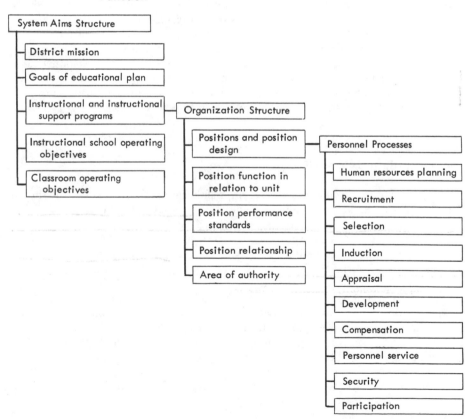

subdivided further into sequential tasks essential to achieving the intent of the process and the larger function of which it is a part. This perception of the personnel function is useful in defining tasks of which it will be composed, in fixing responsibility for their performance, and in communicating to the administrative team the information each member needs to carry out those tasks. In addition, breaking down each of the major functions of a school system (instruction, personnel, logistics, external relations, planning) into operating processes not only compels the central administration to clarify organizational expectations but also assists it in securing consistency among decisions, coordination, and economy of planning efforts. In the sections that follow we shall examine the nature of the several personnel operating processes and consider how each is linked to other personnel processes as well as to other major organizational functions.

STAFFING THE SYSTEM

As was noted previously, an organizational structure is composed of various positions designed to accomplish system goals. A variety of administrative activities is essential to keep those positions staffed with personnel who have the knowledge, skills, and motivation to perform the roles effectively. It is becoming increasingly clear that considerable confusion emerges in an organization when these activities are performed independently. What is needed is an integrated system designed to deal with the total array of personnel activities. In the text following we shall examine the first of several processes designed to systematize the personnel function. These include human resources planning, recruitment, selection, and induction, the intent of which is to attract to and retain in the organization personnel conceptualized in the designs of the various positions to be filled.

EQUAL EMPLOYMENT OPPORTUNITY
AND AFFIRMATIVE ACTION

Before considering various processes comprising the personnel function, it should be brought to the attention of the reader that a variety of external forces affect the personnel policies and procedures of both public and private organizations. These include government legislation, court decisions, unions, economic conditions, labor markets, and political and social change. Of these factors, none is more pervasive than government legislation in the form of Equal Employment Opportunity and Affirmative Action programs. The basic law that regulates employment is the Equal Employment Opportunity Act of 1972, including Title VII of the Civil Rights Act of 1964. The essence of legislation, court decisions, guidelines, and rulings is that equal employment opportunity for all persons regardless of race, color, religion, ethnic origin, sex, or age has become the foundation for any and all facets of the personnel function of an organization.

The equal employment principle is implemented in work organizations through Affirmative Action Programs which are designed to identify, analyze, and establish goals to overcome problems relating to various kinds of personnel discrimination, such as sex discrimination, seniority and discrimination, discrimination in position assignments, employment use of conviction and arrest records, discrimination because of grooming and appearance, height and weight restrictions, and child labor.

Human Resources Process

At the core of the personnel function is a planning process which is concerned with resolving major organization personnel problems such as the following:

- How many positions are needed in the school system, both now and in the future, to achieve organizational expectations?
- What should be the design of each position (both present and proposed) in the organization structure?
- What is the relationship of existing human resources to that required in the projected organization structure?

Examination of the foregoing questions relating to the human resources planning process brings into focus a central fact of organization life: Human resources plans are determined by the goals of the system. Goals determine the educational plan, the quality and quantity of human resources needed to implement programs comprising the plan, the resources to be developed, and the nature of the administrative processes employed to maintain the system.

Operationally speaking, human resources planning will include the following kinds of activities.

- Forecasting community educational demand (who shall be educated, to what extent, for what purpose?).
- Projecting organization structures and designing positions within the structure.
- Projecting the short- and long-term budgetary impact of human resources plans.
- Reviewing appropriateness of contemporary staff deployment practices within the system.
- Preparing an information system to facilitate human resources planning.
- Estimating the impact of collective bargaining on human resources.
- Visualizing the impact of organizational changes on personnel.
- Appraising the results of human resources planning.

While it is important to appreciate that the foregoing description of the human resources planning process conceptualizes a series of sequential and interconnected activities, it is equally important to understand that the process is linked closely to other processes which form the personnel function. The recruitment plan, for example, will be aimless unless it is based on decisions indicating the number and types of positions to be filled as well as the specifications designed to guide efforts to match people and positions. How important the interrelation is between human resources planning and other personnel processes may be judged as we consider the process by which the school systems seek to attract people to positions in the organization structure which need to be filled.

One of the assumptions behind the human resources planning process is that it will provide school officials with a view of the flow of personnel into, through, and out of the organization over time. The personnel flow pattern will provide insights into past experience concerning external recruitment, internal promotions, transfers, separations, and terminations. Data such as the foregoing will establish a basis for forecasting personnel needs and set the stage for initiation of the next step in the personnel function—recruitment.

The recruitment process, as one of the interlocking components of the personnel function, is aimed at bringing into the school system the quality and quantity of people needed to fill position openings. The cruciality of a systems approach to the personnel function may be illustrated clearly by the recruitment process. The human resources planning process, for example, should clarify the question of internal promotion versus external recruitment. In addition, data collected in the planning process should shed considerable light on which sources provide the quality of personnel sought by the system. Further, the human resources planning process establishes in advance the extent to which continuing education programs should be provided to enable personnel within the system to move into upper-level positions. Thus, it is clear that personnel recruitment is perceived not as a separate compartmentalized activity but as a component linked to many other personnel processes, including human resources planning, selection, induction, and development.

The impact of general personnel policies on the recruitment process becomes clear by analysis of the policy considerations organizations must resolve with respect to

- race, creed, national background, age, sex, and physical handicaps of position candidates
- internal promotion via career path
- personnel development programs
- employment of relatives, veterans, part-time and temporary personnel, mothers and working wives, minors, and rehiring of former personnel

Once the school system has settled the human resources policy issues alluded to, and has decided which sources it wishes to use to fill positions which are currently open, the stage is set to complete the recruitment process. This involves plans for organizing and coordinating recruitment activities.

After recruitment tasks have been identified, they are assigned to different people at various levels in the organization and coordinated. This includes (1) establishing communication between the school system and potential candidates to provide the information about the position and to secure information about the candidate, (2) developing a recruitment information system, (3) designing a schedule for recruitment activities, (4) preparing a recruitment budget, (5) managing the recruitment correspondence, (6) systematizing the screening procedures, and (7) tracking the recruitment progress of each candidate.

Thus the recruitment process is conceived to be a centrally planned operation, usually under the direction of an assistant superintendent for personnel or equivalent administrator. To coordinate the recruitment process effectively, consideration should be given to developing procedures for *centralizing* recruitment and screening and *decentralizing* selection. Given this discussion of the recruitment process, let us now examine the collateral process of personnel selection.

Selection Process

The next step in the staffing activity is selection, the process by which the school system goes about matching people and positions. The overall process of matching people and positions resolves itself into a series of subproblems such as the following: (1) What are the requirements of each position to be filled? (2) What are the main specifications needed to fill the positions? (3) To what extent does the individual candidate match position expectations? (4) What is the most feasible and desirable plan for obtaining personnel for the system's short- and long-run needs?

To resolve the foregoing problems relative to personnel selection, some type of selection process must be established and maintained. This process includes (1) using a position guide in which essential data regarding the positions and person specifications are written (the *position specifications* should include facts about position title, primary functions, major responsibility, summary of key duties, special assignments, relationships, area of authority, and the *person specifications* should include facts abouts such qualifications as education, experience, skills, knowledge, abilities, initiative, judgment, personal characteristics); (2) developing an information system which will yield appropriate data for the selection process; (3) appraising the data and the applicants; (4) preparing an eligibility list; (5) nominating personnel for employment; and (6) appointing personnel formally to positions on the basis of nominations by the chief executive. In this process the role of the school principal as indicated in Chapter 14 needs to be made clear and significant.

The *position guide* is one of the tools essential to the selection and other personnel processes. It is assumed that for every position in the system there will be a position guide. More than likely, all position guides will be included in the organization manual. This manual then becomes the formal document for use in human resources planning, recruitment, selection, appraisal, and personnel development.

One of the approaches to be employed in the selection process is based upon the objectives of a given position. *The objective approach* to selection starts with the assumption that a position may include various types of objectives, which are stated as follows in question form:

- What are the standard objectives of the position (as defined in the position guide)?
- What are the problem-solving objectives of the position (as anticipated by the system)?
- What are the innovative or change objectives of the position (as perceived by the system)?

Using the three major categories of position objectives identified, the selection process focuses upon uncovering predictors in the individual's history which would assist the selection team in deciding the extent to which the individual's capabilities are those needed to achieve the position objectives effectively. The standard position requirements, as specified in the position guide, are considered to be inviolate; skills of the candidate to meet the problem-solving and innovative objectives of the positions are judged on an ascending scale of excellence. Selection tools and their application are designed to predict, on the basis of past performance and present potential, the extent to which a candidate will perform effectively in terms of the types of objectives established for the position.

No description of the selection process would be complete without making the observation that the division of activities, such as personnel selection, into a series of steps for which designated personnel are responsible is primarily mechanistic. However elaborate the selection process in a school system, it is not a panacea for solving personnel problems. People may meet the criteria but fail in the position for lack of motivation. In short, because people are human and complex, the selection process is fallible. Consequently, other processes are needed to minimize personnel discontent and to assure a high level of performance once they are on the job. The discussion which follows focuses on organizational efforts needed to facilitate the *adjustment* of individuals after a decision has been made to employ them in the school system.

Induction Process

After an applicant has been selected to fill a position in the school organization, it is to the advantage of both the system and the individual that the latter become adjusted as soon as possible to the position and to the conditions affecting performance in the position. This process of adjustment is known as induction—a systematic organizational effort to minimize problems confronting new personnel so that they can contribute maximally to the work of the school while realizing personal and position satisfaction.

The personnel induction process is designed to resolve the following types of problems encountered to a greater or lesser extent by all inductees:

- Problems relating to the position—organizational expectations of the position, resources needed to perform effectively in the role, and position constraints are illustrative.
- Problems relating to school system—mission, policies, procedures, rules, regulations, and services.
- Problems relating to other system personnel—colleagues, the superior-subordinate relationship, and the people who will have an impact on productivity and need satisfaction.
- Problems involved in becoming acquainted with and making adjustments in the community.
- Problems of a personal nature—finding living accommodations, banking facilities, shopping areas, and so on.

The mobility of school personnel, as well as the problem of turnover, emphasizes the need for continuing efforts to maintain and to improve the induction process. The process may take many forms and involve a wide variety of activities throughout the induction cycle which is designed to assist in adjustments during the pre-appointment stage, the interim stage, and the probationary period. The school system and the community need to implement plans to facilitate the attainment of the goals of the induction program.

The induction process is one that contributes to various human goals of the system, including security, hospitable environment, and placement of personnel in positions in which they will be able to find personal satisfaction and to make effective use of their abilities. The induction process is an organizational acknowledgement that human maladjustment is a prime contributor to system dysfunction. In the text following, our aim is to examine processes in the personnel function designed to improve the performance of personnel once the major problems of induction have been resolved satisfactorily and the inductee is gradually assimilated into the school staff.

IMPROVING PERSONNEL PERFORMANCE

One of the hard realities of organizational life is that the selection process, however perfect, does not ensure that placement of an individual in a position will result automatically in a high degree of person–position compatibility. Every school system is confronted with problems such as the following to maintain suitable levels of performance by people in positions to which they are assigned:

- The selection process may produce a mismatch between person and position.
- The requirements of the position may change.
- The behavior of the individual in the position may change.
- The available supply of personnel to fill the position may be limited.
- Personnel within the school system may be promoted to a new position but need training.
- Newly employed personnel may need assistance.
- New problems, procedures, knowledge, positions, and developments may create a need for continuing education of personnel.
- Social change may lead to modification in organizational objectives, which in turn may create a demand for behavioral changes in personnel.

Analysis of the foregoing conditions leads to the conclusion that personnel development has become a major organizational activity and a key process of the personnel function. It is based on the assumption that every organization must apply increasing amounts of its budget to the development of its human resources. Placement of an individual in a position under this assumption means that the organization takes on the task of assisting him or her, chiefly through two personnel processes, to improve his or her position performances. These processes are now examined.

Appraisal Process

The nucleus of any organizational plan to assist its members to perform effectively in their present positions and to develop personnel to fill new or existing positions is a program that will identify their strengths and weaknesses. Thus, performance appraisal may be defined as one of the several processes of the personnel function designed to arrive at judgments about the past or present performance and future potential of an individual to the school system against the background of his or her total work environment. Considered in this way, the appraisal process may be thought of as one of a network of operating processes, each of which is interrelated and interdependent. This observation can be illustrated by examination of the following activities upon which the appraisal process is focused:

- Place the individual in the system where the individual can realize personal goals and contribute effectively to those of the organization.
- Motivate personnel toward achieving system as well as personal goals.
- Improve performance.
- Uncover abilities.
- Ascertain the potential of the individual to perform various types of tasks.
- Encourage self-development.
- Point up continuing education needs.
- Provide a guide for salary determination.
- Facilitate mutual understanding between superior and subordinate.
- Transfer, demote, promote, or dismiss personnel.
- Test validity of recruitment and selection processes.

The decision elements which enter into the design of an appraisal system, as well as the process by which it is implemented, include the following:

- Upon what assumptions shall the appraisal system rest?
- What shall be the purposes of appraisal?
- What shall be appraised?
- Who shall be appraised?
- Who shall appraise?
- What shall be the methods of appraisal?
- What code of ethics shall govern the appraisal process?
- Where shall the locus of appraisal responsibilities be placed?

Pressures currently bringing about modifications in the traditional performance appraisal system for school personnel are numerous, including *organizational, legal, political, social,* and *economic* changes as well as *client, personnel,* and *theorist* reaction. Mutual goal setting, counseling, progress review, integration of individual and organization goals, and need satisfaction of staff members are but a few of the change and reaction contributions to which modern school systems are heir. Let us now turn our attention to the next sequential step in the personnel function designed to improve personnel performance.

Development Process

By definition, personnel development is focused upon two kinds of activities designed to maintain and improve performance, to enhance commitment, and to increase productivity. These include (1) those programs designed and administered specifically by the school system (formal approaches) and (2) those initiated by personnel (informal approaches). Several dimensions of this definition need elaboration. The first of these dimensions is organizational responsibility for development. Although personnel can and should improve their effectiveness without formal involvement of the system, development of personnel requires systematic organizational planning.

A second dimension of the definition is that staff development embraces all personnel employed by the system, certificated as well as noncertificated. Every individual on the system payroll, according to this concept of development, will be involved at various career stages in some form of continuing education. A third dimension of the definition is that personnel development is aimed at satisfying two kinds of expectations—the contribution required of the individual by the school system and the material and emotional rewards anticipated by the individual staff members as performance residuals. A fourth concept of staff development is that deliberate investment in human capital (skills and knowledge of personnel) represents a valuable asset of the system, one which is essential to its stability as well as to its viability.

Of the emerging concepts and practices relating to staff development in a school system, the following are noteworthy:

- One of the realities of school administration is that in all likelihood there will never be an abundant supply of outstanding talent to fill every position. Consequently, a plan must be maintained to develop those who are in the system as well as those who are recruited.

- Development is aimed at changing the behavior of personnel toward a predetermined goal. The goal is determined by factors relating to the position, the person, and the organization.

- Performance management is emerging as a replacement of the narrower concept of supervision.

- Performance appraisal is basic to the initiation of plans for improving individual performance.

- School systems of the future will grant much more autonomy to local school attendance units than is now the case. Consequently, development programs of the future will be highly decentralized, aimed at making each individual effective in his or her assignment, and enhancing his or her contribution to the goals of the work unit in which he or she is located.

- Development programs in the future will be focused upon goals. The prime concerns of the programs will include these questions:

  What behavior do we wish to change?
  What is the present condition or level of behavior that we wish to change?
  What is the desired condition that we wish to achieve in personnel performance?
  How can we link learning theory to staff development programs?
  What types of training shall be employed (classroom, on-the-job, apprenticeships)?
  What types of newer training technologies shall be employed (computers, projectors, closed-circuit TV, programmed text materials, and video cassettes?)
  What indicators shall we use to evaluate the effectiveness of development programs?

Staff development, then, is viewed as an essential cyclical plan by which the organization maintains and renews itself. Key concepts in the administration of a staff development program include consideration by school officials of the principle that investment in human resources adds to its capital formation in the form of skills and knowledge, that development means changing human behavior, and that learning theory and development plans are inseparable. Having reviewed some of the major concepts of staff development, let us now turn to another process in the personnel function which is equally important in improving staff performance.

Compensation Process

Organizational concern about plans by which personnel are compensated is an ageless activity. A compensation system properly conceived and administered can make an important contribution to attainment of specific objectives of a school system as well as to the individual satisfaction of its members. Goals to which the system can gear its compensation planning include the following:

- Attracting and retaining competent career personnel.
- Motivitating personnel to optimum performance in present positions.
- Creating incentives to growth in performance ability.
- Getting maximum return in service for the economic investment made in the compensation plan.
- Developing personnel confidence in the intent of the organization to build equity and objectivity into the compensation plan.
- Making the plan internally consistent and externally competitive.
- Relating compensation levels to importance and difficulty of positions.
- Making salaries commensurate with the kinds of personnel the organization requires.
- Establishing a compensation structure conducive to the economic, social, and psychological satisfactions of personnel.

To achieve the compensation goals listed, a systematic process is essential to determine the worth of work and the worth of people who do the work. The compensation process by which this is achieved is shown graphically in Chart 17.4.

Compensation policy is also an important tool in achieving the compensation

CHART 17.4 The Compensation Process

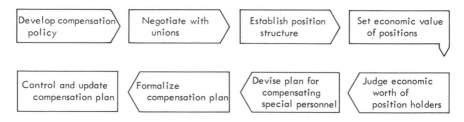

goals of the system noted. The policy guides following illustrate their importance to the development and implementation of derivative compensation plans.

- Contemporary thought and practices governing compensation systems embrace a compensation structure consisting of salaries, wages, collateral benefits, and noneconomic benefits (psychic income).
- The compensation structure includes personnel in every capacity, regardless of income level or position responsibility.
- Quality of performance should be rewarded.
- The individual position and the objectives established for it establish a departure from conventional salary administration procedure.

In addition to the foregoing considerations, a number of other interrelated factors affect the amount of the paycheck an individual receives from the school system. These include compensation legislation, prevailing compensation practices, collective negotiations, supply of and demand for personnel, and the system's ability and willingness to pay as well as the standard and cost of living. While the foregoing capsulization of compensation points up important variables which affect annual compensation levels in a school system, some factor or combination of factors may be more important than others at a given time. In effect, to a considerable extent, compensation is a situational matter.

MAINTAINING AND IMPROVING PERSONNEL SERVICE

The flow of personnel into and out of a school system is endless. To make it possible for the system to have *uninterrupted and effective* service in each position in the structure, plans designed for this purpose are indispensable. The fact that staff members do become mentally and physically ill, that they do experience work- and nonwork-connected accidents, and that their productivity is affected by physical conditions of employment leads to the inevitable conclusion that organizational plans are essential to keeping the system staffed continuously. Chart 17.5 has been included to illustrate key goals of personnel service maintenance as well as the salient provisions needed for achieving the goals.

The process by which problems relating to maintenance and improvement of personnel service are dealt with varies from, but has much in common with, arrangements for making and carrying out other organizational decisions. If the procedures for achieving the objectives of personnel service are analyzed carefully, it will be noted that they are to a considerable extent *repetitive*. It is clear, for example, that problems relating to leaves of absence, health, substitute service, and safety are aspects of personnel administration that confront administrators daily. Consequently, the administration of personnel service, as conceptualized in Chart 17.5, calls for isolation of the recurring elements of these problems and for standardizing, to the extent possible, the manner in which they are treated. The school system can ill afford to wait, for example, until a classroom teacher is hospitalized, or until death in the family of a staff member occurs, before deciding what organizational provisions shall govern these events.

Personnel services represent an area of educational administration suited ideally

```
┌─────────────────────────────────────┐
│   Objectives of Personnel Service    │
├─────────────────────────────────────┤
│ Improve system ability to perform    │
│    function                          │
│ Improve physical, psychological,     │
│    organizational environment        │    ┌──────────────────────────────────┐
│ Prevent accidents                    │    │   Procedures for Achieving Goals   │
│ Control personnel costs              │    ├──────────────────────────────────┤
│ Contribute to personnel emotional    │    │ Leaves of absence                  │
│    security                          │    │ Health and medical services        │
│ Comply with statutory requirements   │    │ Substitute service                 │
│ Contribute to personnel financial    │    │ Safety and working conditions      │
│    security                          │    └──────────────────────────────────┘
│ Reduce personnel turnover            │
│ Establish program limits             │
│ Provide personnel opportunity for    │
│    development                       │
└─────────────────────────────────────┘
```

CHART 17.5   Personnel Service by Objectives

to the application of standing plans such as standard procedures, rules, regulations, and policies, all of which are designed to deal with recurring problems. Standing plans with regard to personnel services not only simplify that task of deciding how a specific personnel situation is to be resolved but also assure a degree of consistency, dependability, and quality of decision throughout the school system as a whole.

The fact should not go unnoticed that the components of personnel service— leaves of absence, substitute service, health and medical service, and safety and working conditions—are usually considered to be items for collective bargaining. As such, they are reviewed annually and considered to be essential provisions to which all organizational personnel are entitled. So viewed, it is incumbent upon school systems to plan personnel services provisions in a way that they are as conducive as possible to this objective.

PERSONNEL SECURITY

Throughout history educators have struggled to gain work-related provisions which would protect them against arbitrary treatment, ensure continuing employment, enable them to exercise freedom of thought and expression on and off the job, and protect them against postemployment financial insecurity. The struggle to achieve these ends has been long and difficult. While the principle of personnel security is well established in many nations throughout the Western world, and particularly in the United States, the gap between principle and practice has not been eliminated completely. Chart 17.6 illustrates the relationship between objectives of personnel security and the tools generally employed to achieve them. The discussion which follows is focused upon five dimensions of personnel security— tenure, academic freedom, protection against arbitrary treatment, retirement, and individual adaptation. Of these dimensions, most are generated by either legislative or system action, such as tenure, retirement, Social Security, grievance procedures,

```
┌──────────────────────────────────────┐
│  Objectives of Personnel Security  ╲   │
│                                     ╲  │      ┌──────────────────────────────────────┐
│   Academic freedom                   ╲ │      │  Procedures for achieving security   │
│   Position security                    ╲│      │     objectives                       │
│   Financial security                    │─────▶│     Tenure provisions                │
│   Protection against arbitrary          │      │     Retirement provisions            │
│      treatment                        ╱ │      │     Grievance machinery              │
│   Freedom of thought, expression,    ╱  │      │     System personnel plans           │
│      action                         ╱   │      │     Transfer, promotion              │
│   Individual organization          ╱    │      └──────────────────────────────────────┘
│      adaptation                   ╱     │
└──────────────────────────────────────┘
```

CHART 17.6 Personnel Security by Objectives

and academic freedom. One dimension of personnel security which cannot be achieved by legislative or judicial action may be classified as individual adaptation.[1] The latter dimension is the sense of security achieved by the individual when able to perform his or her role effectively in the system. The inner security and self-confidence developed by an individual on the job is generated by a number of provisions which are part of the design of the personnel function. The nature of position performance management exercised on behalf of the individual staff member, opportunities for development, fair treatment, and general organizational climate contribute in varying degrees to the maturation of personnel in the roles to which they are assigned and to the kind of individual–organizational fit to which the system aspires.

Tenure of professional personnel. The concept of tenure for professional personnel in education is well established, salient features of which include (1) completion of a specified probationary period, (2) tenure for personnel who meet performance standards during the probationary period, and (3) an orderly procedure for dismissal of personnel.

While it is true that tenure for teachers is accepted in both principle and practice, the decade of the 1970s has been witness to various challenges to efforts at the legislative level to eliminate tenure for teachers. The emerging major argument against tenure is that teachers should not be permitted to have the tenure privilege as well as the privilege of negotiating the conditions under which they will work. These two types of privileges, according to legislative reaction, are in conflict with one another. Thus, so the argument goes, teachers must choose one privilege or the other; they should not be permitted to exercise both privileges. It is an issue which will be contested vigorously on both sides as demands escalate for higher salaries and collateral benefits of education personnel.

Academic freedom. Freedom of thought and expression are crucial concerns in the administration of the personnel function. The right to exercise intellectual freedom in the classroom is basic to freedom of learning. So essential is the con-

---

[1] Other dimensions of the personnel function related to security and discussed elsewhere in this section included collateral benefits, position and financial security, and collective bargaining.

cept of academic freedom to the development of free minds for free people that safeguards are needed in school systems to ensure conditions conducive to the teaching–learning process. Threats to personal and academic freedom of school personnel cannot be dealt with effectively unless protective measures are established by the board of education. Much can be accomplished by the board to ensure academic freedom for its personnel if it develops plans for receiving and examining criticisms relating to the personal and academic freedom of staff members; for developing administrative machinery to deal systematically with attacks on personnel, teaching methods, and the educational program; for protecting personnel so that they are able to exercise personal and academic freedom in the roles of educator and as citizen.

Protection against arbitrary treatment. Since the dawn of work organizations, some personnel have suffered from arbitrary treatment by their superiors in the form of actual or threatened loss of position, status, power, income, privileges, and freedom of action or speech. Efforts of personnel to minimize arbitrary treatment, as well as social legislation designed to ensure worker rights beyond receipt of pay for services rendered, have brought into being protective arrangements which make organizational exercise of this form of personnel control more difficult. An administrative tool which has been devised and frequently employed to protect personnel against arbitrary treatment is the grievance system. Under this system there is an established procedure for identifying and initiating action to deal with grievances. Systematization of grievance handling is conducive to minimization of discontent and dissatisfaction. The very existence of a grievance system is, in itself, an assurance to the individual staff member that the rights and privileges that he or she has been guaranteed will be protected.

Retirement. The provision of retirement benefits for educational personnel is in keeping with similar arrangements for other groups of public and private employees. Most retirement funds call for contributions to a retirement fund at specified rates by the members as well as by the district and the state. Retirement benefits are based generally upon a predetermined fraction of the average compensation for the last several years of employment. Federal Social Security arrangements have, on the one hand, supplemented teacher retirement benefits and, on the other, escalated the combined cost of both retirement and Social Security to the point where the question of the ability of personnel to afford both plans has become an important administrative and social issue. Three criteria are usually employed to test the provisions of a retirement system: (1) Are the retirement funds fully vested? (2) Is the contribution rate adequate? and (3) Are retirement contributions protected against adverse economic conditions, such as inflation and deflation? One of the most valuable services that school systems can render to personnel relative to retirement is advice about what needs to be done to prevent the retirement system from drifting into obsolescence. New concepts are constantly emerging regarding the operation of retirement systems, such as the variable annuity, age of retirement, vesting, and relative size of contributions by employee, employer, and the state. Continuous appraisal and modification of retirement systems is an administrative responsibility of high priority, as personnel now consider retirement benefits an important element of their compensation for working and the equivalent of a property right to which they will be heirs in their postemployment period.

Reduction in force. A major personnel security problem caused by declining enrollments, beginning in the 1970s and continuing into the 1980s, is the necessity for school organizations to reduce the size of the school staff. The security issue revolves around the method employed to determine which personnel shall be terminated. Although the time-honored approach to resolving the reduction in force problem has been to resort to the seniority principle (last to be hired, first to be fired), this practice, vigorously defended by unions, is not without its critics. Opponents of the seniority principle point to the fallacy of ignoring personnel competency in making personnel reductions. Newly appointed teachers frequently raise objections to joining a union because they allege that in situations in which reduction in force is involved, the union forsakes competence for seniority.

Various palliatives to ease the confusion and rancor that can accompany an RIF have been employed, including early retirement, plans for reemployment after layoff, and assistance in finding employment for the unemployed.

The upshot of RIF has been considerable, including state legislation to govern RIF procedures, court decisions, and comprehensive personnel plans in school systems included to clarify the RIF process and to minimize security of personnel threatened by continuing decline in enrollments.

Personnel Participation

The human goals of a school system, as conceptualized in Chart 17.7, include organizational citizenship in decision making. The basic assumption behind the concept of personnel participation in shaping system destiny may be stated as follows: There is a strong, positive relationship between the extent of personnel participation in the affairs of the system and their willingness to contribute to achievement of organization goals. This relationship extends from performance management involving superior and subordinate to systemwide decisions affecting the status and working conditions of staff members.

The concern of the discussion which follows is to focus upon selected personnel activities which have a considerable impact on the extent to and manner in which personnel participation becomes a reality. *The collective negotiations process,* which is also a dimension of personnel participation related to the manner in

CHART 17.7 Conceptualization of the Human Goals of a School System

Organizational climate conducive to optimum personnel development
Fair, courteous, considerate treatment
Absence of discrimination
Grievance machinery
Protection against arbitrary treatment
Equality of opportunity
Economic security
Full utilization of personnel talent
Effective leadership
Organizational citizenship
Full information

which decisions regarding conditions of work are negotiated and administered, is discussed in detail in Chapter 18.

Organizational Democracy

No discussion of personnel participation in the affairs of a school system would be complete without reference to the application of democratic ideals to personnel administration.

One of the essential assumptions of institutions which adhere to democratic principles is that those who plan the conditions of work and those who do the work should be involvéd in determining what the conditions of work ought to be. As illustrated in Chart 17.8, we may specify two categories of personnel participation: (1) superior–subordinate participation in performance management and (2) staff participation in matters affecting their own welfare or that of the total system. The ultimate aim of personnel participation in decision making is to improve the nature of the decisions which are made, either in the manner in which the individual performs the position role or in the resolution of systemwide problems and issues which affect all personnel. Included in the anticipated by-products of personnel participation are that it will motivate members to cooperate voluntarily in role performance, to exercise greater initiative in performance improvement, to develop more positive attitudes toward superiors and toward the organization, and to engage in a higher level of organizational citizenship. In brief, personnel participation, properly planned, should contribute to both the satisfaction of individual needs and to fulfillment of organizational expectations.

SOME IMPORTANT PROBLEMS AND ISSUES

Some of the salient issues relating to personnel in education include the following:

- Is a tenure law in the best interests of teachers? in the best interests of education?
- Is the use of paraprofessional personnel defensible?

CHART 17.8   Illustration of Types of Personnel-
Organization Participation

Individual Participation in Developing	Group Participation in Developing
Major goals of position	District mission
Position guide	Educational goals
Performance standards for position	Programs
	General objectives
Position relationships	Behavioral objectives
Performance appraisal process	Personnel goals
Superior – subordinate program review	Personnel policies, procedures
Performance objectives	Union – organization relationship
Career path	

- How can the concept of differentiated staffing be employed effectively?
- How should the personnel function in a school system be organized?
- How can a school system deal rationally with the inordinately intense enthusiasm for personnel "accountability"?
- What can be done about the lag in school organizations in developing information systems for better management of human resources?
- How can legislative and collective bargaining barriers be removed to improve human performance?
- How can unions and school systems cooperate more effectively to resolve human problems of members?
- What approaches should be employed to improve affirmative action programs?
- Are there more effective approaches to resolving reduction in force problems than those currently advocated?
- What can be done to reverse the dramatic rise of teacher absenteeism?

Are Tenure Laws Essential?

As the trend toward collective organization of teaching personnel intensifies, so do demands for the elimination of state tenure laws. The experience under a tenure law in Pennsylvania makes it possible to understand the concerns of legislators, school boards, administrators, and citizens in general about the consequences of tenure laws. The main points made in two studies of the Pennsylvania law are as follows:

- Under this law, during the period from 1940 to 1970—thirty years—only 65 teachers have been dismissed for all the reasons permissible.
- During this same thirty-year period, only 193 tenure cases have been processed which led to the 65 dismissals.
- In this same period, only 38 demotions have been accomplished under the law.
- When averaging these actions over the thirty-year period, out of a total tenured population of about 100,000 persons, slightly more than 2 teachers per year have been dismissed statewide, and only 1 teacher per year, statewide, has been reduced in salary or position. Normal personnel standards suggest that the minimum numbers involved in dismissal, demotion, or transfer to other types of work for ineffective work performance should be considerably larger.
- The second study (1971–1976) indicates that 11 teacher dismissal cases due to incompetence were appealed to the secretary of education during the five-year period. This represents .000097 percent of the teaching staff. Dividing this percentage by 5 gives a yearly figure for teacher incompetence cases of .000019 percent of the teachers in Pennsylvania. On an annual basis, the probability of a teacher's being charged with incompetence was one in a half million.[2]

[2] Pennsylvania School Boards Association, "Tenure Must Go," *Information Legislative Service,* 10, no. 10 (March 10, 1972), 8–9, and Harry J. Finlayson, "Incompetence and Teacher Dismissal," *Phi Delta Kappan,* 61, no. 1 (September, 1979), 69.

The criticisms of tenure laws are numerous, including (1) the inordinately high price that a student must pay for such protection against social discipline, (2) the high price that good teachers must pay for the damage that incompetent teachers do to the operation of the educational program, and (3) the general intent or mission of the school system that cannot be achieved under tenure laws. Consequently, the arrangement which teachers are now enjoying—*contractual protection* as well as *legislative protection*—appears to be in for increasing attack and probable modification in the near future.

Should tenure legislation be modified so that it will become a part of the negotiations process between teachers' organizations and boards of education? Will teachers' organizations take essential steps to reduce their ranks of those deemed incompetent?

How Can Personnel Absenteeism Be Reduced?

Recent studies have suggested that personnel absenteeism in education has now become a serious problem, perhaps as pervasive as it is outside of educational institutions.[3] These studies lead to a series of questions regarding the control of personnel absenteeism, including the following:

- To what extent do the absence of clearly defined standards and disciplinary procedures in school systems encourage personnel absenteeism? What minimum standards and practices should prevail governing absenteeism?
- What are the responsibilities of middle- and top-level management in designing, implementing, maintaining, and evaluating the absence control system?
- What guidelines should be established for incorporating absence data into the personnel information system?
- How can cooperation between unions and school systems be improved to make the absence control program effective? To encourage consistent personnel attendance?

How Can Personnel Administration Be Improved?

The human resources function in the 1980s will be called upon to resolve numerous problems resulting from extensive political, economic, social, and institutional change. Working life in America is undergoing revolutionary changes wherein organizational members insist upon determining the conditions under which they work, upon greater system concern for their individual needs, and upon deemphasizing the work ethic, career orientation, and organizational stability.

The root causes of ever-increasing difficulty in resolving human problems in educational and other work organizations include top executive posture, leadership deficiencies, absence of effective strategic and operational planning, and inattention to plans for conducting the human resources function effectively. Any strategy for resolving the contemporary human problems in organizations will need to recon-

---

[3] Educational Research Service, Inc., *Employee Absenteeism: A Summary of Research* (Arlington, Va.: The Service, 1980), p. 1.

sider these matters: how to restructure the personnel function so that it is responsive to the people it is supposed to serve, how to improve the scope and quality of personnel service, and how to provide for the continuing growth and development of those responsible for administering the personnel function.

SELECTED REFERENCES

Castetter, William B., *The Personnel Function in Educational Administration* (3rd ed.). New York: Macmillan Publishing Co., Inc., 1981.

Deutsch, Arnold R., *The Human Resources Revolution: Communicate or Litigate.* New York: McGraw-Hill Book Company, 1979.

Glueck, William F., *Personnel: A Diagnostic Approach,* rev. ed. Dallas, Tex.: Business Publications, Inc., 1978.

Harris, Ben M., Kenneth E. McIntyre, Vance C. Littleton, and Daniel F. Long, *Personnel Administration in Education: Leadership for Improvement.* Boston, Mass.: Allyn & Bacon, Inc., 1979.

Mathis, Robert L., and John H. Jackson, *Personnel: Contemporary Perspectives and Applications* (2nd ed.). St. Paul, Minn.: West Publishing Company, 1979.

Stockard, James G., *Rethinking People Management: A New Look at the Human Resources Function.* New York: American Management Association, 1980.

18

COLLECTIVE BARGAINING
and ADMINISTRATION*

In Chapter 17 we examined the personnel function and its relationship to educational governance. Various processes of the personnel function were analyzed in
terms of their interface or points of contact with the totality of the function as well
as their contribution to improving individual and organizational performance. In
this chapter we will consider in greater detail the personnel process referred to as
collective bargaining.

The topic of collective bargaining will be examined in five parts. In the first
section, the nature and significance of collective bargaining in the public sector is
presented. The second section is concerned with functions collective bargaining is
designed to accomplish. The third section focuses on those factors which influence
the collective bargaining process, including organizational, legal, political, social,
and economic variables. A model of the collective negotiations process is presented

---

*Prepared in large part by William B. Castetter, professor of education, University of Pennsyl-
vania.

in the fourth section, including contract negotiations and contract administration. In the fifth section some of the major issues in this field are reviewed.

NATURE AND SIGNIFICANCE
OF COLLECTIVE BARGAINING

Of the major twentieth-century developments in public education, including the reorganization of school administrative units, desegregation, affirmative action, fluctuations in pupil enrollments, and staff professionalization, none has had more impact on the administrative process and the conditions of work than the development of collective bargaining.

A review of union development in twentieth-century America indicates that there have been three major periods signaling the emergence of three different, though related, parts of the labor force.

1900–mid-1930s	Skilled artisans
1930s–mid-1950s	Semi- and unskilled workers in mass manufacturing
1960s–1980s	White-collar and service-economy personnel

Wisconsin, in 1959, became the first state to enact a public sector labor relations law which made collective bargaining mandatory for municipalities.[1] In subsequent years, public employee unionism has spread to include teachers, nurses, police and firefighters, social workers, librarians, members of service associations, and, more recently, administrative or supervisory personnel in educational institutions.[2]

Collective bargaining may be defined as a continuous process in which representatives of a defined group meet with system representatives to negotiate, jointly, an agreement defining the terms and conditions of employment and its interpretation and administration, concerning a specific period of time. The bargaining pattern followed by teachers is somewhat sequential, from bargaining over and obtaining increases in salary and collateral benefits to working conditions and job security and issues of educational policy.[3]

Several summary statements, developed to enable the reader to identify some of the major characteristics of the collective bargaining process, are examined here to provide background information on the nature of collective bargaining and its relevance to personnel administration.

- The collective bargaining process consists essentially of two subprocesses: *agreement negotiation* and *agreement administration*.
- The collective bargaining process is different from other personnel processes, such as human resources planning, recruitment, selection, induction, appraisal, and development. It is different because it transcends organizational bound-

[1] Anthony M. Cresswell and Michael J. Murphy, eds., *Education and Collective Bargaining* (Berkeley, Calif.: McCutchan Publishing Corporation, 1976), p. 15.

[2] William P. Knoester, "Administrative Unionization: What Kind of Solution?" *Phi Delta Kappan,* 59, no. 6 (February 1978), 419–22.

[3] Lorraine McDonnell and Anthony Pascal, *Organized Teachers in American Schools* (Santa Monica, Calif.: The Rand Corporation, 1979), p. vii.

aries and because it influences and is influenced by external forces over which the system has little control. A collective bargaining agreement in California, for example, may have far-reaching consequences for school systems across the state and nation. Community attitudes, court decisions, legislation, and political activities have considerable influence on the nature of contract negotiation and agreement.

- Collective bargaining is essentially a competitive as well as a cooperative process. While these two aspects of bargaining do not occur simultaneously, it is possible for both parties to cooperate in some areas and to compete in others.
- In both common and statutory law, strikes by public personnel have traditionally been illegal. In recent years several states have legalized public employee strikes if no emergency or major inconveniences are involved.
- One of the important characteristics of collective bargaining in the United States, as compared with that in other nations, is that it is highly decentralized; that is, most contracts in both public and private sectors are negotiated by a union and a single employer. Public sector *federal* labor relations laws are regulated by executive orders issued by the president alone. Labor relations for public personnel at state and local levels are governed by state labor relations laws which specify whether collective bargaining is mandated, permitted, or prohibited and which vary from state to state and city to city. Any negotiated agreement must be within the governing board's lawful authority.
- If more than one personnel association is recognized by the board of education, each of the units separately designates its negotiating representative. Many school systems may have one negotiating unit for teachers, one for maintenance and operating personnel, and one for secretarial and clerical workers. Coalition negotiation involves a systemwide entity representing all personnel, even though they belong to separate work categories.
- Collective bargaining imposes restrictions on both the system and the union or personnel association. Unilateral action is prevented. The system must negotiate with the designated representative(s).

Development of unionism in public education has brought about changes of profound significance. One important change is the shift from an era of unilateralism in decision making relative to the conditions of work to one of bilateralism. Consultation and bargaining about matters of employment are bringing about a redistribution of authority to the extent that union–system relations are an accepted aspect of contemporary governance in public education. There have been other changes of significance. They include the following.

Political power. Congress created a separate Department of Education in 1979, largely through the political efforts of the National Education Association. In addition, federal aid to education has increased substantially through political pressures of the association.[4] At the state level, statewide teacher groups have been instrumental in securing passage of legislation relating to improved state support of public education, in compensation and working conditions, and in favorable collective bargaining statutes.

[4] See Eugene H. Methvin, "The NEA: A Washington Lobby Run Rampant," *Reader's Digest,* 113 (November 1978), 97–101.

Contract attainment. Generally speaking, teacher groups have made substantial gains in both compensation and noncompensation areas. Salary and collateral benefit improvements have been achieved through collective bargaining as have gains in provisions governing class size, performance appraisal, reduction in force, length and compostiion of the school day, grievance procedures, assignment and transfer, the addition and use of support personnel, student discipline, instructional policies, and personnel development. Although these gains have not been universal, the significance of collective bargaining efforts is that teachers are continuing to gain greater influence over the conditions of work in the systems in which they are employed.

Redesign of administrative machinery. Acceptance of the collective bargaining principle by school systems has forced changes in school administrative structures and processes. To cope with union activism, school systems have developed improved approaches to the personnel function in general and to the collective bargaining process in particular. Consequently, school systems have matured in their planning and operation of the human resources function.

Organizational jurisprudence. A major achievement of collective bargaining in public education has been the creation of a system of jurisprudence, wherein the organization and its members designate in contractual form their rights and obligations and a process for settling disputes which arise over contractual interpretation. What is emerging is greater reliance upon professional unionism to achieve member goals rather than upon the array of methods previously used by professionals, such as informal consultation with school systems, lobbying, publication of professional journals, promulgation of codes of ethics, and dependence upon passage of state legislation governing salaries, tenure, leaves of absence, and retirement.

Thus, the collective bargaining process, despite considerable public dissatisfaction with both the economic consequences and public inconveniences which it engenders, as well with some of the prevailing shortcomings in state labor relations laws, is not only an extensive and complex activity; its proper conduct is essential to organizational effectiveness and unity. The school system has much to gain by developing in its administrative structure plans to coordinate the total human resources function and to consider the unique opportunities for innovation and social invention through the dynamics of a bargaining relationship.

FUNCTIONS OF COLLECTIVE BARGAINING

The purpose of a work organization such as a school system is to meet the needs of both the system and the needs of the people who serve the system. The collective bargaining process is designed to serve some of the fundamental elements of a democratic society. The more significant of these ideals, expressed in the form of rights, have been summarized as follows:

- The right to be treated as an individual and respected as a person.
- The right of every individual to a voice in his/her own affairs, which includes the right to contribute to the best of his/her ability in the solution of common problems.

- The right of every individual to recognition for his/her contribution to the common good.
- The right of every individual to develop and make use of his/her capabilities.
- The right of every individual to fairness and justice in all relationships with superiors.[5]

While the foregoing ideals serve as moral and ethical standards for meeting the needs of system members, there is a considerable gap in the extent to which such needs are met. Determinants of militancy among teachers include career dissatisfaction, role conflict, and job tension. Issues such as job autonomy, participation in decision making, salary, and other conditions of professional practice are likely to have a major influence on the level of attitudinal militancy that surfaces in any given organization.[6] In brief, it would appear that one of the key functions of collective bargaining is to minimize the mismatch between what system members demand from their roles and what their roles actually provide.

It is probable that unions serve several direct as well as indirect functions for their members. Beyond the central role of increasing the economic status of organization members, unions in the public sector have broadened their functions to include protecting members' rights, ensuring position security, bargaining for collateral benefits such as insurance in various forms (health, accident, life, dental, retirement), extending opportunities for socialization, improving the personnel justice system, and engaging in lobbying for the resolution of problems affecting member welfare.

It is also probable that the 1980s will bring new problems to unions, new pressures for a different kind of leadership, and new forms of relationships with employers. Critics of unions in the public sector claim that contemporary union hierarchies have won power and prestige in different times but have not been able to, indeed, do not perceive the implications of, a fast-changing economy, a radically altered work force, the needs of a new breed of system member, the technological revolution, the generation of women that is changing in the workplace, changes in the progress and work ethic, and the demand for changes in roles, the pattern for which was set in a distant era. Thus, not only is the concept of work changing, but the modern organization member, born of affluence, is different from his or her predecessors. To resolve the problems of work and the worker of the future, unions will face continuous pressures to perform more than the economic function.

VARIABLES INFLUENCING COLLECTIVE BARGAINING

As new developments in collective bargaining in the public sector emerge, efforts are being made to understand factors, forces, and conditions which generate such changes. While it is clear that a complex network of variables influences the process, the extent of these variables' significance and nature of their interconnections have

---

[5] Ernest C. Miller, ed., *Human Resources Management—The Past Is Prologue* (New York: American Management Association, 1979), p. 221.

[6] Joseph A. Alutto and James A. Belasco, "Determinants of Attitudinal Militancy Among Teachers and Nurses," in *Education and Collective Bargaining*, p. 91.

yet to be explored fully. This section is designed to widen the discussion of the collective bargaining process in terms of variables which are assumed to affect its conduct. An understanding of the variables which operate in the workplace and their influence upon the manner in which working conditions and system–union relationships are established and maintained is essential to attainment of adequate individual and group performance—the ultimate goal of organizations.

Chart 18.1 portrays those variables which it is reasonable to suppose have a direct or indirect influence on part or all of the collective bargaining process. The illustration is designed partly to describe what is already known about factors which influence collective bargaining behavior and partly to suggest hypothetical variables and interrelationships which may be tested by further research.

Chart 18.1 includes ten clusters of variables and is intended to draw attention to their existence and to discuss the pattern of linkages among them. The meaning of most of the variables should be clear, but a few explanatory remarks about some of them may help. The *organizational variable* refers to the size of the system, geographic location, posture of the system on human resources, administrative and supervisory style and techniques, and the quality of union–system relationships. The *judicial variable* focuses upon court decisions and administrative rulings of state regulatory agencies relative to matters brought before them for judicial interpretation. The *government variable* covers federal and state policies, legislation, and dispute-resolving mechanisms governing union–system relations. The *political*

CHART 18.1   Types of Variables Assumed to Influence
the Collective Bargaining Process

variable has been included to indicate that the union, the system, and the public may bring political pressure to bear to resolve conflict and strikes. The *media variable* refers to those situations in which the media, through use of newspapers, radio, and television attempt to explain or to influence the outcome of union-system contract negotiations. The *economic variable* includes the state of the economy, the standard of living and the cost of living in a given community, the economic status of system personnel, and community ability and willingness to meet union contractual demands. The *social variable* takes into consideration community attitude toward education, toward unionism, and toward the particular issues which arise in any union–system effort to consummate a working agreement. This variable also includes the existence of power groups and opinion wielders within the community who bring pressures to bear on the collective bargaining process. The *technology variable* relates to the technical content of the tasks performed in a school system. The more complex the instructional, administrative, supervisory, and support technology, the greater the professionalization and training required of the personnel who perform the tasks. As technology advances, changes in skills, modification in work stations, and changes in the number and types of personnel needed affect personnel status and sense of belonging. Traumatic social, professional, and economic dislocations alter various aspects of the organization and find their way to the bargaining table. The *student variable* is prevalent in contract negotiations in the sense that either party claims its primary objective to be the enhancement of student welfare. Moreover, it is not uncommon for student athletes and students whose college entrance may be affected directly or indirectly by the collective negotiations process to insert their group representatives into contract disputes and strikes. The *union variable* perceives unions to vary in objectives, membership, degree of militancy, and quality of leadership, each of which has the potential for affecting the nature of the collective bargaining process.

The list of variables could be extended. The import of their existence is that there is a variety of internal and external factors capable of affecting the collective bargaining process. These forces in our society are constantly evolving and changing. One role of educational administration is the acquisition of knowledge and assessment of the primary variables which are at work in the collective bargaining process and the selection and application of tools, techniques, and methods appropriate to the particular situation as determined by situational analyses.

THE COLLECTIVE BARGAINING PROCESS

The process aspect of collective bargaining consumes the major portion of this chapter. While the reader will probably have concerns about how unionism in the public sector got to be where it is and how its background influences its present behavior, about federal and state statutory bargaining law, about the behavioral basis for unions, and about union organizing campaigns, space limitations make it necessary to direct our primary focus upon the collective bargaining process.[7]

In common parlance, collective bargaining usually refers to two forms of union-

---

[7]For fuller treatment of these aspects of collective bargaining, see John A. Fossum, *Labor Relations: Development, Structure, Process* (Dallas, Tex.: Business Publications Inc., 1979).

system activity: negotiations for a new contract and administration of an existing agreement. These two key clusters of activities comprise what is generally described as the collective bargaining process. This process varies widely from one organization to another. In smaller systems, the process may be limited to discussion and acceptance of a standard agreement. Elaborate planning by both parties, prolonged negotiations, and conflict frequently attend the process, especially in larger or pattern-setting systems.

Chart 18.2 illustrates key activities usually associated with the collective bargaining process. In addition to the two key clusters of process activities shown in Chart 18.2, the reader should note two characteristics: (1) the sequential and cyclical nature of the process and (2) the opportunity in either of the cluster of activities for informal consultation between parties on matters of mutual concern.

Contract Negotiations

Chart 18.3 indicates that contract negotiations include a wide range of activities, beginning with prenegotiations planning and ending with the formalizing of an agreement which binds both parties to certain conditions during a stipulated period of time. Between the prenegotiation and contract-signing phases, various strategies and tactics are employed by both parties to achieve desired goals.

Prenegotiations planning. Chart 18.3 portrays bilateral activities likely to occur in the prenegotiation phase of the bargaining process. Using Chart 18.3 as a backdrop for examining what takes place in the planning stages of the process, we note a commonality that characterizes prenegotiation activities. Both sides analyze the existing agreement to identify those elements they wish to modify; they search for satisfactory and unsatisfactory experiences in administering the existing agreement; they consider requests of their constituents to add to or alter existing contractual arrangements.

Until recent years, the significance of careful planning for contract negotiations has not been appreciated fully by school executives. Unions have been much more perspicacious about the need to spend time, effort, and funds in preparing plans to

CHART 18.2   Model of the Collective Bargaining Process

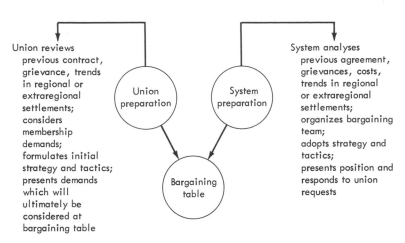

Prenegotiation Activities in the
Collective Bargaining Process

Union reviews
  previous contract,
  grievance, trends
  in regional or
  extraregional
  settlements;
  considers
  membership
  demands;
  formulates initial
  strategy and tactics;
  presents demands
  which will
  ultimately be
  considered at
  bargaining table

Union
preparation

System
preparation

Bargaining
table

System analyses
  previous agreement,
  grievances, costs,
  trends in regional
  or extraregional
  settlements;
  organizes bargaining
  team;
  adopts strategy and
  tactics;
  presents position and
  responds to union
  requests

CHART 18.3   Prenegotiation Activities in the Collective Bargaining
Process

achieve the kind of contract perceived to meet their needs. Contract negotiation is a
complex activity, involving the acquisition of pertinent information, the organization of a bargaining team with the essential conceptual, technical, and interpersonal
skills to deal with issues which will be under consideration, and the formulation of
a philosophy of negotiations which should prevail during union–system bargaining
sessions.

Planning to reach a contract settlement on terms favorable to both the system
and the union is a continuous and complex cyclical activity. This includes monitoring the existing agreement, anticipating the prospective problems, ascertaining the
significant factors to negotiate, defining the objectives and strategy, exploring the
effective bargaining techniques, maintaining the system's right to manage, appraising the effectiveness of different negotiating styles, deciding what to do about the
economic and noneconomic issues in the forthcoming contract, gathering facts and
observations to be employed in the negotiations, and packaging the proposal to be
presented at the bargaining table. An urgent reason for effective planning by both
parties is the increasing complexity and growing number of critical issues to be
negotiated. Although economic issues usually constitute the core of agreement
discussions, noneconomic issues such as organizational justice, performance appraisal, tenure, reduction in force, nonteaching functions, class size, personnel
security, and student discipline have become important contractual considerations.
In addition, social issues related to education are becoming bargainable items,
especially those involving equal opportunity employment, discrimination, integration, staff balance, decentralization, transfer, and community control of attendance
units. Consequently, the bargaining table has become an extension of the school
board meeting, whereby new plans are proposed and those in existence are subjected to critical examination.

Public access to collective bargaining. One contemporary development in the public sector likely to influence planning activities is public access to bargaining sessions. Collective bargaining in the past has not been under close public scrutiny. With the advent of rising costs and declining enrollments, decline in public confidence in the schools, questions about student achievement, reduction in staff, and student discipline, public demands for more information about and for participation in contract negotiation has emerged. Among the forms of public access which have been identified are sunshine bargaining, public review of system and union proposals prior to actual bargaining, citizen representation on the school board's bargaining team, and formation of parent unions.[8] Although the effect of public presence and participation in collective bargaining has not been examined extensively, this development portends changes in planning for and behavior in contract negotiations.

Organizing for negotiations. Prior to initiation of contract negotiations, both union and system organize activities to achieve their expectations. Decisions are made by each side as to the representatives responsible for conducting the negotiations, what information will be needed by those who negotiate, who gathers, refines, stores, and retrieves essential information, who is responsible for plans and action in the event of a strike, and how the total bargaining effort is to be coordinated.

Chart 18.4 illustrates system and union organization structures with emphasis upon the manner in which the system identifies roles and relationships among personnel responsible for various tasks.

- The hypothetical system organization structure, as outlined in Chart 18.4, consists of two mechanisms: a policy committee and a negotiating team.
- The system central policy committee develops policy recommendations for consideration by the board of education. It advises the board on systemwide personnel policies related to collective bargaining and on strategies and tactics to be adhered to in formal or informal bargaining sessions.
- The composition of the bargaining team should have representation from the board of education, the immediate superintendency, and administrative extensions of the superintendency. Some organization structures include a public representative.
- As shown in Chart 18.4, a team rather than a single individual should represent the system, even though responsibility for actual negotiations may be delegated to a single individual (prime negotiator). The team is conceived to consist of a group of individuals with a variety of skills to resolve a series of complex problems.
- The chief executive is not placed in the role of prime negotiator. He or she coordinates, on behalf of the board, all activities involved in and all decisions affecting the contractual agreement.

While it is not the intent of the text to indicate that one type of bargaining model is superior to others, the point of the foregoing discussion is to emphasize the need for planning, for the chief executive to coordinate planning and decision

[8] Robert E. Doherty, ed., *Public Access: Citizens and Collective Bargaining in the Public Schools* (Ithaca: New York State School of Industrial and Labor Relations, 1979).

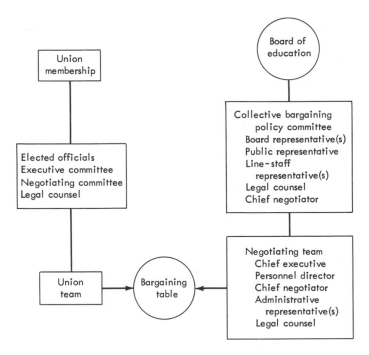

CHART 18.4   Illustration of Bargaining Organization
Structures

making, and for the inclusion of a variety of skills on both the policy and negotiating committees.

Information for bargaining. Issues to be resolved at the bargaining table are influenced to a considerable extent by the quality of pertinent information available to both parties. Although various options are open to the system to allocate responsibilities for the identification, acquisition, refinement, storage, retrieval, dissemination, communication, and integration of bargaining information, one plausible approach is to assign this role to the personnel function. Reasons in favor of this approach include (1) unity of function—the personnel function is usually assigned the task of initiating, maintaining, and improving the personnel information system; (2) most of the issues on the bargaining table have personnel implications; (3) the personnel office has the responsibility for coordinating the collective bargaining process with other personnel processes discussed in Chapter 17. If the system does not have a personnel director, responsibility for coordinating and processing information should be assigned to a single individual within the central administration. This individual will call upon various line-and-staff personnel to make certain analyses and to request information needed by the negotiating team. Preparation of a negotiations handbook containing data on practically any subject on which discussion and negotiation is anticipated is illustrative of one activity involved in the role relating to negotiation information.

A	B	C	D	E	F
Union and system present proposals	Union and system respond to proposals	Proposals are modified	Subgroups form to reexamine proposals	Nonagreement or tentative agreement results	Ratification occurs

CHART 18.5   Outline of Bargaining Stages

Bargaining stages. As prenegotiation planning is completed, the stage is set for a series of bargaining events. These events or stages are shown in Chart 18.5 beginning with either party presenting contract proposals for consideration. Generally on some issues there are wide differences in perceptions as to their acceptability. The initial proposals represent bargaining postures which are modified as the bargaining process proceeds. Both parties respond to the demands, being influenced by a host of factors including pressures from the union membership, the public, power groups, and related elements. As proposals are modified, both sides devise mechanisms to reexamine and to resubmit reshaped proposals for further examination. When the bargaining process moves into the stage at which vital issues are considered to work out reasonable alternatives to initial and perhaps subsequent proposals, the end result can be nonagreement or tentative agreement. Both parties submit proposals to their reference groups for reaction and response. If there is mutual agreement, the process moves into the formal or ratification stage. If nonagreement occurs, the process may move laterally into mediation, strike, or arbitration before a final settlement is reached.

Bargaining behavior. Interest in and concern with union and system bargaining behavior has now developed into a research area toward which increasing effort is being directed. During the bargaining stages (beginning, middle, end), a complex social process is in operation during which negotiators' behavior reflects individual, group, and organizational characteristics. Walton and McKersie have identified the kinds of bargaining relationships likely to prevail during the negotiations process:

- *Distributive bargaining.* Goals of both parties in conflict. Total views are assumed to be fixed, so that "one person's gain is another's loss."
- *Integrative bargaining.* Goals not perceived as conflicting; problems perceived as areas of mutual concern.
- *Attitudinal structuring.* Activities in and surrounding negotiations that serve to change attitudes and relationships.
- *Intraorganizational bargaining.* Activities designed to bring expectations of both parties in line with those of the chief negotiators.[9]

The foregoing framework assumes that negotiations consist of four systems of acitivity, each with its own function for the interacting parties, its own internal logics, and its own identifiable set of instrumental aids or tactics.

[9] Richard E. Walton and Robert B. McKersie, *A Behavioral Theory of Labor Negotiations* (New York: McGraw-Hill Book Company, 1965), pp. 475–477.

The traditional form of negotiation in school systems is considered to be distributive. Far less prevalent is the integrative type which involves less of an offensive-defensive position and more of a cooperative approach to fact-finding, problem exploration, and agreement resolution.

The import of the foregoing discussion is that the posture which either party brings to the process is critical to the outcome. Factors which influence the process include leadership, feelings about the joint relationship, union influence, and attitudes toward employing integrative bargaining.

Strategy and tactics. Bargaining behavior involves employment of two kinds of plans—strategy and tactics. Strategic planning is future oriented, directed toward development of organizational purposes and their attainment. From the standpoint of the school system, strategy in collective bargaining is concerned with the kinds of educational services it intends to deliver to its clients, policies by which the services are developed and delivered, and means of enlisting the voluntary cooperation of system personnel to accomplish these broader aims. One strategic aim of the system is to enable each of its members to derive a suitable standard of living, a sense of dignity and worth, and meaning in an increasingly complex society. Thusly viewed, bargaining strategy is conceived as a guide to system behavior which focuses on its strategic aims. By way of illustration, the strategic aim of the system for its human resources may be to

- Establish working conditions, position security, and personal recognition that will make the system a desirable place in which to work and plan a career.
- Provide development opportunities to enable individuals to advance within the system.
- Provide incentives to motivate personnel to perform effectively and efficiently.
- Establish a reward system to attract and retain competent personnel.

The major strategic goals of the union are considered to be higher salaries and benefits, personnel security, union security, and increased membership. At any given time, some of the foregoing goals must be forsaken in light of the economic, political, and social realities which prevail when the contract is being negotiated. It should be noted that the union or the professional group which it represents may also see as its ultimate goal improved educational services, improved policies regarding the services, and the further development of personnel to increase their effectiveness.

The tactics of collective bargaining include behavior engaged in by either party to achieve either short- or long-run objectives. Some actions are taken prior to negotiations, others at the bargaining table. There is no set pattern by which both parties maneuver to make accommodations called for by their common and opposing interests. If the system adopts an affirmative strategy to improve conditions under which its personnel perform services, it is clear that this cannot be accomplished ordinarily in a single agreement. Tactics in this situation may well be directed toward securing agreement on a series of subgoals which contribute to the broad strategic aims mentioned earlier.

When two parties meet at the bargaining table, the *facts* of the situation are paramount. This is to say that neither side can choose freely the issues to be negotiated or the tactics to be employed in settling them. Different conditions require different tactics. Some bargaining problems are long standing and recurring. The facts or conditions, both internal and external, pertaining to current issues will determine the kinds of negotiations that take place and their final outcome.

Scope of bargaining. The number of clauses in a union-system contract depends to a considerable extent on what both parties agree to as bargainable items. The number of items over which unions and school systems bargain continue to increase and may be categorized into the following groups:

- *Economic issues.* Form of compensation, its magnitude, and method of determination.
- *Personnel security.* Assignments, transfers, promotions, dismissals, reductions in force, grievance procedures.
- *Conditions of employment.* School calendar and working hours, class size, support personnel, student discipline, teacher safety.
- *Professional issues.* Personnel development and evaluation, pupil evaluation and achievement, academic freedom.
- *Union security.* Assurance for unions' existence and stability usually through insistence on withholding of personnel dues by the system from their pay and forwarding the amount directly to the union. Another form of union security to be negotiated is a clause for controlling membership by requiring all personnel to become union members as a condition of continued employment or the payment of a service fee for nonunion members. Some union security contract clauses are aimed at greater union control over hiring, supervising, and discharging personnel.
- *System rights.* The sytem's insistence upon conract language which permits it to carry out its legal, social, and moral obligations without union interference, including size of staff, selection, evaluation, and discipline. These issues are complex, especially where matters of statutory adherence are involved and when extreme pressures are generated from state-level union leaders whose goals are often unrelated to the goals of the system and the diverse needs of its personnel.
- *Contract duration.* General preference of school boards for longer contracts because of the instability caused by frequent negotiations as well as the time, effort, and, expenditure of funds committed to this form of bargaining versus unions' apprehension about longer contracts, especially during a period of increasing economic growth.

Frequently the bargaining ritual begins with the union's presenting an extensive and expensive package of proposals. The system counters with its own proposals, which are usually fewer but far apart from those of the union. This phase of bargaining sets the stage for trading material as negotiations reach the later stages. In effect, this behavior disguises the real intent of both parties and gives room for probing, maneuvering, tempting, and scaling down some proposals or abandoning them altogether when it appears propitious to do so.

The scope of bargaining in those states having statutes regulating collective bargaining in the public sector is defined in general rather than in specific terms. The statutes tend to forbid agreements that conflict with state statutes or provisions of municipal home rule charters. Typical of such statutes are those which do not require public employers to bargain over matters of inherent managerial policy, which shall include but shall not be limited to such areas of discretion or policy as the functions and programs of the public employer, standards of services, its overall budget, utilization of technology, the organizational structure, and selection and direction of personnel. Public employers in most states are not required to bargain with units of first-level supervisors or their representatives, such as principals and superintendents. Where state bargaining laws exist, they do not require either party to agree to a proposal or require the parties to make concessions.

Some states have statutory mechanisms for reviewing scope of bargaining issues when both parties disagree as to bargainable items. This mechanism is a labor relations board or its equivalent. Thereafter, the courts must determine whether the impact of the issue on the interest of the employer outweighs its effect on the basic policy of the system as a whole.

Legislatures remain aloof from passing laws regarding the scope of bargaining that contain a precise list of specific items which are or are not bargainable. Such a list would never be complete, because of unforeseen and unanticipated issues which may arise in the future. In effect, further definition of the scope of bargaining other than legislative guidelines ultimately becomes a matter for the courts to decide.

Collective bargaining impasse. Contract negotiation has been depicted as an uninterrupted series of steps from the presentation of proposals to contract agreement. Disputes or impasses arise frequently, however, between representatives of the public employer and public employees. When the system and the union cannot agree on the terms of a new contract, an impasse exists and the methods for resolving such situations include mediation, fact-finding, arbitration, and strikes or lockouts. In states with bargaining statutes, the steps to resolve an impasse are usually prescribed by law. In states without such laws, systems are generally free to decide at the bargaining table which impasse tactics will be employed. Of the several options mentioned for resolving an impasse *during the bargaining process,* three involve third-party involvement: mediation, fact-finding, and arbitration. Mediation is a process in which a neutral third party, usually one with mediation expertise, is invited in by both parties to help remove an impasse to the negotiations. The role of the mediator is advisory, its primary purpose being to keep the negotiations from deteriorating and to develop a neutral approach which will enable the union and system to resolve the impasse by themselves in their own way.

A second form of third-party involvement in contract negotiations is fact-finding, wherein both sides agree to invite a neutral individual or panel to investigate the unresolved issues and report the results. The role of the fact finder may vary, depending upon the law or the bargaining agreement. The options usually include the capability of the fact finder to point out settlement possibilities or to make specific suggestions for impasse resolution. In some states fact finding panels may hold hearings, take oral or written testimony, and utilize subpoena power. Usually a time frame is specified in the statutes during which findings and facts are reported, publicized, and communicated to both parties, who must then decide whether or not they will accept the recommendations.

The third form of third-party involvement in contract negotiations is referred to as arbitration, the step taken when mediation or fact-finding do not lead to removal of the impasse. Public sector arbitration during contract negotiations is referred to as *interest arbitration*. Grievance arbitration, which will be discussed in the text following is employed *after a contract is signed* when the meaning of contract clauses are in dispute.

Interest arbitration during contract negotiations may be voluntary or compulsory. Both parties may agree to submit the unresolved issues to a third party voluntarily, but they are not obligated to accept the arbitrator's decision. If compulsory arbitration is required by law, the decision of the arbitrator is bilaterally binding. It may be inferred that (1) each approach places increasingly greater constraints on bargaining behavior and (2) only one (binding arbitration) seeks to guarantee a solution to the impasse. For various reasons, binding arbitration has not been embraced by boards of education, including the making of sometimes questionable decisions by an uninformed third party, delegation of legal prerogatives of elected officials to nonelected agents, and the excessive costs which may be associated with such externally mandated decisions.

Strikes and lockouts are resorted to when third-party involvement fails to resolve the bargaining impasse. A strike may be defined as the concerted withdrawal of services by system membership. It is a refusal by personnel to work and represents a form of economic pressure to force the employer to meet union contractual demands. A lockout, on the other hand, is initiated by the system and represents a refusal by the system to permit its personnel to continue employment. A report by the American Association of School Administrators in 1975 indicates that the reward system is at the heart of most work stoppages in public education, despite claims to the contrary.[10] A 1979 report on teacher strikes indicated that payoff from strikes vary markedly. Some resulted in large gains; others caused teachers to settle for less than they had been offered prior to the strike. The difference in payoff, according to the report, seems to depend upon the strength of the teachers' organization and how skillfully it uses the strike as a response to impasse.[11]

In summarizing the foregoing review on procedures for resolving impasses, it has been noted that parties may settle disputes by their own devices, by mediation, by fact-finding, by arbitration, by strikes, and by lockouts. Of these options, the most effective is resolution by both parties without outside intervention. Legal impasse procedures have not been as effective as their proponents claim. The strike, too, is viewed as a high-risk venture, in which the immediate and long-range losses are often far greater than the economic benefits which may accrue.

Contract agreement. Eventually, either before of after a work stoppage, a contractual agreement will be reached. The agreement usually emerges in stages—informal agreement by key negotiators, proposed settlement before full negotiating committees of both sides, reduction of agreement to contract language, and formal ratification and approval by the system and the union. Viewed from the perspective of union membership, the act of contract ratification is helpful in these ways: (1) ratification requires union negotiators to explain the outcome and to influence its acceptance, and (2) membership acceptance enhances enforcement by the union, system, and arbitrators.

---

[10] American Association of School Administrators, *Work Stoppage Strategies,* Executive Handbook Series No. 6 (Arlington, Va.: The Association, 1975), p. 5.

[11] McDonnell and Pascal, *Organized Teachers in American Schools,* pp. 64–65.

In the model of the collective bargaining process illustrated in Chart 18.2, the process was viewed as having two major characteristics: (1) contract bargaining and (2) contract administration. Having covered the first stage of this process, let us turn our attention now to the administration of the contract.

Contract communication. One of the first steps taken by the administrative team of the system upon formal agreement approval is to communicate in detail and to interpret system responsibilities and rights inherent in contract clauses. The system head ensures that all unit heads who direct the work of union members know the meaning of the contract language so that the contract itself is nonthreatening to either party. Denigration of either party through administration of the contract destroys the working relationship and maintains tension. Achieving congruence between the union and the system requires exerted effort in managing the contract and in understanding the needs, views, and pressures of both parties.

Contract evaluation. In addition to clarifying the terms of the contractual agreement and helping personnel to become knowledgeable about its impact on their employment, their rights, and responsibilities, another aspect of contract administration deserves mention. This is evaluation, one of the basic elements of the administrative process designed to determine how well performance conforms to plan. It is concerned with the effects of all plans and procedures in relation to their contribution to system purposes. Evaluation of the collective bargaining process is an activity indispensable to system effectiveness and efficiency. The system needs to know, for example,

- What are the strengths and weaknesses of the existing agreement?
- What are the sources of irritation and dispute in administering the agreement?
- What is the impact of the agreement on the motivation of personnel?
- What has been the history of grievance procedures during contract administration?
- What steps should be taken to improve contract administration?
- What is the nature of feedback about the contract from unit administrators?

Plans for monitoring and evaluating the impact of a negotiated contract on both the individual member and its effect upon the human resources policies of the total system are of large importance.

Contract administration and grievance procedures. Once a contract agreement has been formally approved by the union and system, both parties are bound by its terms for its duration. Because of the manner in which contract clauses are written, because they are frequently subjected to different interpretations, because of changing or unforeseen circumstances, or because of ambiguities created deliberately, disputes arise. Mechanisms resorted to in resolving these disputes include grievance procedures, grievance arbitration, and strikes.

Grievance procedure. <u>A grievance is a formal dissatisfaction between employee and employer, arising from alleged missapplication, misinterpretation, violation, or inequitable application of the terms of the contract agreement</u>. The grievance is expressed formally through an identified procedure contained in the statutes or contractual agreement. Characteristics of a grievance procedure, as illustrated in Chart 18.6, include

- A series of steps through which a grievance may be appealed to several system levels for resolution. The grievance can be settled at any stage.
- Stated time limits for the presentation of grievances.
- Provision for broader review of the grievance as it moves through the line of appeal.
- Provision for arbitration as a final step in settling an unresolved grievance.

Actually, the possibilities for settlement of a grievance are the same as those available for settling a bargaining impasse. These include arbitration (giving a third party the authority to issue a binding decision), mediation (using a third party to help both parties reach an agreement voluntarily), and strike (work stoppage or cessation of service).

The usefulness of formal grievance machinery in school systems, whether unionized or not, is hardly debatable. Such machinery serves various purposes, but its most vital role is the creation of a system of organizational jurisprudence whereby disputes about conditions of employment are dealt with through a rational, systematic process. The security of every individual is enhanced when there is assurance that one can appeal employment discontent or dissatisfaction. In the eyes of the union member, the procedure is his or her most tangible link with the collective bargaining process, a reward for payment of dues, for picketing and striking, for supporting union principles. It is the rampart of position protection in the course of a working career.

ISSUES AND TRENDS

The brief examination of collective bargaining in public education in this chapter is scarcely sufficient to provide adequate explanation of its many ramifications or the variety of pressures which are bringing into focus existing and emerging issues and trends of critical importance. Table 18.1 provides an overview of the extent and variety of important issues in collective bargaining. These issues, it should be noted, are created by a variety of pressures both internal and external to the system. The pressures include demographics, economics, legislation, and decline of public confidence in its schools. The economics of education, highlighted by unemployment and inflation, continue to make it difficult for public school officials to meet union demands for salaries and benefits. Enrollment decline has resulted in staff reductions for significant numbers of teachers and other educational personnel, which affect union membership, stability, costs, and give rise to protracted disputes within the union and with boards of education.

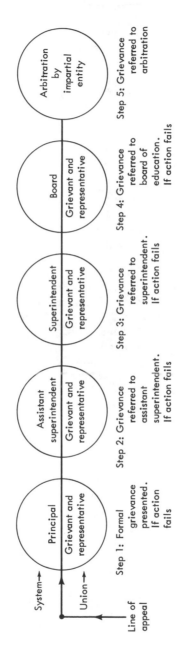

CHART 18.6   Illustration of a Grievance Procedure

TABLE 18.1   Some Major Issues in Collective Bargaining

POLITICAL	ECONOMIC	ADMINISTRATIVE
Strikes in the public sector	Compensation: basic	Reductions in force
Coalition bargaining	salary, extra pay, over-	Performance appraisal
Geographical bargaining,	time, collateral benefits,	Tenure
regional and statewide	cafeteria plan, quasi-	Academic freedom
Federal bargaining	benefits	Grievance procedures
legislation	Form, amount, and	School day and year
Union security	method of determining	Class size
Use of union funds for	method of foregoing	Support personnel
political purposes	elements of compensa-	Assignment
Scope of bargaining	tion are perennial	Transfer
Grievance arbitration	issues	Promotion
Unions for adminis-		Development of personnel
trators		Student discipline
Public access to		Personnel productivity
bargaining		
Picketing		
Unfair practices		
Conflict of interest		
Judicial review		
Personnel security		

In effect, collective bargaining in the public sector is now being subjected to close scrutiny, partly because of the current economic, social, political, and moral difficulties confronting the nation and partly because of public dissatisfaction with collective bargaining laws, negative consequences frequently generated by the bargaining process, and the militant posture of unions which comes as a culture shock to some segments of the citizenry. Insofar as some of the major union-system disputes are concerned, such as strikes and injunctions, performance effectiveness, staff size, and tenure-related problems, the present arrangements for their resolution are not working to the public's satisfaction.

Demographic, economic, political, social, and organizational pressures currently impacting on collective bargaining in the public sector will change in some respects future bargaining strategies and tactics. The future of labor relations in the public sector, according to a report of the Bureau of National Affairs, will be along lines such as the following:

- The number of public employee unions and organizations will continue to grow.
- Interunion conflicts will be created as more groups compete for employee membership.
- Unions will continue to work for the enactment of comprehensive bargaining laws and the refinement of existing ones.
- A federal bargaining law to set minimum standards for public sector bargaining or to include public employees under the National Labor Relations Act may be passed.

- Strikes by teachers and other public employees will not increase in number but may become more severe.
- Increased binding arbitration will stimulate a number of effects. Employers will be pressed to fund awards they cannot afford while taxpayers will demand greater accountability of public services. This may lead to a reversal of the current tendency to favor unions and to subsequent cutbacks in benefits.
- Employees will continue to bargain for fringe benefits while employers will strengthen bargaining pressure in areas such as residency requirements.
- Union security provisions, such as dues checkoffs, will become more common and will provide additional funds for political and organizing activities.
- The use of grievance arbitration will increase.
- Confrontation between employers and employees will continue, but a greater sophistication will be demonstrated in collective bargaining and greater cooperation will be demonstrated in nonbargaining activities such as management–labor committees.
- Future relationships between employers and employees will take economic, political, military, technical, and international developments into account.[12]

Despite all the changes occurring in the world and their profound impact upon public and private organizations, and despite imperfections in and difficulties created by collective bargaining, there are no signs on the horizon to indicate that the practice will disappear from the organizational scene. On the other hand, current bargaining practices in the public sector are not immutable. As public managment continues to explore new opportunities to structure union–system relationships directed toward more efficient and effective service to the public at costs which are affordable, movement of professional unionism can be anticipated toward attainment of longer-run goals, including not only economic security but adequate income in relation to quality of service rendered. When professional unionism assumes a greater role in school reform, particularly in the improvement of teaching and learning, then economic reward for individual merit will become the hallmark of the union member, and those systems which reward everyone equally will become organizational relics—customs whose original environment has disappeared.

The foregoing considerations suggest that the design for future union–system relationships in educational institutions might well include the following assumptions:

- The burden of correcting existing imperfections in current union–system relations must be assumed by four parties to the relationship—the system, the union, government, and the individual. Reform in labor relations cannot be assumed totally by any single element.
- There will be increased interest among professional and semiprofessional union personnel in bargaining over matters different in both substance and implication from prevailing patterns among skilled and unskilled workers in the private or public sectors. Thus, the assumption that professional unionism in the public sector will move away from the classic and compulsive posture of contractual uniformity of bargained working conditions is not without

[12] Bureau of National Affairs, *Negotiating the Future: Labor Relations in the Public Sector, 1979–2029.* (Washington, D.C.: Bureau of National Affairs, 1979).

merit. As protective and economic assurances are achieved by personnel, relief from current tensions in relations between systems and unions about seniority, about reduction in force, about the reward system, about power distribution, and about personnel who are either aided or impeded by bargained conditions, may well be achieved through relaxation of the policy of contractual uniformity.

• There are indications to support the assumption that forces are at work to change the primary functions of central governing bodies of professional unions. Union strategy at the local level in some instances is moving toward a collaborative rather than an adversary relationship. Thus, the future may be witness to modification of the classic central union role as the protagonist of contractual uniformity and toward identification of alternative patterns of economic and protective arrangements. In brief, as the professional moves toward greater diversity and choice in the conditions of employment, union governing bodies will have to choose whether to remain in the background or move to the foreground of changes in the world of work.

Each of these assumptions, it should be noted, directs attention to the likelihood that contemporary concepts of collective bargaining for professionals will undergo partial modification, that practices will tilt away from classic bargaining approaches in the private sector, and that there will be a continuation of certain features of existing work systems.

In sum, the evolutionary process of change, which is so intensively and pervasively at work in the twentieth–century society, is moving toward changes not only in the conditions of work but in search of solutions to improve the manner in which the conditions are determined. Further, probable changes in professional unions create new challenges and opportunities for educational leadership by those representing the system in negotiations.

SELECTED REFERENCES

Aboud, Antone, and **Grace Street Aboud,** *The Right to Strike in Public Employment,* Key Issues Series No. 15. Ithaca: New York State School of Industrial and Labor Relations, 1974.

Castetter, William B., *The Personnel Function in Educational Administration* (3rd ed.). New York: Macmillan Publishing Co., Inc., 1981.

Cresswell, Anthony M., and **Michael J. Murphy,** *Teachers, Unions, and Collective Bargaining in Public Education.* Berkeley, Calif.: McCutchan Publishing Corporation, 1979.

Doherty, Robert E., *Industrial and Labor Relations Terms: A Glossary,* ILR Bulletin No. 44 (4th ed.). Ithaca: New York State School of Industrial and Labor Relations, 1979.

Dunlop, John T., and **Walter Galenson,** eds., *Labor in the Twentieth Century.* New York: Academic Press, Inc., 1978.

Hamner, W. Clay, and **Frank L. Schmidt,** *Comtemporary Problems in Personnel* (rev. ed.). Chicago: St. Clair Press, 1977.

Hanslowe, Kurt L., David Dunn, and **Jay Erstling,** *Union Security in Public Employment: Of Free Riding and Free Association,* IPE Monograph No. 8. Ithaca: Institute of Public Employment, New York State School of Industrial and Labor Relations, 1978.

Mathis, Robert L., and **John H. Jackson,** *Personnel: Contemporary Perspectives and Applications* (2nd ed.). St. Paul, Minn.: West Publishing Company, 1979.

19

FINANCE *and* BUSINESS ADMINISTRATION

Boards of education expect the administrators of the public schools to have an extensive knowledge of financing and business administration of the public schools. It is also essential that all professional employees of the public schools, including teachers, have a knowledge of the basic concepts of educational financing and business administration. As was pointed out in Chapter 4, the pluralistic, collegial concept of educational administration requires that all persons involved in implementing policies should participate in formulating those policies. The practice of collective negotiations is now spreading throughout the nation.[1] Teachers cannot participate intelligently in collective negotiations relating to salaries, fringe benefits, pupil-teacher ratios, and similar matters unless they are aware of the financial resources of the board and the financial impact of their proposals.[2] If the teachers are to participate effectively in budget making, they must have some knowledge

[1] See Ralph B. Kimbrough and Michael Y. Nunnery, *Educational Administration* (New York: Macmillan Publishing Co., Inc., 1976), Chap. 15.
[2] See Chapter 8, The Politics of Education.

of the need for business administration services such as school plant operation and maintenance, school transportation, school food service, accounting, reporting, and so on.

It is beyond the scope of this chapter to present an analysis of even the basic concepts of school financing and business administration. However, the attempt is made to present a brief description of some of the areas of school financing and business administration in which prospective school administrators, teachers, and other professional school personnel are vitally concerned.

TRENDS IN SCHOOL EXPENDITURES

The financing of the public schools from public funds began in New England in colonial days. However, schools in the New England colonies were only partly financed from public funds. Before 1800, in all other states education was considered a family or church responsibility except for paupers. The sixteenth section of each township in the Northwest Territory was set aside for the support of education by the Ordinances of 1785 and 1787, but very little school revenue was derived from these lands prior to 1800. Therefore, prior to the beginning of the nineteenth century, the schools in all states, except the New England states, were financed primarily from philanthropy, fees, and rate bills.

Tax-supported public schools were not generally available in the United States during the first quarter of the nineteenth century. However, during the period 1830 to 1860 constitutional and statutory authority for tax-supported public schools was generally established in the Middle Atlantic and Midwestern states. Legal authorization for tax-supported public schools was not generally provided in the Southern and some of the Western states until the last quarter of the nineteenth century.

Despite the fact that legal authorization for tax-supported public schools had been provided in most states except the Southern states by the middle of the nineteenth century, the actual provisions for public education were very meager. According to the seventh census of the United States in 1850, only about half the children of New England were provided free education, one sixth in the West, and one seventh in the Middle States.[3] Therefore, constitutional and statutory authorization for tax-supported public schools did not result in substantial tax revenues for the public schools in most states for many years. In the South, with few exceptions, free education was provided only for paupers. Even in the New England, Middle Atlantic, and Western states, public education was confined largely to the elementary grades and tax funds were usually supplemented by fees and rate bills. It has been a long and arduous struggle to provide free public elementary and secondary education in the United States. Actually, free, tax-supported public schools did not become generally available in the United States until well into the first quarter of the twentieth century. In fact, secondary education, especially in rural areas, did not become generally available until after World War I.[4]

[3] Newton Edwards and Herman G. Richey, *The School in the American Social Order* (Boston: Houghton Mifflin Company, 1963), p. 292.
[4] *Ibid.*, Chap. 9.

World War I had a significant impact on the financing of education. That war ended a long period of international isolation. We were rapidly becoming the greatest industrial nation in the world and a major migration from the farms to the cities began following that war. It became generally apparent to the people that a type of education that would suffice for an agrarian society was quite inadequate for a technological, industrialized society. This became even more apparent following World War II. The provisions for public education, including financing, have been extended steadily since the period following World War I.

The data presented in Table 19.1 show some important trends in educational expenditures between 1930 and 1980. Expenditures per pupil in average daily attendance increased from $474 to $2,419 in terms of the purchasing power of 1979 dollars. This is a real increase of 410 percent in per pupil expenditures between 1930 and 1980. Education is given a much higher priority in the allocation of our resources today than it was fifty years ago. In 1930 only 2.2 percent of the gross national product was allocated to the support of the public schools, whereas in 1980 we allocated 4.0 percent for that purpose. It is noted from Table 19.1 that we allocated 4.4 percent of the gross national product to the support of the public schools in 1974-1975 and that it had decreased to 4.0 percent in 1979-1980. This reduction in the percentage of GNP allocated to the support of the public schools since 1975-1976 was due primarily to the decline in school enrollment between 1975 and 1980. However, part of that decline was no doubt due to the great increase in inflation since 1976 which resulted in public resistance to increases in taxes not only for education but practically all governmental services.

Special Factors Affecting Trends in Expenditures for the Public Schools

Table 19.2 shows that expenditures per pupil increased only 1.4 percent per year between 1929-1930 and 1939-1940. These were the depression years. However, expenditures per pupil increased 6.0 percent per year between 1959-1960 and 1969-1970. These were relatively prosperous years with a mixed economy. The data in Table 19.2 suggest that improvement in the financing of the public schools come slowly either in times of depression or in times of inflation. The consumer price index declined 16 percent between 1929-1930 and 1939-1940 and increased 98 percent between 1969-1970 and 1979-1980. These were the two decades during the fifty years following 1930 during which expenditures per pupil increased the least.

Although expenditures per pupil continued to increase during the 1970-1980 decade, classroom teachers' salaries actually decreased during that period of time. The Research Service of the National Education Association reported that the average salary of classroom teachers in current dollars was $8,635 in 1969-1970 and $16,001 in 1979-1980.[5] In 1979 dollars of purchasing power, the average salary of classroom teachers in 1969-1970 was $17,097 as compared with $16,001 in 1979-1980. Therefore, in terms of purchasing power, classroom teachers' salaries

[5]National Education Association, *Estimates of School Statistics, 1979-80* (Washington, D.C.: National Education Association, 1980), p. 16.

TABLE 19.1 Trends in Total Expenditures for the Public Schools (includes all items for current expense, capital outlay, and interest on school indebtedness)

Year	Expenditures in Current Dollars (millions)	Percent of Gross National Product Expended for the Public Schools	Average Daily Attendance (thousands)	Expenditures Per Pupil in Current Dollars	Consumer Price Index (1967=100)	Expenditures Per Pupil in Terms of Purchasing Power of 1979 Dollars
1929–30	$ 2,307	2.2	21,165	$ 109	50.0	$ 474
1939–40	2,331	2.6	22,042	106	42.0	541
1949–50	5,768	2.2	22,284	259	71.4	789
1959–60	15,613	3.2	32,477	481	87.3	1,198
1969–70	40,683	4.3	41,934	970	109.8	1,921
1974–75	62,340	4.4	41,476	1,503	147.7	2,212
1979–80	92,924	4.0	38,419	2,419	217.4	2,419

SOURCE: Data on expenditures and average daily attendance from the Office of Education except for the year 1979–1980, which was estimated by the National Education Association. Data on the price index are from the *Survey of Current Business*. The price index and gross national product are for the calendar year in which the school year began.

TABLE 19.2 Percentage Increase in Expenditures Per Pupil in Average Daily Attendance in Dollars of the Same Purchasing Power (data computed from Table 19.1)

Period of Time	Total Percentage Increase in Expenditures Per Pupil	Percentage Increase in Expenditures Per Pupil Per Year	Total Percentage Increase in Consumer Price Index	Annual Percentage Increase in Consumer Price Index
1929–30 to 1939–40	14%	1.4%	−16%	−1.6%
1939–40 to 1949–50	46	4.6	70	7.0
1949–50 to 1959–60	52	5.2	22	2.2
1959–60 to 1969–70	60	6.0	25	2.5
1969–70 to 1979–80	26	2.6	98	9.8

declined $1,096 or 6.4 percent between 1969-1970 and 1979-1980. The pupil-teacher ratio decreased from approximately 21 to 1 in 1969-1970 to 18 to 1 in 1979-1980. This explains the fact that expenditures per pupil increased in constant dollars during that decade and teachers' salaries actually declined.

What is the outlook for the financing of the public schools during the years 1980-1990? If a high rate of inflation continues, no doubt there will be great difficulty in meeting the financial needs of the public schools. Taxpayer resistance to the burden of paying taxes increases in times of inflation. Data presented in *U.S. News and World Report* show that federal taxes increased 76.3 percent between 1974 and 1979, state taxes rose 68.6 percent, local taxes rose 51.6 percent, and the grand total of all taxes rose 69.4 percent.[6] The consumer price index increased 47.2 percent between 1974 and 1979.

The National Retired Teachers Association and American Association of Retired Persons (NRTA-AARP) reported that thirty-two states had enacted eighty statutes reducing either state or local taxes which became effective in 1979-1980.[7] This organization of the elderly supported all those tax-relief measures.

The age composition of the population is changing and this will affect the willingness of the population to levy taxes for education and other functions of government. The U.S. Bureau of the Census has estimated that approximately 34,300,000 persons in the United States in 1980 were sixty years of age and over. This age group constituted 16 percent of the total population in 1980. The number of persons sixty years of age and over increased 19 percent between 1970 and 1980, whereas the total population increased only 9 percent. The retired population on fixed incomes suffers more than does any other sector of the population from inflation. Their support of tax relief and opposition to tax increases is quite understandable.

Attention has already been directed to the fact that teachers' salaries during the 1970s have not kept pace with inflation. Furthermore, increases in the salaries and wages of most other members of the working population have not kept pace

[6] Economic Unit, *U.S. News and World Report,* "How Deep a Bite Taxes Really Take," April 14, 1980, pp. 56–57.

[7] Joint State Legislative Committees, National Retired Teachers Association and American Association of Retired Persons, *State Laws Enacted Pertaining to the Interests of the Elderly, 1979* (Washington, D.C.: NRTA–AARP, 1979), pp. 19–29.

with increases in the rate of inflation. The problems of providing financing adequate to meet the needs of the public schools and other governmental services will continue to be difficult in the future in periods of either inflation or depression.

SOME IMPORTANT ISSUES IN PUBLIC SCHOOL FINANCING

Equity to pupils and equity to taxpayers are goals of school financing that have been sought for many years. The role of the federal government in attaining these goals has been discussed in Chapter 10. Therefore, the issues of school financing discussed in this chapter are confined to state and local financing of the public schools.

The Equalization of Educational Opportunity— Providing Equity for Pupils

All fifty states receive federal funds for the support of the public schools. In 1979-1980, approximately 9 percent of the revenue receipts of the public schools was provided by the federal government, 48 percent by state governments, and 43 percent by local governments.[8]

When state and local revenue only is considered, approximately 53 percent was provided by the states in 1979-1980 and 47 percent by local governments. The state provided only 17 percent of state and local school revenue in 1929-1930 as compared with 53 percent in 1979-1980. Therefore, there was a marked trend during the fifty years following 1930 to increase the proportion of school revenue provided by the state. This trend toward providing a higher percentage of school revenue has been supported by two principal objectives: (1) to promote the equalization of educational opportunity and (2) to provide a more equitable system of taxation for the support of the public schools. These two objectives will be discussed in order.

At this writing, the public schools in forty-nine states were administered by approximately 16,000 local school districts. Hawaii provides no local tax support for its public schools, and it does not have local school districts with the taxing powers of school districts in other states. The local school districts within each state vary widely in the value of property subject to taxation. In states with large school units such as county units, the taxable wealth per pupil may be six to ten times as much in the most wealthy districts as in the least wealthy districts. In states with small districts, the variation may be more than 30 to 1. In such states, the expenditure per pupil may vary as much as 3 or 4 to 1 if the state does not have an equitable plan for school financing. Approximately 98 percent of local tax revenue for the public schools is derived from property taxes. Obviously it is impossible to finance equal educational opportunity within a state entirely by local property taxes unless property taxes are made excessive or even confiscatory in the districts that are rich in numbers of children and poor in wealth.

The need to use the taxing power of the state to equalize educational oppor-

---

[8] National Education Association, *Estimates of School Statistics, 1979-80* (Washington, D.C.: National Education Association, 1980), p. 34.

tunity within a state has been pointed out by scholars in educational finance from almost the beginning of this century. For example, Cubberley in 1905, Updegraff in 1922, Strayer in 1923, Mort in 1924, and Morrison in 1930 were the pioneers who authored important publications urging that the state use its taxing power to equalize educational opportunity.[9]

The equalization of educational opportunity within a state is not a simple task. To those not familiar with the financing of the public schools, it might seem that the obvious solution is to provide the same amount of revenue per pupil in all districts of the state. This policy will not attain the goal of equalizing educational opportunity for the following reasons:

1. The educational needs of pupils vary widely, and educational opportunity cannot be equalized by giving all pupils the same type of educational program.

2. The costs per pupil for exceptional education, vocational education, and the education of the culturally different or culturally deprived are much higher than the cost per pupil of the basic educational program. School districts vary widely in the composition of their student populations.

3. Costs per pupil for an equivalent quality of education vary widely due to sparsity or density of population. Sparsity of population forces many boards of education to operate small schools which lack economies of scale resulting in higher cost per pupil. In some urban districts, the cost of living may be higher than the state average.

4. Districts vary widely in the percentage of the pupil population that must be transported.

The measurement of educational need and the computation of variations in the unit costs for equivalent educational programs and services is a problem which requires continuous study in each state if educational opportunities are really equalized. It is beyond the scope of this book to describe the technology used in these studies. Following, however, are the principal devices used by the states to provide for cost differentials in educational programs.

Weighted pupils. The pupil is weighted in the state finance plan in proportion to variations in cost per pupil. For example, if the state financing plan provides for $1,500 per pupil in the basic program and it is computed that the cost per pupil for vocational education is two times as much as the cost per pupil of the basic program, the full-time equivalent vocational pupil is given a weight of 2 and $3,000 is included in the state finance program for that pupil. This same weighting technique can be used for providing for cost variations due to sparsity or density. State assistance for school transportation is usually provided for under a separate weighting system based on the density or sparsity of transported pupils.

[9] See Ellwood P. Cubberley, *School Funds and Their Apportionment* (New York: Teachers College, Columbia University, 1905); Harlan Updegraff, *Rural School Survey in New York State: Financial Support* (Ithaca, N.Y.: By the author, 1922); George D. Strayer and Robert Murray Haig, *The Financing of Education in the State of New York* (New York: Macmillan Publishing Co., Inc., 1923); Paul R. Mort, *The Measurement of Educational Need* (New York: Teachers College, Columbia University, 1924); and Henry C. Morrison, *School Revenue* (Chicago: University of Chicago Press, 1930).

The adjusted instruction unit. Some states allocate state funds by instruction units which are based on the number of pupils per teacher. Let us assume that the state program provides one instruction unit for each twenty-four pupils in the basic program and one vocational teacher for each twelve equivalent full-time vocational pupils. That policy would be equivalent to giving vocational pupils a weight of 2. This technique can also be used to provide for cost variations due to sparsity or density.

Categorical grants. Some states provide categorical grants for high-cost programs such as vocational education and exceptional education. The purpose of these grants is to provide for the excess costs of high cost programs. This policy is not considered as desirable as the use of weighted pupils or adjusted instruction units to provide for high-cost programs and conditions beyond the control of boards of education which cause extra costs for equivalent educational programs.

Providing Equity for Taxpayers

Legally public school education is a state responsibility. Therefore, it is inequitable to require the taxpayers in school districts of limited wealth to pay higher taxes than do the taxpayers in other districts to provide equivalent educational opportunities. To be equitable to taxpayers, the state finance plan must be fiscally neutral. In other words, the quality of a child's education should not be made dependent on the resources of the school district or on the pocketbook of his or her parents.[10]

Furthermore, the tax itself, regardless of the level of government levying it, should be equitable. Due has stated that a tax is usually considered equitable if it meets the following criteria: "(1) equals are treated as equals (that is, persons in the same relevant circumstances should be taxed the same amount); (2) the distribution of the overall tax burden should be based on ability to pay as measured by income, wealth and consumption; (3) persons in the lowest income groups should be excluded from tax on the grounds that they have no taxpaying capacity; and (4) the overall distribution of the tax structure should be progressive or at least proportional in nature."[11] If ability to pay is considered the most important criterion of equity, the most equitable taxes in order are personal income taxes, corporate income taxes, sales and gross receipts taxes, and property taxes. In 1979 these four taxes provided 90 percent of the total of all federal, state, and local tax revenue excluding Social Security taxes. Any plan of state financing which requires that most of the public school revenue be obtained from the property tax is inequitable to taxpayers because of the regressive nature of the property tax. However, the regressiveness of the property tax can be reduced greatly by legislation providing for a "circuit breaker." The circuit breaker is designed to relieve persons in the lowest income brackets of the excessive burden of the property tax. For example, circuit breaker legislation may provide that, if property taxes on a

[10] See *Serrano* v. *Priest*, 5 Cal. 3d 584, 487 P.2d 1241 (1971).

[11] John F. Due, "Alternative Tax Sources for Education," Chap. 10 in *Economic Factors Affecting the Financing of Education*, eds. Roe L. Johns et al. (Gainesville, Fla.: National Educational Finance Project, 1970).

homestead exceed 5 percent of the homeowner's income, the excess will be rebated by the state to the homeowner, and, if 15 percent of the rent paid by a renter for his or her home exceeds 5 percent of the renter's income, the excess will be rebated to the renter. Some states limit the "circuit breaker" to the elderly. To be effective in reducing the regressiveness of the property tax, it should apply to all ages.

Alternative Plans for Financing the Public Schools from State and Local Revenues

Which plans of state support most adequately provide for equity to pupils and equity to taxpayers? It is beyond the scope of this book to present an extensive analysis of alternative plans of state support.[12] Following is a brief summary of some of the advantages and disadvantages of different plans of school financing. Attention however is directed to the fact that no plan of school financing is equitable to pupils unless it is financed adequately to meet educational needs.

Full state financing. This plan equalizes educational opportunity and could be considered equitable to pupils. It is also equitable to taxpayers, assuming that the state system of taxation is equitable. However, many people fear that this plan would destroy local control of education and that eventually it would result in a mediocre level of quality of education.

Flat grant state financing. Under this plan the state allocates the same amount of money per unit of educational need to each district regardless of variations in wealth per pupil. This plan is not equitable to either pupils or taxpayers unless the flat grant approaches the full cost of education. The higher the percentage of total school revenue provided by the state under the flat grant plan, the more equitable the plan to both pupils and taxpayers. However, as the flat grant approaches 100 percent of total school revenue, it has the same disadvantages as does full state funding.

State equalization plans. Under state equalization plans, the state-assured school program is financed by a combination of state and local revenues under which the state allocates state funds per unit of need in inverse relationship to per pupil wealth. In other words, districts with low per pupil wealth receive more state funds per pupil or per unit of need than do districts with a higher wealth per pupil. There are two principal variations in state equalization plans as follows: (1) a fixed-level state-assured educational program and (2) a variable-level assured program.

The fixed-level assured program plan is commonly known as the foundation program plan of state support. Under this plan the state assures the same level of foundation program per unit of need in all districts and also requires a uniform local tax effort to finance part of the cost of the state-assured program. From the total cost of the state-assured program is deducted the amount of local funds raised by the required local tax effort and the remainder is paid from state funds.

[12] For an extensive analysis, see Roe L. Johns and Kern Alexander, eds. *Alternative Programs for Financing Education,* Vol. 5 of the National Educational Finance Project (Gainesville, Fla.: The National Educational Finance Project, 1971).

For example, suppose that the state assures a foundation program of $1,500 per weighted pupil and requires a local levy of 10 mills on the equalized valuation in support of the foundation program or assured program. Let us assume that in district A the required local levy produces $500 per weighted pupil. The state will provide $1,000 in state equalization funds for that district. This plan is equitable to both pupils and taxpayers if the level of the state-assured program is high enough to provide a high-quality educational program and if the tax effort required to support the foundation program leaves but a small amount of leeway to local boards of education to levy taxes for school support in addition to the taxes required to finance the foundation program. Most authorities on school finance recommend that boards of education have this leeway to preserve local control of education and to stimulate local educational innovations.

The variable-level assured program plan is commonly called the district power equalizing plan of state support. Under this plan, the level of the state-assured program is determined by the level of local tax effort made by the local school district, but districts making the same local tax effort would have the same level of state-assured program. For example, let us assume under the power equalizing plan the state assures that the district will have available from state and local funds $150 per weighted pupil per mill of levy. Using district A again for purposes of comparison, let us assume that it levies 10 mills of local tax. It would raise $500 in local funds and receive $1,000 in state funds per weighted pupil. However, if district A levies 12 mills of local taxes, the state-assured program will be $1,800 per weighted pupil, $600 of which amount will be provided from local funds and $1,200 from state funds. This plan is equitable to taxpayers but inequitable to pupils. It is fiscally neutral; that is, the quality of the educational program in a district does not depend on the wealth of a district. However, the quality of the educational program in a district depends on the tax effort made by the district, and therefore this plan does not equalize educational opportunity. The level of local tax effort made for the public schools depends on many factors such as the educational level of the parents, the percentage of pupils of school age attending private schools, the percentage of the voting population over sixty years of age, the municipal tax overburden, and other factors. A plan that makes the quality of education in a district dependent upon these factors is very inequitable to pupils. Sometimes percentage equalizing, guaranteed yield, and guaranteed tax base plans are devised so as to provide variable-level state-guaranteed programs depending upon the level of the local tax effort made by the district.[13]

Advocates of finance plans that make the level of the educational program dependent upon the level of local tax effort argue that this plan promotes local home rule. Opponents of plans of this type argue that they stimulate an increase in the local property tax which is the most regressive of all major taxes and therefore that, in addition to being inequitable to pupils, it is also inequitable to taxpayers.

The voucher plan. Under this plan, the state issues a voucher for each pupil of school age to parents of the pupils. This voucher finances the entire cost of the

[13] See Esther O. Tron, *Public School Finance Programs, 1975-76* (Washington, D.C.: U.S. Government Printing Office, 1976), pp. 9-13.

state-guaranteed program. The vouchers may be cashed at either public or private schools.[14] No state has yet adopted this plan. Advocates of this plan argue that it will break up the monopoly of the public schools and give parents a choice in the type of education they desire for their children. Opponents of this plan argue that it will destroy the public school system, that it will segregate the pupils by race and social class, that it will be fiscally inefficient, and that it will generally lower the quality of education.

Court Decisions

The provisions for school financing have been challenged recently in the courts in a number of states. The primary basis of these challenges was that the state plan of school financing did not equalize educational opportunity because it made the quality of a child's education a function of the wealth of the district and that it therefore denied equal protection under the law violating provisions of both the state and federal constitutions.

The most famous of these cases is *Serrano v. Priest* in California.[15] In 1971 the Supreme Court of California ruled that education was a "fundamental interest" and that equal protection was denied when the state school financing "system conditions the full entitlement of such interest on wealth, classifies its recipients on the basis of their collective affluence and makes the quality of a child's education depend on the resources of his school district and ultimately upon the pocketbook of his parents." The court then ruled that the provisions for school financing in California violated both the state and the federal constitutions.

Shortly thereafter, a three-judge federal court in Texas, in *Rodriguez v. San Antonio Independent School District*,[16] held that the Texas plan of school financing violated both the state and federal constitutions. The reasoning in the *Rodriguez* decision followed the *Serrano* decision very closely. In 1973, the U.S. Supreme Court held that the Texas finance law did not violate the U.S. Constitution. The court, however, did not endorse the Texas plan of financing but suggested that it was the responsibility of the states to remedy the inequities in their school finance plans.

By the end of 1979, courts in a number of other states, including Wyoming, Minnesota, New Jersey, Kansas, West Virginia, Colorado, Connecticut, New York, and Washington, had held that the plans of school financing in these states violated either the state or federal constitution or both.[17]

These court decisions are destined to have a major impact on school financing. The ruling of the U.S. Supreme Court that the Texas finance plan did not violate the U.S. Constitution will not prevent state courts from ruling that their plans for school financing violate their state constitutions. These decisions have greatly stimulated the study of school financing in the United States and have highlighted dramatically the inequalities of educational opportunity in the nation.

[14] See Milton Friedman, *Economics and the Public Interest* (New Brunswick, N.J.: Rutgers University, 1955), p. 35.

[15] *Serrano* v. *Priest,* 5 Cal. 3d 584, 487 P.2d 1241 (1971).

[16] *Rodriguez* v. *San Antonio Independent School District,* D. Supp. (W.D. Texas, 1971).

[17] For a description and analysis of some of these cases, see Kern Alexander, *School Law* (St. Paul, Minn.: West Publishing Company, 1980).

SCHOOL BUSINESS ADMINISTRATION

The development and execution of sound policies of school business administration are essential to the success of the educational enterprise. The chief executive of the school system must be competent in school business administration as well as in curriculum and instruction. Nothing will destroy the leadership potential of the chief school executive more quickly than incompetent business administration. An external audit presenting proof that he or she has been responsible for extravagant or improper expenditures, or that he or she has violated state or federal laws in the use of school funds, or that the accounting records of the school system do not show the financial condition of the school system or do not show the purposes for which all school funds were expended may subject the chief executive to indictment and dismissal. Furthermore, such justified criticisms destroy the confidence of the public in the school system and those responsible for its administration.

In small school systems, the superintendent of schools must also perform the duties of school business administration. In school systems of sufficient size, the board of education generally employs an assistant superintendent for business affairs who is directly responsible to the superintendent of schools. Although the superintendent under this arrangement delegates the administration of business affairs to the assistant superintendent, the superintendent must continue to exercise appropriate supervision over business affairs because, if something goes wrong, he or she will also be held responsible.

The primary purpose of business administration is to help assure that maximum educational returns will be received per dollar invested in education. The purpose definitely is not to hold educational expenditures to a minimum, though too often that concept has prevailed. Economical efficient administration does not mean parsimonious administration. Business administration should be the servant of the educational program, not the master. Leaders of business and industry have long known that the investment of additional funds in an enterprise will frequently return more profits per dollar invested than could be obtained from a smaller investment. There is much evidence available showing that this same principle applies to the educational enterprise. On the other hand, the wasteful or unnecessary expenditure of funds does not bring the desired returns in either business or education.

In Chapter 7, the importance of planning was emphasized. In no area of educational administration is planning more important than in business administration. As is pointed out in the following paragraphs, business administration services are essential if educational planning is made effective.

Management of Resources

The Association of School Business Officials, after extensive study, developed a useful conceptualization of resource management called ERMS or educational resources management system.[18] The association conceptualized business adminis-

---

[18]William H. Curtis, *Educational Resources Management System* (Chicago: Research Corporation of the School Business Officials, 1971).

tration services as a component of the total educational system provided for the purpose of facilitating the attainment of educational objectives. ERMS was explained as follows:

> An ERM System should be viewed as a basic conceptualization of a planning, programming, budgeting, evaluating system (PPBES) application. The system is designed for the management of educational resources in local school districts.[19]

The ERMS conceptualization had its origin in the planning, programming, and budgeting systems (PPBS) used in industry and the federal government. The association adapted PPBS to education, renamed it PPBES, and described it as an educational resources management system. Following are the basic assumptions upon which ERMS is based:

1. The resources available to a school district are less than equal to the demands of that district.
2. The school district exists to produce a set of outcomes—to achieve certain objectives expressed as specific changes in characteristics of the learners.
3. Objectives of a school district can be achieved theoretically in a multitude of ways (program plans), some of which are more effective than others.
4. Productivity of a school district can be increased by the organization of learning activities and supporting services into programs specifically directed toward achieving previously defined goals and objectives.
5. Better decisions regarding the selection of program plans and greater benefits from their operation result when the costs thereof are considered on a long-term (multi year) basis.
6. Better decisions regarding the selection of program plans and greater benefits from their application result when outcomes are related methodically to objectives.[20]

The processes of the ERM System were considered by the association to be planning, programming, budgeting, and evaluating. Those processes were defined as follows:

1. Planning is the process of guiding internal change so that the school adapts effectively to the dynamic society of which it is a part.
2. Programming is the process of developing program plans.
3. Budgeting is the process which includes in addition to final reconciliation of programs and available resources according to established priorities, the preparation of the budget documents, the approval by a board of education, and the execution of the budgetary plans.
4. Evaluating is the process of assessing the attainment of objectives and the worth of programs.[21]

[19] *Ibid.*, p. 37.
[20] *Ibid.*, pp. 37–39.
[21] *Ibid.*, pp. 45–51.

It is interesting to note that the Association of School Business Officials is using the systems approach in its recommendations for the establishment of a management system. Business management, per se, is seen not as an end in itself but as a means to attain educational objectives.

Management Information Systems

Educational administrators are being urged by the business community and many legislators to install management information systems. There is no doubt that educational administrators and boards of education need relevant information when they are making management decisions. This has always been true. However, some of the enthusiasts for management information systems assume that such a system, when installed in a school system, can be programmed in a computer so as to give optimum answers to all educational problems without the necessity of thinking and evaluating on the part of educational administrators, teachers, and boards of education. This is an erroneous assumption.

The implementation of PPBES involves research. Planning involves the determination of purposes and goals and the projection of the possible consequences of the acceptance of alternate purposes and goals. The intelligent selection of purposes and goals cannot be done without the availability of needed information. Programming cannot be accomplished without considering alternate programs. This requires cost-effectiveness and cost–benefit analyses. These analyses cannot be made without relevant information. Adequate budgeting requires information concerning programs, object, function, locus, revenues, and so forth. Evaluation requires the measurement of actual output as compared with expected output. This requires appropriate information. A management information system is designed to obtain the information necessary for planning, programming, budgeting, and evaluating. It is pointed directly to the implementation of these processes. Electronic data processing (EDP) is not an information management system (MIS) although it is essential to that system. EDP is simply the processing of information whereas MIS is "a planned arrangement for assuring that appropriate data are communicated in the proper form to the correct decision points at the appropriate time so that it facilitates organizational and managerial planning and operational decision making."[22]

Much has been written in recent years concerning management by objective (MBO). State legislators especially have been interested in this approach. The MBO approach is quite useful in business and industry where the attainment of objectives can be determined objectively. MBO is also quite useful in managing such school business administration services as transportation, school food service, and maintenance and operation of the school plant. However, the MBO approach cannot be applied to the attainment of some important educational objectives which cannot be measured by standardized tests.

The most important element in school business administration is the development and administration of the budget. Those topics will be discussed next.

[22] Robert L. Granger, *Educational Leadership* (Scranton, Pa.: Intext Educational Publishers, 1971), pp. 177–178.

A school budget is an aggregate of educational plans with an estimate of the receipts and expenditures necessary to finance the services and facilities required to provide the desired educational programs. School budgets are usually made for a period of one fiscal year, although budgetary needs are sometimes projected for some years into the future. The school fiscal year should include a complete scholastic year to simplify the estimating of expenditures. Furthermore, the school fiscal year should coincide with the tax levying and collecting year, so that the flow of revenue may coincide with the flow of expenditures during the school year. The most commonly used fiscal year, and perhaps the best for boards of education, is the year beginning July 1 and ending June 30. A fiscal year beginning on January 1 is particularly unsuited to school operations, because fractions of two different operating years must be budgeted within one fiscal year.

All school systems in the United States now operate on some type of budget. These budgets may vary all the way from simple lump-sum estimates of receipts and expenditures listed on a few sheets of paper to comprehensive documents of a hundred pages or more setting forth detailed programs and estimates of receipts and expenditures with accompanying material fully interpreting the budget. The budgetary process may be nothing more than ascertaining the revenue that will be available and allocating it in such a manner as to minimize complaints. On the other hand, the budgetary process may involve carefully studying educational needs, estimating the revenue necessary to meet educational needs, and planning the procurement of the necessary revenue to implement the educational program agreed upon. The latter type of budgetary process has been found to be most effective in promoting the development of adequate educational programs.

The school budget is the instrument through which the people can determine both their educational and their financial policy. Therefore, effective school budgeting must include

1. the preparation of the budget in such a manner as to provide an educational program that gives effect to educational policies previously determined
2. the budget document, which may be defined as a systematic plan and statement that forecasts the expenditures and revenues of a school system during a stated period of time
3. the presentation, consideration, and adoption of the budget
4. the administration of the budget
5. the appraisal of the budget

Once the educational program is agreed upon, estimates can be prepared indicating the probable costs. The word "costs" is used deliberately, because there are different costs for different levels of quality in many components of the educational program. Therefore, several alternative budgets and subbudgets should be prepared before the final budget is adopted. These alternative budgets will show the additional costs necessary to provide additional services or a higher quality of service. Whenever possible data on cost benefit or cost effectiveness for alternatives should be provided for those participating in making the budget. Representative citizen committees, classroom teachers, principals, supervisors, and other interested parties should be given adequate opportunity to share with the board and the superintendent the responsibility of developing the educational plan. Representative advisory groups should be given broad opportunities to study alternative educational plans and to present their recommendations to the board. This process results in communitywide participation in the educational planning and budget making. Only through the process of participation in the planning can there be genuine understanding of the budget.

As was mentioned previously, the formal budget should incorporate a definite statement of the educational program in the form of a programmed budget as well as a statement of receipts and expenditures in terms of required function and object accounts. Other interpretive material might include various types of unit cost analyses, data for comparable school systems, trends in receipts and expenditures adjusted for variations in the purchasing power of the dollar, and any other information that will help the board and the public to make intelligent decisions concerning the budget.

There should be a centralized administration of the budget. No budget can be kept in balance if numerous persons make expenditures without preauthorization. The superintendent or his or her representative must have the responsibility for administering the budget.

If the budget is to have any meaning, it must be put in operation. A budget is not an effective instrument for implementing the educational program if it is filed away and referred to only at long intervals. Programs must be organized; persons must be employed; supplies must be purchased; buildings must be constructed, equipped, maintained, and operated; and many types of services must be provided. These and many other things all cost money, and unless the budget serves as a real guide there will be no money left for others. The choice then is to fail to finance certain items in the budget or to incur a deficit. Either alternative prevents the full achievement of educational goals. Therefore, the budget is the instrument used to keep all expenditures in balance, in order that the total educational plan is made a reality.

THE INDIVIDUAL AND SOCIAL BENEFITS OF EDUCATION

It seems appropriate to end this chapter with a brief discussion of the individual and social returns from the investment in education. It is possible to measure in dollars part of the individual and social benefits of education, but most of these benefits cannot be measured in dollars. These benefits will be discussed in order.

Individual Benefits of Education

The U.S. Bureau of the Census reported in 1979 that the average annual earnings of males of all races eighteen years of age and over in 1977 was as follows: (1) elementary school dropout, $9,770, (2) elementary school graduate, $11,836, (3) high school dropout, $12,678, (4) high school graduate, $14,600, (5) college one to three years, $16,207, (6) college graduate four years plus, $20,966, (7) college graduate five years plus, $25,650.[23] The average annual income of females in 1977

[23] Adapted from U.S. Bureau of the Census, Current Population Reports, *Consumer Income,* Series P-60 (Washington, D.C.: U.S. Government Printing Office, March 1979), Table 48, p. 195.

was as follows: (1) elementary school dropout, $5,923, (2) elementary school graduate, $6,814, (3) high school dropout, $7,144, (4) high school graduate, $8,590, (5) college one to three years, $9,626, (6) college graduate four years plus, $12,516, (7) college graduate five years plus, $14,571. These data confirm only what is common knowledge—that income is highly associated with level of education. However, a comparison of the income of females with the income of males of the same educational level reveals that females have not yet attained equality of economic opportunity.

Two pioneer studies of the individual returns of an investment in education were made by Becker and Schultz. Becker found that the rate of return on the investment in college education by urban white males, including income foregone by students was 10 percent before taxes in 1950.[24]

Schultz estimated the rate of return for the entire labor force in 1957.[25] He computed the rate of return of investment in elementary education to be 35 percent; high school education, 10 percent; and college education, 11 percent. Numerous studies of the individual benefits of education have been made by other researchers, and, although the rates of return found by these researchers vary, in general they confirm the findings of Becker and Schultz.[26]

Many of the individual benefits of education cannot be measured in dollars. Education is a consumption as well as a producer good. An adequate level of education broadens one's cultural horizons. For example, a relatively uneducated person has only a limited capacity to enjoy art, music, and literature. Furthermore, the educated person is better equipped to change vocations or positions and to deal with the complexities of this modern technological civilization. For example, a person may be thrown out of his or her job due to automation. If that person has a limited education, the difficulty of learning a new job is much greater than is that for someone with an education adequate for the times.

Social Benefits of Education

Not all educational returns accrue to the benefit of the individual. Actually the social or indirect returns of education are probably greater than are the individual returns. That is the principal justification for supporting education by taxation. It is impossible to compute a dollar figure showing the social and indirect benefits of education. Following, however, are some of these benefits.

1. As was pointed out, level of income is highly correlated with level of education. Those with higher incomes pay higher taxes. Psacharopoulos has estimated that the social rate of return on the public investment in high school completion versus elementary school is 7.4 percent and 3.6 percent

[24] Gary S. Becker, "Underinvestment in College Education," *American Economic Review, Papers and Proceedings,* 90 (May 1960), 346–354.

[25] Theodore W. Schultz, "Education and Economic Growth" in *Social Forces Influencing American Education,* National Society for the Study of Education, 60th Yearbook (Chicago: University of Chicago Press, 1961), Chap. 3, pp. 46–88.

[26] An exception is C. Jencks, *Inequality, A Reassessment of the Effects of Family and Schooling in America* (New York: Basic Books, Inc., Publishers, 1972). Jencks concluded that the socioeconomic level of the family determined the differences among persons in income rather than differences in education. The findings of this highly controversial book have not been accepted by most of the scholars of the economics of education.

on completion of four years of college versus high school due solely to higher taxes paid by those with higher levels of education.[27]

2. The percentage of unemployment is a function of educational level. In 1976 unemployment among youths sixteen to twenty-four years of age was 22.2 percent for white high school dropouts and 37.1 percent for black high school dropouts; for white high school graduates, 10.8 percent, and for blacks, 23.6 percent; for white college graduates, 7.1 percent, and for blacks, 3.6 percent.[28]

3. The amount of crime committed is related highly to educational level. In 1970, elementary school graduates only, comprised 13.4 percent of the total population and 16.2 percent of the inmates of correctional institutions, high school graduates comprised 34.0 percent of the total population and 19.1 percent of the inmates of correctional institutions, and college graduates comprised 11.0 percent of the total population and only 1.0 percent of the inmates of correctional institutions.[29]

4. There is a high correlation between educational attainment and political participation. Political participation by the electorate is essential to the functioning of a democratic form of government. In the 1976 presidential election, only 51.4 percent of elementary school graduates voted whereas 59.4 percent of high school graduates and 79.8 of college graduates voted.[30]

Many other social and indirect benefits of education could be cited. Education is an investment in people. The productivity of the economy is highly dependent on the educational capital of the people. The quality of life of the people and the very survival of the nation depend to a considerable extent on the quantity and quality of education provided.

SOME IMPORTANT PROBLEMS AND ISSUES

There are many unresolved issues in school business adminstration and school financing. Two of those issues are discussed briefly in the following paragraphs.

How Should Local Tax Effort in Support of the State-Assured Program Be Measured?

State-assured programs of education, either fixed level or variable level, require local school districts to make local tax effort in proportion to taxpaying ability or capacity to fund that program jointly. The required local tax effort is usually

---

[27] George Psacharopoulos, "Spending on Education in an Era of Economic Stress: An Optimist's View" (unpublished paper presented at Conference on *Financing Education in the Future,* Orlando, Florida, April 1980), p. 17.

[28] Adapted from the National Center for Educational Statistics, *The Condition of Education, 1978* (Washington, D.C.: U.S. Government Printing Office, Office of Education, 1978), p. 14.

[29] Adapted from U.S. Department of Commerce, Bureau of the Census, "Persons in Institutions and Other Group Quarters," *Statistical Abstract of the U.S.,* 94th annual ed. (Washington, D.C.: U.S. Government Printing Office, 1973), Table 178.

[30] U.S. Department of Commerce, Bureau of the Census, "Voting and Registration in the Election of November 1976," *Current Population Reports,* Series P-20, No. 332 (Washington, D.C.: U.S. Government Printing Office, 1978).

computed in terms of a specified tax levy on the equalized assessed valuation or a guaranteed yield per mill of levy on the equalized valuation. There are some who argue that the equalized value of property is an inadequate measure of local tax-paying ability. It is insisted that per capita or per pupil income is a better measure of local taxpaying ability. Those holding that point of view recommend that income be combined with equalized valuation of property in determining local taxpaying ability required to support the state-assured program, regardless of whether the board can levy a local income tax.

Others argue that the local tax effort required for joint state–local funding of the state-assured program is not a measure of local taxpaying ability but rather a measure of the accessibility that the board of education has to local tax revenues. Those holding that point of view recommend that income be included in the measure of local tax effort only if the board of education has the legal authority to levy a local income tax for schools. They would also include in the measure of local tax effort local revenue from other tax resources, such as a local sales tax or local payroll tax, if the board has the authority to levy such taxes for the public schools.

Many municipalities have high municipal taxes for municipal purposes. These taxes, sometimes called "the municipal overburden," make it difficult in many cities to obtain taxpayer approval of the local taxes needed for school support. Some authorities on public finance argue that the excessive municipal overburden be deducted from the required local tax effort required of school districts. Others recommend that the state government contribute directly to necessary municipal services such as fire and police protection and thereby eliminate excessive municipal overburden without introducing undesirable complications in the state aid formula for schools.

What other arguments can be advanced either for or against the conflicting points of view described?

Should the Local School Budget Be Approved by Some Agency Other Than the School Board?

A board of education is fiscally independent when it is directly responsible to the people for its financial program and its educational policies. A board of education is fiscally dependent when its budget is subject to review, revisions, or approval by any noneducational agency or commission.

The principal arguments that have been advanced for fiscal independence of school boards are as follows:

1. Schools should be kept free of partisan policies.
2. Education is a state function. An intermediary authority standing between the state and the local school board makes it impossible for the board to be in fact responsible to the state and the people.
3. Fiscal control of school boards by noneducational governmental agencies leads to *de facto* control of educational policies.
4. Control of school affairs by municipal or other noneducational local

governmental agencies often leads to coercion in professional and technical matters and in the management of expenditures.

5. Fiscal independence leads to greater stability and continuity in educational planning.

6. Fiscal dependence leads to competition for the local tax dollar, thereby intensifying controversies between local governmental agencies and school authorities.

7. Fiscal dependence complicates school administration.

8. Fiscal independence is the only sure way to protect school funds from diversion to nonschool purposes.

9. There is no evidence that fiscal dependence results in greater economy and efficiency.

10. The people should be able to express themselves on the important problem of education without having issues confused by a mixture with other governmental problems.

11. Separation of fiscal control from responsibility for educational results violates the basic administrative principle that authority and responsibility should go together.

12. It is desirable to keep educational control close to the people to preserve the elements of democratic government and to provide for the freedom essential for adaptability, adjustment, and invention.

The principal arguments that have been advanced for fiscal dependence of school boards are as follows:

1. There is a place for a unified and coordinated local financial structure. Intergovernmental relations are more complex and there is much duplication of effort and overlapping of functions when schools are independent of local government.

2. Determination of expenditures for all purposes should permit the weighing of the relative merits of each service. This recommends a single legislative authority.

3. Coordination of services in which the schools and local government are mutually interested is facilitated.

4. School services when delegated to local control and responsibility are in reality legitimate aspects of local government, the same way as police protection, public health, and similar services are of general social significance.

The research on fiscal independence versus dependence affords little objective evidence to support either set of arguments. It is doubtful if this issue can ever be resolved by objective evidence, because it involves the determination of the relative importance of different social values. The determination of relative social values is a philosophical problem, and philosophical propositions do not readily lend themselves to statistical evaluation.

If one believes that centralization of the fiscal planning of all governmental services has greater social value than does more direct determination of educational policy by the people, that person will support fiscal dependence of boards of education. If one believes that the decentralized determination of educational policy is of greater social value than is centralized fiscal management, that person will support the fiscal independence of school districts.

SELECTED REFERENCES

Alexander, Kern, and K. Forbis Jordan, eds., *Educational Need and the Public Economy.* Gainesville: The University Presses of Florida, 1976.

Candoli, I. Carl, Walter G. Hack, John R. Ray, and Dewey H. Stollar, *School Business Administration: A Planning Approach.* Boston: Allyn & Bacon, Inc., 1978.

Cohn, Elchanan, *The Economics of Education.* Cambridge, Mass.: Ballinger Publishing Co., 1979.

Curtis, William H., *Educational Resources Management System.* Chicago: Association of School Business Officials, 1971.

Johns, Roe L., and Kern Alexander, eds., *Alternative Programs for the Financing of Education,* Vol. 5, National Educational Finance Project. Gainesville, Fla.: National Educational Finance Project, 1971.

——, and Edgar L. Morphet, *The Economics and Financing of Education.* Englewood Cliffs, N.J.: Prentice-Hall, Inc., 1975.

Nelson, D. Lloyd, and William W. Purdy, *School Business Administration.* Lexington, Mass.: D. C. Heath & Co., 1971.

Wise, Arthur E., *Rich Schools, Poor Schools.* Chicago: University of Chicago Press, 1968.

INDEX